Macintosh™
Revealed

Volume One: Unlocking the Toolbox

R E L A T E D   T I T L E S

Macintosh™
Revealed

Volume One: Unlocking the Toolbox

Second Edition

Stephen Chernicoff

HAYDEN BOOKS

A Division of Macmillan Computer Publishing

11711 North College, Carmel, Indiana 46032 USA

For

Ann,

who likes the one with the mouse.

SECOND EDITION
FIFTH PRINTING—1990

International Standard Book Number: 0-672-48400-5
Library of Congress Catalog Card Number: 85-8611

Acquisitions Editor: *Michael McGrath*
Macintosh Library Cover Design: *Jim Bernard*
Cover Art: *Celeste Design*
Index: *Ted Laux*
Composition: *McFarland Graphics & Design, Inc.*

Printed in the United States of America

Preface

If you're reading this book, you probably don't need to be told that Apple Computer's Macintosh is an extraordinary personal computer. It does things you may never have seen a computer do before, in ways you'd never even imagined. If you've wondered what goes on behind the scenes to make the magic happen, this book is for you. By the time you've finished it, the inner workings of the Macintosh will stand revealed before your eyes, and you'll be able to use its built-in User Interface Toolbox to perform the same magic in your own programs.

One thing must be said, however, right at the outset: the Toolbox is for experienced programmers, not beginners. To get the most out of this book, you should have some previous experience (the more the better) in at least one high-level programming language. The programming examples given here are written in Pascal, but the general principles they embody are applicable in other languages as well. If Pascal isn't your native programming tongue, you should at least be able to pick up enough of it to follow the logic of the programming examples and apply them in your own preferred language. The book will offer a few hints to help you over the rough spots, but in general it's assumed that you're already acquainted with the syntax and semantics of standard Pascal. (For hard-core bit bangers, there's also information on how to use the Toolbox in assembly language.)

The only other assumption is that you want to know how the Macintosh user interface works from the inside. Whether you're a professional software developer, a college student, a midnight hacker, or just the kind of person who likes to take watches apart and see what makes them tick, read on and behold the Macintosh revealed.

STEPHEN CHERNICOFF
Berkeley, California

v

Acknowledgments

No book is ever the product of one person working alone—especially a book of the size and complexity of this one. These are some of the people who helped me bring the book to completion, and to whom I owe a special debt of gratitude and appreciation:

First and forever, to my wife, **Helen,** whose love and understanding through the ordeal of living with an author have brought new meaning to the word "patience"; and to my parents, **Murray and Annette Chernicoff,** for their unwavering encouragement and support.

To **Chris Espinosa** and **Mike Murray,** who, as my managers at Apple, graciously afforded me the freedom to pursue this project as an independent agent.

To **Mike McGrath, Ronnie Groff, Mary Picklum,** and **Nancy Ragle** of Hayden Book Company, professionals all in the noblest sense of the word, whose contributions were manifold and invaluable.

To **Don Herrington, Jennifer Ackley,** and **Wendy Ford** of Howard W. Sams & Co., for their aid in preparing the second edition.

To **David Cásseres** of Apple Computer, for his indispensable assistance with the programming examples and his wise and thoughtful counsel throughout.

To **Scott Knaster** of Apple Computer, for his thorough technical review of the manuscript and his inexhaustible patience with my questions, intelligent and otherwise.

To **Steven Smith** of CommuniTree Group, who executed the illustrations with imagination and panache.

And finally, to the men and women of Apple Computer's Macintosh Division, as talented and creative a group of people as I have ever been privileged to work with; and to **Steven Jobs,** erstwhile chairman of the board of Apple Computer and general manager of the Macintosh Division, who provided the vision and inspiration for these remarkable people to bring Macintosh to reality.

Contents

vii

CHAPTER

All the Tools You Need

What sets the Macintosh apart from other personal computers is its revolutionary *user interface*. In plain English, an *interface* is a junction or boundary where two things meet. In computerese, it refers to the set of rules and conventions by which one part of an organized system (like the Macintosh) communicates with another. Wherever two components of the system come together, they exchange information by way of an interface.

The Macintosh system consists partly of hardware (physical components such as chips, circuits, and other electronic and mechanical devices) and partly of software (programs). The most important component of all is the human being "out there," peering at the screen and fiddling with the mouse and keyboard. This flesh-and-blood component of the system is known, in technical parlance, as the *user*. So the user interface is the set of conventions that allow the human user to communicate with the rest of the system.

In the past, user interfaces were typically based on a screen full of text characters (usually displayed in garish green) and a keyboard for typing them. To tell the computer what to do, you had to memorize a complex command language, so you could press exactly the right keys in exactly the right order. If your actions didn't conform to what the computer expected of you, it would tell you so in terms ranging from curt to unintelligible. On

1

the whole, it was sometimes hard to tell that the human was the boss and the computer the servant, instead of the other way around.

Macintosh changes all that. In place of the time-honored character screen and keyboard, it uses a high-resolution, "bit-mapped" display and a hand-held pointing device, called a *mouse*. The result is a whole new way of communicating between people and computers. The bit-mapped screen can present information in vivid visual form, using pictorial "icons," elaborate graphical effects, and varied patterns and textures. Text can be depicted exactly as it will appear on the printed page—in black characters on a white background, with a variety of typefaces, sizes, and styles. The mouse provides a direct, natural way of giving commands, by pointing and manipulating images directly on the screen instead of typing arcane command sequences from the keyboard.

The programmers at Apple have put a great deal of thought and effort into how best to take advantage of these features to produce a user interface that feels natural and comfortable. The result of their efforts is the User Interface Toolbox, a body of tightly engineered, lovingly hand-crafted machine-language code that's built into every Macintosh in *read-only memory (ROM)*. With it, you can write programs that use overlapping windows, pulldown menus, scroll bars, dialog boxes, and all the other wonders you see on the Macintosh screen. This book will teach you how.

Strictly speaking, the contents of the Macintosh ROM are divided into three parts: the Macintosh Operating System, which handles low-level tasks such as memory management, disk input/output, and serial communications; the QuickDraw graphics routines, which are responsible for everything displayed on the screen; and the User Interface Toolbox, which implements the higher-level constructs of the user interface, such as windows and menus. As a rule, we'll be using the term *Toolbox* to refer loosely to the entire body of built-in code that's available to a running program; only occasionally will we use it in the narrower sense of the user-interface code alone, as distinct from the Operating System and QuickDraw.

How This Book Is Organized

The book is divided into two volumes. Volume One, *Unlocking the Toolbox* (which you now have in your hands), presents the underlying foundations on which the Toolbox is built:

- Chapter 2, "Putting the Tools to Work," introduces the basic conventions for calling the Toolbox from an application program and discusses a number of general-purpose Toolbox facilities that you'll find useful in your programs.
- Chapter 3, "Thanks for the Memory," tells how the Macintosh's memory is laid out and how to allocate memory space for your program's needs.
- Chapter 4, "Any Port in a Storm," presents the fundamental concepts behind the QuickDraw graphics routines.
- Chapter 5, "Quick on the Draw," shows how to use QuickDraw to draw on the screen.
- Chapter 6, "Summoning Your Resources," introduces the important subject of resources, one of the cornerstones of the Macintosh software design.
- Chapter 7, "Getting Loaded," covers the way programs are started up and how code is loaded into memory for execution.
- Chapter 8, "Upstanding Characters," tells how character text is represented inside the computer and displayed on the screen.

Once you've mastered these fundamentals, you'll be ready for Volume Two, *Programming with the Toolbox*. There you'll learn about the various parts of the Macintosh user interface and how they work: events (the mechanism for monitoring the user's actions with the mouse and keyboard), windows, menus, cut-and-paste text editing, controls (including scroll bars), alert and dialog boxes, and disk input/output.

Because the Toolbox includes such a broad range of facilities and features, it's impossible to cover them all in this book. We've tried to include those features that most programmers will need for most applications, but unavoidably, some topics had to be left out because of time and space limitations. Some of these missing topics, such as printing, sound, and desk accessories, will be covered in our forthcoming Volume Three, and the most recent additions to the Macintosh family, the Macintosh SE and Macintosh II, in Volume Four. The ultimate, comprehensive source of information on the Toolbox is Apple's own *Inside Macintosh* manual.

A central feature of Volume Two is a fully worked example program, a simple interactive text editor named MiniEdit, which serves two purposes. First, it illustrates concretely how to use the various parts of the Toolbox. Second, once you understand how it works, you can use it as a "shell" within which to develop your own application programs. The example program already includes all the Toolbox calls needed to implement the standard features of the user interface—for instance, to display pulldown menus when the user presses the mouse in the menu bar, or move windows around on the screen when the user drags them by their title bars—so it can save you from having to "reinvent the wheel" every time you write a program of your own. By returning the mail-order form provided in Volume Two, you can order a software disk containing the source code of the MiniEdit program. Then instead of writing your own programs from scratch, you can just modify the existing program for whatever application you choose.

How to Use This Book

With the exception of Chapter 1, each chapter in this book consists of two complementary parts: the basic text of the chapter and the subsequent reference sections. They are designed to be used in parallel. The text chapters are intended to be read more or less sequentially, from beginning to end. Their purpose is to give you an overall conceptual understanding of the Toolbox and how to use it, without attempting to cover all the minute details. Cross-references enclosed in square brackets, such as [2.1.1], will lead you to the relevant reference sections, where you'll find detailed descriptions of individual Toolbox procedures, functions, constants, variables, and data types. When you encounter one of these for the first time, follow the cross-reference to the reference section for the details. Together, the text and reference sections will teach you step by step what you need to know to use the Toolbox in your own programs.

After you've learned the basic concepts, you'll find the reference sections useful on their own for refreshing your memory or looking up specific facts and details. The reference sections are organized for quick reference rather than sequential reading. Although their structure generally parallels that of the text chapters, they don't always treat topics in exactly the same order or build logically on what's gone before. Thus you may find some of the material in the reference sections hard to follow at first, because it refers to topics you haven't yet learned. Try not to let this bother you—just skip the parts that don't make sense and come back to them later when you're better prepared to understand them. You'll also find some subjects covered in the reference sections that aren't discussed at all in the text chapters; once you've acquired a working knowledge of the Toolbox, you can come back and pick up these extra topics by browsing the reference sections on your own.

What's in the Reference Sections

Each reference section is headed by a set of Pascal declarations defining the Toolbox entities—procedures, functions, constants, variables, and data types—discussed in that section. The declarations give the names of the entities being defined, along with additional information you need in order to use them, such as the number, order, and types of a procedure's parameters, the type of value a function returns, or the names and types of a record's fields. Following the declarations are a series of notes explaining the meaning and use of the Toolbox entities being discussed. Finally, most reference sections end with a box containing further information of interest to assembly-language programmers only.

For the benefit of readers unfamiliar with Pascal, let's look at a few examples of the reference declarations and how to read them. Program 1-1 shows a typical Pascal type declaration of the kind you'll find in the reference sections. (This one, in fact, is taken from section [5.2.1].) The declaration says that PenState is the name

```
type
   PenState = record
               pnLoc  : Point;    {Current location of graphics pen in local coordinates}
               pnSize : Point;    {Width and height of pen in pixels}
               pnMode : INTEGER;  {Transfer mode for line drawing and area fill}
               pnPat  : Pattern   {Pen pattern for line drawing}
            end;
```

Program 1-1 A type declaration

of a record type with four components, or *fields.* The first field is
named pnLoc and holds a value of type Point; the second, pnSize,
also holds a Point; the third is named pnMode and is of type INTEGER;
and the fourth, pnPat, is of type Pattern. To the right of each field
definition is a comment (enclosed in the Pascal comment brackets
{ and }) describing the meaning of that field: for instance, field
pnLoc represents the current location of the graphics pen in local
coordinates. (We'll be learning about the graphics pen in Chapter
5 and the meaning of "local coordinates" in Chapter 4.) If
thePenState is the name of a record in your program of type PenState,
the expression

    thePenState.pnLoc

denotes a value of type Point giving the pen location in local
coordinates.

```
procedure MoveTo
               (horiz : INTEGER;   {Horizontal coordinate to move to, in pixels}
                vert  : INTEGER);  {Vertical coordinate to move to, in pixels}
```

Program 1-2 A procedure declaration

Program 1-2 shows an example of a procedure declaration,
taken from reference section [5.2.4]. This declaration defines the
procedure MoveTo, used to reposition the graphics pen to a new
set of coordinates. The procedure accepts two parameters named
horiz and vert, both of type INTEGER; as the explanatory comments
state, these represent the pen's new horizontal and vertical coor-

```
function EqualPt
            (point1 : Point;               {First point to be compared}
             point2 : Point);              {Second point to be compared}
                : BOOLEAN;                 {Are they equal?}
```

Program 1-3 A function declaration

dinates, respectively. To move the pen to coordinates h and v, you would use the statement

```
MoveTo (h, v)
```

Program 1-3 shows the declaration for the Toolbox function EqualPt, taken from reference section [4.4.1]. This function compares two points and tells whether they're equal. Like the procedure declaration we just looked at, a function declaration defines the names and types of the parameters the function expects you to supply. In addition, it also specifies the type of value the function returns as a result, following the colon (:) on the last line of the declaration. In this case the function accepts two parameters named point1 and point2, both of type Point, and returns a result of type BOOLEAN. You might call this function with a statement such as

```
equalFlag := EqualPt (firstPoint, secondPoint)
```

where equalFlag is a variable of type BOOLEAN declared in your program, and firstPoint and secondPoint are of type Point.

If you compare the procedure and function declarations shown in our reference sections with those given in Apple's *Inside Macintosh* manual, you'll find that the names of the parameters are often different. Since you don't actually use the parameter names when you call a routine in your program, the names given in the declaration have no effect on the way the routine is used—so we've taken the liberty of changing many of the names to suggest more clearly the meaning or purpose of the parameters.

Names that you *do* use directly in your own program, such as those of constants and variables or of the fields in a record, are of course listed the same way in our reference sections as in the Apple documentation. Even here, however, you may notice slight variations in capitalization style; these make no difference, since Apple's Pascal compiler doesn't distinguish between corresponding upper- and lowercase letters.

Some Terms and Conventions

Before we get started, let's explain some of the terms and conventions we'll be using. The microprocessor used in the Macintosh (the Motorola MC68000, usually just called the "68000" for short) works with data items of three different sizes: *bytes* of 8 bits each, *words* of 16 bits (2 bytes), and *long words* of 32 bits (2 words, or 4 bytes). All memory addresses are long words, 32 bits in length, of which only the last 24 bits are actually significant. Each address designates a single 8-bit byte in memory. As a rule, word-length and long-word data items in memory must begin at an even-numbered byte address, known as a *word boundary*.

Throughout the book, we use an alternate computer voice typeface as a kind of implicit quotation mark to distinguish actual program code from ordinary body text. This convention is also used occasionally for characters typed on the Macintosh keyboard or displayed on the screen.

In keeping with the convention used in many programming languages (including Apple's versions of Pascal and assembly language for the Macintosh), we use a dollar sign ($) to denote hexadecimal (base-16) constants. For instance, the constant $43 represents the same numerical value as decimal 67 (4 sixteens plus 3). As usual, the letters A to F stand for hexadecimal digits with numerical values from 10 to 15—so the hexadecimal constant $BD stands for 11 sixteens plus 13, or decimal 189.

We've already mentioned that section numbers enclosed in square brackets, such as [2.1.1], denote cross-references to the designated reference section. References to Volume Two are prefixed with a roman numeral II and a colon: for instance, [II:2.1.1] refers to Volume Two, section 2.1.1.

> Throughout the text chapters, you'll see shaded boxes like this one. These "by-the-way" boxes enclose side comments, helpful hints, exceptional cases, and other material subordinate to the main discussion.

Several chapters end with a section titled "Nuts and Bolts." This section is for miscellaneous topics that don't fit anywhere else in the chapter—the little unclassified odds and ends rattling around in the bottom of the Toolbox. In general these are minor points of only limited interest, or things that are useful only in unusual or highly specialized circumstances.

> In this new Macintosh Plus edition, you'll often see Toolbox routines or features identified in the reference sections as "available only on Macintosh Plus." This designation is understood to apply also to the Macintosh 512K Enhanced, Macintosh SE, Macintosh II, or to any other Macintosh that includes the newer 128K or any later ROM.

That about does it for the preliminaries—it's time to get down to the business at hand. If you're ready to see the Macintosh revealed, read on and let's get started!

CHAPTER

2

Putting the Tools to Work

Like a genie in a bottle, the Toolbox waits patiently inside every Macintosh, ready to perform its wonders for any program that cares to summon it. But before it will serve you, you need to know how to call it forth and command it to do your bidding. In this chapter, we'll start learning the spells needed to make the Toolbox work its magic. We'll learn about the underlying trap mechanism that's used at the machine-language level to call the Toolbox routines in the Macintosh ROM, as well as the higher-level calling conventions used in Pascal and assembly language. Then we'll talk about some nonstandard features of Apple's version of Pascal that are particularly useful for programming with the Toolbox. Finally we'll discuss some of the general-purpose utility routines that are included in the Toolbox for things like working with character strings, low-level bit manipulation, arithmetic operations, and reading or setting the date and time on the Macintosh's built-in clock chip.

The Language Problem

Exactly how you go about using the Toolbox depends on the language you're programming in. The Toolbox doesn't care what language you use, as long as you follow the proper rules and conventions to communicate with it. At the underlying machine level, these rules are always the same; but in a higher-level language, like Pascal or Basic or C, you normally don't have to deal with them directly. Instead, each language has its own way of representing Toolbox calls and its own set of conventions that you, as a programmer, have to follow.

When Apple first began developing the software for the Macintosh, there wasn't any Macintosh to develop it on. Fortunately, Mac's big sister Lisa (now known as the Macintosh XL) was around to lend a hand. The Lisa already had a complete software development system based on the same microprocessor used in the Macintosh, the Motorola MC68000. This Lisa programming environment, with its Pascal compiler and 68000 assembler, became the *de facto* standard for programming the Macintosh. All of Apple's own Mac software—including the Toolbox itself—was written in Lisa Pascal or assembly language, compiled or assembled on a Lisa, and "ported" to the Macintosh to run. So was all the application software produced by independent developers under special pre-release licenses from Apple. In those early days, if you wanted to program the Macintosh, you had to have a Lisa to do your programming on.

Since Macintosh was released, that situation has changed rapidly. A growing number of languages are now available for programming directly on the Macintosh, including Pascal, Basic, Fortran, Cobol, C, Lisp, Logo, and Forth. Most of these systems include some sort of facility for calling the Toolbox routines in the Macintosh ROM from within a running application program. Apple itself has introduced the Macintosh Programmer's Workshop, a complete development environment that includes both Pascal and C compilers and a 68000 assembler, along with an interactive program editor, linker, symbolic debugger, and full Toolbox support.

Because the Toolbox has its historical roots in the Lisa development system, its internal data formats and calling conventions are based on those of Lisa Pascal. In a sense, Pascal is the Toolbox's "native language." We'll be using it for all our programming examples in this book, and our descriptions of Toolbox routines and data structures will be given in Pascal form (along with additional information on how to use them in assembly language). If you're writing in another language, you'll have to consult your documentation to find out how to convert the information given here into the form you need.

> At the time this book was written, no Macintosh-based Pascal compiler was yet available. The example program MiniEdit that forms the core of Volume Two was actually compiled on a Lisa and ported to the Macintosh for execution. In theory, compilers such as TML's MacLanguage Series Pascal, Borland International's Turbo Pascal for the Mac, Think Technologies' Lightspeed Pascal, and Apple's own Macintosh Programmer's Workshop (MPW) Pascal are supposed to be completely compatible with the original Lisa Pascal at the language level. In practice, however, there may be slight differences. Please forgive any confusion that may arise because of such minor language incompatibilities. (As any programmer knows, there's no difference between theory and practice in theory, but often a great deal of difference between theory and practice in practice!)

The Trap Mechanism

At the machine level, all calls to Toolbox routines have to be translated into subroutine jumps to the appropriate addresses in the Macintosh ROM. The way this is done is rather ingenious. It's based on a feature of the 68000 processor called the *emulator trap*, which is used to add new operations to the processor's instruction set. These new operations look like ordinary machine instructions, but the processor doesn't actually execute them directly: their effects are "emulated" in software instead of hardware. The Macintosh uses such emulated instructions to represent all Toolbox operations built into the ROM.

A *trap* (also called an *exception*) occurs when the processor detects an error or abnormal condition in the course of executing a program. This causes it to suspend normal execution and save the address of the next instruction to be executed, along with some additional information about the processor's internal state. It then executes a *trap handler* routine to deal with the abnormal condition. On completion, the handler routine restores the internal state of the processor, using the state information and return address saved earlier, and resumes normal execution from the point of suspension.

Traps can occur for a variety of reasons, such as an attempt to divide by zero, a reference to an illegal address, or an interrupt signal from an input/output device. Each type of trap has its own trap handler. The addresses of the various trap handlers are called *trap vectors*, and are kept in a *vector table* in the first kilobyte of memory. When a trap occurs, the processor fetches the vector for that type of trap from the vector table and uses it to locate the proper handler routine to execute.

In particular, an *emulator trap* occurs when the processor, in the course of program execution, encounters an instruction word that it doesn't recognize as a valid machine-language instruction. On the Macintosh, the trap vector for such unimplemented instructions is set up to point to a handler routine called the *Trap Dispatcher*. The Trap Dispatcher locates the offending instruction, examines its bit pattern to determine what Toolbox operation it represents, and jumps to the corresponding Toolbox routine in ROM. On completion, the Toolbox routine will return control to the program instruction following the trap.

The unimplemented instruction used to represent a Toolbox operation is called a *trap word* (see Figure 2-1). As the name implies, a trap word is always one word (16 bits) long. Its first 4 bits are always 1010 (hexadecimal $A), the pattern that the 68000 processor recognizes as an unimplemented instruction. This is followed by a bit that classifies it as either a *Toolbox trap* dealing with the higher-level elements of the Macintosh user interface (windows, menus, and so forth) or an *Operating System* (or *OS*) *trap* representing some lower-level operation such as memory management or input/output. The particular operation is identified by a *trap number* in the last 8 bits of the word (for OS traps) or the last 9 bits (for Toolbox traps). The remaining bits are flags giving additional information to the Trap Dispatcher about how to carry out the operation; the details needn't concern us here.

a. Toolbox Trap Word Format

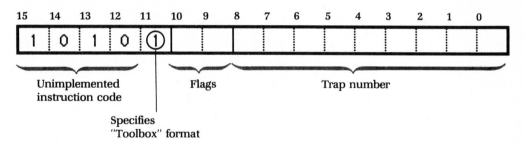

b. Operating System Trap Word Format

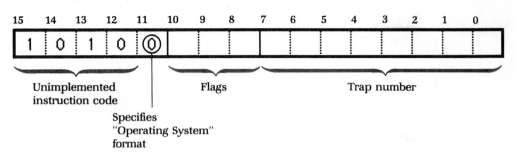

Figure 2-1 Format of a trap word

The Trap Dispatcher locates the ROM routine for a given Toolbox operation by looking it up in a table in memory called the *dispatch table*. The 8- or 9-bit trap number taken from the trap word is actually an index to an entry in the dispatch table, which in turn gives the address of the corresponding routine in ROM. The ROM itself contains a compressed version of its own dispatch table, which is used to reconstruct the actual table in RAM whenever the system is started up. This makes it easy to upgrade the machine as newer versions of the ROM appear: all that's needed is to substitute the new ROM chips for the older ones, and everything will work just as before, even though all the Toolbox routines may be at different locations in the new ROM.

The Macintosh Plus has two separate dispatch tables: one for Toolbox traps, with room for up to 512 entries, and another for OS traps, with a capacity of 256. Each entry in either table holds the actual memory address of a Toolbox or Operating System routine. On older Macintosh models, Toolbox and OS traps share the same dispatch table, limiting the number of traps to 512 for the two categories combined. To save space, entries in this combined table are encoded into a more compact form than just a raw address, and have to be decoded to find the actual location of the routine. Again, the details aren't important here: all that matters is that each entry in the dispatch table somehow leads the Trap Dispatcher to the correct address of the corresponding routine in memory.

A further wrinkle in the dispatch mechanism is that some Toolbox and Operating System routines may actually reside in RAM rather than ROM—for instance, to fix bugs discovered after the ROM code was already "frozen." In this case the corrected version of the routine is loaded into RAM from the disk when the system is started up, and the relevant entry in the dispatch table is "patched" to lead to the proper RAM address. This arrangement is completely transparent to the running application program, which needn't know or care whether a given routine happens to reside in ROM or RAM.

The Macintosh Plus takes advantage of the extra capacity afforded by its 128K ROM and dual dispatch table to add a whole range of new features and facilities to the Toolbox that weren't available on earlier models. These new features must be used with caution, however. Any program that relies on them is limited to the Macintosh Plus (or the Macintosh 512K Enhanced, Macintosh SE, Macintosh II, or any other Macintosh that includes the 128K or later ROM); they will crash the system if you attempt to use them with the old 64K ROM. All such features are identified as "available only on the Macintosh Plus" in the reference notes at the end of each chapter of this book. (This designation is understood to apply to any machine equipped with ROM version $75 or greater.)

If you want your program to run on all models of Macintosh, you have to take suitable precautions. Of course, you could just play safe and avoid the new features altogether—but then what's the point of having them in the first place? Another approach is to use the Toolbox routine Environs [3.1.3] to check the version number of the ROM in the machine you're running on, and use the new features only if you know they're available. Don't threaten your users with The Bomb!

The Stack

Routines written in Pascal receive their parameters and return their results on a *pushdown stack* in memory. To understand how the stack works, picture a stack of trays in a self-service cafeteria. Trays are always added or removed at the top of the stack, never at the bottom; the base of the stack remains fixed on the counter top. The next tray to be removed is always the last one added, so the stack grows and shrinks in "LIFO" order (last in, first out).

A program's subroutines (procedures and functions) also behave in LIFO fashion: the last routine called is always the first to return to its caller. This means that their parameters and private storage can be kept in a contiguous area of memory that grows and shrinks at one end, just like the stack of trays on the lunch counter (see Figure 2-2). One end of this area (the *base* of the stack) remains fixed in memory, while items are added or removed at the other end (the *top*). One of the processor's registers, address register A7, is reserved for use as the *stack pointer:* this register always holds the address of the top of the stack.

When you call a routine in Pascal (or any other language that follows the same calling conventions), the compiler generates machine instructions to "push" the parameter values you supply onto the top of the stack, along with the routine's *return link* (the instruction address where execution will continue when the routine is finished). If the routine is a function, space is also reserved on the stack for the result value that it will return. The

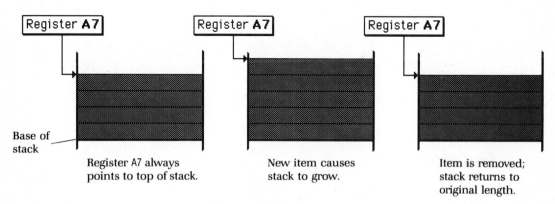

Register A7 always points to top of stack.

New item causes stack to grow.

Item is removed; stack returns to original length.

Figure 2-2 The stack

routine can then allocate additional stack space for its own local variables, if any.

If this routine in turn calls any others, the space for *their* parameters and local variables will be added to the top of the stack above those of the calling routine. Before returning control to the point of call, each routine "pops" its parameters, local variables, and return link from the stack, leaving it in the same state it was in before the routine was called. (In the case of a function, it leaves its result on the top of the stack for the calling routine to do with as it pleases.)

The Pascal Interface

All of the Toolbox routines and data structures that we'll be discussing in this book are defined in a set of Pascal *interface units*. A *unit* is a collection of precompiled constant, type, procedure, and function declarations that can be incorporated wholesale into any Pascal program. The units that make up the Toolbox interface are provided as part of most Pascal-based software development systems. They include the following units:

- MemTypes defines a set of basic, general-purpose data types that are used by all the other units.
- OSIntf contains the interface to the Macintosh Operating System.
- QuickDraw contains the interface to the QuickDraw graphics routines.
- ToolIntf contains the interface to the User Interface Toolbox proper.
- PackIntf contains the interface to the disk-based subroutine packages that supplement the Toolbox; these are discussed further in Chapter 7.

There are also a few other units for specialized uses not covered in this book, such as printing, floating-point arithmetic, transcendental functions, the AppleTalk network, and three-dimensional graphics; see Volume Three and *Inside Macintosh* for information.

Each unit consists of two files: a text *interface file* containing the declarations that make up the unit in Pascal source form, and an *object module* containing the corresponding compiled code. To use the Toolbox in Pascal, you name the interface units in a **uses** declaration:

   uses MemTypes, OSIntf, QuickDraw, ToolIntf, PackIntf;

This makes all the constant, variable, type, and routine names declared in the units available to your program at compilation time, just as if they were Pascal standard identifiers like INTEGER or SQRT. (Of course, you only need to include those units that you actually use in your program: if you don't use any of the routines in the disk-based packages, for instance, you can omit the PackIntf unit from your **uses** declaration.) After compiling your program, you link it with the corresponding object modules to incorporate the compiled code of the units; for further information on this process, see the documentation provided with whatever software development system you're using.

> Instead of a **uses** declaration, some Pascal systems use a $i ("include") directive or some other method for including precompiled units in your program. See your Pascal documentation for details.

Stack-Based and Register-Based Routines

Most of the Toolbox routines are *stack-based:* they accept their parameters and return their results on the stack, as described in the preceding section. This allows the Pascal compiler to generate the same machine instructions to set up the parameters for these predefined routines that it would use for an ordinary Pascal routine defined in your program. Remember, though, that routines in ROM have to be called through the trap mechanism we discussed earlier, rather than by jumping directly to a memory address in the normal way. The Toolbox interface units use a special "inline declaration" for all stack-based ROM routines, telling the compiler to place an appropriate trap word in-line—that is, directly into the compiled object code—instead of the usual JSR (Jump to Subroutine) instruction.

Not all the ROM routines are stack-based, however; some of them are *register-based* instead. In general these are Operating System routines that perform relatively low-level operations such as memory management and file input/output, and were originally intended to be called only from assembly language rather than

Pascal. So instead of using the stack like a Pascal routine, they pass their parameters and results directly in the processor's registers.

Later it was decided that some of these register-based routines would be useful in Pascal as well as assembly language, so they were added to the Pascal interface. Because of the difference in calling conventions, however, an extra level of indirection had to be introduced. When you call a register-based routine in Pascal, what you're actually calling is a special *interface routine* that mediates between the stack- and register-based calling conventions. The interface routine moves the parameters from the stack, where the Pascal calling program leaves them, to the registers where the ROM routine expects to find them; then it traps to the ROM routine. On return from the trap, it moves the results, if any, back from the registers to the stack for the Pascal program's benefit. The interface routine serves as a kind of "glue" between your Pascal program and the register-based routine in ROM, and is sometimes referred to as a "glue routine."

> When you use the Pascal interface units, you don't have to worry about the distinction between stack- and register-based routines. You simply use the normal Pascal syntax for all your routine calls, and the interface units see to it that everything gets fixed up to work the way you expect. The difference between stack- and register-based routines is really important only if you're using the Toolbox in assembly language, as discussed in the next section.

The Assembly-Language Interface

To call a Toolbox routine in assembly language, you use a *trap macro* that expands into the proper trap word for that routine. For example, to call the routine HidePen [5.2.3], which hides the "graphics pen" that the Toolbox uses to draw lines on the screen, you would use the instruction

```
_HidePen
```

When assembled, this macro produces the trap word $A896, which causes a trap to the HidePen routine in ROM.

The trap macros are defined in a set of assembly-language files that you incorporate into your program with an .INCLUDE directive:

- SysTraps, containing the macros for calling Operating System routines
- QuickTraps for the QuickDraw graphics routines
- ToolTraps for the User Interface Toolbox
- PackMacs for the disk-based packages

There's also a set of *definition files* that use .EQU directives to define assembly-language constants and addresses of global variables for use with the Toolbox:

- SysEqu for constants and variables relating to the Operating System
- QuickEqu for those relating to QuickDraw
- ToolEqu for those relating to the Toolbox proper
- SysErr for Operating System error codes

The assembly-language macro and definition files are included with both the Consulair Macintosh Development System (MDS) and Apple's own Macintosh Programmer's Workshop (MPW).

You'll find the names of all the trap macros (along with the corresponding trap words) listed in summary boxes at the ends of the reference sections following each chapter. Trap macro names always begin with an underscore character (_), followed by the name of the routine. The routine name is generally spelled the same way as in Pascal, but there are occasional exceptions; these are noted where appropriate in the reference sections. The reference sections also list useful Toolbox constants, addresses of global variables, field offsets within Toolbox data structures, and so forth, taken from the definition files.

> Be warned that the values of constants, and especially the addresses of global variables, may be subject to change in future versions of the Toolbox. To stay on the safe side, always refer to them by name, rather than relying on the values and addresses shown in our reference sections.

Before calling a Toolbox routine with a trap macro, you have to set up its parameters the way it expects to find them. For stack-based routines, this means pushing the parameters onto the stack in the order they're listed in the routine's Pascal definition. All parameter values must be in the same data formats used by the Pascal compiler:

- Integers are 2 bytes long, long integers 4 bytes, both in two's-complement form.
- All pointers (including handles, discussed in Chapter 3) are 4 bytes long.
- Booleans occupy 2 bytes on the stack, with the actual value in bit 8, the low-order bit of the first byte: 1 for TRUE, 0 for FALSE. The other 15 bits are ignored.
- Single characters (type CHAR) occupy 2 bytes, with the ASCII character code in the second byte. The first byte is ignored.
- Character strings are represented on the stack by a 4-byte pointer to the actual string in memory. The format of the string itself is described later in this chapter and in reference section [2.1.1].
- Data structures such as records and arrays are usually represented by a 4-byte pointer to the structure in memory. However, if the contents of the structure are no more than 4 bytes long, they're stored directly on the stack in place of the pointer.
- All variable parameters, regardless of type, are represented by a 4-byte pointer giving the address of the variable in memory.

The routine will remove its parameters from the stack before returning, so there's no need for you to do this yourself. If the routine is a function, you must reserve stack space for its result by decrementing the stack pointer the appropriate number of bytes *before* pushing the parameters; on return from the trap, you'll find the result on top of the stack.

For register-based routines, of course, you have to set up the parameters in the appropriate registers rather than on the stack. Register usage conventions for all such routines are given in the reference sections; if no register information appears, you can assume the routine is stack-based.

A few of the routines listed in the reference sections don't reside in ROM, but belong to the Pascal interface itself. These routines are inaccessible via the trap mechanism and so are unavailable in assembly language. In general, they exist only to provide a way of doing something in Pascal that can be done more directly and easily at the assembly-language level, such as by reading or setting a global variable. Routines in this category are identified wherever applicable in the reference sections.

Extended Features of Pascal

The version of the Pascal language supported by Apple's MPW and compatible systems has a few nonstandard features that we'll be using in our programming examples. One of these is the data type LONGINT ("long integer"), representing integers of twice the normal length: 32 bits including sign, instead of only 16. This provides a range of ±2147483647, compared with ±32767 for ordinary integers. You can apply all the standard arithmetic operators to long-integer operands as well as to ordinary integers. An ordinary integer will automatically be converted to the equivalent long integer if you combine it with a long integer in an arithmetic expression, or assign it to a long-integer variable, or pass it to a routine that expects a long integer as a parameter.

Many of the Toolbox routines accept long-integer parameters or return long-integer results. Since memory addresses in the 68000 processor are 32 bits long, this type is particularly useful for working with addresses and related quantities, such as the lengths of memory blocks. For the same reason, all pointers on the Macintosh (including handles, which we'll learn about in the next chapter) are 32 bits long.

The built-in function ORD is a standard Pascal function for converting any scalar value to a corresponding integer: for instance, a character to its equivalent integer character code. On the Macintosh, ORD will also accept a pointer and return the equivalent long-integer address. For converting in the other direction, there's a built-in function named POINTER that accepts a long integer representing a memory address and converts it into a pointer to that address. The result is a "blind pointer" similar to the standard

Pascal constant NIL: it can be assigned to a variable of any pointer type, regardless of the underlying base type the variable is declared to point to.

The ORD and POINTER functions can be used in combination to convert from one pointer type to another. For instance, if you've declared

```
var
  this : ThisPtr;
  that : ThatPtr;
```

where ThisPtr and ThatPtr are two different pointer types, you can convert one into the other by writing

```
this := POINTER(ORD(that))
```

or

```
that := POINTER(ORD(this))
```

ORD converts the original pointer to a long-integer address, then POINTER takes it back into a blind pointer that you can assign to a variable of the other type.

However, Apple's Pascal compiler provides a more direct way to convert data values (including pointers) from one type to another. Just use the name of the target type as a function, giving it as a parameter the value to be converted to that type. In the example above, for instance, you could convert the pointers directly with the statements

```
this := ThisPtr(that)
```

or

```
that := ThatPtr(this)
```

This technique is known as *typecasting*. It doesn't change the underlying data representation (in this case, the memory address that the pointers point to)—only the high-level data type that it's considered to represent. We'll see many examples of this technique later on, particularly when we begin to develop our example program MiniEdit in Volume Two.

Another useful feature is the @ operator, which produces a pointer to whatever variable or routine you give it as an operand. Once again, the result is a blind "pointer to anything." For instance, if you declare

```
var
  aThing    : Thing;
  aThingPtr : ^Thing;
```

then the statement

```
aThingPtr := @aThing
```

sets aThingPtr to point to the address of variable aThing. After you've executed this assignment, the expression

```
aThingPtr^
```

(which denotes whatever aThingPtr points to) is equivalent to the variable aThing itself. You can use this expression on either side of an assignment statement, or anywhere else that variable aThing could be used: for instance, if something is another variable of type Thing, the statement

```
something := aThingPtr^
```

is equivalent to

```
something := aThing
```

and

```
aThingPtr^ := something
```

is equivalent to

```
aThing := something
```

The @ operator can be applied to routines (that is, procedures or functions) as well as to variables. Some of the Toolbox routines and data structures have parameters or fields of type ProcPtr [2.1.1], representing a pointer to a program routine. You can use the @

operator to create such routine pointers: for example, if `Twiddle` is the name of a routine in your program, then the expression

```
@Twiddle
```

denotes a pointer to it. You can assign this routine pointer to a variable of type `ProcPtr`, embed it in a data structure, or pass it to any Toolbox routine that expects a `ProcPtr` as a parameter.

Technically, though, a `ProcPtr` is just defined as a pointer to a byte in memory—presumably the address of the first instruction in the routine. This means that there's no way in Pascal to "open up" the `ProcPtr` and execute the underlying routine it points to. That can only be done at the machine- or assembly-language level, either by the Toolbox or by an assembly-language routine of your own, using a `JSR` (Jump to Subroutine) instruction.

One thing to watch out for is that the @ operator doesn't work properly on "nested" routines (those whose definitions are embedded within another routine). Make sure you use it only on routines that are defined at the top level of your program.

Another built-in function that's sometimes handy is `SIZEOF`, which accepts a variable of any type as a parameter and returns the number of bytes that variable occupies in memory. If the parameter is the name of a type, `SIZEOF` gives the number of bytes occupied by a value of that type. For instance, if x is an integer variable, then the expressions `SIZEOF(x)` and `SIZEOF(INTEGER)` both have the value 2 (since an integer is 2 bytes long).

In some versions of Pascal, the SIZEOF function won't accept a type name as a parameter. To find the size of a given type, you have to use a dummy variable of that type instead of the type itself. For example, instead of writing

    SIZEOF(Thing)

you might declare a variable

    var
        something : Thing;

and then write

    SIZEOF(something)

One last feature worth mentioning is EXIT, which allows you to take an immediate return from the middle of a procedure or function. The remainder of the routine is skipped, and control returns immediately to the point of call. This feature is useful, for instance, for escaping from a routine on detecting an error condition of some sort; we'll be using it for this purpose in our MiniEdit program in Volume Two.

The EXIT feature isn't available in some versions of Pascal. You can achieve the same effect by using an (ugh!) goto to jump to an (ugh!) label at the very end of the routine you're exiting from.

General-Purpose Utilities

In the rest of this chapter, we'll be talking about some of the general-purpose utility routines that are included in the Toolbox. Generally, these are simple, straightforward operations dealing with such things as character strings, bit-level manipulation, and arithmetic. These topics aren't essential to your overall understanding of the Toolbox: if you're in a hurry, you might just want to skim this section for a general idea of the utilities available, then refer back later when you need more detailed information.

Strings

For working with strings of character text, the Toolbox uses the same data format as Apple's Pascal compiler. A string is stored internally as a variable-length data structure consisting of 1 byte giving the length of the string in characters, followed by the characters themselves (Figure 2-3). Since the character count is 1 byte long, it can accommodate strings of up to 255 characters. The actual character codes used to stand for the various characters will be given in Chapter 8.

Strings of this form are normally represented in the Toolbox interface by the data type Str255 [2.1.1], used for things like the titles of windows and the names of menu items. Declared variables of this type always take up 256 bytes of memory, regardless of the actual length of the string. Those that are allocated dynamically or embedded in Toolbox data structures take up only as many bytes as are needed to hold the actual characters (along with the length byte, of course). For instance, the string 'Snark' would be 6

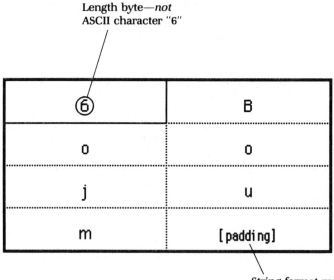

Figure 2-3 Internal string format

bytes long: 1 byte for the character count and 5 more for the characters of the string. However, the string must always occupy a whole number of words—that is, an even number of bytes. If the number of bytes actually needed is odd, an extra, unused byte is added at the end for "padding." So the string 'Boojum' would take up 8 bytes altogether: 1 for the character count, 6 for the characters, and 1 more to keep the overall length even. The empty string takes up 2 bytes of memory: a character count of 0 and a byte of padding.

The Toolbox function EqualString [2.1.2] compares two strings and returns a Boolean result telling whether they're equivalent. You can specify whether you want corresponding upper- and lowercase letters to be considered the same or different. A similar function, RelString (available only on the Macintosh Plus), also tells whether one string alphabetically precedes or follows another. The UprString routine [2.1.2] converts all letters in a string to uppercase while leaving all other characters unchanged.

The Macintosh character set includes a variety of accented letters and diacritical marks for use in foreign languages. The EqualString, RelString, and UprString routines all accept Boolean parameters telling them whether to take such foreign characters into account or whether to ignore them or remove them from the string. There's also an International Utilities Package for adapting a program to the needs of foreign languages and countries. This package includes a more sophisticated string comparison routine named IUEqualString (IU for "International Utilities") that can be customized to the spelling conventions used in a particular language. (For instance, in German it can be set up to treat the umlauted vowels ä, ö, and ü as equivalent to the combinations ae, oe, and ue.) See the *Inside Macintosh* manual for information on the International Utilities Package.

Bit-Level Operations

For testing or changing single bits in memory, the Toolbox includes routines named BitSet to set a bit to 1, BitClr to clear it to 0, and BitTst to test its current value [2.2.1]. These routines all accept two parameters: a pointer to a base address and a bit number relative to that address. Bits are numbered consecutively throughout memory, beginning with 0 for the leftmost (high-order)

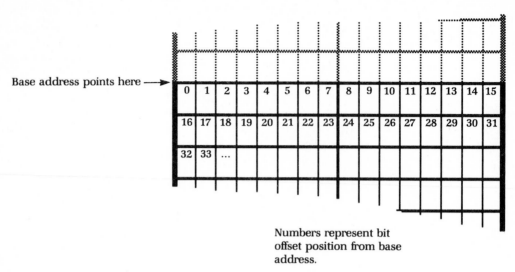

Base address points here →

Numbers represent bit
offset position from base
address.

Figure 2-4 Bit numbering for single-bit operations

bit at the designated base address (Figure 2-4). Thus bit numbers
0 to 7 refer to the byte at the base address itself, 8 to 15 refer to
the following byte, and so on through consecutive bytes of
memory. You can designate a bit at any distance forward from the
given base address by making the bit number as big as you like,
but negative bit numbers are not allowed.

> Notice that this bit-numbering convention is the reverse of the one
> usually used on the 68000 processor, where bits are numbered from
> right to left within a byte or word.

The utility routines BitAnd, BitOr, BitXOr, and BitNot [2.2.2] perform
the standard bitwise logical operations on 32-bit operands. BitShift
[2.2.2] shifts its operand a specified number of bit positions in
either direction. The shift is a logical one, in which bits shifted
out at one end of the operand are lost and 0s are shifted in at the
other end. HiWord and LoWord [2.2.3] extract the high-order and
low-order 16 bits, respectively, of a 32-bit operand.

The StuffHex procedure [2.2.4] "stuffs" consecutive bytes of
memory, beginning at a specified destination address, with the

contents defined by a string of hexadecimal digits. The string should contain no characters other than 0 to 9 and A to F. In particular, it should *not* begin with the leading dollar sign ($) usually used to denote hexadecimal constants.

> StuffHex is a dangerous operation that can easily get you in trouble if you use it carelessly. It does no range or validity checking, just blindly stores into the specified locations in memory. If you give it the wrong destination pointer, the consequences can be catastrophic. Be careful what you stuff and where you stuff it!

Arithmetic Operations

The Toolbox includes facilities for working with 32-bit fixed-point numbers. Type Fixed [2.3.1] is defined as equivalent to the built-in Pascal type LONGINT, but is interpreted in a different way. Instead of a full 32-bit integer, a fixed-point number is considered to have a "binary point" in the middle, splitting it into a 16-bit integer part and a 16-bit fraction. A pair of conversion functions, Long2Fix and Fix2Long [2.3.1], convert numerical values between the two types. The FixRatio routine [2.3.2] divides two 16-bit integers and produces a 32-bit Fixed result. You can add and subtract fixed-point numbers in the usual way, with the standard arithmetic operators $+$ and $-$, but for multiplication and division you have to use the special Toolbox functions FixMul and FixDiv [2.3.2].

The FixRound function [2.3.1] converts a positive fixed-point number to the nearest 16-bit integer. There's also a routine named LongMul [2.3.5] that multiplies two 32-bit long integers and produces a 64-bit integer result. The conversion routines NumToString and StringToNum [2.3.7] convert between long integers and their equivalent representations as strings of decimal digits.

> The Macintosh Plus Toolbox includes a new numerical type, Fract [2.3.3], representing 32-bit fixed-point numbers with 2 integer and 30 fractional bits. Values of this type thus range between -2 and $+2$ at intervals of 2^{-30}. There are routines for converting between the new fractions and the older fixed-point numbers [2.3.3], for multiplying, dividing, and finding square roots of fractions [2.3.4], and for finding fractional sines and cosines of fixed-point quantities [2.3.4].

```
function Randomize (range : INTEGER)          {Desired range of random numbers}
                    : INTEGER;                {Random number between 0 and (range - 1)}



    { Generate random numbers over a specified range. }



var
    rawResult : LONGINT;                      {"Raw" random number received from Toolbox}



begin {Randomize}

    rawResult := ABS(Random);                 {Get random number between 0 and 32767 [2.3.5]}
    Randomize := (rawResult * range) div 32768  {Scale to specified range}

end;  {Randomize}
```

Program 2-1 Generate random numbers

Finally, there's a Random function [2.3.8] that returns a different integer result each time you call it. The results are distributed uniformly over the entire range of integer values, from −32768 to +32767. Program 2-1 shows how to scale the result to the range you need: to generate an integer between 0 and (range − 1), convert the "raw" result you receive from the Random function to a positive value, multiply by range, and divide by the original range of 32768. Notice the use of a LONGINT variable for the intermediate result.

The method used to generate random numbers is based on a "seed" value kept in a global variable named RandSeed [2.3.8], which is changed each time you call the Random function. The sequence of numbers is really only "pseudo-random," since you can reproduce the same sequence again by starting out with the same seed value. The seed is ordinarily initialized to a standard value of 1 at the beginning of your program; if you want to produce a different sequence of random numbers each time the program is run, you have to change this setting to start with a different seed each time. The easiest way to do this is to initialize the seed to the current setting of the clock chip (see next section) at the time the program is started.

Date and Time

The Macintosh has a built-in clock chip that continuously keeps track of the current date and time. The clock chip is powered independently by a battery, and continues to keep time even when the machine's main power is switched off. The date and time are expressed internally as a total number of seconds since the beginning of time, which according to Apple's painstaking research occurred at midnight, January 1, 1904. You can read the clock in this "raw" form with the Toolbox routine GetDateTime or set it with SetDateTime [2.4.1].

Often, however, it's more convenient to work with a *date and time record* [2.4.2], which has separate fields for the year, month, day of the month, day of the week, hour, minute, and second. To read or set the clock in this form, use GetTime or SetTime [2.4.2] instead of GetDateTime or SetDateTime. There's also a pair of utility routines named Secs2Date and Date2Secs [2.4.3] for converting between raw seconds on the one hand and date and time records on the other.

To convert the date and time into a readable character string for human consumption, use IUDateString and IUTimeString [2.4.4]. These routines accept the clock reading in raw seconds and return a string representing the date or time of day, respectively. You can ask for the date in any of three formats: short

12/18/84

long

Tuesday, December 18, 1984

or abbreviated

Tue, Dec 18, 1984

and the time with seconds included

1:47:22 PM

or without

1:47 PM

REFERENCE

2.1 Elementary Data Structures

2.1.1 Strings and Procedures

Definitions

```
type
    Str255  = STRING[255];        {Any text string, maximum 255 characters}
    ProcPtr = Ptr;                {Pointer to a procedure or function [3.1.1]}
```

Notes

1. Str255 stands for a string of text with a maximum length of 255 characters.

2. The first byte (element 0) gives the length of the string in characters; the remaining 1 to 255 bytes contain the characters themselves.

3. Declared variables of type Str255 always take up 256 bytes of memory. Those allocated dynamically (for instance, with NewPtr or NewHandle [3.2.1] or with NewString, GetString, or SetString [8.1.2]), or embedded in

34

Toolbox data structures, include just enough bytes to hold the length count and the actual characters of the string.

4. The string must always physically occupy a whole number of 16-bit memory words. If necessary, an unused byte of "padding" is added at the end to fill out the physical length to an even number of bytes.

5. ProcPtr is a pointer to a procedure or function.

6. To denote a ProcPtr to a given routine, prefix the name of the routine with the pointer operator @.

2.1.2 String Operations

 Definitions

```
function   EqualString
              (string1      : Str255;       {First string to be compared}
               string2      : Str255;       {Second string to be compared}
               caseCounts   : BOOLEAN;      {Distinguish upper- and lowercase?}
               marksCount   : BOOLEAN)      {Include diacritical marks?}
               : BOOLEAN;                   {Are the two strings equivalent?}

function   RelString
              (string1      : Str255;       {First string to be compared}
               string2      : Str255;       {Second string to be compared}
               caseCounts   : BOOLEAN;      {Distinguish upper- and lowercase?}
               marksCount   : BOOLEAN)      {Include diacritical marks?}
               : INTEGER;                   {Which string comes first?}

procedure  UprString
              (var theString : Str255;      {String to be converted}
               stripMarks    : BOOLEAN);    {Eliminate diacritical marks?}

const
   SortsBefore = −1;                        {First string precedes second}
   SortsEqual  =  0;                        {Strings are equivalent}
   SortsAfter  = +1;                        {First string follows second}
```

Notes

1. EqualString compares two strings for equality and returns a Boolean result; RelString tells which of two strings precedes the other alphabetically.

2. RelString returns the value SortsBefore if the first string precedes the second, SortsEqual if the two strings are equivalent, SortsAfter if the first follows the second.

3. If caseCounts is FALSE, corresponding upper- and lowercase letters are considered identical for purposes of comparison; if TRUE, they're considered different.

4. If marksCount is TRUE, foreign-language accents and diacritical marks are taken into account in the comparison; if FALSE, they're disregarded.

5. A more sophisticated form of string comparison, allowing for specialized spelling conventions used in foreign languages, is available through the IUEqualString routine of the International Utilities Package. See *Inside Macintosh* for details.

6. RelString is available only on the Macintosh Plus.

7. UprString converts a string to full capitals, replacing any lowercase letters with their uppercase equivalents.

8. Characters other than letters of the alphabet are left unchanged.

9. If stripMarks is TRUE, foreign-language accents and diacritical marks are removed from the converted string.

10. The trap macro for EqualString is **named** _CmpString ("compare string").

11. When called from assembly language, these routines are register-based: see register usage information below.

12. In assembly language, the Boolean parameters are represented by flag bits in the trap word: 1 for TRUE, 0 for FALSE. caseCounts and marksCount correspond to bits 10 and 9, respectively, of the _CmpString and _RelString traps, and stripMarks to bit 9 of the _UprString trap. The trap macros accept optional parameters named CASE and MARKS for setting these flag bits to 1: for example,

```
_UprString        ,MARKS
_CmpString        ,CASE
_RelString        ,MARKS,CASE
```

Assembly Language Information

Trap macros:

(Pascal) Routine name	(Assembly) Trap macro	Trap word
EqualString	_CmpString	$A03C
RelString	_RelString	$A050
UprString	_UprString	$A854

Register usage:

Routine	Register	Contents
EqualString	A0.L (in)	pointer to string1
	A1.L (in)	pointer to string2
	D0.L (in)	high word: length of string1
		low word: length of string2
	D0.L (out)	= 0 if strings equal
		≠ 0 if unequal
RelString	A0.L (in)	pointer to string1
	A1.L (in)	pointer to string2
	D0.L (in)	high word: length of string1
		low word: length of string2
	D0.L (out)	= −1 if string1 precedes string2
		= 0 if strings are equivalent
		= +1 if string1 follows string2
UprString	A0.L (in)	pointer to theString
	D0.B (in)	length of theString
	A0.L (out)	pointer to theString

Assembly-language constants (Macintosh Plus only):

Name	Value	Meaning
SortsBefore	1	First string precedes second
SortsEqual	0	Strings are equivalent
SortsAfter	−1	First string follows second

2.2 Bit-Level Operations

2.2.1 Single Bit Access

Definitions

```
procedure  BitSet
              (bitsPtr     : Ptr;            {Pointer to bits [3.1.1]}
               bitNumber : LONGINT);         {Number of bit to be set to 1}

procedure  BitClr
              (bitsPtr     : Ptr;            {Pointer to bits [3.1.1]}
               bitNumber : LONGINT);         {Number of bit to be cleared to 0}

function   BitTst
              (bitsPtr     : Ptr;            {Pointer to bits [3.1.1]}
               bitNumber : LONGINT)          {Number of bit to be tested}
                 : BOOLEAN;                  {Is bit set to 1?}
```

Notes

1. These routines operate on single bits in memory.

2. BitSet sets a bit to 1; BitClr clears it to 0; BitTst tests it and returns a Boolean result representing its value.

3. bitsPtr is a pointer to a base address in memory (the elementary data type Ptr is defined in [3.1.1]). bitNumber identifies a single bit relative to the base address.

4. Bits are numbered from left to right within each byte; notice that this is the reverse of the usual 68000 convention.

5. bitNumber can have any nonnegative value, and can designate a bit at any distance in memory from the base address. Bit numbers 0 to 7 refer to the byte designated by the base address, 8 to 15 refer to the byte following it, and so on through consecutive bytes of memory.

6. Negative bit numbers are not allowed.

7. BitTst returns TRUE for a 1 bit, FALSE for a 0 bit.

Assembly Language Information

Trap macros:

(Pascal) Routine name	(Assembly) Trap macro	Trap word
BitSet	_BitSet	$A85E
BitClr	_BitClr	$A85F
BitTst	_BitTst	$A85D

2.2.2   Logical Operations

Definitions

```
function BitAnd
        (bits1 : LONGINT;           {First operand}
         bits2 : LONGINT)           {Second operand}
          : LONGINT;                {Bitwise "and"}

function BitOr
        (bits1 : LONGINT;           {First operand}
         bits2 : LONGINT)           {Second operand}
          : LONGINT;                {Bitwise "or"}

function BitXOr
        (bits1 : LONGINT;           {First operand}
         bits2 : LONGINT)           {Second operand}
          : LONGINT;                {Bitwise "exclusive or"}

function BitNot
        (bits : LONGINT)            {Bits to be complemented}
          : LONGINT;                {Bitwise complement}

function BitShift
        (bits       : LONGINT;      {Bits to be shifted}
       shiftCount : INTEGER)        {Number of places to shift}
          : LONGINT;                {Result of shift}
```

Notes

1. These routines perform bitwise logical operations on 32-bit (long-word) operands.

2. For BitAnd, BitOr, and BitXOr, each bit of the result is obtained by applying the given logical operation to the bits found at the corresponding position in the two operands.

3. For BitNot, each bit of the result is the logical complement of the corresponding bit in the operand. That is, each 1 bit in the operand is transformed into a 0 bit in the result, and vice versa.

4. The result returned by BitShift is obtained by shifting the operand bits by the number of bit positions specified by shiftCount.

5. shiftCount is interpreted modulo 32.

6. Positive shift counts shift to the left, negative to the right.

7. BitShift performs a *logical* shift. Bits shifted out at one end of the operand are lost; positions vacated at the other end are filled with 0s.

Assembly Language Information

Trap macros:

(Pascal) Routine name	(Assembly) Trap macro	Trap word
BitAnd	_BitAnd	$A858
BitOr	_BitOr	$A85B
BitXOr	_BitXOr	$A859
BitNot	_BitNot	$A85A
BitShift	_BitShift	$A85C

2.2.3   Word Access

Definitions

```
function HiWord
          (longWord : LONGINT)      {32-bit operand}
              : INTEGER;            {High-order 16 bits}

function LoWord
          (longWord : LONGINT)      {32-bit operand}
              : INTEGER;            {Low-order 16 bits}
```

Notes

1. These routines extract and return the high- and low-order 16-bit words of a 32-bit long word.

2. HiWord and LoWord can be used to extract the integer and fractional parts, respectively, of a fixed-point number [2.3.1].

Assembly Language Information

Trap macros:

(Pascal) Routine name	(Assembly) Trap macro	Trap word
HiWord	_HiWord	$A86A
LoWord	_LoWord	$A86B

2.2.4   Direct Storage

Definitions

```
procedure  StuffHex
           (destPtr   : Ptr;        {Pointer to data structure to be stuffed}
            hexString : Str255);    {String representing data in hexadecimal}
```

Notes

1. StuffHex stores "raw" bits into any designated data structure in memory.

2. destPtr is a pointer to the beginning of the destination data structure. The specified data will be "stuffed" into consecutive locations beginning at this address.

3. hexString is a string representing the data to be stuffed, in hexadecimal form.

4. hexString should contain no characters other than the hexadecimal digits 0-9 and A-F. It should *not* begin with a dollar sign ($).

5. Nominally, the maximum length of hexString is 255 hexadecimal digits. However, since data structures generally must consist of a whole number of 16-bit words, the effective maximum is actually 252 digits, or 63 words.

6. *BEWARE:* No range checking of any kind is performed.

Assembly Language Information

Trap macro:

(Pascal) Routine name	(Assembly) Trap macro	Trap word
StuffHex	_StuffHex	$A866

2.3   Arithmetic Operations

2.3.1   Fixed-Point Numbers

Definitions

```
type
    Fixed = LONGINT;                        {Fixed-point number}

function Long2Fix
        (theNumber : LONGINT)               {Long integer to be converted}
        : Fixed;                            {Fixed-point equivalent}

function Fix2Long
        (theNumber : Fixed)                 {Fixed-point number to be converted}
        : LONGINT;                          {Long-integer equivalent}

function FixRound
        (theNumber : Fixed)                 {Fixed-point number to be rounded}
        : INTEGER;                          {Number rounded to an integer}
```

Notes

1. Type Fixed represents a 32-bit fixed-point number, with 16 bits before the binary point and 16 bits after it.

2. The value of a fixed-point number is equivalent to that of the corresponding long integer divided by 65536 (2^{16}).

3. Use HiWord and LoWord [2.2.3] to extract the integer and fractional parts of a fixed-point number, respectively.

4. Long2Fix and Fix2Long convert between fixed-point numbers and long integers.

5. FixRound rounds a fixed-point number to the nearest integer.

6. On earlier Macintosh models, FixRound doesn't work properly for negative values: to round a negative fixed-point number, multiply it by −1, round with FixRound, then multiply the result back by −1. This problem has been corrected on the Macintosh Plus.

Assembly Language Information

Trap macros:

(Pascal) Routine name	(Assembly) Trap macro	Trap word
FixRound	_FixRound	$A86C
Long2Fix	_Long2Fix	$A83F
Fix2Long	_Fix2Long	$A840

2.3.2 Fixed-Point Arithmetic

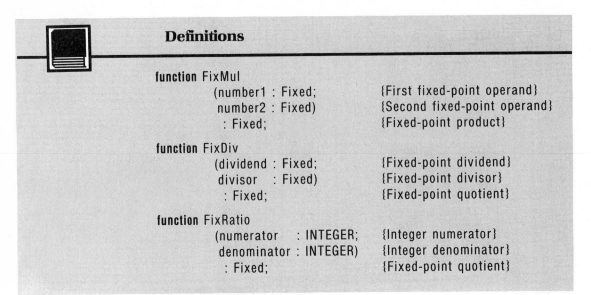

Definitions

function FixMul	
(number1 : Fixed;	{First fixed-point operand}
number2 : Fixed)	{Second fixed-point operand}
: Fixed;	{Fixed-point product}
function FixDiv	
(dividend : Fixed;	{Fixed-point dividend}
divisor : Fixed)	{Fixed-point divisor}
: Fixed;	{Fixed-point quotient}
function FixRatio	
(numerator : INTEGER;	{Integer numerator}
denominator : INTEGER)	{Integer denominator}
: Fixed;	{Fixed-point quotient}

Notes

1. FixMul and FixDiv multiply and divide two fixed-point numbers and produce a fixed-point result.

2. FixDiv is available only on the Macintosh Plus.

3. FixRatio divides two integers and produces a fixed-point result.

4. To add and subtract fixed-point numbers, just use the standard operators + and −.

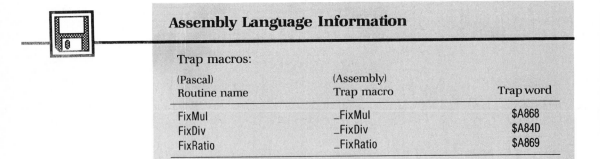

Assembly Language Information

Trap macros:

(Pascal) Routine name	(Assembly) Trap macro	Trap word
FixMul	_FixMul	$A868
FixDiv	_FixDiv	$A84D
FixRatio	_FixRatio	$A869

2.3.3 Fractions

Definitions

```
type
    Fract = LONGINT;

function Fix2Frac
        (theNumber : Fixed)      {Fixed-point number to be converted}
            : Fract;             {Fraction equivalent}

function Frac2Fix
        (theNumber : Fract)      {Fraction to be converted}
            : Fixed;             {Fixed-point equivalent}
```

Notes

1. Type Fract represents a 32-bit fixed-point number, with 2 bits before the binary point and 30 bits after it.

2. The value of a fraction is equivalent to that of the corresponding long integer divided by 1073741824 (2^{30}).

3. Fix2Frac and Frac2Fix convert between fractions and fixed-point numbers [2.3.1].

4. Type Fract and the routines that operate on it are available only on the Macintosh Plus.

Assembly Language Information

Trap macros:

(Pascal) Routine name	(Assembly) Trap macro	Trap word
Fix2Frac	_Fix2Frac	$A841
Frac2Fix	_Frac2Fix	$A842

2.3.4 Fraction Arithmetic

Definitions

function FracMul
          (fraction1 : Fract;   {First fractional operand}
          fraction2 : Fract)   {Second fractional operand}
          : Fract;   {Fractional product}

function FracDiv
          (dividend : Fract;   {Fractional dividend}
          divisor   : Fract)   {Fractional divisor}
          : Fract;   {Fractional quotient}

function FracSqrt
          (theNumber : Fract)   {Fractional operand}
          : Fract;   {Fractional square root

Notes

1. FracMul and FracDiv multiply and divide two fractions and produce a fractional result.

2. To add and subtract fractions, just use the standard operators + and −.

3. FracSqrt finds the square root of a fractional quantity.

4. FracSqrt interprets its parameter as an *unsigned* quantity: that is, negative fractions between −2 and 0 are treated as positive values between +2 and +4.

5. These routines are available only on the Macintosh Plus.

Assembly Language Information

Trap macros:

(Pascal) Routine name	(Assembly) Trap macro	Trap word
FracMul	_FracMul	$A84A
FracDiv	_FracDiv	$A84B
FracSqrt	_FracSqrt	$A849

2.3.5   Long Multiplication

Definitions

```
type
  Int64Bit = record
                hiLong : LONGINT;        {High-order 32 bits}
                loLong : LONGINT         {Low-order 32 bits}
             end;

procedure LongMul
             (number1    : LONGINT;      {First 32-bit operand}
              number2    : LONGINT;      {Second 32-bit operand}
              var product : Int64Bit);   {Returns 64-bit product}
```

Notes

1. LongMul multiplies two 32-bit long integers and produces a 64-bit result.

Assembly Language Information

Trap macro:

(Pascal) Routine name	(Assembly) Trap macro	Trap word
LongMul	_LongMul	$A867

2.3.6   Trigonometric Functions

Definitions

```
function FracSin
        (theAngle : Fixed)          {Fixed-point angle in radians}
          : Fract;                  {Fractional sine}

function FracCos
        (theAngle : Fixed)          {Fixed-point angle in radians}
          : Fract;                  {Fractional cosine}

function FixATan2
        (denominator : LONGINT;     {Denominator of tangent}
         numerator   : LONGINT)     {Numerator of tangent}
          : Fixed;                  {Fixed-point arc tangent in radians}
```

Notes

1. FracSin and FracCos find the fractional sine and cosine of a given angle.
2. FixATan2 finds the arc tangent of a given ratio (that is, the angle whose tangent is equal to that ratio).
3. The ratio is specified by giving a long-integer numerator and denominator. Notice that the denominator is given first (unlike FixDiv [2.3.2] and FracDiv [2.3.4], which take the numerator first).
4. All angles are expressed in fixed-point form, in *radians* (not degrees).
5. These routines are available only on the Macintosh Plus.

Assembly Language Information

Trap macros:

(Pascal) Routine name	(Assembly) Trap macro	Trap word
FracSin	_FracSin	$A848
FracCos	_FracCos	$A847
FixATan2	_FixATan2	$A818

2.3.7   Binary/Decimal Conversion

Definitions

```
procedure  NumToString
              (theNumber    : LONGINT;      {Number to be converted}
           var theString : Str255);         {Returns equivalent string}

procedure  StringToNum
              (theString      : Str255;      {String to be converted}
           var theNumber: LONGINT);          {Returns equivalent number}
```

Notes

1. These routines convert a number between its internal binary representation and its external representation as a decimal character string.

2. The string consists entirely of decimal digits (0-9), except possibly for a leading sign (+ or −).

3. NumToString doesn't produce a + sign for positive numbers, but StringToNum will accept one.

4. NumToString suppresses leading zeros except in the case of the numerical value 0, which produces the one-character string '0'.

5. The magnitude of the string provided to StringToNum should not exceed $2^{31} - 1$ (2147483647).

6. The binary/decimal conversion routines are not actually part of the Toolbox proper; they're contained in a package, the Binary/Decimal Conversion Package, that resides in the system resource file (or in ROM on a Macintosh Plus) and is automatically loaded into memory when needed. Package routines are defined in the interface file PackIntf. See Chapter 7 for further information on the package mechanism.

7. The trap macros for these routines expand to call _Pack7 [7.2.1] with the routine selectors given below.

Assembly Language Information

Trap macros and routine selectors:

(Pascal) Routine name	(Assembly) Trap macro	Trap word	Routine selector
NumToString	_NumToString	$A9EE	0
StringToNum	_StringToNum	$A9EE	1

Register usage:

Routine	Register	Contents
NumToString	D0.L (in)	theNumber
	A0.L (out)	pointer to theString
StringToNum	A0.L (in)	pointer to theString
	D0.L (out)	theNumber

2.3.8 Random Numbers

Definitions

```
function Random
        : INTEGER;        {Random number}

var
    RandSeed : LONGINT;   {"Seed" for random number generation}
```

Notes

1. Random returns a different integer each time it's called, distributed uniformly over the interval from −32768 to +32767.

2. The sequence of numbers generated is "pseudo-random": the same sequence can be duplicated by starting with the same "seed" value in the global variable RandSeed.

3. RandSeed is initialized to 1 by the QuickDraw initialization procedure InitGraf [4.3.1].

4. RandSeed is actually a QuickDraw global variable [4.3.1]. To access it in assembly language, find the pointer to QuickDraw's globals at the address contained in register A5, then locate the variable relative to that pointer using the offset constant RandSeed (below). See Chapter 3 and [4.3.1, note 4] for further discussion.

Assembly Language Information

Trap macro:

(Pascal) Routine name	(Assembly) Trap macro	Trap word
Random	_Random	$A861

QuickDraw global variable:

Name	Offset in bytes	Meaning
RandSeed	−126	"Seed" for random number generation

2.4   Date and Time

2.4.1   Date and Time in Seconds

Definitions

```
procedure  GetDateTime
           (var seconds : LONGINT);   {Returns current date and time in "raw" seconds}
function   SetDateTime
           (seconds : LONGINT)        {New date and time in "raw" seconds}
              : OSErr;                 {Result code [3.1.2]}
const
  ClkRdErr = −85;                      {Unable to read clock}
  ClkWrErr = −86;                      {Clock not written correctly}
```

Notes

1. These routines read and set the current date and time in the Macintosh's built-in clock chip.

2. The user can set the date and time with the Alarm Clock or Control Panel desk accessory.

3. The date and time are expressed as a total number of "raw" seconds since midnight, January 1, 1904. This value can be converted to a date and time record with Secs2Date [2.4.3], or to an equivalent character string with IUDateString and IUTimeString [2.4.4].

4. The function result returned by SetDateTime is an Operating System result code [3.1.2].

5. When called from assembly language, SetDateTime is register-based; see register usage information below.

6. GetDateTime is not available in assembly language via the trap mechanism. Instead, the current reading of the clock chip is directly accessible in the global variable Time.

Assembly Language Information

Trap macro:

(Pascal) Routine name	(Assembly) Trap macro	Trap word
SetDatetime	_SetDateTime	$A03A

Register usage:

Routine	Register	Contents
SetDateTime	D0.L (in) D0.W (out)	seconds result code

Assembly-language global variable:

Name	Address	Meaning
Time	$20C	Current date and time in "raw" seconds

2.4.2   Date and Time Records

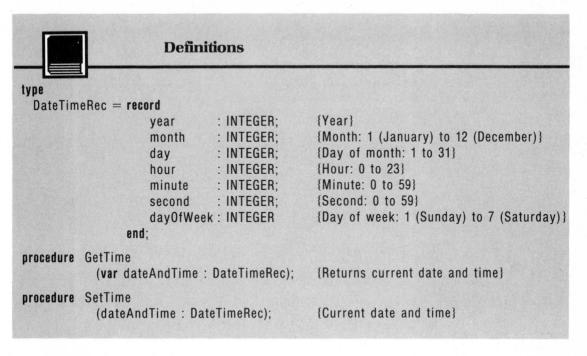

Definitions

```
type
  DateTimeRec = record
                year       : INTEGER;     {Year}
                month      : INTEGER;     {Month: 1 (January) to 12 (December)}
                day        : INTEGER;     {Day of month: 1 to 31}
                hour       : INTEGER;     {Hour: 0 to 23}
                minute     : INTEGER;     {Minute: 0 to 59}
                second     : INTEGER;     {Second: 0 to 59}
                dayOfWeek : INTEGER       {Day of week: 1 (Sunday) to 7 (Saturday)}
           end;
procedure GetTime
          (var dateAndTime : DateTimeRec);    {Returns current date and time}

procedure SetTime
          (dateAndTime : DateTimeRec);        {Current date and time}
```

Notes

1. GetTime and SetTime read and set the current date and time in the Macintosh's built-in clock chip.

2. The user can set the date and time with the Alarm Clock or Control Panel desk accessory.

3. The date and time are represented in the form of a record of type DateTimeRec.

4. These routines are not available in assembly language via the trap mechanism. Instead, you can read the clock chip directly via the global variable Time or set it with SetDateTime [2.4.1] and convert between "raw" seconds and date and time records with Secs2Date and Date2Secs [2.4.3].

Assembly Language Information

Field offsets in a date and time record:

(Pascal) Field name	(Assembly) Offset name	Offset in bytes
year	dtYear	0
month	dtMonth	2
day	dtDay	4
hour	dtHour	6
minute	dtMinute	8
second	dtSecond	10
dayOfWeek	dtDayOfWeek	12

2.4.3   Date and Time Conversion

Definitions

```
procedure Secs2Date
          (seconds         : LONGINT;        {Date and time in "raw" seconds}
       var dateAndTime : DateTimeRec);   {Returns equivalent date and time record}

procedure Date2Secs
          (dateAndTime : DateTimeRec;       {Date and time record}
       var seconds   : LONGINT);        {Returns equivalent in "raw" seconds}
```

Notes

1. These routines convert the date and time between "raw" seconds, as reported directly by the built-in clock chip [2.4.1], and the more convenient form of date and time records [2.4.2].

2. When called from assembly language, these routines are register-based: see register usage information below.

Assembly Language Information

Trap macros:

(Pascal) Routine name	(Assembly) Trap macro	Trap word
Secs2Date	_Secs2Date	$A9C6
Date2Secs	_Date2Secs	$A9C7

Register usage:

Routine	Register	Contents
Secs2Date	D0.L (in)	seconds
	A0.L (out)	pointer to dateAndTime
Date2Secs	A0.L (in)	pointer to dateAndTime
	D0.L (out)	seconds

2.4.4   Date and Time Strings

Definitions

```
type
    DateForm = (ShortDate, LongDate, AbbrevDate);

procedure IUDateString
        (seconds      : LONGINT;   {Date and time in "raw" seconds}
         format       : DateForm;  {Format desired for date}
         var theString : Str255);  {Returns equivalent character string}

procedure IUTimeString
        (seconds      : LONGINT;   {Date and time in "raw" seconds}
         withSeconds  : BOOLEAN;   {Include seconds in string?}
         var theString : Str255);  {Returns equivalent character string}
```

Notes

1. These routines convert a date and time in "raw" seconds, as reported by ReadDateTime [2.4.1], to a character string representing the corresponding calendar date or time of day.

2. These routines are not actually part of the Toolbox proper; they're contained in a package, the International Utilities Package, that resides in the system resource file and is automatically loaded into memory when needed. Package routines are defined in the interface file PackIntf. See Chapter 7 for further information on the package mechanism, and *Inside Macintosh* for more on the International Utilities Package.

3. The exact formats used for dates and times may vary from one country to another, under the control of the International Utilities Package. The formats shown below are the standard ones for American use.

4. The format parameter to IUDateString identifies the format desired for the date, as in the following examples:

Short:	6/ 8/84
	10/15/84
Long:	Friday, June 8, 1984
	Monday, October 15, 1984
Abbreviated:	Fri, Jun 8, 1984
	Mon, Oct 15, 1984

5. Dates in the short format carry leading blanks or zeros if necessary, so that they're always the same length (8 characters in the standard American format).

6. The withSeconds parameter to IUTimeString specifies whether to include a seconds field in the time, as in the following examples:

With seconds:	10:47:13 AM
	3:23:08 PM
Without seconds:	10:47 AM
	3:23 PM

7. Times, whether with or without seconds, carry leading blanks or zeros if necessary, so that they're always the same length (8 or 11 characters in the standard American format).

8. The trap macros for these routines expand to call _Pack6 [7.2.1] with the routine selectors given below.

Assembly Language Information

Trap macros:

(Pascal) Routine name	(Assembly) Trap macro	Trap word	Routine selector
IUDateString	_IUDateString	$A9ED	0
IUTime String	_IUTimeString	$A9ED	2

Assembly-language constants:

Name	Value	Meaning
ShortDate	0	Short form of date
LongDate	1	Long form of date
AbbrevDate	2	Abbreviated form of date

CHAPTER

3

Thanks for
the Memory

This chapter is about memory: how it's organized and how to manage it. We'll learn what's where in the Macintosh's memory, how to allocate blocks of memory for a program's use, how to refer to those blocks from within the program, how to copy and combine them, and how to release them when they're no longer needed. These are basic techniques that you'll use in every program you write for the Macintosh.

Memory Organization

The original Macintosh has 64 kilobytes—that is, 64 times 1024, or 65,536 bytes—of *read-only memory* (ROM), containing the built-in code of the Toolbox. The new Macintosh Plus doubles the ROM size to 128K. ROM addresses begin at hexadecimal $400000 and run up to $40FFFF or $41FFFF, depending on the model. Since its contents are permanent and unchangeable, this portion of memory is not available for general use by a running program.

When we talk about memory allocation, we're really referring only to the remaining *read/write memory* (commonly known by the misleading term "random-access memory," or RAM). The original "Skinny Mac" has 128K of RAM, occupying addresses $0-$1FFFF; the "Fat Mac" has 512K, from $0-$7FFFF. The Macintosh Plus has a full megabyte (1024K, or 1,048,576 bytes), running from

59

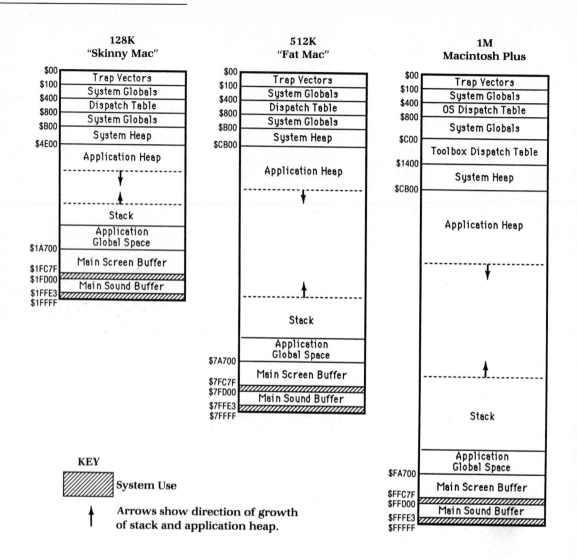

Figure 3-1 Memory organization

$0-$FFFFF, and can be expanded to 2, 2.5, or even 4 megabytes; future models will have even more memory. The Toolbox is designed to adapt automatically to different memory configurations, so that the same program can run without change on all models of the machine and will automatically make use of whatever amount of RAM is available.

Figure 3-1 shows how RAM is laid out. On all models of

Macintosh, addresses $0-$FF hold the 68000 processor's trap vectors, which we discussed in the last chapter. The Toolbox keeps its *system globals* (memory locations reserved for its own private use) at addresses $100-$3FF and $800-$AFF ($800-$BFF on the Macintosh Plus). On older models, the dispatch table, which holds the ROM addresses of the various Toolbox and Operating System routines, is at addresses $400-$7FF. On the Macintosh Plus, this area is reserved for the OS dispatch table only; the Toolbox has a separate table of its own, running from $C00-$13FF.

All of the addresses given in this chapter may differ in future models of the Macintosh.

At the end of memory are the *screen buffer*, containing the bits that define the image to be displayed on the Macintosh screen, and the *sound buffer*, which controls the sounds emitted by the built-in speaker. Table 3-1 shows the addresses of the screen and sound buffers in the various models. Just before these buffers in memory is the *application global space*, which contains the application program's global variables and other information about the program as a whole. The space between the end of the system globals and the beginning of the application globals is available for dynamic memory allocation.

Table 3-1 Buffer addresses

Model	Memory size	Main screen buffer	Main sound buffer	Alternate screen buffer	Alternate sound buffer
Skinny Mac	128K	$1A700-$1FC7F	$1FD00-$1FFE3	$12700-$17C7F	$1A100-$1A3E3
Fat Mac	512K	$7A700-$7FC7F	$7FD00-$7FFE3	$72700-$77C7F	$7A100-$7A3E3
Macintosh Plus	1M	$FA700-$FFC7F	$FFD00-$FFFE3	$F2700-$F7C7F	$FA100-$FA3E3

Although most programs will use the main screen and sound buffers at the addresses just given, there are also alternate buffers available for unusual needs, at the locations shown in Table 3-1. Since the application global space is always located right before the lowest-addressed screen or sound buffer in use, using either or both of the alternate buffers lowers the position of the global space in memory and reduces the space available for dynamic allocation accordingly. For the alternate sound buffer, the reduction is $600 bytes, or 1.5K; for the alternate screen buffer, it's $8000 bytes, or 32K.

The Application Global Space

The application global space holds three kinds of information pertaining to a program: its *global variables, application parameters,* and *jump table* (see Figure 3-2). The space needed for these varies from one program to another, and is allocated at the time the program is started up. (We'll have more to say about how this is done, and about the contents and purpose of the jump table, in Chapter 7; we'll be discussing the application parameters in just a minute.)

At the machine-language level, the processor's address register A5 always holds a pointer to the beginning of the application parameters. If you're programming in a higher-level language such as Pascal, of course, you never have to think about processor registers; your language software will see to it that A5 is properly maintained. Even so, you should understand how this register is used at the machine level. The Toolbox initializes A5 when a program is started, and uses it as a base address from which to locate everything in the application global space: global variables at negative offsets from A5, application parameters and the jump table at positive offsets. (The global variables are allocated in the reverse of the order they're declared. That is, the first variable declared is last in memory, at the smallest negative offset from the base address in A5.)

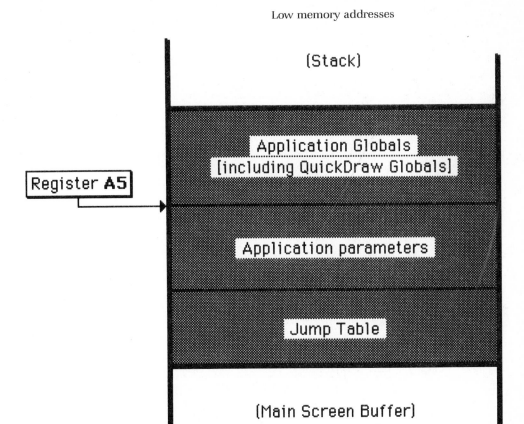

Low memory addresses

(Stack)

Application Globals
[including QuickDraw Globals]

Register **A5**

Application parameters

Jump Table

(Main Screen Buffer)

High memory addresses

Figure 3-2 Application global space

If you're using assembly language, you have to remember that register A5 is special and be careful not to disturb its contents. If you absolutely must "borrow" this register temporarily, be sure to restore it from the system global CurrentA5 [3.1.3] before calling any Toolbox routine.

This "A5 world" is a vestige of the Lisa Pascal environment from which much of the Macintosh software grew. On the Lisa, the application parameters held important descriptive information about the program that was used by various parts of the system.

Most of these parameters are no longer used on the Macintosh, but a few are still needed by parts of the Toolbox that preserve traces of their Lisa origins. To keep these archaic parts of the Toolbox happy, space (normally 32 bytes) is still reserved for the application parameters when a program is started up, and a pointer to them is placed in A5.

Only two of the application parameters are actually used on the Macintosh (Figure 3-3). At address 0(A5) (that is, at an offset of 0 bytes from the base address in register A5) is a pointer that the QuickDraw graphics routines use to find their global variables; we'll return to this subject in Chapter 4. At 16(A5) is the *startup handle*, used by the Finder to tell the program what files to open on starting up. (We'll be learning what a handle is later in this chapter; the Finder startup handle is discussed in Chapter 7.) The rest of the 32-byte application parameter area is reserved for possible future use.

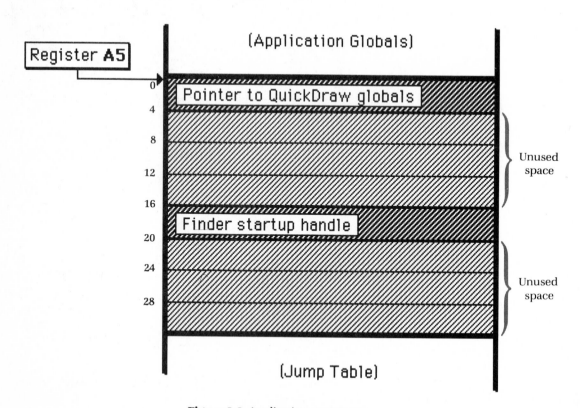

Figure 3-3 Application parameters

The Stack and the Heap

As noted earlier, the space available for dynamic memory allocation runs from the end of the system globals to the beginning of the application globals. This area is shared between two different forms of allocation, the *stack* and the *heap*, which grow toward each other from opposite ends of the space (see Figure 3-4). The stack is used mainly for holding parameters, local variables, return addresses, and other temporary storage associated with a program's routines (procedures and functions). If you're an assembly-language programmer, you already know all about the stack and how to use it. In Pascal and other higher-level languages, all stack management is handled for you automatically and you needn't concern yourself with it; all you really need to know is that every variable you declare by name in one of your program's routines implicitly resides on the stack. The memory space needed to hold such a variable is allocated on entry to the routine that declares it, and released again on exit.

> The stack actually grows backward in memory, from higher- toward lower-numbered addresses. If you're an experienced programmer, you should be used to this sort of thing—you also probably draw your trees with their roots at the top and their leaves at the bottom!

Unlike stack space, space in the heap is allocated and released only by explicit request, never implicitly, even in high-level languages. These requests can be issued in whatever order the program requires, and are not tied to the program's subroutine call structure like the stack. If stack space is allocated in LIFO order ("last in, first out"), heap allocation might be called LIOF: "last in, OK, fine." The heap extends forward from the end of the system globals, and is divided into two parts, the *system heap* and the *application heap*.

As you might expect, the system heap is used by the system software for its own private memory needs. It begins right after the end of the system globals, and has a fixed size of $4300 bytes (16.75K) on a Skinny Mac, $C000 bytes (48K) on a Fat Mac, or $B700 bytes (45.75K) on a Macintosh Plus. Its contents aren't destroyed

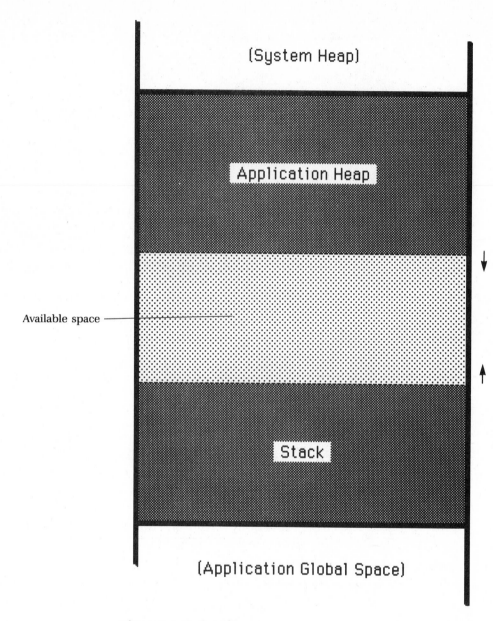

Figure 3-4 Stack and heap

when one program ends and another is started; this allows the system to maintain its private data structures from one program to the next.

> The sizes given for the system heap are correct as of the time of writing. These sizes may vary in future releases of the system software.

The application heap is for your program's use; it contains the code of the program itself and any data structures that the Toolbox creates on your behalf, as well as space that you allocate explicitly for your own data. The application heap follows the system heap in memory, and is reinitialized every time a new program is started. This destroys its previous contents and gives each program a brand-new, empty heap to work with. The initial size of the application heap is $1800 bytes (6K), but it can grow bigger as the program runs if more space is needed.

> Technically, what we're calling the system heap and application heap are actually *heap zones*. The Toolbox can maintain any number of heap zones: if you want, you can subdivide your original application heap into two or more separate zones and allocate space from each of them independently. This is an unusual thing to do, though, and we won't go into it any further here; see Apple's *Inside Macintosh* manual if you want the details. Unless you explicitly specify otherwise, all the memory allocation operations described in this chapter will automatically apply to the single application heap zone.

Handles and Master Pointers

You can allocate space from the heap in *blocks* of any size; when you no longer need a block, you should release it so that the space can be reused for another purpose. As blocks are allocated and released, the available free space tends to become fragmented into lots of little blocks scattered randomly throughout the heap. Such fragmentation can sometimes make it impossible to allocate a block of a given size even though the needed amount of free space

Before   After

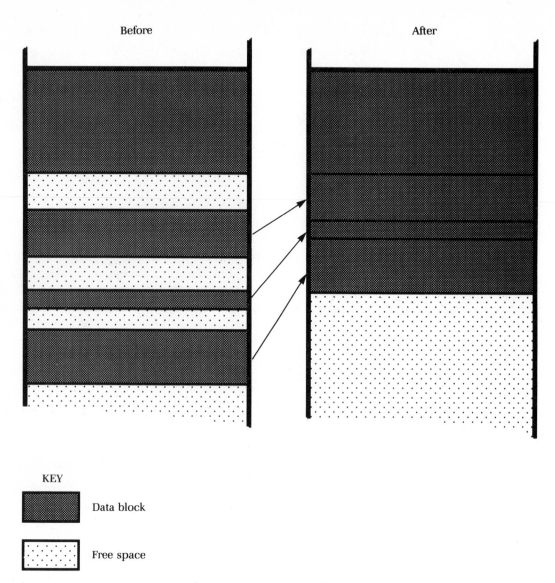

KEY

Data block

Free space

Figure 3-5 Heap compaction

is available, because no single free block is big enough. When this happens, the Toolbox tries to create a block of the needed size by moving all the allocated blocks together and coalescing the free space into one big block. This is known as *compacting* the heap (see Figure 3-5).

Figure 3-6 Dangling pointer

For heap compaction to work, there must be a way to keep track of the allocated blocks as they're moved from one location to another. Suppose you ask the Toolbox to allocate a block; it gives you back a pointer to the new block, which you save in a variable or embed in a data structure of some kind. Later, the heap is compacted and the block is moved to a different location (see Figure 3-6). This leaves your pointer pointing to where the block used to be instead of where it is; what's actually there now is anybody's guess. Trying to follow this "dangling pointer" is now a one-way ticket to the Twilight Zone.

The solution to this problem is simple and elegant. Instead of giving you a pointer when it allocates a block, the Toolbox keeps its own *master pointer* to the block and gives you a pointer to the master pointer, known as a *handle* to the block (Figure 3-7). Like the block itself, the master pointer resides in the heap; but unlike the block, the master pointer is never moved, even when the heap is compacted. Since it remains at a known, fixed location, the Toolbox can easily update it whenever the block is moved, so that it always points correctly to the block's current location. When you need to refer to the block, you do it by double indirection: the handle leads you to the master pointer, which in turn leads you to the block. Since the master pointer never moves, you'll never lose track of the block, no matter where or how often it's moved within the heap.

Figure 3-7 Handle and master pointer

Relocatable and Nonrelocatable Blocks

Blocks that are referred to by handles are called *relocatable* blocks, since they can safely be moved around within the heap. You create a relocatable block by calling the Toolbox routine NewHandle [3.2.1], specifying the size of the block in bytes. For instance, suppose your program defines a data type named Thing. To allocate a new Thing from the heap, you would use a statement like

thatThing := NewHandle(SIZEOF(Thing))

(Recall that the SIZEOF function, applied to a type name, gives the number of bytes occupied by a value of that type.) NewHandle will allocate heap space for a block of the requested size and also for its master pointer, set the master pointer to point to the block, and give you back a pointer to the master pointer—that is, a handle to the block. Thus the expression

thatThing^

denotes the master pointer, and

thatThing^^

refers to the underlying Thing itself. If a Thing is a record with a field named widget, you can access the field with the expression

    thatThing^^.widget

Once you allocate a block, its size isn't frozen forever. You can make it bigger or smaller at any time with the Toolbox routine SetHandleSize [3.2.3]. (When you make a block bigger, things may have to be moved around in the heap to make room; but of course the master pointers will be fixed up properly, so all your handles will remain correct.) To find out the current size of a block, use GetHandleSize [3.2.3]. When you're all through with a block, release it by calling DisposHandle [3.2.2] to make its space available for reallocation.

You can also create *nonrelocatable* blocks, which will never be moved even during heap compaction. To allocate such a block, use NewPtr [3.2.1] instead of NewHandle:

    otherThing := NewPtr(SIZEOF(Thing))

Since the block will never be moved, there's no need for a master pointer—so NewPtr doesn't create one. Instead of a handle, it just gives you back a pointer directly to the block itself (Figure 3-8). You can then use this pointer to refer to your Thing by single rather than double indirection

    otherThing^

and access its fields with expressions like

    otherThing^.widget

Like a relocatable block, a nonrelocatable one can be lengthened or shortened at any time. You can change its size with SetPtrSize [3.2.3], find out its current size with GetPtrSize [3.2.3], and release it when the time comes with DisposPtr [3.2.2].

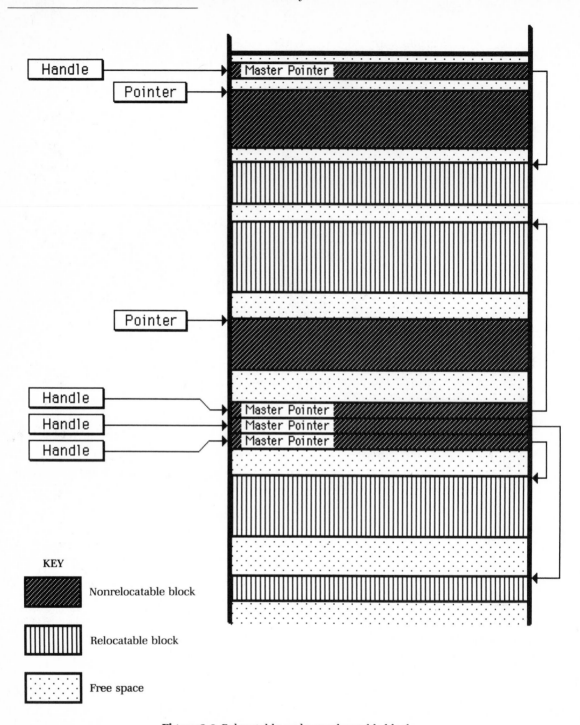

Figure 3-8 Relocatable and nonrelocatable blocks

Elementary Data Types

The Toolbox interface defines general-purpose data types [3.1.1] for talking about pointers and handles. Type Ptr stands for a pointer to an arbitrary byte in memory, and Handle for a pointer to a Ptr. Both are based on the underlying type SignedByte, which represents a single memory byte as an integer between −128 and +127. (There's also an alternate type just named Byte, which represents a byte as an unsigned integer between 0 and 255.) For specifying the size of a block on the heap, there's the type Size, equivalent to a long integer (LONGINT).

The heap allocation routines NewPtr and NewHandle return results of type Ptr and Handle, respectively—that is, a pointer or a handle to a SignedByte. In order to access a block's contents, you have to convert these to some other type that more specifically describes the block's internal structure.

For instance, suppose your program defines the following types:

```
type
  LinkHandle = ^LinkPtr;
  LinkPtr    = ^Link;
  Link       = record
                 data : INTEGER;
                 next : LinkHandle
               end;
```

To allocate a new Link record from the heap and store into its data field, you can't simply declare a variable

```
var
  theLink : LinkHandle;
```

and write something like

```
theLink := NewHandle(SIZOF(Link));
theLink^^.data := 0
```

The first of these statements is not a valid assignment, because the types don't match: NewHandle returns a general Handle (a handle to a SignedByte), whereas the variable theLink expects a LinkHandle (a handle to a Link record). Nor can you correct the problem by changing the declared type of theLink:

```
var
    theLink : Handle;
```

Now the second statement

```
theLink^^.data := 0
```

is invalid, because theLink^^ is now a SignedByte instead of a Link, and so doesn't have a field named data.

The solution is to use the "typecasting" technique described in Chapter 2 to convert the general Handle you get from the Toolbox into a LinkHandle that you can work with:

```
var
    the Handle : Handle;
    the Link    : LinkHandle;

    . . . ;

    theHandle := NewHandle(SIZEOF(Link));
    theLink    := LinkHandle(theHandle);

    theLink^^.data := 0
```

(Actually, of course, you could do it in one step by dispensing with the intermediate variable theHandle and simply writing

```
theLink := LinkHandle(NewHandle(SIZEOF(Link)))
```

We did it in two steps here just to make sure it's clear exactly what's going on.)

Error Reporting

Strictly speaking, the memory management routines are part of the Macintosh Operating System, rather than the Toolbox proper. Along with other Operating System routines, most of them post a *result code* of type OSErr [3.1.2] to report errors or signal successful completion. At the machine level, the result code is returned in a register—the lower half of D0, to be precise. To allow you to access it from Pascal, the interface unit OSIntf includes a special function named MemError [3.1.2] that returns the result code posted by the last memory management operation.

> Notice, however, that MemError is part of the *interface* to the memory management routines, not one of the routines actually built into ROM. Other languages may have different mechanisms for accessing Operating System result codes, or none at all. You'll have to consult your own language documentation for details.

Result codes are always less than or equal to 0. A value of 0 (NoErr) means the routine was able to complete its job successfully; a negative result code means that it was prevented from doing so because of an error. The most important error reported by the memory management routines is MemFullErr, which means that an allocation operation failed for lack of heap space.

> If you're programming in assembly language, you can just look in register D0 for the result code returned by a memory management (or other Operating System) routine. However, not all such routines do in fact post a result code in this register; the register usage information in the Reference Handbook will tell you which ones do and which don't.
>
> Before returning from any Operating System trap, the Trap Dispatcher sets the processor's condition codes to reflect the result code (if there is one) by executing the instruction
>
> ```
> TST.W D0
> ```
>
> You can then just branch on the condition codes without performing a test of your own: for example,
>
> ```
>     MOVEQ D0,#blockSize      ; Indicate size of block
>     _NewHandle               ; Allocate block
>       BMI  Error             ; Branch on error
> ```

Locking Blocks

Whenever you allocate a block from the heap, you can choose whether to make it relocatable (with NewHandle) or nonrelocatable (with NewPtr). In general you should use relocatable blocks whenever possible, since this allows the Toolbox to make the most efficient use of the available heap space. However, relocatable blocks also have their costs, in both space and time: they take up an extra 4 bytes for the master pointer and require an extra memory fetch to access, because of the second level of indirection. Usually this is a negligible price to pay, but sometimes that extra memory reference can be costly, if it occurs inside a tight inner loop or some other part of your program where speed is critical.

In such cases, you can save time by converting the block's handle to a copy of the master pointer

```
masterPtr := theHandle^
```

and then referring to the block by single indirection

```
masterPtr^
```

within the loop. This is known as *dereferencing* the handle (a general term meaning to convert any pointer into the thing it points to). However, keep in mind that all you have is a *copy* of the master pointer, not the master pointer itself. If the heap is compacted and the block is moved, the Toolbox will only update the actual master pointer; the copy will be left pointing into the Twilight Zone.

To keep your pointers from dangling, you can *lock* the block before dereferencing its handle. This temporarily prevents the block from being moved, even if the heap is compacted. You can then safely dereference the handle and refer to the block by single indirection. When you're through with your critical program section, you can discard your copy of the master pointer and *unlock* the block, so that it can again be moved around to make room in the heap for other blocks. The Toolbox routines for locking and unlocking a block are HLock and HUnlock [3.2.4]; Program 3-1 shows how to use them in dereferencing a handle. (Notice that only a relocatable block can be locked; this makes it *temporarily* unmovable, while a nonrelocatable block is *permanently* unmovable.)

```
{ Skeleton code to illustrate use of a dereferenced handle.  }

type
   LinkHandle = ^LinkPtr;
   LinkPtr    = ^Link;

   Link      = record
                   data : INTEGER;
                   next : LinkHandle
                end;

var
   theHandle : Handle;                         {Untyped handle for creating the block}
   theLink   : LinkHandle;                      {Typed handle for referring to the block}
   masterPtr : LinkPtr;                         {Typed pointer for dereferencing the handle}

begin

   theHandle := NewHandle(SIZEOF(Link));        {Allocate a relocatable block [3.2.1]}
   theLink   := POINTER(ORD(theHandle));        {Convert to typed handle}

   . . . ;

   HLock (theLink);                             {Lock the block [3.2.4]}

      masterPtr := theLink^;                    {Dereference the handle}

      while . . . do
         begin
            . . . ;
            ...masterPtr^...;                   {Use single indirection inside loop}
            . . .
         end;

   HUnlock (theLink);                           {Unlock the block [3.2.4]}

   . . .

end
```

Program 3-1 Dereferencing a handle

Certain Pascal constructs involving handles can also cause Apple's compiler to generate dangling pointers. For example, a **with** statement based on a relocatable record

```
with aHandle^^ do
  begin
    . . .
  end
```

will lead to trouble if the underlying record is moved or purged because of memory allocation performed inside the body of the statement. To avoid problems, you always should lock the block with

```
HLock (aHandle)
```

before executing such a **with** statement and then unlock it again afterward.

Similarly, any call to a routine that can do heap allocation may cause trouble if you pass it a field of a relocatable record as a variable

```
ARoutine (aHandle^^.field)
```

or assign its result to such a field

```
aHandle^^.field := ARoutine (. . .)
```

Instead of locking the block in these cases, you can use a temporary variable:

```
temp := aHandle^^.field;
ARoutine (temp)
```

or

```
temp := ARoutine (. . .);
aHandle^^.field := temp
```

Keep in mind that many Toolbox routines allocate heap space behind the scenes, without your being aware of it. To stay on the safe side, you should assume that any Toolbox call is "dangerous" and take suitable precautions.

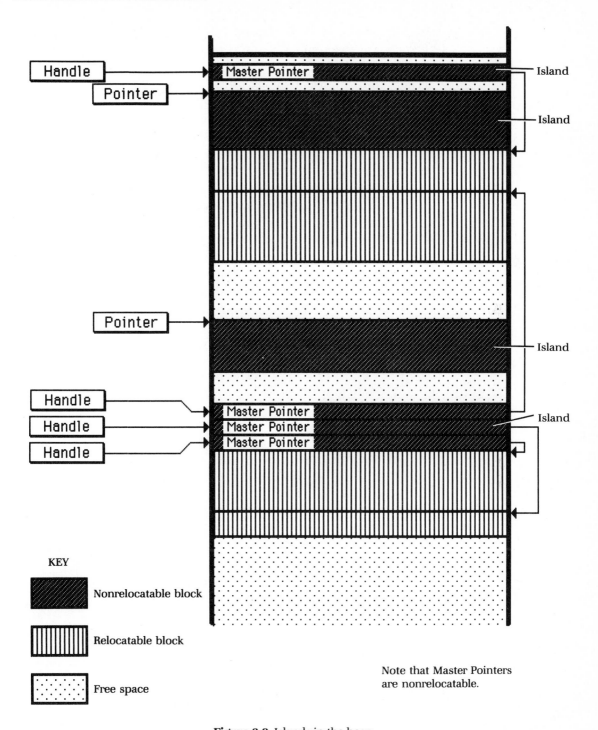

Figure 3-9 Islands in the heap

In general, try not to keep a block locked any longer than you have to, and remember to unlock it again as soon as you safely can. An unmovable block, whether it's temporarily locked or permanently nonrelocatable, forms an 'island'' in the heap that can interfere with compaction and prevent the available free space from being coalesced (Figure 3-9). You can avoid this problem, however, by arranging to keep all the unmovable blocks together at the beginning of the heap, out of the way of the movable ones. For nonrelocatable blocks, the Toolbox does this automatically: it allocates them as near as possible to the start of the heap, moving other blocks out of the way if necessary to make room. To do the same for a relocatable block (if you know it will be locked for long periods of time), you can use the Toolbox routine ResrvMem [3.2.5]. This routine creates space near the beginning of the heap for a block of a specified size, but doesn't actually allocate the block. You have to follow it with a call to NewHandle to do the actual allocation:

```
ResrvMem (blockSize);
theHandle := NewHandle (blockSize)
```

If you're only locking a block for a short time, you can keep it out of the way by moving it to the end of the heap instead of the beginning, using the Toolbox routine MoveHHi [3.2.5]:

```
MoveHHi (theHandle);
HLock    (theHandle)
```

Notice that MoveHHi operates on a block that already exists, whereas ResrvMem just clears the heap space for a block about to be created.

Copying and Combining Blocks

The Toolbox includes a number of utility routines for copying and combining blocks in the heap. HandToHand [3.2.6] creates a new relocatable block that's a copy of another. You give it a variable containing a handle to the block you want to copy; it returns a handle to the copy in this same variable (see Figure 3-10). For

result := HandToHand (theHandle)

Figure 3-10 HandToHand

example, if thisHandle is a handle to the block to be copied, the statements

```
thatHandle := thisHandle;
resultCode := HandToHand(thatHandle)
```

make thatHandle a handle to the fresh copy.

> Notice that HandToHand, as well as the other routines discussed in this section, returns its result code as a function result rather than through the MemError function.

PtrToHand and PtrToXHand [3.2.6] both copy an existing non-relocatable block to a brand-new relocatable one. You can copy an entire block or just part of one; both routines accept a byteCount parameter that tells how many bytes of the original block to copy. (However, the portion you copy must always start at the beginning of the original block. Notice also that you can make a partial copy of a nonrelocatable block only; a relocatable block must be copied

result := PtrToHand (fromPtr, toHandle, byteCount)

Figure 3-11 PtrToHand

in its entirety, using HandToHand.) PtrToHand creates a new master pointer to the copy and returns a pointer to it (a handle) through a variable parameter (Figure 3-11), while PtrToXHand (X for "existing") sets an existing master pointer to point to the copy (Figure 3-12). In the case of PtrToXHand, the previous contents of the master pointer are lost; normally you'll want to give it an empty handle (a pointer to a NIL master pointer) to be "stuffed" with the address of the newly created copy.

HandAndHand and PtrAndHand [3.2.7] are used to combine existing blocks by appending a copy of one block onto the end of another. The block you're appending to is always relocatable, and is lengthened to include the appended information. You can append a copy of either a relocatable block (HandAndHand, Figure 3-13) or all or part of a nonrelocatable block (PtrAndHand, Figure 3-14); in either case, the original block being copied remains intact.

The most general copying utility of all is BlockMove [3.2.6], which just copies "raw" bytes between memory locations. Watch your step—this is a dangerous operation! It doesn't check for errors, just blindly copies the bytes. The source and destination pointers you give it aren't restricted to the heap, but can lie

result := PtrToXHand (fromPtr, toHandle, byteCount)

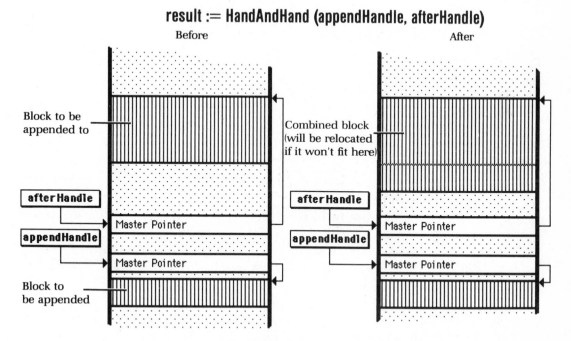

Figure 3-12 PtrToXHand

result := HandAndHand (appendHandle, afterHandle)

Figure 3-13 HandAndHand

result := PtrAndHand (appendHandle, afterHandle, byteCount)

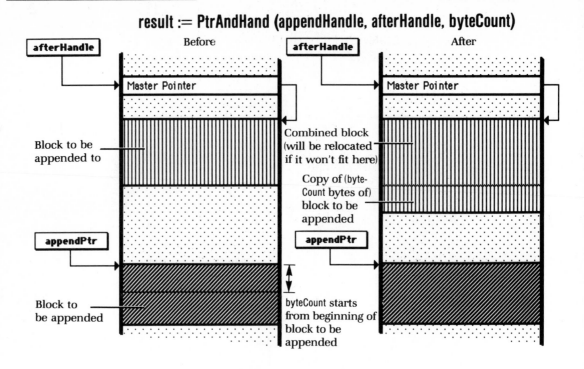

Figure 3-14 PtrAndHand

anywhere in memory. Give it the wrong parameters and it will cheerfully reduce your program to a pile of rubble.

Purging Blocks

If the Toolbox can't find room for a requested block even after compacting the entire heap, its next step is to try expanding the size of the heap itself. From its initial size of 6K bytes, the heap can grow in increments of 1K at a time, but only up to a certain limit. Recall that the heap and the stack grow toward each other from opposite ends of the same area in memory (Figure 3-4). The Toolbox imposes a limit on the heap's expansion to prevent it from colliding with the stack. This *application heap limit* is initially set to allow a maximum stack depth of 8K bytes, but you can adjust it to your program's needs with the Toolbox routine SetApplLimit [3.3.4]. GetApplLimit [3.3.4] tells you the current setting of the application heap limit; StackSpace [3.3.4] tells how much more space is available for the stack to grow before colliding with the heap.

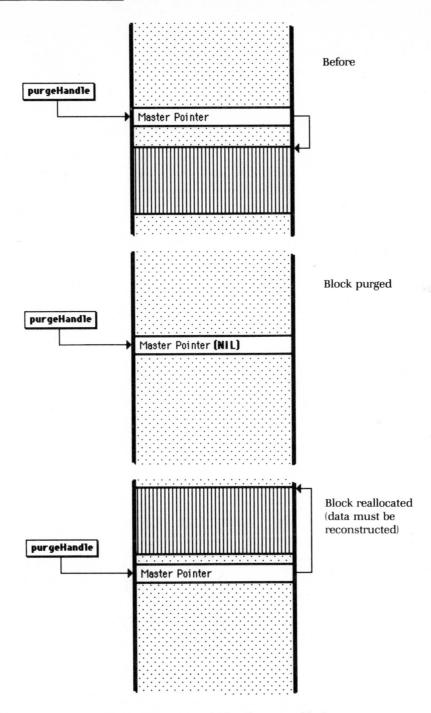

Figure 3-15 Purging and reallocating a block

If the needed space can't be created by expanding the heap, the Toolbox will try to make room by *purging* existing blocks from the heap. Only relocatable blocks can be purged; the block is simply removed from the heap and its space is made available for reallocation. The block's master pointer remains allocated, but is set to NIL to show that the block no longer exists in the heap. All former handles to the block continue to point to this same master pointer, but since the master pointer now points nowhere, the handles are considered *empty*.

The Toolbox will never purge a block from the heap without your permission. A block is always *unpurgeable* when it's first created; you can make it *purgeable* with the Toolbox routine HPurge, and unpurgeable again with HNoPurge [3.2.4]. Before attempting to access a purgeable block, you have to test its handle to see if it's been purged. If the handle is empty (that is, if it points to a NIL master pointer), you have to *reallocate* the block with the Toolbox routine ReallocHandle [3.3.3] before you can access it. This allocates fresh space for the block and updates the master pointer to point to it (see Figure 3-15). However, it does nothing to restore the information the block contained before it was purged; you have to do that for yourself after reallocating the block.

Since all relocatable blocks are unpurgeable at first, you needn't worry about checking for an empty handle and reallocating the block unless you've explicitly made the block purgeable.

The Toolbox routine EmptyHandle [3.3.3] unconditionally purges a block from the heap, even if the block is marked unpurgeable. By calling this routine, you tacitly "give permission" for the block to be purged; the Toolbox will assume you know what you're doing and will obediently purge the block, whether it's purgeable or not. (The block must be unlocked, however.)

REFERENCE

3.1 Memory Basics

3.1.1 Elementary Data Types

Definitions

```
type
    Byte       =      0..255;      {Any byte in memory}
    SignedByte = −128..127;        {Any byte in memory}

    Ptr        = ^SignedByte;      {General pointer}
    Handle     = ^Ptr;             {General handle}

    Size       = LONGINT;          {Size of a heap block in bytes}
```

Notes

1. Both Byte and SignedByte designate an arbitrary byte in memory, as either an unsigned or a signed 8-bit integer.

2. Ptr represents a general, untyped pointer to any byte in memory; Handle represents an untyped handle, a pointer to a master pointer.

3. Size is a long integer representing the size of a heap block in bytes.

3.1.2 Error Reporting

Definitions

```
type
    OSErr = INTEGER;              {Operating System result (error) code}

const
    NoErr         =     0;        {No error; all is well}
    MemFullErr    = −108;         {No room; heap is full}
    NilHandleErr  = −109;         {Illegal operation on empty handle}
    MemWZErr      = −111;         {Illegal operation on free block}
    MemPurErr     = −112;         {Illegal operation on locked block}
    MemLockedErr  = −117;         {Attempt to move locked block}

function MemError
            : OSErr;             {Result code of last memory operation}
```

Notes

1. OSErr represents an integer result code returned by an Operating System routine (such as those dealing with memory allocation).

2. The MemError function returns the result code posted by the last call to a memory allocation routine.

3. A result code of NoErr means that all is well; no error has occurred.

4. MemFullErr means that not enough heap space is available to satisfy an allocation request.

5. NilHandleErr means that a requested operation can't be performed because the specified handle is empty (points to a NIL master pointer).

6. MemWZErr means that a memory allocation routine that operates on already-allocated blocks was given a free block instead. (The WZ in MemWZErr stands for WhichZone, a low-level routine that tells which heap zone a given block is in. Although WhichZone itself is not covered in this book, it's called by many of the routines that are.)

7. MemPurErr means that an attempt was made to purge a locked block.

8. MemLockedErr means that an attempt was made to move a locked block to a new location within the heap.

9. The MemError function isn't available in assembly language. On return from most memory allocation routines, the result code is in the lower 16 bits of register D0 and the processor's condition codes are set accordingly.

Assembly Language Information

Assembly-language constants:

Name	Value	Meaning
NoErr	0	No error; all is well
MemFullErr	−108	No room; heap is full
NilHandleErr	−109	Illegal operation on empty handle
MemWZErr	−111	Illegal operation on free block
MemPurErr	−112	Illegal operation on locked block
MemLockedErr	−117	Attempt to move locked block

3.1.3   Machine Configuration

Definitions

```
procedure  Environs
              (var romVersion   : INTEGER;     {Version number of installed ROM}
               var machineType : INTEGER);     {Type of machine}

function   TopMem
              : Ptr;                           {Pointer to end of memory}

const
   MacXLMachine = 0;                           {Macintosh XL (Lisa)}
   MacMachine   = 1;                           {Skinny Mac, Fat Mac, or Mac Plus}
```

Notes

1. Environs returns information about the machine on which a program is being run.

2. The variable parameter romVersion returns the version number of the ROM code installed in the machine. Unmodified Skinny and Fat

Macs have ROM version $69 (decimal 105); the initial Macintosh Plus ROM is version $75 (decimal 117).

3. Features identified in these reference notes as "available only on the Macintosh Plus" should be used only on machines with ROM version $75 or greater.

4. The machineType parameter returns an integer code identifying the type of machine the program is running on: 0 for a Macintosh XL (a Lisa computer running under the MacWorks emulator software) or 1 for a true Macintosh.

5. Machine codes and ROM versions for the Macintosh SE and Macintosh II are given in Volume Four.

6. The ROM version returned for a Macintosh XL is that of the ROM image installed by the MacWorks emulator at system startup.

7. TopMem returns a pointer to the first address beyond the end of physical RAM memory (*not* the last address actually existing in memory). For example, in a 1-megabyte Macintosh Plus, whose last byte of physical memory is at address $FFFFF, TopMem returns a pointer to address $100000.

8. These routines are part of the Pascal Toolbox interface, not part of the Toolbox itself. They don't reside in ROM and can't be called from assembly language via the trap mechanism.

9. In assembly language, the global variable MemTop holds the address one byte beyond the end of physical RAM. The other system globals listed below hold the boundary addresses of various important areas in memory.

10. To find the ROM version and machine type in assembly language, look at the memory word beginning eight bytes past the beginning of ROM (that is, at an address 8 greater than that contained in the system global ROMBase). On a true Macintosh, this word will contain the value $00vv, where vv is the version number of the ROM; on a Macintosh XL, it will contain $vvFF. See Volume Four for information on the Macintosh SE and Macintosh II.

Assembly Language Information

Assembly-language global variables:

Name	Address	Meaning
SysZone	$2A6	Pointer to start of system heap
ApplZone	$2AA	Pointer to start of application heap
HeapEnd	$114	Pointer to end of application heap
CurStackBase	$908	Pointer to base of stack
CurrentA5	$904	Base pointer for application globals
BufPtr	$10C	Pointer to end of application global space
ScrnBase	$824	Pointer to start of screen buffer
SoundBase	$266	Pointer to start of sound buffer
MemTop	$108	Pointer to end of physical memory
ROMBase	$2AE	Pointer to start of ROM

3.2   Heap Allocation

3.2.1   Allocating Blocks

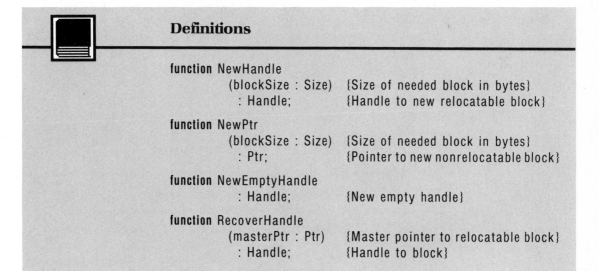

Definitions

```
function NewHandle
        (blockSize : Size)    {Size of needed block in bytes}
        : Handle;             {Handle to new relocatable block}

function NewPtr
        (blockSize : Size)    {Size of needed block in bytes}
        : Ptr;                {Pointer to new nonrelocatable block}

function NewEmptyHandle
        : Handle;             {New empty handle}

function RecoverHandle
        (masterPtr : Ptr)     {Master pointer to relocatable block}
        : Handle;             {Handle to block}
```

Notes

1. NewHandle allocates a new relocatable block and returns a handle to it; NewPtr allocates a new nonrelocatable block and returns a pointer to it.

2. blockSize gives the size of the needed block in bytes.

3. The block allocated by NewHandle is initially unlocked and unpurgeable.

4. If necessary, both NewHandle and NewPtr may compact the heap, expand it, or purge blocks from it.

5. Both routines post the error code MemFullErr [3.1.2] if a block of the requested size can't be allocated.

6. In case of an error, a NIL handle or pointer is returned.

7. NewEmptyHandle allocates a new master pointer, sets it to NIL, and returns a pointer to it (an empty handle).

8. RecoverHandle reconstructs a relocatable block's handle from a copy of its master pointer.

Assembly Language Information

Trap macros:

(Pascal) Routine name	(Assembly) Trap macro	Trap word
NewHandle	_NewHandle	$A122
NewPtr	_NewPtr	$A11E
NewEmptyHandle	_NewEmptyHandle	$A166
RecoverHandle	_RecoverHandle	$A128

Register usage:

Routine	Register	Contents
NewHandle	D0.L (in)	blockSize
	A0.L (out)	function result
	D0.W (out)	result code
NewPtr	D0.L (in)	blockSize
	A0.L (out)	function result
	D0.W (out)	result code
NewEmptyHandle	A0.L (out)	function result
	D0.W (out)	result code
RecoverHandle	A0.L (in)	masterPtr
	A0.L (out)	function result
	D0.L (out)	unchanged

3.2.2 Releasing Blocks

Definitions

procedure DisposHandle
    (theHandle : Handle);   {Handle to relocatable block to be deallocated}

procedure DisposPtr
    (thePtr : Ptr);   {Pointer to nonrelocatable block to be deallocated}

Notes

1. DisposHandle and DisposPtr deallocate a relocatable or nonrelocatable block, respectively. The space occupied by the block becomes available for reuse.

2. All handles or pointers to the deallocated block become invalid. Don't use them after deallocating the block.

Assembly Language Information

Trap macros:

(Pascal) Routine name	(Assembly) Trap macro	Trap word
DisposHandle	_DisposHandle	$A023
DisposPtr	_DisposPtr	$A01F

Register usage:

Routine	Register	Contents
DisposHandle	A0.L (in)	theHandle
	A0.L (out)	0
	D0.W (out)	result code
DisposPtr	A0.L (in)	thePtr
	A0.L (out)	0
	D0.W (out)	result code

3.2.3   Size of Blocks

Definitions

function	GetHandleSize	
	(theHandle : Handle)	{Handle to a relocatable block}
	: Size;	{Size of block in bytes}
function	GetPtrSize	
	(thePtr : Ptr)	{Pointer to a nonrelocatable block}
	: Size;	{Size of block in bytes}
procedure	SetHandleSize	
	(theHandle : Handle;	{Handle to a relocatable block}
	newSize : Size);	{New size of block in bytes}
procedure	SetPtrSize	
	(thePtr : Ptr;	{Pointer to a nonrelocatable block}
	newSize : Size);	{New size of block in bytes}

Notes

1. GetHandleSize and GetPtrSize return the size of a block in bytes.

2. SetHandleSize and SetPtrSize change the size of a block to newSize bytes. The block may be either lengthened or shortened.

3. If necessary to lengthen a block, SetHandleSize and SetPtrSize may compact the heap, expand it, or purge blocks from it.

4. If the room needed to lengthen a block can't be found, SetHandleSize and SetPtrSize post the error code MemFullErr [3.1.2].

5. GetHandleSize and SetHandleSize post the error code NilHandleErr [3.1.2] if the given handle is empty (points to a NIL master pointer).

6. All four routines post the error code MemWZErr [3.1.2] if the specified block is free (not allocated).

7. In case of an error, GetHandleSize and GetPtrSize return 0 as the block size.

8. In assembly language, the condition codes on return from the _GetHandleSize and _GetPtrSize traps are not valid, since they reflect only the lower 16 bits of register D0 and these routines return a result in the full 32-bit register (see table below). To test the status of D0 after the trap, use your own TST.L instruction.

Assembly Language Information

Trap macros:

(Pascal) Routine name	(Assembly) Trap macro	Trap word
GetHandleSize	_GetHandleSize	$A025
GetPtrSize	_GetPtrSize	$A021
SetHandleSize	_SetHandleSize	$A024
SetPtrSize	_SetPtrSize	$A020

Register usage:

Routine	Register	Contents
GetHandleSize	A0.L(in)	theHandle
	D0.L (out)	if ≥ 0, function result if < 0, result code
GetPtrSize	A0.L (in)	thePtr
	D0.L (out)	if ≥ 0, function result if < 0, result code
SetHandleSize	A0.L (in)	theHandle
	D0.L (in)	newSize
	D0.W (out)	result code
SetPtrSize	A0.L (in)	thePtr
	D0.L (in)	newSize
	D0.W (out)	result code

3.2.4   Properties of Blocks

Definitions

```
procedure HLock
          (theHandle : Handle);        {Handle to a relocatable block}

procedure HUnlock
          (theHandle : Handle);        {Handle to a relocatable block}

procedure HPurge
          (theHandle : Handle);        {Handle to a relocatable block}

procedure HNoPurge
          (theHandle : Handle);        {Handle to a relocatable block}

procedure HSetRBit
          (theHandle : Handle);        {Handle to a relocatable block}

procedure HClrRBit
          (theHandle : Handle);        {Handle to a relocatable block}

function  HGetState
          (theHandle : Handle)         {Handle to a relocatable block}
           : SignedByte;               {Current properties of block}

procedure HSetState
          (theHandle : Handle;         {Handle to a relocatable block}
           properties : SignedByte);   {New properties of block}
```

Notes

1. HLock locks a relocatable block; HUnlock unlocks it. A locked block can neither be moved nor purged from the heat.

2. HPurge makes a relocatable block purgeable; HNoPurge makes it unpurgeable. An unpurgeable block can't be purged, but can be moved within the heap.

3. On creation, a relocatable block is unlocked and unpurgeable.

4. HSetRBit marks a relocatable block for special treatment as a resource; HClrRBit clears this property. Resources are discussed in Chapter 6.

5. The lock, purge, and resource bits are all kept in the high-order byte of the block's master pointer. The assembly-language constants Lock,

Purge, and Resourc are bit numbers within this byte, for use with the BTST, BSET, BCLR, and BCHG instructions.

6. HGetState returns the current state of a master pointer's flag bits; HSetState changes them.

7. The definitions or locations of these flags may be subject to change in future versions of the Toolbox. It's safer to use the Toolbox routines described here than to manipulate the flags directly for yourself.

8. Before using a master pointer in assembly language, the flag bits must be masked off. The assembly-language global variable Lo3Bytes holds a mask for extracting the actual memory address from the low-order 3 bytes of the master pointer.

9. All of these routines will post the error code NilHandleErr [3.1.2] if the given handle is empty (points to a NIL master pointer), or MemWZErr if the specified block is free (not allocated).

Assembly Language Information

Trap macros:

(Pascal) Routine name	(Assembly) Trap macro	Trap word
HLock	_HLock	$A029
HUnlock	_HUnlock	$A02A
HPurge	_HPurge	$A049
HNoPurge	_HNoPurge	$A04A
HSetRBit	_HSetRBit	$A067
HClrRBit	_HClrRBit	$A068
HGetState	_HGetState	$A069
HSetState	_HSetState	$A06A

Register usage:

Routine	Register	Contents
HLock	A0.L (in)	theHandle
	D0.W (out)	result code
HUnlock	A0.L (in)	theHandle
	D0.W (out)	result code
HPurge	A0.L (in)	theHandle
	D0.W (out)	result code
HNoPurge	A0.L (in)	theHandle
	D0.W (out)	result code
HSetRBit	A0.L (in)	theHandle
	D0.W (out)	result code
HClrRBit	A0.L (in)	theHandle
	D0.W (out)	result code
HGetState	A0.L (in)	theHandle
	D0.B (out)	function result
HSetState	A0.L (in)	theHandle
	D0.B (in)	properties
	D0.W (out)	result code

Bit numbers in a master pointer's flag byte:

Name	Value	Meaning
Lock	7	Bit number of lock bit
Purge	6	Bit number of purge bit
Resourc	5	Bit number of resource bit

Assembly-language global variable:

Name	Address	Meaning
Lo3Bytes	$31A	Mask for extracting address from a master pointer

3.2.5 Block Location

Definitions

procedure ResrvMem	
(blockSize : Size);	{Size of needed block in bytes}
procedure MoveHHi	
(theHandle : Handle);	{Handle to a relocatable block}
procedure MoreMasters;	

Notes

1. ResrvMem reserves space for a block of a requested size as near as possible to the beginning of the heap, by moving existing blocks upward, expanding the heap, or purging blocks if necessary.

2. ResrvMem doesn't actually allocate a block, just creates space for it near the beginning of the heap. The block must then be allocated explicitly with NewHandle or NewPtr [3.2.1].

3. Call ResrvMem before allocating any relocatable block that will be locked for long periods of time, to minimize interference with heap compaction.

4. It isn't necessary to call ResrvMem for nonrelocatable blocks (or for resources with the ResLocked attribute [6.4.2]), since they're automatically allocated near the beginning of the heap.

5. MoveHHi moves an existing relocatable block as near as possible to the end of the heap, moving other blocks downward if necessary to make room.

6. Call MoveHHi before locking a block, to minimize interference with heap compaction.

7. MoveHHi is available in assembly language, via the trap mechanism, only on the Macintosh Plus. On earlier models it isn't built into ROM, but is part of the Pascal interface unit OSIntf.

8. MoreMasters allocates a new block of master pointers.

9. MoreMasters doesn't allocate any relocatable blocks; just the master pointers that will later be used to point to them. The master pointers themselves are nonrelocatable.

10. Master pointers are normally allocated in blocks of 64 at a time; one such block is allocated for you automatically at program startup.

11. To minimize heap fragmentation, it's generally a good idea to call MoreMasters at the very beginning of your program, as many times as necessary to preallocate all the master pointers you anticipate you'll need. This is particularly important in programs that make extensive use of code segments (see Chapter 7). It's better to waste a little heap space by preallocating too many master pointers than to fragment the heap by preallocating too few.

12. Both ResrvMem and MoreMasters will post the error code MemFullErr [3.1.2] if a block of the needed size can't be allocated or reserved.

13. MoveHHi will post the error code NilHandleErr [3.1.2] if the given handle is empty (points to a NIL master pointer), or MemLockedErr if the specified block is locked.

Assembly Language Information

Trap macros:

(Pascal) Routine name	(Assembly) Trap macro	Trap word
ResrvMem	_ResrvMem	$A040
MoveHHi	_MoveHHi	$A064
MoreMasters	_MoreMasters	$A036

Register usage:

Routine	Register	Contents
ResrvMem	D0.L (in)	blockSize
	D0.W (out)	result code
MoveHHi	A0.L (in)	theHandle
	D0.W (out)	result code
MoreMasters	D0.W (out)	result code

3.2.6   Copying Blocks

Definitions

function	HandToHand	
	(**var** theHandle: Handle)	{Handle to relocatable block to be copied}
	: OSErr;	{Result code}
function	PtrToHand	
	(fromPtr : Ptr;	{Pointer to nonrelocatable block to be copied}
	var toHandle : Handle;	{Returns handle to relocatable copy}
	byteCount : LONGINT)	{Number of bytes to be copied}
	: OSErr;	{Result code}
function	PtrToXHand	
	(fromPtr : Ptr;	{Pointer to nonrelocatable block to be copied}
	toHandle : Handle;	{Handle to be set to relocatable copy}
	byteCount : LONGINT)	{Number of bytes to be copied}
	: OSErr;	{Result code}
procedure	BlockMove	
	(fromPtr : Ptr;	{Pointer to data to be copied}
	toPtr : Ptr;	{Pointer to destination location}
	byteCount : Size);	{Number of bytes to be copied}

Notes

1. HandToHand, PtrToHand, and PtrToXHand all copy an existing block. The result in each case is a relocatable block, newly allocated from the heap.

2. HandToHand copies a relocatable block. On entry, theHandle designates the block to be copied; on exit, it returns a handle to the copy.

3. PtrToHand and PtrToXHand both copy all or part of a nonrelocatable block, designated by the parameter fromPtr.

4. The byteCount parameter tells how many bytes of the block to copy, and must not exceed the overall size of the block. The portion to be copied always starts at the beginning of the block.

5. For PtrToHand, toHandle is a variable parameter that returns a handle to the copy. For PtrToXHand, it's an existing handle (a pointer to an existing master pointer), which will be set to point to the copy.

6. All three routines may compact the heap, expand it, or purge blocks from it in order to make room for the copy.

7. All three routines return the error code MemFullErr [3.1.2] if there isn't enough room in the heap for the copy.

8. The result code is returned as the function result; it is *not* posted in the usual way and is not available through MemError [3.1.2].

9. BlockMove copies byteCount bytes of "raw" data between two arbitrary locations in memory, designated by the pointers fromPtr and toPtr.

10. *BEWARE:* BlockMove does no error checking of any kind.

Assembly Language Information

Trap macros:

(Pascal) Routine name	(Assembly) Trap macro	Trap word
HandToHand	_HandToHand	$A9E1
PtrToHand	_PtrToHand	$A9E3
PtrToXHand	_PtrToXHand	$A9E2
BlockMove	_BlockMove	$A02E

Register usage:

Routine	Register	Contents
HandToHand	A0.L (in)	theHandle
	A0.L (out)	theHandle
	D0.W (out)	result code
PtrToHand	A0.L (in)	fromPtr
	D0.L (in)	byteCount
	A0.L (out)	toHandle
	D0.W (out)	result code
PtrToXHand	A0.L (in)	fromPtr
	A1.L (in)	toHandle
	D0.L (in)	byteCount
	A1.L (out)	toHandle
	D0.W (out)	result code
BlockMove	A0.L (in)	fromPtr
	A1.L (in)	toPtr
	D0.L (in)	byteCount
	D0.W (out)	result code

3.2.7   Combining Blocks

Definitions

```
function HandAndHand
        (appendHandle : Handle;      {Handle to relocatable block to be appended}
         afterHandle   : Handle)     {Handle to relocatable block to append to}
         : OSErr;                    {Result code}

function PtrAndHand
        (appendPtr   : Ptr;          {Pointer to nonrelocatable block to be appended}
         afterHandle : Handle;       {Handle to relocatable block to append to}
         byteCount   : LONGINT)      {Number of bytes to append}
         : OSErr;                    {Result code}
```

Notes

1. Both of these routines append a copy of one block to the end of another.

2. The block appended to is always an existing relocatable block.

3. For HandAndHand, the block to be appended is an existing relocatable block. For PtrAndHand, it's all or part of an existing nonrelocatable block; the byteCount parameter tells how many bytes to append, and must not exceed the overall size of the block. The portion to be copied always starts at the beginning of the block.

4. Both routines may compact the heap, expand it, or purge blocks from it in order to allocate more space for the destination block.

5. Both routines return the error code MemFullErr [3.1.2] if there isn't enough room in the heap to lengthen the destination block.

6. The result code is returned as the function result; it is *not* posted in the usual way and is not available through MemError [3.1.2].

Assembly Language Information

Trap macros:

(Pascal) Routine name	(Assembly) Trap macro	Trap word
HandAndHand	_HandAndHand	$A9E4
PtrAndHand	_PtrAndHand	$A9EF

Register usage:

Routine	Register	Contents
HandAndHand	A0.L (in)	appendHandle
	A1.L (in)	afterHandle
	A1.L (out)	afterHandle
	D0.W (out)	result code
PtrAndHand	A0.L (in)	appendPtr
	A1.L (in)	afterHandle
	D0.L (in)	byteCount
	A1.L (out)	afterHandle
	D0.W (out)	result code

3.3   Heap Management

3.3.1   Available Space

Definitions

```
function   FreeMem
              : LONGINT;                      {Total free bytes in the heap}
function   MaxBlock
              : LONGINT;                      {Largest contiguous block obtainable by compaction}
procedure  PurgeSpace
           (var totalBytes  : LONGINT;   {Total free bytes obtainable by purging}
            var contigBytes : LONGINT);  {Largest contiguous block obtainable by purging}
```

Notes

1. FreeMem returns the total number of free bytes in the heap.

2. Because of heap fragmentation, it may not actually be possible to allocate a block this big.

3. MaxBlock returns the size in bytes of the largest contiguous block that could be obtained by compacting the heap, without expanding it or purging any blocks.

4. PurgeSpace returns the total number of free bytes and the size of the largest contiguous block that could be obtained by purging and compacting the heap.

5. The values returned for totalBytes and contigBytes include the amount of existing free space before purging or compaction.

6. These operations do not actually purge or compact the heap.

Assembly Language Information

Trap macros:

(Pascal) Routine name	(Assembly) Trap macro	Trap word
FreeMem	_FreeMem	$A01C
MaxBlock	_MaxBlock	$A061
PurgeSpace	_PurgeSpace	$A162

Register usage:

Routine	Register	Contents
FreeMem	D0.L (out)	function result
MaxBlock	D0.L (out)	function result
PurgeSpace	A0.L (out) D0.L (out)	contigBytes totalBytes

3.3.2   Reclaiming Free Space

Definitions

function	CompactMem	
	(sizeNeeded : Size)	{Size of needed block in bytes}
	: Size;	{Size of largest free block after compaction}
procedure	PurgeMem	
	(sizeNeeded : Size);	{Size of needed block in bytes}
function	MaxMem	
	(**var** growBytes : Size)	{Returns maximum bytes by which heap can expand}
	: Size;	{Size of largest free block in heap}

Notes

1. CompactMem does a complete or partial compaction of the heap; PurgeMem purges all blocks that are relocatable, unlocked, and purgeable; MaxMem reclaims all available heap space by purging all purgeable blocks and compacting the entire heap.

2. CompactMem and PurgeMem terminate when a free block of at least sizeNeeded bytes is found or created, or when the entire heap has been compacted or purged. The block is not actually allocated.

3. CompactMem returns the size in bytes of the largest free block found or created during compaction.

4. MaxMem returns the size in bytes of the largest available free block after purging and compacting the entire heap.

5. The growBytes parameter returns the number of additional bytes by which the heap can expand. The heap is not actually expanded.

6. If a free block of the specified size can't be found, PurgeMem will post the error code MemFullErr [3.1.2].

Assembly Language Information

Trap macros:

(Pascal) Routine name	(Assembly) Trap macro	Trap word
CompactMem	_CompactMem	$A04C
PurgeMem	_PurgeMem	$A04D
MaxMem	_MaxMem	$A11D

Register usage:

Routine	Register	Contents
CompactMem	D0.L (in)	sizeNeeded
	D0.L (out)	function result
PurgeMem	D0.L (in)	sizeNeeded
	D0.W (out)	result code
MaxMem	A0.L (out)	growBytes
	D0.L (out)	function result

3.3.3   Purging Blocks

Definitions

```
procedure  EmptyHandle
             (theHandle : Handle);      {Handle to relocatable block to be purged}

procedure  ReallocHandle
             (theHandle  : Handle;      {Empty handle to be reallocated}
              sizeNeeded : Size);       {Size of block to be allocated in bytes}
```

Notes

1. EmptyHandle purges a relocatable block from the heap.

2. The purged block's master pointer remains allocated, but is set to NIL. All existing handles to the block become empty.

3. The designated block is purged even if it's marked as unpurgeable; however, a locked block will not be purged.

4. ReallocHandle reallocates space for a purged block; the sizeNeeded parameter tells how many bytes to allocate.

5. The master pointer pointed to by theHandle is updated to point to the reallocated block. All existing handles to the block become valid again.

6. If theHandle already points to an existing block, that block is deallocated before updating the handle.

7. ReallocHandle may compact the heap, expand it, or purge blocks from it in order to make room for the reallocated block. If the needed space can't be found, it will post the error code MemFullErr [3.1.2].

8. Both EmptyHandle and ReallocHandle will post the error code MemPurErr or MemWZErr [3.1.2] if they're given the handle of a locked block or one that's free (unallocated).

Assembly Language Information

Trap macros:

(Pascal) Routine name	(Assembly) Trap macro	Trap word
EmptyHandle	_EmptyHandle	$A02B
ReallocHandle	_ReallocHandle	$A027

Register usage:

Routine	Register	Contents
EmptyHandle	A0.L (in)	theHandle
	D0.W (out)	result code
ReallocHandle	A0.L (in)	theHandle
	D0.L (in)	sizeNeeded
	A0.L (out)	theHandle, or 0 if block not reallocated
	D0.W (out)	result code

3.3.4 Heap Expansion

Definitions

procedure SetApplLimit
            (newLimit : Ptr); {Pointer to new application heap limit}

function GetApplLimit
            : Ptr;   {Current application heap limit}

procedure MaxApplZone;

function StackSpace
            : LONGINT;   {Amount stack can grow}

Notes

1. SetApplLimit sets the *application heap limit,* which controls how far the application heap can be expanded; GetApplLimit returns the current heap limit.

2. newLimit is a *limit pointer* to an address one byte beyond the maximum to which the heap can be expanded. All allocatable space beyond this address is reserved for the stack.

3. Notice that newLimit is a pointer to an address in memory; it is *not* a number of bytes representing the maximum size of the heap.

4. The application heap limit is initially set to allow 8K bytes for the stack.

5. GetApplLimit is part of the Pascal Toolbox interface, not part of the Toolbox itself. It doesn't reside in ROM and can't be called from assembly language via the trap mechanism. Instead, the application heap limit is accessible directly in the assembly-language global variable ApplLimit.

6. MaxApplZone expands the application heap to its maximum permissible size, as defined by the current application heap limit.

7. MaxApplZone is available in assembly language, via the trap mechanism, only on the Macintosh Plus. On earlier models it isn't built into ROM, but is part of the Pascal interface unit OSIntf.

8. StackSpace returns the number of additional bytes by which the stack can grow before colliding with the application heap limit.

Assembly Language Information

Trap macros:

(Pascal) Routine name	(Assembly) Trap macro	Trap word
SetApplLimit	_SetApplLimit	$A02D
MaxApplZone	_MaxApplZone	$A063
StackSpace	_StackSpace	$A165

Register usage:

Routine	Register	Contents
SetApplLimit	A0.L (in)	newLimit
	D0.W (out)	result code
MaxApplZone	D0.W (out)	result code
StackSpace	D0.L (out)	function result

Assembly-language global variable:

Name	Address	Meaning
ApplLimit	$130	Application heap limit

CHAPTER

Any Port in a Storm

At the heart of the Macintosh user interface lies a remarkably fast and versatile set of graphics routines called QuickDraw. Everything you see on the Macintosh screen—text, pictures, windows, menus—is put there by QuickDraw. When you call a Toolbox routine, say, to draw a window at a certain location on the screen, the Toolbox in turn calls QuickDraw to do the actual drawing. When the Toolbox text-handling routines need to display text in a window, they use QuickDraw to draw the characters. The basic principles of QuickDraw are fundamental to the way the rest of the Toolbox works.

Your program can also call QuickDraw directly. For instance, after the Toolbox has drawn a window's frame for you, you use QuickDraw to fill in the window's contents. Although QuickDraw is mainly for drawing on the screen, you can also use it for other purposes, such as printing on a dot-matrix printer or preparing animation frames off-screen and then transferring them to the screen all at once. In this chapter we'll discuss the underlying principles and concepts behind QuickDraw. In Chapter 5 we'll learn how to use it for actual drawing on the screen.

111

Initializing QuickDraw

Before attempting any QuickDraw operation, you first have to call InitGraf [4.3.1] to initialize QuickDraw's global variables and internal data structures. As we mentioned in the last chapter, QuickDraw locates its globals by means of a pointer at address 0(A5) in the application parameters area of the program's "A5 world." When you initialize QuickDraw you supply this pointer as a parameter; InitGraf stores it at address 0(A5), where the rest of the QuickDraw routines expect to find it.

Figure 4-1 shows how QuickDraw's global variables are arranged in memory. The pointer at 0(A5) points to the first of the QuickDraw globals, ThePort [4.3.1]. Recall, though, that global variables are always allocated in the reverse of the order they're declared. So this "first" global is physically positioned *last* in memory, with all the other globals located at *negative* offsets from the pointer. In Pascal, the space for the QuickDraw globals is automatically reserved in your program's application globals area, and all your own references to the variables are directed to the corresponding addresses in this area. To make sure everything works right, you should always pass a pointer to ThePort as the parameter to InitGraf:

    InitGraf (@ThePort)

In assembly language you can technically place the QuickDraw globals anywhere you like in memory, provided that you reserve enough space for them. (The number of bytes you need is defined in the assembly-language interface as a constant named GrafSize [4.3.1].) The normal practice is to handle the QuickDraw globals the same way they're treated in Pascal: that is, to include them as part of the program's own global variables and place them in the application global space, as in Figure 4-1.

In any case, since the globals are located with a simple pointer instead of a handle, you'd better make sure they're nonrelocatable. The pointer you pass to InitGraf must be the address of the *last* 4 bytes in this space, which will hold the variable ThePort. Then make sure you direct your own references to the QuickDraw globals to the proper offsets relative to this same pointer.

Low memory addresses

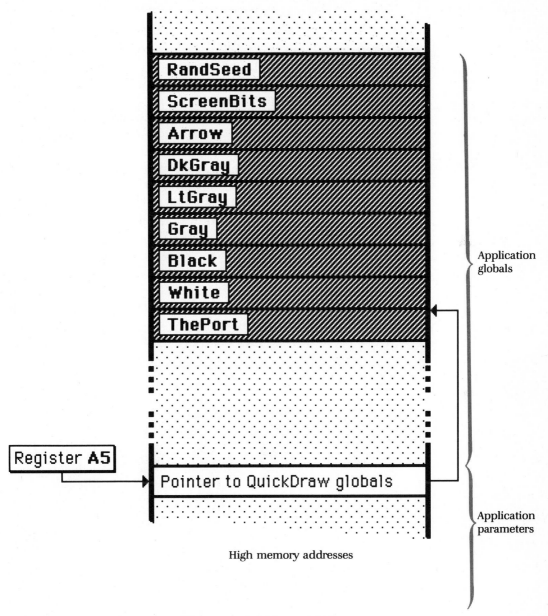

Figure 4-1 QuickDraw globals

Bits, Pixels, and Images

QuickDraw manipulates graphical images made up of white and black dots called *pixels* (short for "picture elements"). The pixels are arranged in a two-dimensional array of rows and columns to form the image, as shown in Figure 4-2. When displayed on the Macintosh screen, each pixel appears as a square, white or black dot approximately 1/72 of an inch on each side.

Internally, a graphical image is stored in the computer's memory as a collection of bits called a *bit image*. Each bit represents one pixel of the image: 0 for a white pixel, 1 for a black one. Notice that bits and pixels aren't the same thing. A pixel is an element of a graphical image; a bit is its internal representation in the computer's memory. In casual reference the distinction is often blurred, however, and we speak loosely of drawing bits on the screen or setting pixels in memory.

To work with a bit image in Pascal, you group the bits into 16-bit memory words. You can then treat each word as an integer and define the bit image as an array of integers. For example, the bit image in Figure 4-2, which consists of 10 rows of 16 bits each,

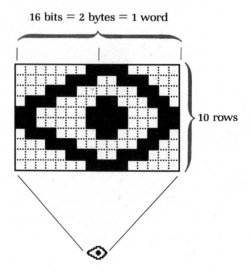

Figure 4-2 A graphical image

might be declared as

```
var
    anImage : array [1..10] of INTEGER;
```

with each element of the array representing one row of the image.

This image conveniently happens to be exactly 16 pixels wide, but of course this won't always be the case. When represented in bits, however, each row of an image must consist of some whole number of 16-bit words. If the image's width is not a multiple of 16 pixels, there will be some unused bits at the end of each row. These extra bits are just "padding" added to fill out the row to a whole number of words. For example, the image shown in Figure 4-3 is 18 pixels wide by 12 high. To represent it in bits, you have to allow two full words (32 bits) for each row

```
var
    otherImage : array [1..12, 1..2] of INTEGER;
```

leaving 14 bits unused at the end of the row.

The number of *bytes* (not words or bits) in each row is called the image's *row width*. Since each row must be a whole number of words and a word is 2 bytes, the row width is always an even number. For the image in Figure 4-2, the row width is 2 bytes; in Figure 4-3, it's 4 bytes.

The most important bit image of all is the *screen image,* which defines what the user sees displayed on the Macintosh screen. The screen is 512 pixels wide by 342 high, a total of 175,104 pixels. Its internal representation, the screen image, is equivalent to an array of type

```
array [1..342, 1..32] of INTEGER
```

—that is, it consists of 342 rows of 32 words (512 bits) each.

The screen image occupies 175,104 bits (21,888 bytes, or 10,944 words) at a certain fixed block of locations in the computer's memory. This special area of memory is the *screen buffer,* which we've already mentioned in our discussion of memory organization in Chapter 3. The Macintosh's video display circuitry automatically "paints" the contents of the screen buffer onto the screen 60 times each second. When you ask QuickDraw to draw

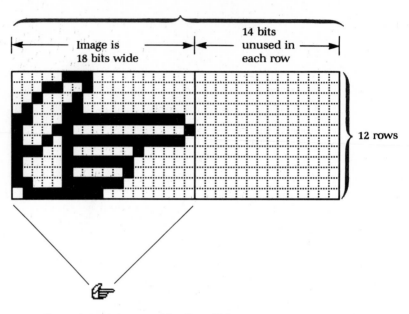

Figure 4-3 Bit image with unused bits

something on the screen, it does so by storing the appropriate bits into the screen buffer in memory.

> The screen dimensions given above, and used throughout this book, apply equally to the 128K Skinny Mac, the 512K Fat Mac, and the 1-megabyte (or larger) Macintosh Plus. The Macintosh XL (Lisa) has a larger screen: 720 pixels by 364, totaling 262,080 bits (32,760 bytes, or 16,380 words). The new large-screen displays have more pixels yet, and future models will undoubtedly have still different screen sizes.

In principle, you can store bits directly into a bit image by writing them as hexadecimal constants and assigning them to elements of the array. For instance, to set row 6 of anImage (declared earlier) to alternating black and white pixels, you could write

anImage[6] := $AAAA

(since the hexadecimal digit $A is equivalent to binary 1010). However, storing directly into individual words is not the recommended way of drawing in a bit image. It's generally safer and more convenient to use QuickDraw's specialized drawing routines—after all, drawing into bit images is what QuickDraw is for!

If you must store a specific sequence of bits into a bit image, the easiest way is to use the utility procedure StuffHex [2.2.4]. For example, to set anImage to the image shown in Figure 4-2, you could write

```
StuffHex (@anImage, CONCAT('01E0',
                           '0738',
                           '1C0C',
                           '70C6',
                           'C1E3',
                           'C1E3',
                           '70C6',
                           '1C0C',
                           '0738',
                           '01E0'))
```

(Here, since a string constant isn't allowed to run across a line break, we've split the string into pieces and joined them together with the built-in Pascal function CONCAT.)

Coordinates, Points, and Rectangles

Since a bit image may have to contain some unused bits at the end of each row to fill out a whole number of 16-bit words, you have to tell QuickDraw how many bits of each row really "count" and how many are just padding. You do this by specifying a *boundary rectangle* for the bit image, as shown in Figure 4-4. The width and height of the boundary rectangle define the dimensions of the actual image, in pixels. Bits in the bit image that lie beyond the right edge of the boundary rectangle are ignored, and it doesn't matter what they contain; the same goes for any extra rows below the rectangle's bottom edge.

The boundary rectangle also imposes a system of coordinates on the bit image. QuickDraw measures coordinates on a grid of horizontal and vertical lines drawn *between* the pixels (not

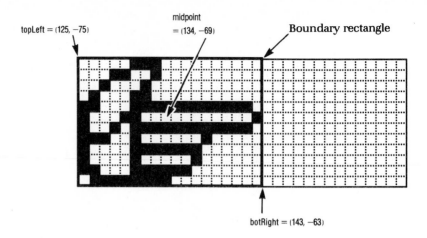

Figure 4-4 Bit image with boundary rectangle

through them), as in the figure. The top-left corner of the boundary rectangle is always assumed to be positioned just outside the first pixel in the image. This top-left corner is called the *origin* of the boundary rectangle, and you can give it any integer coordinates you like; in the figure its coordinates are 125 horizontally and −75 vertically. The coordinates of any other point on the grid are then determined relative to that point.

Here are some important things to remember about coordinates in QuickDraw:

- All coordinates are expressed as 16-bit integers, running from a minimum of −32768 to a maximum of +32767.

- Horizontal coordinates increase from left to right, vertical coordinates from top to bottom. This matches the way English is written (whether on the Macintosh screen or on a printed page), but runs counter to the usual mathematical convention that vertical coordinates increase from bottom to top.

- The coordinates on the grid *enclose* the pixels in the image, rather than coincide with them. In Figure 4-4, for example, the top left pixel in the bit image doesn't lie at coordinates 125 and −75, but rather *between* 125 and 126 horizontally and between −75 and −74 vertically. If you think of the coordinate grid as a sheet of graph paper, the pixels fall in the squares between the lines, not at the intersections.

For designating positions on the coordinate grid, QuickDraw provides a fundamental data type named Point [4.1.1]. It's defined as a Pascal variant record structure, so that you can treat the point's horizontal and vertical coordinates either as two separate fields of the record or as a single two-element array indexed by the scalar type VHSelect [4.1.1]. For example, if midpoint is a variable of type Point, you can refer to its horizontal coordinate as either

```
midpoint.h
```

or

```
midpoint.vh[H]
```

and its vertical coordinate as either

```
midpoint.v
```

or

```
midpoint.vh[V]
```

at your convenience. So to set midpoint to the coordinates shown for it in Figure 4-4, you can write either

```
with midpoint do
  begin
    h := 134;
    v := −69
  end
```

or

```
with midpoint do
  begin
    vh[H] := 134;
    vh[V] := −69
  end
```

or you can use the QuickDraw procedure SetPt [4.1.1]:

```
SetPt (midpoint, 134, −69)
```

Notice in the figure that midpoint denotes a point on the coordinate grid, *not* a pixel in the image.

Notice carefully that Point records reverse the customary mathematical convention and place the vertical coordinate before the horizontal. In Pascal this makes no difference, since you always refer to the coordinates by name (h or v). But if you're programming in assembly language, you have to be careful to keep the vertical coordinate first. To further confound the perplexed, notice that the arguments to SetPt (as opposed to the fields of a Point) *are* given in the conventional order, horizontal before vertical. Aren't computers fun?

A rectangle on the coordinate grid can be defined in either of two ways: as a pair of points specifying the top-left and bottom-right corners of the rectangle, or as four integers giving the top, left, bottom, and right coordinates separately. Again, QuickDraw uses a variant record structure, Rect [4.1.2], so you can define your rectangles in whichever way is convenient. If r is a variable of type Rect, all the expressions shown on each line below are equivalent:

```
r.top        r.topLeft.v      r.topLeft.vh[V]
r.left       r.topLeft.h      r.topLeft.vh[H]
r.bottom     r.botRight.v     r.botRight.vh[V]
r.right      r.botRight.h     r.botRight.vh[H]
```

To set r to the boundary rectangle shown in Figure 4-4, you can write

```
with r do
  begin
    top    := −75;
    left   := 125;
    bottom := −63;
    right  := 143
  end
```

or use the QuickDraw procedure SetRect [4.1.2]:

```
SetRect (r, 125, −75, 143, −63)
```

Or, if origin and corner are points with coordinates (125, −75) and (143, −63), respectively, you can use the assignments

```
with r do
  begin
    topLeft  := origin;
    botRight := corner
  end
```

or the QuickDraw procedure Pt2Rect [4.1.2]:

```
Pt2Rect (origin, corner, r)
```

The points you give to Pt2Rect can be any pair of diagonally opposite corners of the rectangle, not necessarily the top-left and bottom-right.

Calculations with Points and Rectangles

QuickDraw includes a wealth of utility routines for performing various calculations on graphical entities. In this section we'll see how to compare points or rectangles for equality, add or subtract their coordinates, and transform or combine them in a variety of ways. In the next section we'll talk about similar operations on two classes of more complex figures, polygons and regions.

You can compare two points or two rectangles to find out whether they're equal with EqualPt [4.4.1] or EqualRect [4.4.5]. Each of these functions takes a pair of arguments (points for EqualPt, rectangles for EqualRect), compares them coordinate by coordinate, and returns a Boolean result: TRUE if the arguments are equal, FALSE if they're unequal. Another useful comparison function is PtInRect [4.4.3], which tests whether a given point lies within a given rectangle.

The procedures AddPt and SubPt [4.4.1] perform simple arithmetic on points. These procedures add or subtract the two points you give them, coordinate by coordinate, and set the coordinates of the second point to the result. The first point is unaffected. (An alternate routine, DeltaPoint [4.4.1], also subtracts one point from another, but returns the difference as a function result instead of altering the coordinates of the second point.)

EmptyRect [4.4.4] tests whether a given rectangle is *empty*.

Remember that the boundaries of a rectangle run *between* the pixels of an image, not through them. If the specified bottom-right corner doesn't lie strictly below and to the right of the rectangle's origin—that is, if

r.top ≥ r.bottom

or

r.left ≥ r.right

—then the rectangle encloses no pixels and is considered empty. In this case, EmptyRect returns a value of TRUE; otherwise it returns FALSE.

OffsetRect [4.4.4] adjusts a rectangle's coordinates by a given horizontal and vertical offset, as shown in Figure 4-5. This is

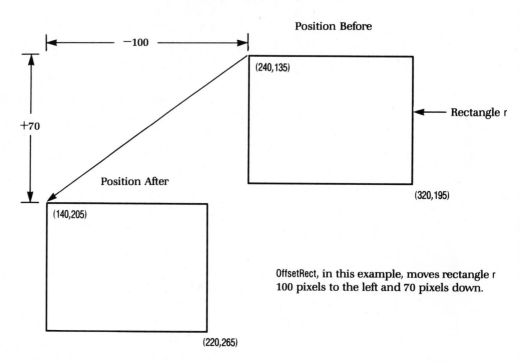

OffsetRect (r, −100, 70)

OffsetRect, in this example, moves rectangle r
100 pixels to the left and 70 pixels down.

Figure 4-5 Offsetting a rectangle

equivalent to moving the rectangle within its coordinate system while keeping its width and height fixed. If the horizontal offset is positive, the rectangle is moved to the right; if it's negative, the rectangle is moved to the left. Similarly, a positive vertical offset moves the rectangle down and a negative offset moves it up.

InsetRect [4.4.4] adjusts a rectangle's size by a horizontal and vertical inset, as shown in Figure 4-6. The left and right edges of the rectangle are both moved inward (toward the center) by the specified horizontal inset, and the top and bottom by the vertical inset. A negative value for either inset adjusts the edges of the rectangle outward instead of inward in that dimension.

> OffsetRect and InsetRect operate on a rectangle as a purely mathematical entity. All they do is adjust the values of the rectangle's coordinates; they have nothing to do with moving or changing pixels in a bit image.

InsetRect (r, 15, 10)

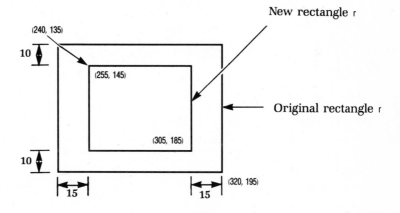

InsetRect, in this example, moves rectangle rs sides in by 15 pixels at the left and right, 10 pixels at the top and bottom.

Figure 4-6 Insetting a rectangle

UnionRect (r1, r2, union)

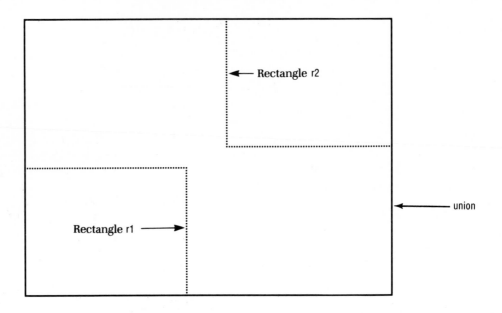

UnionRect returns the smallest rectangle, union, that
contains both rectangles r1 and r2.

Figure 4-7 Union of two rectangles

UnionRect and SectRect [4.4.5] form the union and intersection
of a pair of rectangles and return the result as the value of their
third parameter (resultRect). The union of two rectangles is the
smallest rectangle that encloses them both (see Figure 4-7); the
intersection is the largest rectangle that lies entirely within both
(Figure 4-8). SectRect also returns a Boolean result that's TRUE if the
two rectangles intersect at all (that is, if their intersection is not
empty), FALSE if they don't.

result := SectRect (r1, r2, intersection)

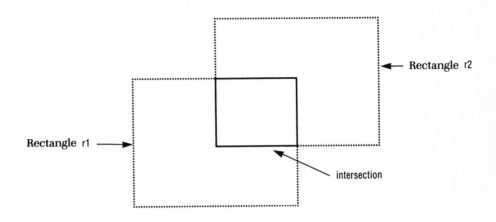

SectRect returns the largest rectangle, intersection, contained within both rectangles r1 and r2.

Figure 4-8 Intersection of two rectangles

Calculations involving two or more points or rectangles are meaningful only if the arguments are expressed in the same system of coordinates. If they aren't, you have to transform them into a common coordinate system before performing the calculation. The procedures LocalToGlobal and GlobalToLocal [4.4.2] are useful for this purpose; they're discussed below under "Local and Global Coordinates."

Polygons and Regions

QuickDraw provides two special types of structure, polygons and regions, that you can use to define and manipulate graphical figures of any shape. A *polygon* can be any shape that you can describe with a closed series of connected straight lines, such as the one in Figure 4-9. ("Connected" means that each line begins

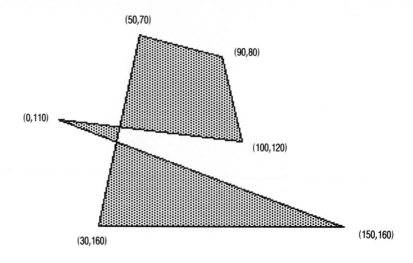

(50,70)

(90,80)

(0,110)

(100,120)

(30,160)

(150,160)

    Area inside polygon

Figure 4-9 A polygon

where the previous one ended; "closed" means that the last line ends where the first one began, so that the figure's outline connects back to where it started.) A *region* is even more general, and can be any shape that can be built up out of simpler shapes such as rectangles, ovals, polygons, and even other regions. It can have curved as well as straight edges, and can even have holes in it or consist of two or more separate pieces (see Figure 4-10).

Both polygons and regions are represented internally by variable-length data structures whose size depends on the figure's complexity. Both structures, Polygon [4.1.3] and Region [4.1.5], begin with a couple of fixed fields, followed by variable-length data to define the figure's shape. The first field (polySize or rgnSize) is an integer giving the overall length of the data structure in bytes. The second (polyBBox or rgnBBox) is the figure's *bounding box,* the smallest rectangle that completely encloses it on the coordinate grid. QuickDraw maintains these fields for you automatically; you can access their contents, but normally you shouldn't store into them yourself.

Entire shaded area can be
defined as one region.

Figure 4-10 A region

The rest of the data structure consists of the variable-length data defining the figure's shape. This part of the structure can't be properly described in a Pascal type definition, so there's no way to access it directly from a Pascal program. You can only manipulate it indirectly, by calling the appropriate QuickDraw routines to do the job for you. You define the shape of a polygon or region by actually drawing it with QuickDraw's various drawing routines. Since drawing is the subject of the next chapter, we'll postpone our discussion of polygon and region definitions until then.

There are QuickDraw routines for performing a full range of calculations on regions:

- EmptyRgn [4.4.7] tests whether a region is empty.
- EqualRgn [4.4.8] tests whether two regions are identical.
- PtInRgn [4.4.3] tests whether a point lies within a given region.
- RectInRgn [4.4.3] tests whether a given rectangle and region intersect.
- OffsetRgn and InsetRgn [4.4.7] are analogous to the rectangle operations OffsetRect and InsetRect, discussed earlier. (There's also an OffsetPoly routine [4.4.6] for polygons.)

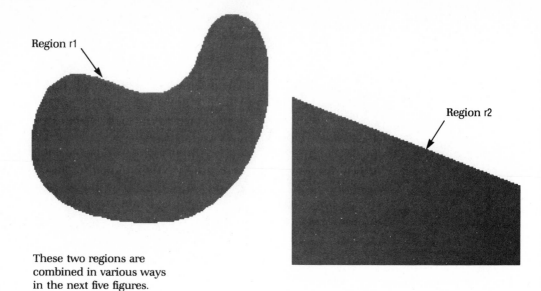

Region r1

Region r2

These two regions are
combined in various ways
in the next five figures.

UnionRgn (rgn1, rgn2, union)

Shaded area shows
resulting region
(union).

Figure 4-11 Union of two regions

SectRgn (rgn1, rgn2, intersection)

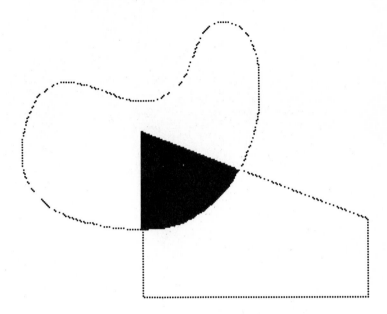

Shaded area shows resulting region (intersection); dotted lines
show boundaries of original regions.

Figure 4-12 Intersection of two regions

- UnionRgn [4.4.8] forms the union of two regions, the set of all pixels that
  lie within either of them (Figure 4-11).
- SectRgn [4.4.8] forms the intersection of two regions, the set of all pixels
  that lie within both of them (Figure 4-12).
- DiffRgn [4.4.8] forms the difference of two regions, the set of all pixels
  that lie within the first but not the second (Figure 4-13).
- XOrRgn [4.4.8] forms the "exclusive or" of two regions, the set of all pixels
  that lie within either one of them but not the other (Figure 4-14).

DiffRgn (rgn1, rgn2, difference)

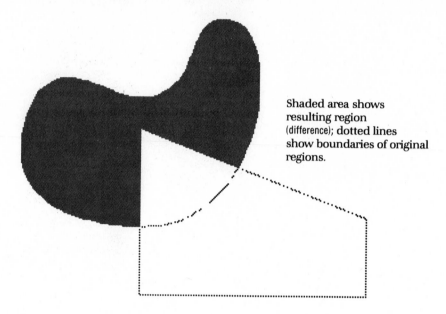

Shaded area shows
resulting region
(difference); dotted lines
show boundaries of original
regions.

DiffRgn (rgn2, rgn1, difference)

Shaded area shows
resulting region
(difference) when
order of the original regions
is switched.

Figure 4-13 Difference of two regions

XOrRgn (rgn1, rgn2, exclusiveOr)

Shaded area shows the
resulting region,
exclusiveOr. (Exclusive or =
union − intersection.)

Figure 4-14 ''Exclusive or'' of two regions

Bit Maps

We said earlier that a bit image needs a boundary rectangle to tell
QuickDraw how many bits of each row really ''count'' and how
many are just padding. This combination of a bit image and a
boundary rectangle is called a *bit map*. Bit maps are the basic
medium in which QuickDraw does all of its drawing. The bit image
provides the bit map's content; the boundary rectangle defines its
extent and gives it a system of coordinates.

Different bit maps can share the same bit image: for example,
every window on the screen has its own bit map, but they all share
the same screen image in memory. The boundary rectangle limits
the portion of the bit image that a particular bit map refers to.
The rest of the image is regarded as padding by this bit map

(though possibly not by others), and is not affected by any operation you perform on the bit map. Notice that, since a given bit map may use just part of a larger, shared bit image, there can be any amount of padding at the end of a row in the image, not necessarily just enough to fill out the row to a multiple of 16 bits.

Conceptually, a bit map could be represented by a record containing two fields: one for the bit image and another for the boundary rectangle. But because of Pascal's strong typing rules, the record definition would have to include the dimensions of the array containing the bit image: for example,

```
type
  BitMap = record
              image  : array [1..12, 1..2] of INTEGER;
              bounds : Rect
           end;
```

Under this definition, a bit map record could refer only to bit images of one particular size—12 rows of 2 words each. To work with images of different sizes, there would have to be a different type of bit map for each size. So instead of including the bit image itself as part of the bit map record, QuickDraw just uses a pointer to the first byte of the image (its *base address*). That way, since pointers have no dimensions, a single type of bit map can refer to bit images of any size.

But now some important information has been lost. The height and width of the boundary rectangle tell how many rows there are and how many bits of each row count as part of the bit map. But QuickDraw also needs to know how many bits of padding to skip at the end of each row, in order to find the beginning of the next row in memory. So the bit map record has to include another field giving the row width of the bit image—the total width of each row in bytes, including padding. Putting all this together, the actual type definition for bit maps is as follows [4.2.1]:

```
type
  BitMap = record
              baseAddr : Ptr;
              rowBytes : INTEGER;
              bounds   : Rect
           end;
```

To create a bit map in your program corresponding to the one shown earlier in Figure 4-4, you might declare

```
var
   theImage : array [1..12, 1..2] of INTEGER;
   theMap   : BitMap;
```

and then write something like

```
StuffHex (@theImage, CONCAT('07000000',
                            '19000000',
                            '22000000',
                            '46000000',
                            'C7FF8000',
                            '8C004000',
                            '97FF8000',
                            'E4080000',
                            '87F00000',
                            '84100000',
                            'C7E00000',
                            '7F800000'));

with theMap do
   begin
      baseAddr := @theImage;
      rowBytes := 4;
      SetRect (bounds, 125, −75, 143, −63)
   end
```

Remember that rowBytes is expressed in *bytes*, not words, so it has to be set to *twice* the number of integers in each row of the bit image.

Like a child with a coloring book, QuickDraw will carefully keep all of its drawing in a bit map "inside the lines" defined by the boundary rectangle. But it has to take your word for where the lines are. Make sure the bit map's base address pointer really points to a bit image in memory, and that the image array is as big as the bit map's row width and boundary rectangle say it is! If it isn't, QuickDraw will "color outside the lines" and ruin your pretty picture. Specifically, the number of bytes allocated for the bit image must not be less than the row width times the height of the boundary rectangle:

SIZEOF(theImage) ≥ theMap.rowBytes *
  (theMap.bounds.bottom - theMap.bounds.top)

Similarly, the width of the boundary rectangle must be no greater than the actual number of bits in each row:

(theMap.bounds.right - theMap.bounds.left)
  ≤ theMap.rowBytes * 8

As the screen image is the most important bit image of all, the most important bit map is the *screen map,* which QuickDraw keeps in a global variable named ScreenBits [4.2.1]. The screen map's base address field points to the beginning of the screen buffer in memory, with a row width of 64 bytes (512 bits). Its boundary rectangle is the same size as the Macintosh screen, 512 pixels wide by 342 high; the origin of the rectangle has coordinates (0, 0), placing its bottom-right corner at (512, 342).

On the Macintosh XL, with its larger screen, ScreenBits has a row width of 90 bytes (720 bits) and a boundary rectangle 720 pixels wide by 364 high. Remember, too, that screen dimensions are different on large-screen displays and may vary on future models of Macintosh. Instead of making dangerous assumptions, always use the screen map's boundary rectangle (ScreenBits.bounds) to find out the screen dimensions for the machine you're running on.

Graphics Ports

There's much more to QuickDraw's drawing environment than just a bit map to draw into. There are foreground and background patterns for filling in areas of an image; a pen size and location for line drawing; a typeface, size, and style for displaying text. Often a program needs to use more than one drawing environment: for example, the program may have several windows on the screen, each with its own pen location, fill patterns, text characteristics, and so forth.

Graphics ports enable you to switch quickly and easily from one drawing environment to another. A graphics port is a complete drawing environment containing all the information needed for QuickDraw drawing operations. Each port has its own bit map, fill patterns, pen properties, and everything else QuickDraw needs to do its job. A program can have as many separate graphics ports as it needs; in particular, every window on the screen has its own port.

All the information associated with a graphics port is kept in a record of type GrafPort [4.2.2], which normally resides in the heap. For obscure reasons shrouded in the mists of antiquity, graphics ports are nonrelocatable objects and are referred to by single indirection, with simple pointers of type GrafPtr [4.2.2] rather than handles. To create a new graphics port, you first allocate a GrafPort record with NewPtr [3.2.1], then open the port for use with OpenPort [4.3.2]:

```
rawPointer := NewPtr(SIZEOF(GrafPort));
newPort    := GrafPtr(rawPointer);
OpenPort (newPort)
```

(where rawPointer is of type Ptr and newPort is of type GrafPtr). OpenPort initializes the port's fields and allocates its internal data structures; always be sure to call this routine after creating a port and before attempting to use it in any way. (Another routine, InitPort [4.3.2], reinitializes the fields of an existing port but doesn't reallocate its internal structures.) When you're finished with a port, remember to release the internal structures with ClosePort [4.3.2] before destroying the port itself:

```
ClosePort (oldPort);
rawPointer := Ptr(oldPort);
DisposPtr (rawPointer)
```

At any given time, exactly one graphics port is in use, called the *current port*. Many QuickDraw routines operate implicitly on the current port, so you have to make sure the port you want is current before calling the routine. You can always find out what port is current with the QuickDraw procedure GetPort or change the current port with SetPort [4.3.3]. (A pointer to the current port is also kept in the global variable ThePort [4.3.3].) If you're working with more than one graphics port, it's a good idea to use GetPort and SetPort in any procedure or function that changes the current port, to save the previous port at the beginning of the routine and restore it again at the end. Program 4-1 illustrates the technique. Any routine written in this way is "transparent" to the setting of the current port: it leaves the same port current on return from the routine as when it was called.

Every graphics port has its own bit map to draw into, kept in the portBits field of the GrafPort record. portBits is the port's "canvas": QuickDraw operations directed to the port will draw into the bit image belonging to this bit map, and the bit map's boundary rectangle establishes the port's coordinate system. When you open or initialize a port, its portBits field is set to a copy of the screen map ScreenBits, with the screen image as its bit image, a row width of 64 bytes (90 on a Macintosh XL), and a boundary rectangle the same size as the screen with its origin at coordinates (0, 0). If necessary, you can then use the QuickDraw routine SetPortBits [4.3.4] to

```
procedure DrawInPort (whichPort: GrafPtr);

   {  Skeleton procedure showing use of GetPort and SetPort to preserve current port setting.  }

   var
      oldPort : GrafPtr;                        {Pointer to previous current port}
      . . . ;

   begin {DrawInPort}

      GetPort (oldPort);                        {Save old port on entry [4.3.3]}

      SetPort (whichPort);                      {Switch to specified port [4.3.3]}

         . . . ;                                {Draw in port}

      SetPort (oldPort)                         {Restore old port on exit [4.3.3]}

   end;  {DrawInPort}
```

Program 4-1 Saving and restoring the current port

change the bit map (for example, to one based on a bit image other than the screen), or change the port's coordinate system by adjusting the bit map's boundary rectangle. Since the port's bit map is only a copy of the screen map, any changes you make to its fields won't affect the screen map itself.

The portRect, visRgn, and clipRgn fields of a graphics port all define *clipping boundaries* for drawing into the port. QuickDraw will automatically confine its drawing activities within the intersection of all these boundaries, as well as the port's boundary rectangle (see Figure 4-15). Any drawing you attempt that lies outside any one of the clipping boundaries will be suppressed (*clipped*) and will have no effect on the bit image.

The *port rectangle* (portRect) defines the portion of the bit map that the port can draw into. For a newly opened or initialized port,

a.

This window obscures part
of the window behind it.

Figure 4-15 Clipping boundaries

b.

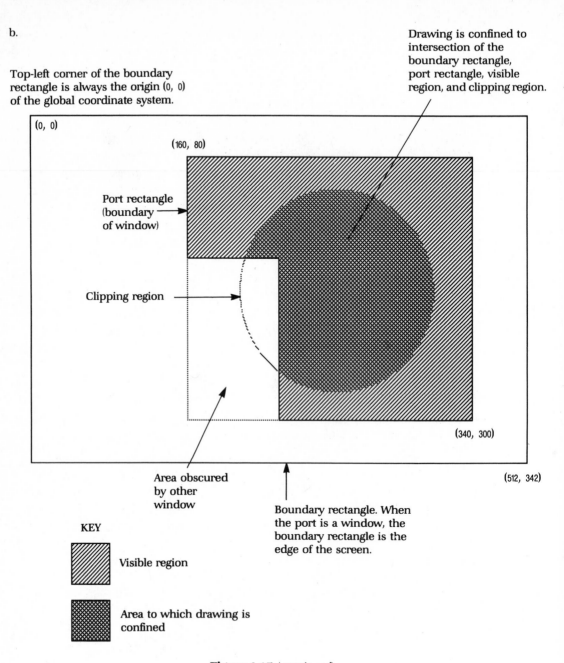

Top-left corner of the boundary rectangle is always the origin (0, 0) of the global coordinate system.

Drawing is confined to intersection of the boundary rectangle, port rectangle, visible region, and clipping region.

Port rectangle (boundary of window)

Clipping region

Area obscured by other window

Boundary rectangle. When the port is a window, the boundary rectangle is the edge of the screen.

KEY

Visible region

Area to which drawing is confined

Figure 4-15 (*continued*)

the port rectangle is a copy of the screen map's boundary rectangle: top-left corner at coordinates (0, 0), bottom-right at (512, 342) or (720, 364) or whatever. You can then change the port rectangle to whatever coordinates are appropriate. For a port belonging to a window on the screen, the port rectangle corresponds to the interior of the window, inside the window's frame. For the window shown in Figure 4-15, the port rectangle extends from coordinates (160, 80) at the top-left to (340, 300) at the bottom-right.

The *clipping region* (clipRgn) is a general-purpose clipping boundary that you can use any way you like. Notice that it's a *region*, not a rectangle, which means you can make it any shape you need. For example, in an adventure game you might use a circular clipping region, as in the figure, to simulate the view through a telescope or a ship's porthole. Opening or initializing a port sets its clipping region to an arbitrarily large rectangular region extending from coordinates (−32768, −32768) to (32767, 32767), sometimes called the "wide-open" region. You can then install a different clipping region with SetClip or ClipRect, or access the port's current clipping region with GetClip [4.3.6]. We'll look at an example that uses a port's clipping region in Chapter 5.

The *visible region* (visRgn) can also be of any shape, but it's there for use by the Toolbox, not by your program. As windows are moved around on the screen, the Toolbox uses this field to keep track of the portion of each window's port rectangle that's exposed to view. Any part of the window that's hidden behind another window is excluded from the visible region, so drawing in that part of the window is suppressed and won't appear on the screen. Figure 4-15 illustrates how a window's visible region is determined by its position on the screen in relation to other, overlapping windows.

Most of the remaining fields of the GrafPort record are discussed in Chapter 5 (bkPat, fillPat, pnLoc, pnSize, pnMode, pnPat, pnVis) and Chapter 8 (device, txFont, txFace, txMode, txSize, spExtra). The fgColor, bkColor, and colrBit fields are reserved for future use with color displays or printers; patStretch, picSave, rgnSave, and polySave are for QuickDraw's private use. grafProcs is used for "customizing" Quick-Draw operations to your own needs; see Volume Three for further information.

Local and Global Coordinates

A port's bit map belongs to just that port and no other. Even ports that draw into the same bit image have separate bit maps based on that same image. For instance, all ports that draw on the screen share the one screen image in the Macintosh's memory, but refer to it through different bit maps. Each has its own boundary rectangle, whose coordinates can be set independently of all the others.

Since the bit map's boundary rectangle determines the coordinate system of the graphics port, it follows that each port has its own coordinate system, called the *local* coordinate system of that port. The origin (top-left corner) of the boundary rectangle always lies just outside the first pixel in the bit image; everything else in the port is measured relative to the coordinates of that point.

Remember, though, that the area of the bit image that a port can draw into is defined by the port rectangle, not by the boundary rectangle of the port's bit map. Often it's more natural to measure your coordinates relative to the port rectangle instead of the boundary rectangle. The QuickDraw procedure SetOrigin [4.3.4] allows you to set a port's local coordinate system in terms of the port rectangle. Like most QuickDraw routines, SetOrigin applies implicitly to the current graphics port. It adjusts (the ten-dollar word is "translates") the port's coordinate system to give the top-left corner of the port rectangle the designated coordinates, hOrigin and vOrigin. In so doing, it recalculates the coordinates of the boundary rectangle, port rectangle, and visible region to keep them all in the same spatial relationships in the new coordinate system. You might call it a case of "simultaneous translation."

For example, Figure 4-16a shows a port belonging to a window on the Macintosh screen, which is partially hidden by another, overlapping window; this is just a repeat of our earlier Figure 4-15b. The boundary rectangle of the port's bit map extends from coordinates (0, 0) at the top-left to (512, 342) at the bottom-right. The port rectangle, representing the interior of the window, extends from (160, 80) to (340, 300). Since the window is partially hidden on the screen, its visible region is limited to the shaded area shown in the figure.

a.

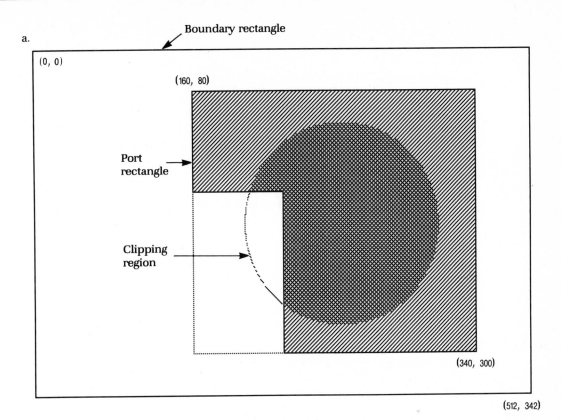

Boundary rectangle

(0, 0)

(160, 80)

Port
rectangle

Clipping
region

(340, 300)

(512, 342)

KEY

Visible region

Area to which drawing is
confined

Figure 4-16 Adjusting coordinates with SetOrigin

b.
[− 160, − 80]
(0, 0)

SetOrigin (−160, −80)

Boundary rectangle

[0, 0]
(160, 80)

Port
rectangle

(340, 300)
[180, 220]

(512, 342)
[352, 262]

Clipping
region

KEY

Visible region

Area to which
drawing is confined

( )   Global coordinates

[ ]   Local coordinates

Figure 4-16 (*continued*)

If you would prefer to express coordinates in this window relative to the window itself instead of the screen, you can write

```
SetOrigin (0, 0)
```

The result is shown in Figure 4-16b. Notice that the port rectangle and the visible region haven't changed their position on the screen; only the coordinate system has been changed. The origin of the boundary rectangle now has coordinates (−160, −80), placing the origin of the port rectangle at (0, 0), as requested. The bottom-right corners of the two rectangles have been recalculated, to keep the sizes of the rectangles the same as before. The window's visible region has also been transformed to the new coordinate system, keeping it in the same relative position on the screen.

Because each port has its own local coordinate system, coordinates expressed in different ports aren't directly comparable. Before performing any calculation involving coordinates taken from different ports, you have to convert them into a common coordinate system. A convenient system to use for such purposes is the *global* coordinate system, in which the point just outside the first pixel of a port's bit image always has coordinates (0, 0).

A port's global coordinate system is independent of the boundary rectangle, and so isn't affected by changes in the local coordinate system. In Figure 4-16a, for instance, the port's local coordinate system coincides with the global system, since the origin of the boundary rectangle has coordinates (0, 0). In Figure 4-16b, the local system has been transformed, but the global system remains the same as before. Expressed in global coordinates, the port rectangle and visible region still have the same coordinates shown for them in Figure 4-16a, even though their local coordinates have been changed to those in Figure 4-16b.

```
{ Program fragment to find the intersection of two windows' port
  rectangles by converting both to global coordinates.  }

var
   portA, portB        : GrafPtr;
   rectA, rectB, inter : Rect;
   nonEmpty            : BOOLEAN;
   . . . ;
```

Program 4-2 Converting to global coordinates

```
begin

   . . . ;

   portA := . . . ;                                {Port A is first window's port}
   portB := . . . ;                                {Port B is second window's port}
   rectA := portA^.portRect;                       {First window's port rectangle [4.2.2]}
   rectB := portB^.portRect;                       {Second window's port rectangle [4.2.2]}

   SetPort (portA);                                {Get into port A [4.3.3]}
   with rectA do
      begin
         LocalToGlobal (topLeft);                  {Convert port rectangle to      }
         LocalToGlobal (botRight)                  {   global coordinates [4.4.2]}
      end;

   SetPort (portB);                                {Switch to port B [4.3.3]}
   with rectB do
      begin
         LocalToGlobal (topLeft);                  {Convert port rectangle to      }
         LocalToGlobal (botRight)                  {   global coordinates [4.4.2]}
      end;

   nonEmpty :=  SectRect (rectA, rectB, inter);    {Find intersection [4.4.5]}
   if nonEmpty
      then                                         {Intersection is nonempty:          }
         begin
            with intersection do
               begin
                  GlobalToLocal (topLeft);         {   convert intersection to          }
                  GlobalToLocal (botRight)         {   port B's local coordinates [4.4.2]}
               end;
            . . .                                  {   and proceed with normal processing}
         end
      else                                         {Intersection is empty:     }
         . . . ;                                   {   handle exceptional case}
   . . .

end
```

Program 4-2 (*continued*)

```
{ Program fragment to find the intersection of two windows' port
  rectangles by converting one to local coordinates of the other }

var
  portA, portB         : GrafPtr;
  rectA, rectB, inter : Rect;
  nonEmpty            : BOOLEAN;
  . . . ;

begin

  . . . ;

  portA := . . . ;                             {Port A is first window's port}
  portB := . . . ;                             {Port B is second window's port}
  . . . ;
  rectA := portA^.portRect;                    {First window's port rectangle [4.2.2]}
  rectB := portB^.portRect;                    {Second window's port rectangle [4.2.2]}

  SetPort (portA);                             {Get into port A [4.3.3]}
  with rectA do
     begin
        LocalToGlobal (topLeft);               {Convert port rectangle to    }
        LocalToGlobal (botRight)               {   global coordinates [4.4.2]}
     end;

  SetPort (portB);                             {Switch to port B [4.3.3]}
  with rectA do
     begin
        GlobalToLocal (topLeft);               {Convert to port B's          }
        GlobalToLocal (botRight)               {   local coordinates [4.4.2]}
     end;

  nonEmpty :=  SectRect (rectA, rectB, inter); {Find intersection [4.4.5]}
  if nonEmpty
     then                                      {Intersection is nonempty: }
        . . .                                  {   handle normal case     }
     else                                      {Intersection is empty:    }
        . . . ;                                {   handle exceptional case}

  . . .

end
```

Program 4-3 Converting between coordinate systems

Global coordinates provide a handy basis of comparison between different ports, provided that the ports are based on the same underlying bit image. For instance, for all ports corresponding to windows on the screen, the global coordinate system measures coordinates with respect to the screen instead of the window.

Suppose you want to find the intersection of two windows on the screen. Since each window's port rectangle is expressed in that window's own local coordinates, you can't just apply SectRect directly to the two rectangles. First you have to convert the rectangles into a common coordinate system. Since the two windows' graphics ports are based on the same bit image (the screen), you can use global coordinates as a common basis of comparison.

QuickDraw provides a pair of utility procedures, LocalToGlobal and GlobalToLocal [4.4.2], for converting between coordinate systems. The local coordinate system involved is always implicitly that of the current port, so you have to make sure the right port is current for each conversion. Program 4-2 shows one way to do the job:

1. Convert both windows' port rectangles into global coordinates.
2. Find the intersection of the two port rectangles in global coordinates.
3. Convert the result back into the local coordinates of one of the two windows.

A slightly more efficient way of doing the same thing is shown in Program 4-3:

1. Convert one window's port rectangle into global coordinates.
2. Convert this same rectangle from global coordinates into the local coordinates of the other window.
3. Find the intersection directly in the second window's local coordinates.

This method requires only two coordinate conversions instead of three.

REFERENCE

4.1   Mathematical Foundations

4.1.1   Points

Definitions

```
type
  VHSelect = (V, H);                          {Selector for coordinates of a point}

  Point    = record
                case INTEGER of

                  0: (v : INTEGER;            {Vertical coordinate}
                      h : INTEGER);           {Horizontal coordinate}

                  1: (vh : array [VHSelect] of INTEGER)   {Coordinates as a two-element array}

             end;

procedure SetPt
            (var thePoint : Point;            {Point to be set}
             hCoord       : INTEGER;          {Horizontal coordinate}
             vCoord       : INTEGER);         {Vertical coordinate}
```

Notes

1. A Point is a data structure representing a point on the QuickDraw coordinate grid.

2. The variant record structure allows the point's coordinates to be accessed as two separate integers

   ```
   thePoint.v
   thePoint.h
   ```

   or as a two-element array

   ```
   thePoint.vh[V]
   thePoint.vh[H]
   ```

3. The vertical coordinate comes first, contrary to the usual mathematical convention.

4. SetPt sets thePoint to a point with coordinates hCoord and vCoord.

5. Notice that the order of the coordinates in a call to SetPt is not the same as in the Point record itself.

Assembly Language Information

Field offsets in a point record:

(Pascal) Field name	(Assembly) Offset name	Offset in bytes
v	v	0
h	h	2

Trap macro:

(Pascal) Routine name	(Assembly) Trap macro	Trap word
SetPt	_SetPt	$A880

4.1.2 Rectangles

Definitions

```
type
  Rect = record
           case INTEGER of
             0: (top     : INTEGER;      {Top coordinate}
                 left    : INTEGER;      {Left coordinate}
                 bottom  : INTEGER;      {Bottom coordinate}
                 right   : INTEGER);     {Right coordinate}

             1: (topLeft  : Point;       {Top-left corner}
                 botRight : Point)       {Bottom-right corner}

         end;
  procedure  SetRect
             (var theRect : Rect;        {Rectangle to be set}
              left        : INTEGER;     {Left coordinate}
              top         : INTEGER;     {Top coordinate}
              right       : INTEGER;     {Right coordinate}
              bottom      : INTEGER);    {Bottom coordinate}

  procedure  Pt2Rect
             (point1      : Point;       {First corner}
              point2      : Point;       {Diagonally opposite corner}
              var theRect : Rect);       {Rectangle to be set}
```

Notes

1. A Rect is a data structure representing a rectangle on the coordinate grid.

2. The variant record structure allows the rectangle's coordinates to be accessed as four separate integers

```
theRect.top
theRect.left
theRect.bottom
theRect.right
```

or as a pair of points

```
theRect.topLeft
theRect.botRight
```

representing the top-left and bottom-right corners.

3. If right ≤ left or bottom ≤ top, the rectangle is considered empty.

4. SetRect sets theRect to a rectangle with coordinates left, top, right, and bottom.

5. Notice that the order of the coordinates in a call to SetRect is not the same as in the Rect record itself.

6. Pt2Rect sets theRect to a rectangle defined by a pair of diagonally opposite points point1 and point2.

7. If point1 and point2 have the same horizontal or vertical coordinate, the resulting rectangle will be empty.

Assembly Language Information

Field offsets in a rectangle record:

(Pascal) Field name	(Assembly) Offset name	Offset in bytes
top	top	0
left	left	2
bottom	bottom	4
right	right	6
topLeft	topLeft	0
botRight	botRight	4

Trap macros:

(Pascal) Routine name	(Assembly) Trap macro	Trap word
SetRect	_SetRect	$A8A7
Pt2Rect	_Pt2Rect	$A8AC

4.1.3 Polygons

Definitions

```
type
  PolyHandle = ^PolyPtr;
  PolyPtr    = ^Polygon;

  Polygon    = record
                 polySize   : INTEGER;            {Length of this data structure in bytes}
                 polyBBox   : Rect;               {Bounding box}
                 polyPoints : array [0..0] of Point  {Variable-length array of vertices}
               end;
```

Notes

1. A Polygon is a variable-length data structure representing an arbitrary polygon on the QuickDraw coordinate plane.

2. The shape of the polygon is defined by a series of connected sides, specified with the line-drawing operations Line and LineTo [5.2.4]. Each side begins where the previous side ended; their endpoints are the polygon's vertices.

3. If the first and last vertices don't coincide, an extra side is added automatically to close the polygon.

4. The dummy field polyPoints stands for a variable-length array of points (not directly accessible in Pascal) representing the polygon's vertices. The Toolbox maintains the contents of this array for you—you'll never need to access or store into it yourself.

5. polySize is the overall length of this Polygon data structure in bytes, including the variable-length polyPoints array.

6. polyBBox is the polygon's *bounding box,* the smallest rectangle that completely encloses it.

Assembly Language Information

Field offsets in a polygon record:

(Pascal) Field name	(Assembly) Offset name	Offset in bytes
polySize	polySize	0
polyBBox	polyBBox	2
polyPoints	polyPoints	10

4.1.4 Defining Polygons

Definitions

```
function   OpenPoly
              : PolyHandle;                        {Handle to new polygon}

procedure  ClosePoly;

procedure  KillPoly
              (thePolygon : PolyHandle);   {Handle to polygon to be destroyed}
```

Notes

1. OpenPoly creates a new Polygon record [4.1.3], opens it for definition, and returns a handle to it.

2. Subsequent calls to the line-drawing routines Line and LineTo [5.2.4] will be accumulated into the Polygon record to define the shape of the polygon.

3. The graphics pen is hidden [5.2.3] while a polygon is open; the line-drawing operations that define the polygon will not appear on the screen.

4. The polygon's outline is infinitely thin, and is unaffected by pen characteristics such as size, pattern, and mode [5.2.1].

5. Only one polygon may be open at a time; don't attempt to open another without closing the one that's already open.

6. ClosePoly closes the polygon currently open for definition, if any.

7. The polygon's bounding box [4.1.3] is recomputed to enclose all of the points in the polygon.

8. The graphics pen is reshown [5.2.3]; subsequent line-drawing operations will appear on the screen instead of being accumulated into the polygon definition.

9. KillPoly destroys a Polygon record and deallocates the memory space it occupies. The polygon is no longer usable after this operation.

10. The trap macro for ClosePoly is spelled _ClosePgon.

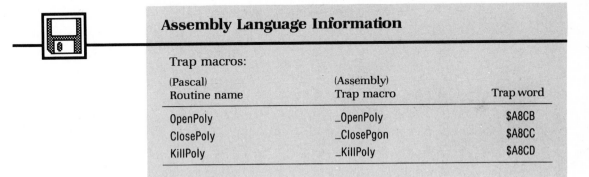

Assembly Language Information

Trap macros:

(Pascal) Routine name	(Assembly) Trap macro	Trap word
OpenPoly	_OpenPoly	$A8CB
ClosePoly	_ClosePgon	$A8CC
KillPoly	_KillPoly	$A8CD

4.1.5 Regions

Definitions

```
type
   RgnHandle = ^RgnPtr;
   RgnPtr    = ^Region;

   Region    = record
                  rgnSize  : INTEGER;    {Length of this data structure in bytes}
                  rgnBBox : Rect;        {Bounding box}
                  {additional data defining shape of region}
               end;
```

Notes

1. A Region is a variable-length data structure representing an arbitrary region on the QuickDraw coordinate plane.

2. The shape of the region is defined by a series of lines and shapes specified with the line-drawing operations Move, MoveTo, Line, and LineTo [5.2.4] and the shape-drawing operations FrameRect [5.3.2], FrameRoundRect [5.3.3], FrameOval [5.3.4], FramePoly [5.3.6], and FrameRgn [5.3.7]. The region's outline is formed by the specified lines and the boundaries of the specified shapes.

3. At the end of the Region record is variable-length data (not directly accessible in Pascal) defining the shape of the region in compact, encoded form. The Toolbox maintains this data for you—you'll never need to access or store into it yourself.

4. rgnSize is the overall length of this Region data structure in bytes, including the variable-length data defining the shape of the region.

5. rgnBBox is the region's *bounding box*, the smallest rectangle that completely encloses it.

6. For a strictly rectangular region, the variable-length data is absent; the bounding box completely defines the shape of the region. In this case rgnSize = 10 (2 bytes for the size and 8 for the bounding box).

Assembly Language Information

Field offsets in a region record:

(Pascal) Field name	(Assembly) Offset name	Offset in bytes
rgnSize	rgnSize	0
rgnBBox	rgnBBox	2
————	rgnData	10

4.1.6 Defining Regions

Definitions

function	NewRgn : RgnHandle;	{Handle to new region}
procedure	OpenRgn;	
procedure	CloseRgn (theRegion : RgnHandle);	{Handle to be set to defined region}
procedure	DisposeRgn (theRegion : RgnHandle);	{Handle to region to be destroyed}

Notes

1. NewRgn creates a new Region record [4.1.5] and returns a handle to it. The new region is initially empty.

2. OpenRgn begins a new region definition; subsequent calls to the line-drawing routines Move, MoveTo, Line, and LineTo [5.2.4] and the shape-drawing routines FrameRect [5.3.2], FrameRoundRect [5.3.3], FrameOval [5.3.4], FramePoly [5.3.6], and FrameRgn [5.3.7] will be accumulated to define the shape of the region.

3. The graphics pen is hidden [5.2.3] while a region is open; the line- and shape-drawing operations that define the region will not appear on the screen.

4. The region's outline is infinitely thin, and is unaffected by pen characteristics such as size, pattern, and mode [5.2.1].

5. Only one region may be open at a time; don't attempt to open another without closing the one that's already open.

6. CloseRgn closes the region definition currently open and sets an existing region to the defined shape.

7. The region must already have been created previously with NewRgn.

8. The graphics pen is reshown [5.2.3]; subsequent line- and shape-drawing operations will appear on the screen instead of being accumulated into the region definition.

9. DisposeRgn destroys a Region record and deallocates the memory space it occupies. The region is no longer usable after this operation.

10. The trap macro for DisposeRgn is spelled _DisposRgn.

Assembly Language Information

Trap macros:

(Pascal) Routine name	(Assembly) Trap macro	Trap word
NewRgn	_NewRgn	$A8D8
OpenRgn	_OpenRgn	$A8DA
CloseRgn	_CloseRgn	$A8DB
DisposeRgn	_DisposRgn	$A8D9

4.1.7 Setting Regions

Definitions

```
procedure SetEmptyRgn
          (theRegion : RgnHandle);        {Handle to region to be set empty}

procedure RectRgn
          (theRegion : RgnHandle;         {Handle to region to be set}
           theRect   : Rect);             {Rectangle to set it to}

procedure SetRectRgn
          (theRegion : RgnHandle;         {Handle to region to be set}
           left      : INTEGER;           {Left coordinate of rectangle to set it to}
           top       : INTEGER;           {Top coordinate of rectangle to set it to}
           right     : INTEGER;           {Right coordinate of rectangle to set it to}
           bottom    : INTEGER);          {Bottom coordinate of rectangle to set it to}

procedure CopyRgn
          (fromRegion : RgnHandle;        {Region to be copied}
           toRegion   : RgnHandle);       {Region to copy it to}
```

Notes

1. SetEmptyRgn sets an existing region to empty, erasing its previous structure.

2. The region remains in existence, but becomes empty (encloses no pixels). The Region record itself [4.1.5] is not destroyed.

3. RectRgn and SetRectRgn both set an existing region to a specified rectangle. For RectRgn, the rectangle is given as a Rect record [4.1.2]; for SetRectRgn, it's given as four separate coordinates.

4. If right ≤ left or bottom ≤ top, the region is set to empty.

5. CopyRgn sets an existing region to the same shape as another.

6. In each case, the destination region (theRegion or toRegion) must already have been created previously with NewRgn [4.1.6].

7. The trap macro for SetRectRgn is spelled _SetRecRgn.

Assembly Language Information

Trap macros:

(Pascal) Routine name	(Assembly) Trap macro	Trap word
SetEmptyRgn	_SetEmptyRgn	$A8DD
RectRgn	_RectRgn	$A8DF
SetRectRgn	_SetRecRgn	$A8DE
CopyRgn	_CopyRgn	$A8DC

4.2   Graphical Foundations

4.2.1   Bit Maps

Definitions

```
BitMap = record
              baseAddr : Ptr;          {Pointer to bit image}
              rowBytes : INTEGER;      {Row width in bytes}
              bounds   : Rect          {Boundary rectangle}
          end;

var
    ScreenBits : BitMap;               {Bit map for Macintosh screen}
```

Notes

1. baseAddr is a pointer to the bit map's *bit image*. The bits of the bit image define the pixels of the bit map.

2. rowBytes is the bit map's *row width*, the number of bytes in each row of the bit image.

3. The row width should always be even, representing a whole number of 16-bit words.

4. bounds is the bit map's *boundary rectangle,* which defines its extent and coordinate system.

5. The first pixel in the bit image lies just inside the top-left corner of the boundary rectangle.

6. The width of the boundary rectangle must not exceed the row width of the bit image in bits (that is, 8 * rowBytes). Its height must not exceed the number of rows in the bit image.

7. Any bits of the bit image that lie beyond the right or bottom edge of the boundary rectangle are ignored.

8. The global variable ScreenBits holds the *screen map,* a bit map representing the Macintosh screen.

9. The screen map's bit image is the screen buffer in memory; its row width is 64 bytes (512 bits); its boundary rectangle extends from coordinates (0, 0) at the top-left to (512, 342) at the bottom-right. (These values may differ on large-screen displays or on future models.) On a

Macintosh XL, its row width is 90 bytes (720 bits) and its boundary rectangle extends from (0, 0) to (720, 364).

10. To access the screen map in assembly language, find the pointer to QuickDraw's globals at the address contained in register A5, then locate the variable relative to that pointer using the offset constant ScreenBits (below). See Chapter 3 and [4.3.1, note 4] for further discussion.

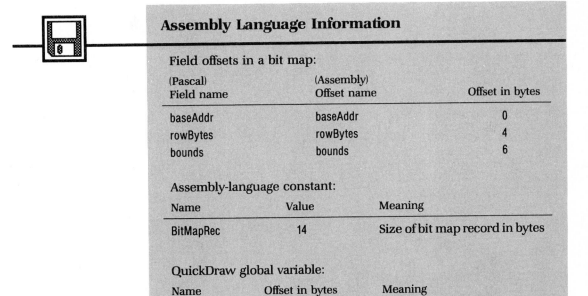

Assembly Language Information

Field offsets in a bit map:

(Pascal) Field name	(Assembly) Offset name	Offset in bytes
baseAddr	baseAddr	0
rowBytes	rowBytes	4
bounds	bounds	6

Assembly-language constant:

Name	Value	Meaning
BitMapRec	14	Size of bit map record in bytes

QuickDraw global variable:

Name	Offset in bytes	Meaning
ScreenBits	−122	Bit map for Macintosh screen

4.2.2   Graphics Ports

Definitions

```
type
  GrafPtr  = ^GrafPort;

  GrafPort = record
             device    : INTEGER;      {Device code for font selection [8.3.1]}
             portBits  : BitMap;       {Bit map for this port}
             portRect  : Rect;         {Port rectangle}
             visRgn    : RgnHandle;    {Visible region}
             clipRgn   : RgnHandle;    {Clipping region}
             bkPat     : Pattern;      {Background pattern [5.1.1]}
             fillPat   : Pattern;      {Fill pattern for shape drawing [5.1.1]}
             pnLoc     : Point;        {Current pen location in local coordinates [5.2.1]}
             pnSize    : Point;        {Dimensions of graphics pen [5.2.1]}
             pnMode    : INTEGER;      {Transfer mode for graphics pen [5.1.3, 5.2.1]}
             pnPat     : Pattern;      {Pen pattern for line drawing [5.1.1, 5.2.1]}
             pnVis     : INTEGER;      {Pen visibility level [5.2.3]}
             txFont    : INTEGER;      {Font number for text [8.2.1, 8.3.1]}
             txFace    : Style;        {Type style for text [8.3.1]}
             txMode    : INTEGER;      {Transfer mode for text [5.1.3, 8.3.1]}
             txSize    : INTEGER;      {Type size for text [8.3.1]}
             spExtra   : Fixed;        {Extra space between words [8.3.1]}
             fgColor   : LONGINT;      {Foreground color}
             bkColor   : LONGINT;      {Background color}
             colrBit   : INTEGER;      {Color plane}
             patStretch: INTEGER;      {Private}
             picSave   : Handle;       {Private}
             rgnSave   : Handle;       {Private}
             polySave  : Handle;       {Private}
             grafProcs : QDProcsPtr    {Pointer to bottleneck procedures (note 15)}
           end;
```

Notes

1. A graphics port is a complete drawing environment containing all the information needed for QuickDraw drawing operations.

2. Graphics ports are nonrelocatable objects in the heap and are always referred to by simple pointers rather than handles.

3. portBits is the bit map that this graphics port draws into.

4. The port's *boundary rectangle* is the same as that of its bit map, portBits.bounds.

5. portRect is the *port rectangle*, the portion of the bit map that the port draws into, in local coordinates.

6. visRgn is the port's *visible region*, the portion of the port rectangle currently exposed to view on the screen. It's maintained privately by the Toolbox to keep track of overlapping windows; never attempt to manipulate this field yourself.

7. clipRgn is the *clipping region*, provided for general-purpose use by the application.

8. All drawing in a port is clipped to the intersection of the port's boundary rectangle, port rectangle, visible region, and clipping region.

9. bkPat and fillPat are the port's *background pattern* and *fill pattern*, used in shape drawing; see [5.1.1].

10. pnLoc, pnSize, pnMode, and pnPat are characteristics of the graphics pen, used in line drawing; see [5.2.1].

11. pnVis is the *pen level*, which controls whether the pen is visible on the screen; see [5.2.3].

12. device, txFont, txFace, txMode, txSize, and spExtra are the port's text characteristics, which control the drawing of text characters; see [8.3.1].

13. fgColor, bkColor, and colrBit are the port's color characteristics, used to control drawing on a color display or printer; see Volume Four for further information.

14. patStretch, picSave, rgnSave, and polySave are used privately by the Toolbox.

15. grafProcs is a pointer to the port's low-level drawing procedures (sometimes called "bottleneck procedures"). These procedures are used to "customize" QuickDraw operations; see Volume Three for further information.

Assembly Language Information

Field offsets in a graphics port:

(Pascal) Field name	(Assembly) Offset name	Offset in bytes
device	device	0
portBits	portBits	2
portRect	portRect	16
visRgn	visRgn	24
clipRgn	clipRgn	28
bkPat	bkPat	32
fillPat	fillPat	40
pnLoc	pnLoc	48
pnSize	pnSize	52
pnMode	pnMode	56
pnPat	pnPat	58
pnVis	pnVis	66
txFont	txFont	68
txFace	txFace	70
txMode	txMode	72
txSize	txSize	74
spExtra	spExtra	76
fgColor	fgColor	80
bkColor	bkColor	84
colrBit	colrBit	88
patStretch	patStretch	90
picSave	picSave	92
rgnSave	rgnSave	96
polySave	polySave	100
grafProcs	grafProcs	104
portBits.bounds	portBounds	8

Assembly-language constant:

Name	Value	Meaning
portRec	108	Size of graphics port record in bytes

4.2.3 Pixel Access

Definitions

function GetPixel
            (hCoord : INTEGER;   {Horizontal coordinate of pixel}
             vCoord : INTEGER)   {Vertical coordinate of pixel}
               : BOOLEAN;   {Is it a black pixel?}

Notes

1. GetPixel returns the state of a designated pixel in the current graphics port.

2. hCoord and vCoord are expressed in the local coordinate system of the current port. The pixel returned will be the one immediately below and to the right of these coordinates.

3. The function result is TRUE for a black pixel, FALSE for a white one.

4. For a graphics port on the screen (such as a window), the result is meaningful only if the given coordinates lie within the port's visible region.

Assembly Language Information

Trap macro:

(Pascal) Routine name	(Assembly) Trap macro	Trap word
GetPixel	_GetPixel	$A865

4.3 Operations on Graphics Ports

4.3.1 Initializing QuickDraw

Definitions

```
procedure  InitGraf
            (globalVars : Ptr);       {Pointer to QuickDraw global variables}
var
    ThePort     : GrafPtr;            {Pointer to current port [4.3.3]}
    White       : Pattern;           {Solid white pattern [5.1.2]}
    Black       : Pattern;           {Solid black pattern [5.1.2]}
    Gray        : Pattern;           {Medium gray pattern [5.1.2]}
    LtGray      : Pattern;           {Light gray pattern [5.1.2]}
    DkGray      : Pattern;           {Dark gray pattern [5.1.2]}
    Arrow       : Cursor;            {Standard arrow cursor [II:2.5.2]}
    ScreenBits  : BitMap;            {Bit map for Macintosh screen [4.2.1]}
    RandSeed    : LONGINT;           {Seed for random number generation [2.3.8]}
```

Notes

1. InitGraf must be called before any other QuickDraw operation, to initialize QuickDraw's global variables and internal data structures.

2. globalVars is a pointer to an area in memory where QuickDraw can store its global variables.

3. In Pascal, globalVars should always be set to @ThePort.

4. In assembly language, QuickDraw's global variables can be placed anywhere in memory where enough space is available. The parameter passed to InitGraf must be the address of the *last* global variable, ThePort, in the last 4 bytes of the space reserved for the globals. InitGraf will store this pointer at the address contained in register A5; all the other globals can then be found at negative offsets relative to this pointer, using the offset constants given in the table below. See Chapter 3 for further discussion.

5. The number of bytes needed for QuickDraw's globals is defined by the assembly-language constant GrafSize.

6. Don't call InitGraf more than once in the same program.

Assembly Language Information

Trap macro:

(Pascal) Routine name	(Assembly) Trap macro	Trap word
InitGraf	_InitGraf	$A86E

Assembly-language constant:

Name	Value	Meaning
GrafSize	206	Size in bytes of QuickDraw global variables

QuickDraw public global variables:

Name	Offset in bytes	Meaning
The Port	0	Pointer to current port
White	−8	Solid white pattern
Black	−16	Solid black pattern
Gray	−24	Medium gray pattern
LtGray	−32	Light gray pattern
DkGray	−40	Dark gray pattern
Arrow	−108	Standard arrow cursor
ScreenBits	−122	Bit map for Macintosh screen
RandSeed	−126	Seed for random number generation

4.3.2   Creating and Destroying Ports

Definitions

```
procedure  OpenPort
              (whichPort : GrafPtr);   {Pointer to port to open}
procedure  InitPort
              (whichPort : GrafPtr);   {Pointer to port to initialize}
procedure  ClosePort
              (whichPort : GrafPtr);   {Pointer to port to close}
```

Initial values of GrafPort fields:

Field	Initial value
device	0 (screen)
portBits	Copy of ScreenBits [4.2.1]
portRect	(0, 0) to (512, 342)
visRgn	Rectangular region (0, 0) to (512, 342)
clipRgn	Rectangular region (−32768, −32768) to (32767, 32767)
bkPat	White [5.1.2]
fillPat	Black [5.1.2]
pnLoc	(0, 0)
pnSize	(1, 1)
pnMode	PatCopy [5.1.3]
pnPat	Black [5.1.2]
pnVis	0 (visible) [5.2.3]
txFont	0 (system font) [8.2.1]
txFace	Plain [8.3.1]
txMode	SrcOr [5.1.3]
txSize	0 (standard size) [8.3.1]
spExtra	0

Notes

1. OpenPort initializes a graphics port and opens it for use; InitPort reinitializes a port that's already been opened.

2. Both routines set the fields of the GrafPort record to their standard initial values, as shown in the table.

3. In both cases, the designated port becomes the current port.

4. The bottom-right coordinates of portRect and visRgn reflect the actual width and height of the screen. These values may vary from those shown, depending on the model of Macintosh and the display device being used.

5. OpenPort allocates space for the port's internal data structures (the visible region and clipping region); InitPort does not.

6. The GrafPort record representing the port must already have been allocated previously with NewPtr [3.2.1].

7. ClosePort destroys a port's internal data structures (visible region and clipping region), but not the GrafPort record itself.

8. Call this routine to deallocate the space occupied by the visible and clipping regions before deallocating the port itself with DisposPtr [3.2.2].

Assembly Language Information

Trap macros:

(Pascal) Routine name	(Assembly) Trap macro	Trap word
OpenPort	_OpenPort	$A86F
InitPort	_InitPort	$A86D
ClosePort	_ClosePort	$A87D

4.3.3 Current Port

Definitions

```
procedure SetPort
            (newPort : GrafPtr);        {Pointer to port to be made current}

procedure GetPort
            (var curPort : GrafPtr);    {Returns pointer to current port}

var
    ThePort : GrafPtr;                  {Pointer to current port}
```

Notes

1. SetPort makes a designated graphics port the current port; GetPort returns the current port.
2. Most QuickDraw operations apply implicitly to the current port.
3. A port must be opened with OpenPort [4.3.2] before it can be made current with SetPort.
4. The global variable ThePort always contains a pointer to the current port.
5. To access variable ThePort in assembly language, find the pointer to QuickDraw's globals at the address contained in register A5; this pointer leads directly to ThePort. See Chapter 3 and [4.3.1, note 4] for further discussion.

Assembly Language Information

Trap macros:

(Pascal) Routine name	(Assembly) Trap macro	Trap word
SetPort	_SetPort	$A873
GetPort	_GetPort	$A874

QuickDraw global variable:

Name	Offset in bytes	Meaning
ThePort	0	Pointer to current port

4.3.4   Bit Map and Coordinate System

Definitions

procedure SetPortBits
        (theBits : BitMap);   {New bit map for current port}

procedure SetOrigin
        (hOrigin : INTEGER;   {New horizontal coordinate of port rectangle}
        vOrigin : INTEGER);   {New vertical coordinate of port rectangle}

Notes

1. SetPortBits assigns a new bit map to the current port.

2. The bit map theBits is stored into the port's portBits field [4.2.2].

3. The rectangle theBits.bounds becomes the port's boundary rectangle and establishes a new local coordinate system for the port.

4. SetOrigin changes the local coordinate system of the current port so as to give the top-left corner of its port rectangle (*not* its boundary rectangle!) the local coordinates hOrigin and vOrigin.

5. The bottom-right corner of the port rectangle, as well as the boundary rectangle and the visible region, are adjusted to keep the same spatial relationships relative to the port rectangle's new origin.

6. The port's clipping region and pen location are not adjusted. Their coordinates remain unchanged, but are now interpreted relative to the new coordinate system; this changes their spatial positions relative to the port rectangle.

7. SetOrigin has no visible effect on the screen.

8. A port's initial bit map (after OpenPort or InitPort [4.3.2]) is a copy of the screen map ScreenBits [4.2.1]. Its initial boundary rectangle, port rectangle, and visible region all extend from coordinates (0, 0) at the top left to the dimensions of the screen at the bottom right.

9. The trap macro for SetPortBits is spelled _SetPBits.

Assembly Language Information

Trap macros:

(Pascal) Routine name	(Assembly) Trap macro	Trap word
SetPortBits	_SetPBits	$A875
SetOrigin	_SetOrigin	$A878

4.3.5   Port Rectangle

Definitions

```
procedure MovePortTo
         (leftGlobal : INTEGER;      {New left edge of port rectangle in global coordinates}
          topGlobal : INTEGER);      {New top edge of port rectangle in global coordinates}

procedure PortSize
         (portWidth  : INTEGER;      {New width of port rectangle}
          portHeight : INTEGER);     {New height of port rectangle}
```

Notes

1. MovePortTo moves the current port's port rectangle to a new position within its bit map.

2. leftGlobal and topGlobal are the new *global* coordinates of the port rectangle's top-left corner, and will be converted to the port's *local* coordinate system.

3. The bottom-right corner of the port rectangle is adjusted so that its width and height remain the same.

4. Unlike SetOrigin [4.3.4], MovePortTo does not affect the port's coordinate system; it simply moves the port rectangle to a new location *within* the existing coordinate system.

5. PortSize adjusts the size of the current port's port rectangle.

6. The coordinates of the port rectangle's bottom-right corner are adjusted to give it the new dimensions portWidth and portHeight. The top-left corner of the rectangle is unchanged.

7. These routines are used by the Toolbox to move and size windows on the screen; application programs normally have no need for them.

8. Neither routine has any immediate visible effect on the screen.

9. A port's initial port rectangle (after OpenPort or InitPort [4.3.2]) extends from coordinates (0, 0) at the top left to the dimensions of the screen at the bottom right.

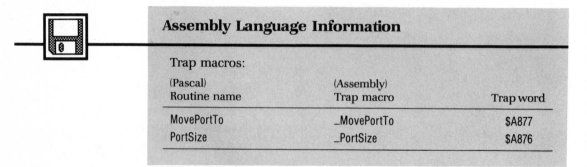

Assembly Language Information

Trap macros:

(Pascal) Routine name	(Assembly) Trap macro	Trap word
MovePortTo	_MovePortTo	$A877
PortSize	_PortSize	$A876

4.3.6 Clipping Region

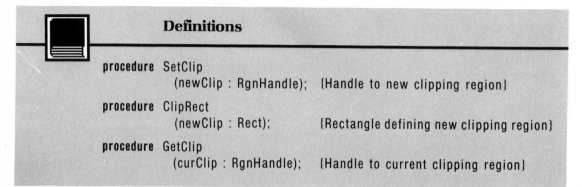

Definitions

```
procedure  SetClip
              (newClip : RgnHandle);    {Handle to new clipping region}
procedure  ClipRect
              (newClip : Rect);         {Rectangle defining new clipping region}
procedure  GetClip
              (curClip : RgnHandle);    {Handle to current clipping region}
```

Notes

1. SetClip sets the current port's clipping region to a specified region, which can be of any shape; ClipRect sets it equivalent to a given rectangle.

2. The handle in the port's clipRgn field is unchanged, but its master pointer is set to point to the new clipping region.

3. SetClip *copies* the region designated by newClip, rather than using the region itself.

4. The new clipping region or rectangle is expressed in the port's local coordinate system.

5. GetClip returns the current port's clipping region in the handle curClip.

6. The handle itself is unchanged, but its master pointer is set to point to a copy of the port's clipping region.

7. A port's initial clipping region (after OpenPort or InitPort [4.3.2]) extends from coordinates (−32768, −32768) at the top left to (32767, 32767) at the bottom right.

Assembly Language Information

Trap macros:

(Pascal) Routine name	(Assembly) Trap macro	Trap word
SetClip	_SetClip	$A879
ClipRect	_ClipRect	$A87B
GetClip	_GetClip	$A87A

4.4   Calculations on Graphical Entities

4.4.1   Calculations on Points

Definitions

```
procedure  AddPt
           (addPoint   : Point;        {Point to be added}
            var toPoint : Point);       {Point to add it to}

procedure  SubPt
           (subPoint       : Point;     {Point to be subtracted}
            var fromPoint : Point);     {Point to subtract it from}

function   DeltaPoint
           (fromPoint : Point;          {Point to subtract from}
            subPoint   : Point)         {Point to be subtracted}
            : LONGINT;                  {Difference between points}

function   EqualPt
           (point1 : Point;             {First point to be compared}
            point2 : Point)             {Second point to be compared}
            : BOOLEAN;                  {Are they equal?}
```

Notes

1. AddPt adds one point to another; SubPt subtracts one point from another.

2. The horizontal and vertical coordinates of the two points are added or subtracted independently.

3. The coordinates of the second point are set to the calculated results; the first point is unaffected.

4. DeltaPoint also subtracts one point from another, but returns the difference as a function result rather than through a variable parameter.

5. Although nominally a long integer, the result is actually a Point record [4.1.1], with the vertical difference in the high-order word and the horizontal difference in the low.

6. EqualPt compares two points for equality and returns a Boolean result.

7. DeltaPoint and EqualPt leave both points unchanged.

Assembly Language Information

Trap macros:

(Pascal) Routine name	(Assembly) Trap macro	Trap word
AddPt	_AddPt	$A87E
SubPt	_SubPt	$A87F
DeltaPoint	_DeltaPoint	$A94F
EqualPt	_EqualPt	$A881

4.4.2   Coordinate Conversion

Definitions

procedure LocalToGlobal
              (**var** thePoint : Point);   {Point to be converted}

procedure GlobalToLocal
              (**var** thePoint : Point);   {Point to be converted}

Notes

1. These two routines convert a point between local and global coordinates.

2. The local coordinate system involved is always that of the current port.

3. In the local coordinate system, the top-left corner of the port's bit image has the coordinates given by the top-left corner of the boundary rectangle.

4. In the global coordinate system, the top-left corner of the bit image has coordinates (0, 0), independent of the boundary rectangle. This provides a convenient basis of comparison between different ports sharing the same bit image, such as the screen.

5. To convert a point from one port's coordinate system to that of another, make the first port current with SetPort [4.3.3], convert the point from local to global coordinates, make the second port current, and convert from global to local coordinates.

6. To convert a rectangle, polygon, or region from one coordinate system to another, use OffsetRect [4.4.4], OffsetPoly [4.4.6], or OffsetRgn [4.4.7].

Assembly Language Information

Trap macros:

(Pascal) Routine name	(Assembly) Trap macro	Trap word
LocalToGlobal	_LocalToGlobal	$A870
GlobalToLocal	_GlobalToLocal	$A871

4.4.3   Testing for Inclusion

Definitions

```
function PtInRect
        (thePoint : Point;          {Point to be tested}
         theRect  : Rect)           {Rectangle to test it against}
         : BOOLEAN;                 {Is the point in the rectangle?}

function PtInRgn
        (thePoint  : Point;         {Point to be tested}
         theRegion : RgnHandle)     {Handle to region to test it against}
         : BOOLEAN;                 {Is the point in the region?}

function RectInRgn
        (theRect   : Rect;          {Rectangle to be tested}
         theRegion : RgnHandle)     {Handle to region to test it against}
         : BOOLEAN;                 {Does the rectangle intersect the region?}

function PinRect
        (thePoint : Point;          {Rectangle to pin to}
         theRect  : Rect)           {Point to be pinned}
         : LONGINT;                 {Point pinned to rectangle}
```

Notes

1. PtInRect and PtInRgn test whether a given point lies inside a given rectangle or region.

2. The test actually applies not to the point itself, but to the *pixel* just below and to the right of it. For example, PtInRect will return TRUE if the given point lies on the top or left edge of the rectangle, but FALSE if it's on the right or bottom edge (since the corresponding pixel is then outside the rectangle).

3. RectInRgn tests whether a given rectangle and region intersect. It returns TRUE if there is at least one pixel that lies inside both the rectangle and the region, FALSE if they have no pixels in common.

4. PinRect "pins" a point to a designated rectangle: that is, if the point lies outside the rectangle, PinRect converts it to the nearest point along the rectangle's boundary.

5. If the point is already inside the rectangle, it's returned unchanged.

6. The resulting point is returned as a long integer, with its vertical coordinate in the high-order word and its horizontal coordinate in the low-order word. Use HiWord and LoWord [2.2.3] to extract the coordinates, or typecasting (Chapter 2) to convert the long integer to a Point.

Assembly Language Information

Trap macros:

(Pascal) Routine name	(Assembly) Trap macro	Trap word
PtInRect	_PtInRect	$A8AD
PtInRgn	_PtInRgn	$A8E8
RectInRgn	_RectInRgn	$A8E9
PinRect	_PinRect	$A94E

4.4.4 Calculations on One Rectangle

Definitions

```
procedure OffsetRect
          (var theRect : Rect;        {Rectangle to be offset}
           hOffset     : INTEGER;     {Horizontal offset in pixels}
           vOffset     : INTEGER);    {Vertical offset in pixels}

procedure InsetRect
          (var theRect : Rect;        {Rectangle to be inset}
           hInset      : INTEGER;     {Horizontal inset in pixels}
           vInset      : INTEGER);    {Vertical inset in pixels}

function  EmptyRect
          (theRect : Rect)            {Rectangle to be tested}
           : BOOLEAN;                 {Is the rectangle empty?}
```

Notes

1. OffsetRect moves a rectangle to a new position within its coordinate system without affecting its width and height.
2. The given horizontal and vertical offsets are added to both the rectangle's top-left and bottom-right corners.
3. A positive horizontal offset moves the rectangle to the right, negative to the left; a positive vertical offset moves the rectangle downward, a negative one moves it upward.
4. This operation is useful for transforming a rectangle from one coordinate system to another.
5. InsetRect shrinks or expands a rectangle while leaving it centered at the same position.
6. The given horizontal and vertical insets are added to the rectangle's top-left corner and subtracted from its bottom-right corner.
7. A positive inset in either dimension shrinks the rectangle in that dimension; a negative inset expands it.
8. If the rectangle becomes empty (right ≤ left or bottom ≤ top), all four of its coordinates are set to 0.
9. EmptyRect tests whether a rectangle is empty.
10. None of these operations has any visible effect on the screen.

Assembly Language Information

Trap macros:

(Pascal) Routine name	(Assembly) Trap macro	Trap word
OffsetRect	_OffsetRect	$A8A8
InsetRect	_InsetRect	$A8A9
EmptyRect	_EmptyRect	$A8AE

4.4.5   Calculations on Two Rectangles

Definitions

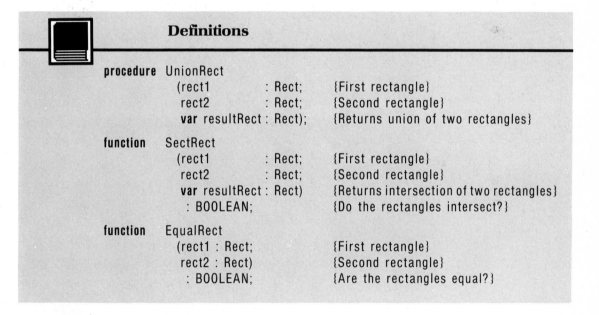

```
procedure  UnionRect
            (rect1          : Rect;      {First rectangle}
             rect2          : Rect;      {Second rectangle}
             var resultRect : Rect);     {Returns union of two rectangles}

function    SectRect
            (rect1          : Rect;      {First rectangle}
             rect2          : Rect;      {Second rectangle}
             var resultRect : Rect)      {Returns intersection of two rectangles}
             : BOOLEAN;                  {Do the rectangles intersect?}

function    EqualRect
            (rect1 : Rect;               {First rectangle}
             rect2 : Rect)               {Second rectangle}
             : BOOLEAN;                  {Are the rectangles equal?}
```

Notes

1. UnionRect forms the union of two rectangles, the smallest rectangle that completely encloses both of them.

2. SectRect forms the intersection of two rectangles, the largest rectangle completely enclosed within both of them.

3. SectRect returns a Boolean result telling whether the intersection of the two rectangles is nonempty (encloses at least one pixel).

4. If the intersection is empty, all four coordinates of resultRect will be set to 0.

5. EqualRect tests whether two rectangles are equal (agree in all four coordinates).

6. For any of these routines to produce meaningful results, both rectangles must be expressed in the same coordinate system.

7. None of these operations has any visible effect on the screen.

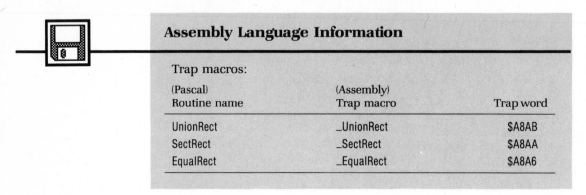

Assembly Language Information

Trap macros:

(Pascal) Routine name	(Assembly) Trap macro	Trap word
UnionRect	_UnionRect	$A8AB
SectRect	_SectRect	$A8AA
EqualRect	_EqualRect	$A8A6

4.4.6 Calculations on Polygons

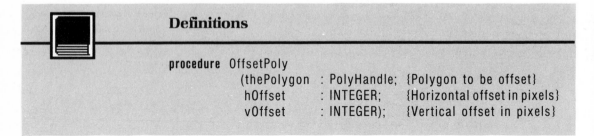

Definitions

```
procedure OffsetPoly
          (thePolygon : PolyHandle; {Polygon to be offset}
           hOffset    : INTEGER;    {Horizontal offset in pixels}
           vOffset    : INTEGER);   {Vertical offset in pixels}
```

Notes

1. OffsetPoly moves a polygon to a new position within its coordinate system without affecting its shape and size.

2. A positive horizontal offset moves the polygon to the right, negative to the left; a positive vertical offset moves the polygon downward, a negative one moves it upward.

3. This operation is useful for transforming a polygon from one coordinate system to another.

4. The operation has no visible effect on the screen.

Assembly Language Information

Trap macro:

(Pascal) Routine name	(Assembly) Trap macro	Trap word
OffsetPoly	_OffsetPoly	$A8CE

4.4.7   Calculations on One Region

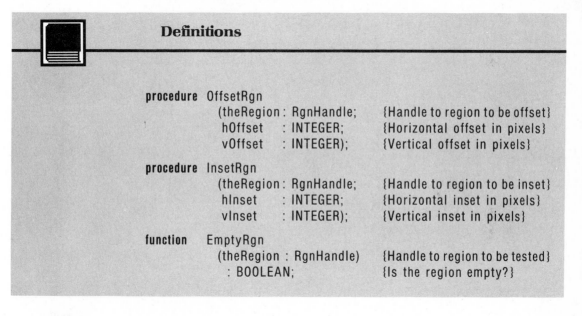

Definitions

```
procedure  OffsetRgn
              (theRegion : RgnHandle;       {Handle to region to be offset}
               hOffset    : INTEGER;        {Horizontal offset in pixels}
               vOffset    : INTEGER);       {Vertical offset in pixels}

procedure  InsetRgn
              (theRegion : RgnHandle;       {Handle to region to be inset}
               hInset     : INTEGER;        {Horizontal inset in pixels}
               vInset     : INTEGER);       {Vertical inset in pixels}

function   EmptyRgn
              (theRegion : RgnHandle)       {Handle to region to be tested}
               : BOOLEAN;                   {Is the region empty?}
```

Notes

1. OffsetRgn moves a region to a new position within its coordinate system without affecting its shape and size.

2. A positive horizontal offset moves the region to the right, negative to the left; a positive vertical offset moves the region downward, a negative one moves it upward.

3. This operation is useful for transforming a region from one coordinate system to another.

4. InsetRgn shrinks or expands a region while leaving it centered at the same position.

5. All coordinates in the region's definition are moved inward (toward the center) by the given horizontal and vertical insets.

6. A positive inset in either dimension shrinks the region in that dimension; a negative inset expands it.

7. EmptyRgn tests whether a region is empty.

8. None of these operations has any visible effect on the screen.

9. The trap macro for OffsetRgn is spelled _OfsetRgn.

Assembly Language Information

Trap macros:

(Pascal) Routine name	(Assembly) Trap macro	Trap word
OffsetRgn	_OfsetRgn	$A8E0
InsetRgn	_InsetRgn	$A8E1
EmptyRgn	_EmptyRgn	$A8E2

4.4.8   Calculations on Two Regions

Definitions

```
procedure UnionRgn
          (region1      : RgnHandle;    {Handle to first region}
          region2       : RgnHandle;    {Handle to second region}
          resultRegion : RgnHandle);   {Handle to be set to union of two regions}

procedure SectRgn
          (region1      : RgnHandle;    {Handle to first region}
          region2       : RgnHandle;    {Handle to second region}
          resultRegion : RgnHandle);   {Handle to be set to intersection of two regions}

procedure DiffRgn
          (region1      : RgnHandle;    {Handle to region to be subtracted from}
          region2       : RgnHandle;    {Handle to region to subtract from it}
          resultRegion : RgnHandle);   {Handle to be set to difference of two regions}

procedure XOrRgn
          (region1      : RgnHandle;    {Handle to first region}
          region2       : RgnHandle;    {Handle to second region}
          resultRegion : RgnHandle);   {Handle to be set to "exclusive or" of two regions}

function  EqualRgn
          (region1 : RgnHandle;         {Handle to first region}
          region2 : RgnHandle)          {Handle to second region}
           : BOOLEAN;                   {Are the regions equal?}
```

Notes

1. UnionRgn forms the union of two regions, the smallest region that completely encloses both of them.

2. SectRgn forms the intersection of two regions, the largest region completely enclosed within both of them.

3. DiffRgn forms the difference of two regions, the portion of the first region that doesn't lie within the second.

4. XOrRgn forms the "exclusive or" of two regions, the difference between their union and intersection.

5. In each case, the destination region resultRegion must already have been previously created with NewRgn [4.1.6].

6. In each case, if the result of the calculation is the empty region, resultRegion will be set to a rectangular region with all four coordinates equal to 0.

7. EqualRgn tests whether two regions are equal (have the same shape, size, and location).

8. Any two empty regions are considered equal.

9. For any of these routines to produce meaningful results, both regions must be expressed in the same coordinate system.

10. None of these operations has any visible effect on the screen.

Assembly Language Information

Trap macros:

(Pascal) Routine name	(Assembly) Trap macro	Trap word
UnionRgn	_UnionRgn	$A8E5
SectRgn	_SectRgn	$A8E4
DiffRgn	_DiffRgn	$A8E6
XOrRgn	_XOrRgn	$A8E7
EqualRgn	_EqualRgn	$A8E3

4.4.9 Scaling and Mapping

Definitions

```
procedure  ScalePt
              (var thePoint : Point;        {Point to be scaled}
               fromRect     : Rect;         {Rectangle to scale it from}
               toRect       : Rect);        {Rectangle to scale it to}

procedure  MapPt
              (var thePoint : Point;        {Point to be mapped}
               fromRect     : Rect;         {Rectangle to map it from}
               toRect       : Rect);        {Rectangle to map it to}

procedure  MapRect
              (var theRect  : Rect;         {Rectangle to be mapped}
               fromRect     : Rect;         {Rectangle to map it from}
               toRect       : Rect);        {Rectangle to map it to}

procedure  MapPoly
              (thePolygon : PolyHandle;     {Polygon to be mapped}
               fromRect   : Rect;           {Rectangle to map it from}
               toRect     : Rect);          {Rectangle to map it to}

procedure  MapRgn
              (theRegion : RgnHandle;       {Region to be mapped}
               fromRect  : Rect;            {Rectangle to map it from}
               toRect    : Rect);           {Rectangle to map it to}
```

Notes

1. ScalePt scales a point by the ratio of the dimensions of two rectangles.

2. Each coordinate of thePoint is scaled by the ratio of toRect to fromRect in the corresponding dimension. That is, the horizontal coordinate of the point is multiplied by the ratio of the rectangles' widths, and the vertical coordinate by the ratio of their heights.

3. MapPt maps a point in one rectangle to the corresponding point in another.

4. The mapping takes into account both the ratio of the rectangles' dimensions and the offset between their top-left corners. The effect is as if rectangle fromRect were moved and stretched or shrunk to coincide with toRect.

5. MapRect, MapPoly, and MapRgn map an entire figure from one rectangle to another by mapping each point of the figure as in MapPt.

6. In each case, the figure should be entirely contained within the rectangle fromRect.

Assembly Language Information

Trap macros:

(Pascal) Routine name	(Assembly) Trap macro	Trap word
ScalePt	_ScalePt	$A8F8
MapPt	_MapPt	$A8F9
MapRect	_MapRect	$A8FA
MapPoly	_MapPoly	$A8FC
MapRgn	_MapRgn	$A8FB

CHAPTER

Quick on the Draw

QuickDraw places a wide variety of drawing facilities at your disposal. You can draw

- *Lines*, using a "pen" of any size and pattern (Figure 5-1a), with a variety of graphical effects.
- *Shapes*, including rectangles with square or rounded corners, circles, ovals, arcs, wedges, and polygons of any shape. All of these can be outlined with any pen or filled with any pattern (Figure 5-1b).
- *Regions* made up of any combination of lines and shapes forming a closed area. A region can have any shape whatever—even one with two or more pieces or with holes in it. For instance, the shaded area in Figure 5-1c could be defined as a single region.
- *Text characters* in a variety of typefaces, sizes, and styles (Figure 5-1d).

In addition, you can take any of these graphical elements and stretch or condense it to any desired proportions, horizontally, vertically, or both ways independently. You can "clip" one element to the boundaries of another—for instance, to make one object appear to be hidden behind another. (This is how the Toolbox makes the windows overlap on your screen.) And you can define *pictures* consisting of any combination of these elements and operations, which you can then treat as a unit and redraw in a single operation.

185

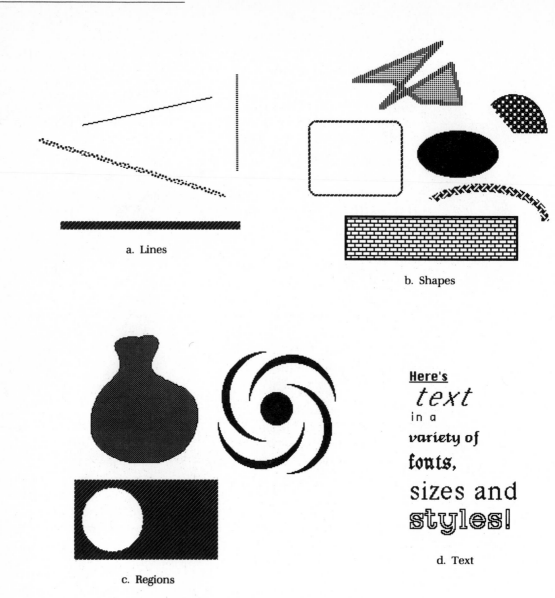

a. Lines

b. Shapes

c. Regions

d. Text

Figure 5-1 QuickDraw graphical elements

Line Drawing

All line drawing in a graphics port is done with the *graphics pen*.
Every port has its own pen; you draw lines in the port's bit map
by moving the pen from point to point on the coordinate grid.

The pen's current location is kept in the pnLoc field of the graphics port [4.2.2]; you can read it out at any time with the QuickDraw procedure GetPen [5.2.4].

The routines for drawing lines with the pen are Move, MoveTo, Line, and LineTo [5.2.4]. MoveTo simply moves the pen to a designated pair of coordinates, without drawing anything; it's like picking the pen up off the paper (that is, the bit map) before moving it. LineTo puts the pen down on the paper and then moves it from its current location to a new set of coordinates, drawing as it goes. The result is a straight line directly from one point to another. The pen is then left at the new location, ready to begin the next line. For example, the statements

```
MoveTo ( 50,  50);

LineTo (150,  50);
LineTo (150, 150);
LineTo ( 50, 150);
LineTo ( 50,  50)
```

draw a square 100 pixels on a side, with its top-left corner at coordinates (50, 50).

Everything the pen draws is clipped to the intersection of the port's boundary rectangle, port rectangle, clipping region, and visible region [4.2.2]. The pen will go anywhere you tell it on the coordinate grid, even outside these boundaries, but only those lines (or parts of lines) that fall inside the clipping boundaries will actually be drawn. Anything drawn outside the clipping boundaries is lost: even if you later enlarge the boundaries, the clipped parts of the drawing won't reappear.

The procedures Move and Line are similar to MoveTo and LineTo, but interpret the coordinates you give as a motion relative to the current pen location, rather than as an absolute location on the coordinate grid. A positive value for the horizontal coordinate moves the pen to the right, negative to the left; a positive vertical coordinate moves the pen downward, a negative one moves it upward. For example, the statements

```
MoveTo (  50,   50);     {Move to starting point}
Line   ( 100,    0);     {Draw 100 pixels to the right, }
Line   (   0,  100);     {  100 down,                    }
Line   (-100,    0);     {  100 to the left,             }
Line   (   0, -100)      {  and 100 up                   }
```

draw the same square as in the previous example.

> When you shift the origin of the coordinate system with SetOrigin [4.3.4], the pen goes along for the ride. The coordinates of the pen remain unchanged, but those coordinates now lie at a new position within the port's bit map. The pen is said to "stick to" the coordinate system. Anything you've already drawn in the port, however, sticks to the image: the existing pixels in the bit image remain the same, but the coordinates of each pixel change because of the change of origin.

Program 5-1 shows a simple example of line drawing. Procedure StopSign draws the stop sign shown in Figure 5-2 into the current graphics port, at any specified location and to any specified scale. The parameters figureTop and figureLeft locate the figure within the port's local coordinate system; scale gives the size of the scale units in which the figure is drawn.

To simplify our drawing operations, we will temporarily transform the coordinate system to give the origin (that is, the top-left corner) of the figure the coordinates (0, 0). First we call GetPort [4.3.3] to get a pointer to the current port, which we use to find the origin of the port rectangle,

```
currentPort^.portRect.topLeft
```

Before transforming the coordinates of this point, we first save it in the variable oldOrigin so that we can later restore the coordinate system to its original state. Then we use SetOrigin [4.3.4] to subtract the coordinates of the figure's origin, figureLeft and figureTop, from those of the port rectangle's origin. This has the effect of subtracting these same two values from the coordinates of every other point in the port as well: in particular, it transforms the point (figureLeft, figureTop), which will be the origin of the figure, to (0, 0) as we want.

Now we're ready to draw the figure: first the octagonal outline of the stop sign, then the two horizontal lines, then each of the letters in turn. All our drawing operations are defined in terms of the specified scale unit; overall, the figure is 18 units wide by 18 high. Finally, we restore the port's original coordinate system with SetOrigin and exit.

```
procedure StopSign (figureTop  : INTEGER        {Top edge of figure in local coordinates}
                    figureLeft : INTEGER;       {Left edge of figure in local coordinates}
                    scale      : INTEGER);      {Size of scale unit in pixels}


{ Example of simple line drawing.  }


var
   currentPort : GrafPtr;                       {Pointer to current port [4.2.2]}
   oldOrigin   : Point;                         {Origin of port rectangle on entry [4.1.1]}


begin {StopSign}

   GetPort (currentPort);                       {Get pointer to current port [4.3.3]}
   oldOrigin := currentPort^.portRect.topLeft;  {Save old origin of port rectangle [4.2.2, 4.1.2]}
   with oldOrigin do
      SetOrigin (h - figureLeft, v - figureTop);  {Offset to origin of figure [4.3.4]}

   MoveTo ( 5 % scale, 0       );               {Draw the octagon [5.2.4]}
   Line   ( 8 % scale, 0       );
   Line   ( 5 % scale, 5 % scale);
   Line   ( 0        , 8 % scale);
   Line   (-5 % scale, 5 % scale);
   Line   (-8 % scale, 0       );
   Line   (-5 % scale, -5 % scale);
   Line   ( 0        , -8 % scale);
   Line   ( 5 % scale, -5 % scale);
```

Program 5-1 Line drawing

```
MoveTo ( 0       ,  5 $ scale);          {Draw the horizontal lines [5.2.4]}
Line   (18 $ scale, 0       );
MoveTo ( 0       , 13 $ scale);
Line   (18 $ scale, 0       );

MoveTo ( 4 $ scale,  7 $ scale);         {Draw the "S" [5.2.4]}
Line   (-2 $ scale, 0       );
Line   ( 0       ,  2 $ scale);
Line   ( 2 $ scale, 0       );
Line   ( 0       ,  2 $ scale);
Line   (-2 $ scale, 0       );

MoveTo ( 7 $ scale,  7 $ scale);         {Draw the "T" [5.2.4]}
Line   ( 0       ,  4 $ scale);
Move   (-1 $ scale, -4 $ scale);
Line   ( 2 $ scale, 0       );

MoveTo (10 $ scale,  7 $ scale);         {Draw the "O" [5.2.4]}
Line   ( 2 $ scale, 0       );
Line   ( 0       ,  4 $ scale);
Line   (-2 $ scale, 0       );
Line   ( 0       , -4 $ scale);

MoveTo (14 $ scale,  7 $ scale);         {Draw the "P" [5.2.4]}
Line   ( 0       ,  4 $ scale);
Move   ( 0       , -4 $ scale);
Line   ( 2 $ scale, 0       );
Line   ( 0       ,  2 $ scale);
Line   (-2 $ scale, 0       );

with oldOrigin do
   SetOrigin (h, v)                      {Restore old origin [4.3.4]}

end;  {StopSign}
```

Program 5-1 *(continued)*

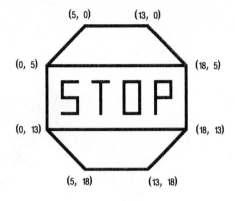

All coordinates are
expressed in scale units.

Figure 5-2 Output of procedure StopSign

Pen Size

The "pen point" that you draw with is always rectangular in shape, but it can be any size you like. When you open or reinitialize a graphics port, its pen is set to the finest possible point, 1 pixel wide by 1 pixel high. You can then change its dimensions with the QuickDraw procedure PenSize [5.2.2]. For example, to make the pen 3 pixels wide by 7 high, you would write

```
PenSize (3, 7)
```

> If you make either dimension of the pen zero or negative, the pen vanishes completely and won't draw anything at all.

A port's pen location always refers to the top-left corner of the pen; the rest of the pen "hangs" below and to the right of those coordinates. It's important to keep this in mind when you use pen sizes bigger than (1, 1). Lines drawn with Line or LineTo don't necessarily end at the coordinates you specify: they extend to include the width and height of the pen as well. For example, in Figure 5-3, a line drawn from coordinates (65, 140) to (80, 145), using a pen 3 pixels wide by 7 high, will extend to coordinates (83, 152), the bottom-right corner of the pen.

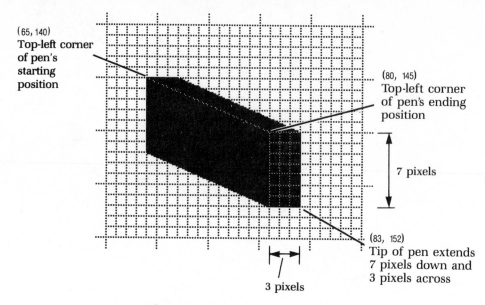

(65, 140)
Top-left corner of pen's starting position

(80, 145)
Top-left corner of pen's ending position

7 pixels

(83, 152)
Tip of pen extends 7 pixels down and 3 pixels across

3 pixels

Figure 5-3 Pen size

Hiding the Pen

The pen draws into a port's bit image only when it's *visible*. It can also be *hidden*, in which case none of your drawing operations have any effect on the image. You can hide the pen with HidePen and later make it visible again with ShowPen [5.2.3]. These routines control the pen's visibility by manipulating the pnVis field of the current graphics port.

You might think that pnVis would be a simple Boolean field: TRUE if the pen is visible, FALSE if it's hidden. Actually, it's an integer called the *pen level:* the pen is hidden if the pen level is negative, visible if it's zero or positive. The pen level is set to 0 when you open a new port, making the pen initially visible. HidePen decrements the level by 1, which hides the pen by making the pen level negative; ShowPen increments the level by 1, undoing the effect of the last HidePen. Notice that this doesn't necessarily cause the pen to become visible again: it just restores the pen level to whatever value it had before the pen was last hidden. In effect, the pen level counts how many times the pen has been hidden and not yet reshown. This allows calls to HidePen and ShowPen to be "nested" to any depth; only when every HidePen has been balanced by a corresponding ShowPen will the pen become visible again.

This arrangement is useful for writing routines that leave the pen in the same state of visibility as when they found it. If a routine needs to hide the pen, it can restore the previous pen level by calling ShowPen before returning. If the pen was visible (PnVis = 0) on entry to the routine, this will make it visible again; if it was already hidden (pnVis < 0), the routine will leave it hidden at the same depth of nesting as before.

> Notice that if the pen level ever becomes greater than 0, decrementing it with HidePen won't make it negative and so won't hide the pen. To keep this from happening, don't ever call ShowPen except to balance a previous call to HidePen. This will keep the pen level from going above 0, so the pen will always hide when you tell it to.

Patterns and Transfer Modes

You can achieve a variety of interesting graphical effects by varying two more of the pen's characteristics, its *pattern* and *transfer mode*. A pattern [5.1.1] is a special bit image, always 8 pixels wide by 8 high, that can be repeated indefinitely to fill an area in a bit map, like identical floor tiles laid end to end (see Figure 5-4). You can use the graphics pen to paint any pattern by setting the *pen pattern* kept in the port's pnPat field [4.2.2]. A port's pen pattern is initially set to solid black, but you can change it to some other pattern

Figure 5-4 Patterns

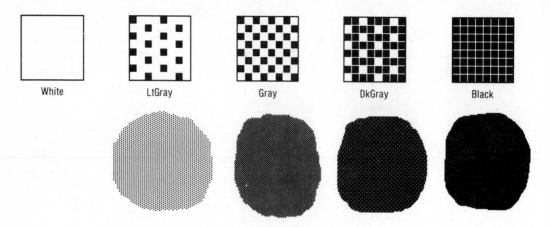

Figure 5-5 Standard fill tones

with PenPat [5.2.2]. The pen will then paint in that pattern, just like the paintbrush tool in MacPaint.

> When you paint with a pattern, QuickDraw automatically aligns each "tile" so that its top-left corner falls at an even multiple of 8 pixels from the origin of the port rectangle. This ensures that adjacent areas of the same pattern will blend into one another without creating visible "seams" along the boundaries.

The Toolbox provides five standard patterns representing a range of tones from solid white to solid black (Figure 5-5). These standard fill tones are available in the global variables White, LtGray, Gray, DkGray, and Black [5.1.2], which are initialized when you call InitGraf [4.3.1]. You can also define your own patterns by storing the desired bits into them with StuffHex [2.2.4]. For example, if myPattern is a variable of type Pattern, the statement

StuffHex (@myPattern, '3C66C39999C3663C')

will set it to the third pattern shown in Figure 5-4.

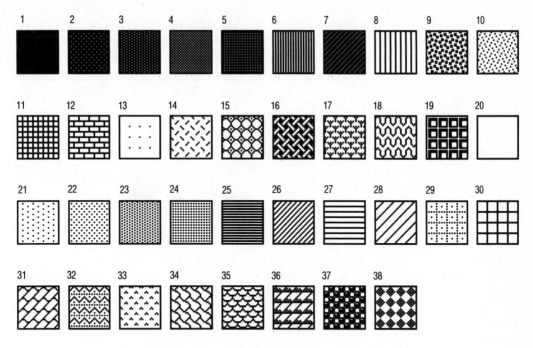

Figure 5-6 Standard pattern list

For a more varied selection than just the five standard fill tones, a *pattern list* is available in the system resource file containing the same 38 patterns that MacPaint offers on its pattern palette (see Figure 5-6). We'll be learning about resources in the next chapter; you can access individual patterns in the list with the Toolbox routine GetIndPattern [5.1.1].

Besides a pen pattern, every graphics port also has a *background pattern* (bkPat) and a *fill pattern* (fillPat). The background pattern is used for erasing things. It's normally solid white, but you can set it to some other pattern with BackPat [5.1.1]. The fill pattern is used privately by QuickDraw for certain shape-drawing operations; you'll never need to set it yourself.

A port's *pen mode* [5.1.3] controls the way the pen paints its pattern into the bit map. There are four basic pen modes, and four more that are variants of the basic ones (see Figure 5-7). The most straightforward is PatCopy, which simply copies the pixels of the pattern directly to the bit map, replacing whatever was there before. The existing pixels of the bit map are simply "painted over" by those of the pattern, both black and white. This is the mode the pen is set to when you open a brand-new graphics port; to switch to one of the other modes instead, use PenMode [5.2.2].

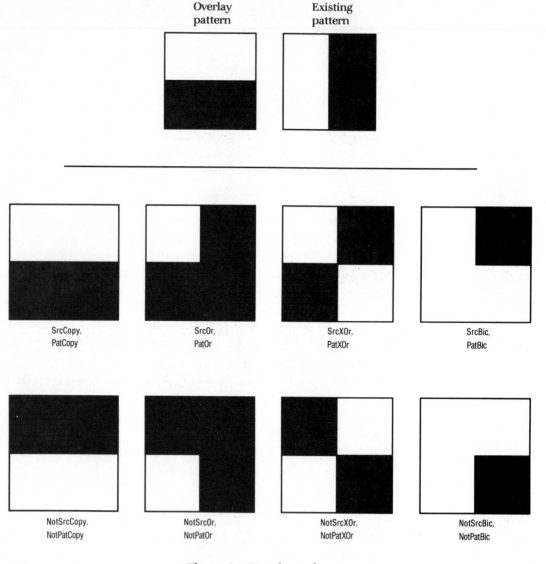

Figure 5-7 Transfer modes

The other three basic pen modes each perform a particular operation on the existing pixels of the bit map. They all use the pattern as a "mask" to select which pixels of the bit map the operation will affect. Wherever the pattern has a black pixel (that is, a 1 bit), the corresponding pixel of the bit map will be affected; a white pixel (0 bit) in the pattern leaves the existing pixel in the bit map unchanged. The pen mode PatOr sets the selected bits in the bit map to black, PatBic ("bit clear") clears them to white, and PatXOr ("exclusive or") inverts them from one color to the other.

The four variant pen modes work the same as the four basic ones, but reverse the roles of the white and black pixels in the pattern. So NotPatCopy paints the inverse of the pattern: white pixels where the pattern has black, and vice versa. NotPatOr, NotPatXOr, and NotPatBic perform the same operations as their counterparts just described, but they affect those pixels in the bit map corresponding to white in the pattern, while leaving those corresponding to black unchanged. (The bits of the pattern itself aren't inverted, they're just interpreted the opposite way.)

Together, the pen's location, size, pattern, and mode make up the port's *pen state*. If you have to change any of the pen's characteristics for any reason, you can save the old state with GetPenState and restore it later with SetPenState [5.2.1]. The routine PenNormal [5.2.2] resets the pen to its initial state: 1 pixel wide by 1 high, with a solid black pattern and a pen mode of PatCopy.

Direct Bit Transfer

QuickDraw's fundamental drawing operation, on which all the others are based, is CopyBits [5.1.4]. It copies pixels directly from any rectangle in one bit map (the source) to any rectangle in another (the destination), in any of the eight transfer modes and with optional scaling and clipping. You can use CopyBits to "stamp" a copy of a small bit image into a designated location in another. For example, to stamp the pointing hand of Figure 4-3, which we defined in the last chapter as a bit map named theMap, into a larger bit map named theCanvas at coordinates (85, 60), you could write

```
SetRect (atRect, 85, 60, 103, 72);
CopyBits (theMap, theCanvas,
          theMap.bounds, atRect,
          SrcCopy, NIL)
```

(In this example the rectangle you're copying from is theMap.bounds, the entire boundary rectangle of the source bit map; you could also specify a smaller source rectangle to transfer just a part of the bit map instead of the whole thing.)

Notice that the transfer mode in the example is specified as SrcCopy, not PatCopy as in the preceding section. CopyBits has its own set of eight *source transfer modes* [5.1.3], analogous to the *pattern transfer modes* used with the graphics pen. It's important to keep the two kinds of transfer mode straight, and to use the right kind in a given situation. The pattern modes are for painting patterns with the pen; the source modes are for transferring bits from one bit map to another. As we'll see when we talk about character text in Chapter 8, the characters in a font are also represented in the form of a bit map, so source transfer modes are used for "painting" text characters as well.

Another thing to notice in the example above is that the destination rectangle atRect has the same dimensions as the source rectangle theMap.bounds, 18 pixels wide by 12 high. This means the source map will be copied directly, pixel for pixel, to the destination. The two rectangles aren't required to be the same size, however. If they aren't, the source pixels will be stretched or condensed to fit the destination rectangle. For instance, if you used a destination rectangle twice as wide and three times as high, 36 pixels by 36,

```
SetRect (atRect, 85, 60, 121, 96)
```

the source image would be scaled accordingly and would come out looking as in Figure 5-8.

Scaling an image to a different-size rectangle works best if both dimensions of the destination rectangle are exact multiples or divisors of the source dimensions. Otherwise the image tends to come out looking distorted and ugly, like text scaled to an unavailable point size in MacPaint or MacWrite.

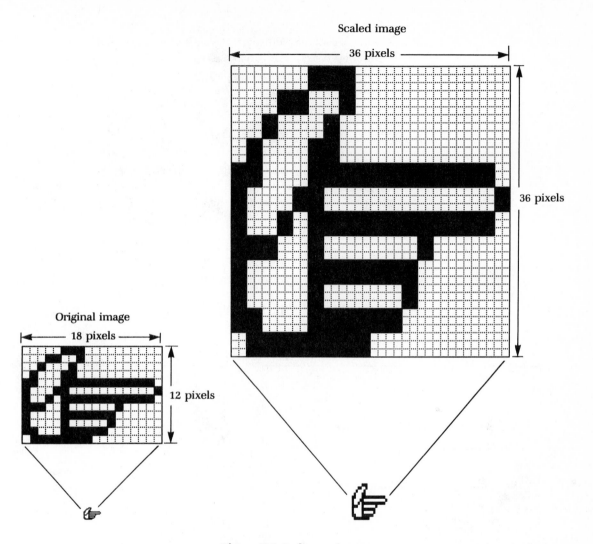

Figure 5-8 Scaling an image

QuickDraw has utility routines for mapping standard figures such as points, rectangles, polygons, and regions from one rectangle to another [4.4.9]. These routines transform each point in the original figure, relative to the origin of the source rectangle, to the corresponding coordinates relative to the origin of the destination rectangle, scaled by the ratio of the two rectangles' widths and heights (see Figure 5-9). For polygons and regions, the source rectangle is normally the figure's bounding box (polyBBox [4.1.3] or rgnBBox [4.1.5]). There's also a ScalePt routine [4.4.9] that scales a point by the proportion between two rectangles' dimensions, without reference to their origins (Figure 5-10).

The last parameter to CopyBits is an arbitrary clipping region, expressed in the coordinate system of the destination bit map.

MapPoly (thePolygon, fromRect, toRect)

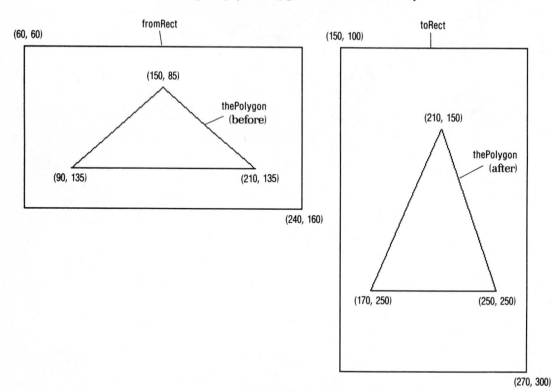

Figure 5-9 Mapping a figure

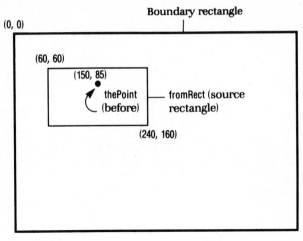

a. Source rectangle and point before mapping or scaling

MapPt (thePoint, fromRect, toRect)

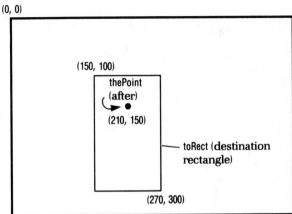

b. The new position of thePoint (210, 150) is mapped with reference to the origin of the destination rectangle (150, 100).

ScalePt (thePoint, fromRect, toRect)

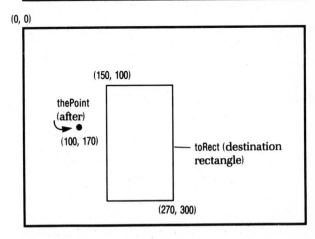

c. The new position of thePoint (100, 170) is scaled without reference to the origin of the destination rectangle.

Figure 5-10 Scaling and mapping a point

You can use this to confine the bit transfer within any desired boundary of any shape—only those bits that lie inside the given boundary will actually be transferred. If you don't want to specify a clipping region, you can set this parameter to NIL, as in our example above. However, CopyBits will *always* clip automatically to the boundary rectangle of the destination bit map, and in the common case where the destination is the bit map belonging to the current graphics port (ThePort.portBits), it will also clip to the port's port rectangle, visible region, and clipping region.

The Macintosh Plus also has an alternate bit-transfer routine named CopyMask [5.1.4]. Instead of using a clipping region to confine the transfer operation, CopyMask accepts a rectangular portion of a third bit map to be used as a mask. Pixels are copied from the source bit map to the destination only in those positions where the mask has a black pixel; where the mask pixel is white, the destination pixel is left unchanged. Unlike the original CopyBits, CopyMask doesn't accept a mode parameter, but just does a straight copy (equivalent to transfer mode SrcCopy). Also, it won't scale one rectangle to another of a different size: the source, mask, and destination rectangles must all have the same dimensions for the transfer to work properly.

A specialized form of bit transfer is ScrollRect [5.1.5], which shifts the contents of a rectangle within the current port by a given horizontal and vertical distance. As the name suggests, this operation is useful mainly for scrolling the contents of a window on the screen. The results are clipped to the specified rectangle, as well as to the usual clipping boundaries (boundary rectangle, port rectangle, clipping region, and visible region). Pixels scrolled out of the rectangle at one end are lost forever; the empty space vacated at the other end is "erased" by filling it with the port's background pattern, normally solid white (see Figure 5-11).

It's then your responsibility to fill in this cleared area with whatever new information may have been scrolled into the window. As we'll see in the chapter on windows in Volume Two, this involves adding the area to the window's *update region*. ScrollRect supports this chore by returning a handle to the affected region through its updateRgn parameter; you can then add the region to

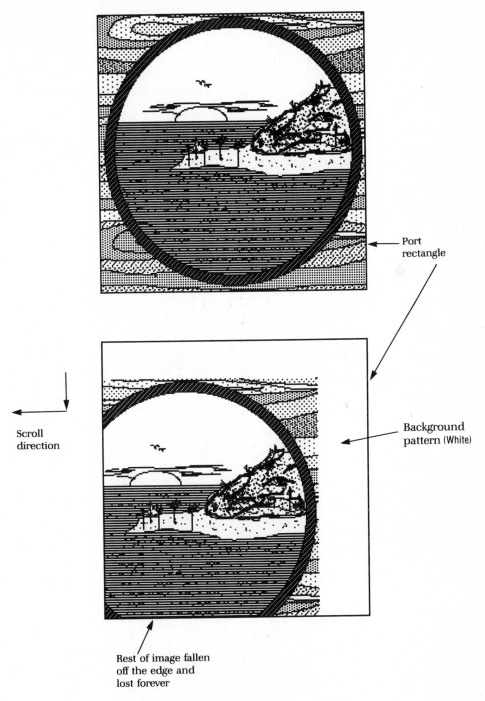

Port
rectangle

Scroll
direction

Background
pattern (White)

Rest of image fallen
off the edge and
lost forever

Figure 5-11 Scrolling a rectangle

the window's update region with the window-management routine
InvalRgn [II:3.4.2].

Icons

One particularly important category of bit images used extensively
in the Macintosh user interface are *icons*. These are images of a
standard size, 32 pixels by 32, used (among other things) to
represent objects on the Macintosh desktop that the user can
manipulate directly with the mouse (see Figure 5-12). There isn't
any special data type representing an icon; it's just a block of 1024

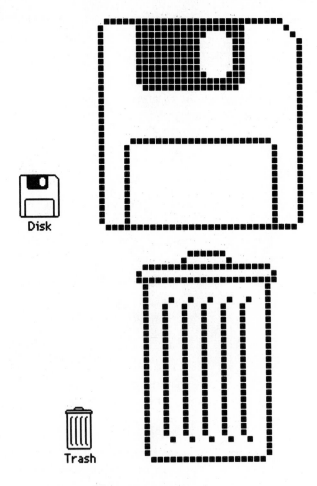

Figure 5-12 Icons

bits (128 bytes, or 64 words) that resides in the heap and is referred to by a handle.

Icons are commonly stored in resource files (Chapter 6) and read in with the Toolbox routine GetIcon [5.4.4], but you can also create one for yourself as an

`array [1..32] of LONGINT`

and fill in its bits with StuffHex [2.2.4]. You can then draw the icon anywhere in the current port with PlotIcon [5.4.4]. (The new Macintosh Plus routine CopyMask [5.1.4] is also useful for drawing icons.)

Drawing Shapes

In addition to simple line drawing and bit transfers, QuickDraw can also perform a range of drawing operations on a wide variety of standard shapes:

- Rectangles and squares, with both square and rounded corners
- Ovals and circles
- Arcs and wedges
- Polygons
- Regions of any shape

Shape-drawing operations are always performed in the current graphics port, and the shapes to be drawn must be specified in the coordinate system of that port. There are five standard drawing operations [5.3.1]:

- *Framing* the shape (drawing its outline)
- *Painting* the shape with the port's current pen pattern
- *Filling* the shape with any other designated pattern
- *Erasing* the shape (filling it with the port's background pattern)
- *Inverting* the shape (changing white pixels to black and vice versa)

Even though some of these operations (framing and painting) use the current pen characteristics, they're independent of the pen location and don't change it in any way. However, these operations *are* affected by the pen *level*, and have no effect on the bit map if the pen is hidden. As usual, all drawing operations are clipped to the port's boundary rectangle, port rectangle, clipping region, and visible region.

Rectangles

The simplest of all QuickDraw shapes is the rectangle, which we discussed in Chapter 4. To illustrate how the various shape-drawing operations work, let's look at how they apply to rectangles [5.3.2]. The equivalent operations on other shapes work in the same general way.

The FrameRect routine (Figure 5-13) draws the outline of a rectangle without affecting its interior. The outline is hollow: whatever was inside the rectangle before the operation will still show through afterward. The outline is drawn with the port's graphics pen, so its appearance depends on the current pen size, pattern, and mode. The pen is then returned to wherever it was before, so the operation has no overall effect on its location.

> In framing a shape, QuickDraw automatically adjusts for the current pen size to keep its drawing confined "within the lines." The outline that's drawn won't extend beyond the shape's boundary at the right and bottom, regardless of the pen's size. In general, QuickDraw drawing operations never affect any pixels outside the boundary of the shape being drawn. (The one exception to this rule, as we'll see later, occurs when you frame a polygon.)

FrameRect (r)

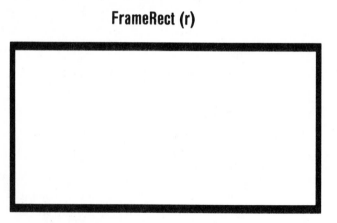

Figure 5-13 Framing a rectangle

PaintRect (r)

Figure 5-14 Painting a rectangle

PaintRect, FillRect, and EraseRect all fill a rectangle with a pattern—both its outline and its interior. PaintRect (Figure 5-14) uses the port's current pen pattern and pen mode; FillRect (Figure 5-15) uses a pattern you supply as an argument, with a transfer mode of PatCopy; EraseRect (Figure 5-16) uses the port's background pattern and the PatCopy mode.

Finally, InvertRect (Figure 5-17) inverts all existing pixels within the rectangle, changing white to black and black to white. The entire rectangle is affected, both outline and interior.

Program 5-2 illustrates the use of these rectangle-drawing operations to produce a dynamically changing work of "abstract art." The results (Figure 5-18) are reminiscent of the rectilinear style of the Dutch painter Piet Mondrian. To keep things simple, we adjust the origin of the current port's port rectangle (presumably a window on the screen) to coordinates (0, 0), after first saving the previous coordinates in variable oldOrigin for later restoration. Then we begin generating random rectangles based on the width and height of the port rectangle, using our earlier Randomize function (Program 2-1). Notice how we use Pt2Rect [4.1.2] to form the rectangle, so that we don't have to worry about the relative positions of the two points that define it: they can be any two diagonally opposite

FillRect (r, Gray)

Figure 5-15 Filling a rectangle

EraseRect (r)

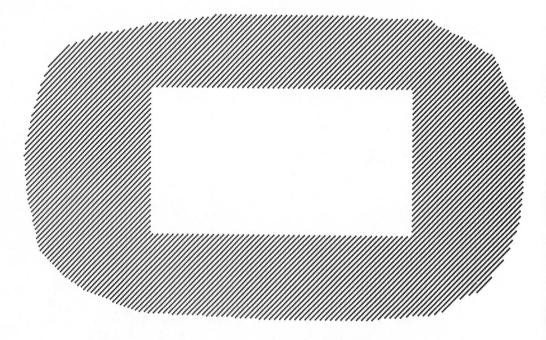

Figure 5-16 Erasing a rectangle

InvertRect (r)

Figure 5-17 Inverting a rectangle

corners of the rectangle, not necessarily the top-left and bottom-right.

The most interesting graphical effects are produced by using the InvertRect operation to paint the rectangle on the screen. If we inverted all our rectangles, however, the image would soon become fragmented into tiny slivers of black and white with no discernible shape or pattern. The effect is more pleasing if we throw in a PaintRect or EraseRect every so often to restore part of the image to solid black or solid white (assuming those are the port's current fill and background patterns). To decide which drawing operation to use, we call Randomize again with a range determined by the constant opRange. On the average, out of every opRange rectangles we generate, we'll paint one black, erase one to white, and invert the rest. The specific value we choose for opRange controls the degree of visual fragmentation we're willing to tolerate: the higher the value, the more fragmentation.

To slow things down to mere human speed, we pause to

```
procedure Mondrian;


   { Example of simple shape drawing using rectangles.  }


   const
      opRange     = 10;                    {Constant controlling degree of visual fragmentation}
      delayInterval = 500;                 {Length of delay between rectangles}


   var
      currentPort : GrafPtr;               {Pointer to current port [4.2.2]}
      oldOrigin   : Point;                 {Origin of port rectangle on entry [4.1.1]}
      windowWidth : INTEGER;               {Width of port rectangle}
      windowHeight : INTEGER;              {Height of port rectangle}
      corner1     : Point;                 {First corner of rectangle to be drawn [4.1.1]}
      corner2     : Point;                 {Second corner of rectangle to be drawn [4.1.1]}
      randomRect  : Rect;                  {Rectangle to be drawn [4.1.2]}
      operation   : INTEGER;               {Drawing operation to use}
      delayCount  : INTEGER;               {Counter for delay between rectangles}


   begin {Mondrian}

      GetPort (currentPort);               {Get pointer to current port [4.3.3]}
      with currentPort^.portRect do
         begin
            oldOrigin    := topLeft;       {Save old origin of port rectangle [4.1.2]}
            windowWidth  := right - left;  {Find dimensions of port rectangle [4.2.2]}
            windowHeight := bottom - top
         end;
      SetOrigin (0, 0);                    {Use origin of (0, 0) for convenience [4.3.4]}
```

Program 5-2 Drawing rectangles

```
repeat

    with corner1 do
       begin
          h := Randomize (windowWidth);        {Generate random coordinates    }
          v := Randomize (windowHeight)        {   for first corner [Prog. 2-1]}
       end;
    with corner2 do
       begin
          h := Randomize (windowWidth);        {Generate random coordinates    }
          v := Randomize (windowHeight)        {   for second corner [Prog. 2-1]}
       end;
    Pt2Rect (corner1, corner2, randomRect);    {Combine to form rectangle [4.1.2]}

    operation := Randomize (opRange);          {Generate random drawing operation [Prog. 2-1]}
    case operation of
       0:
          PaintRect  (randomRect);             {Fill with pen pattern (normally black) [5.3.2]}
       1:
          EraseRect  (randomRect);             {Fill with background pattern (normally white) [5.3.2]}
       otherwise
          InvertRect (randomRect)              {Invert colors [5.3.2]}
       end; {case}

    for delayCount := 1 to delayInterval do    {Wait a while . . . }
       {nothing}

until Button;                                  {Stop when mouse button is pressed [II:2.4.2]}

with oldOrigin do
    SetOrigin (h, v)                           {Restore old origin [4.3.4]}

end;   {Mondrian}
```

Program 5-2 *(continued)*

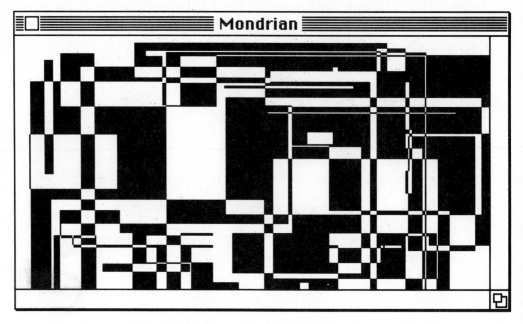

Figure 5-18 Output of procedure Mondrian

count up to a constant delayInterval after drawing each rectangle; we can, of course, vary the length of the delay by changing the value of this constant. (A better way to control a program delay is with the Toolbox routines Delay or TickCount, which we'll be learning about in Volume Two.)

Then we go back to generate and draw another rectangle, and continue to repeat the cycle until the user presses the mouse button. (The Toolbox function Button, also covered in Volume Two, returns a Boolean value of TRUE if the mouse button is down at the time of call, FALSE if it isn't.) When the button is finally pressed, the last order of business before leaving procedure Mondrian is to restore the origin of the port rectangle to its previous coordinates, leaving the port's coordinate system set the way we found it.

Ovals

The oval-drawing routines [5.3.4] all accept a rectangle as a parameter. Instead of drawing the rectangle, however, they draw an oval inscribed *within* the rectangle (see Figure 5-19). The rectangle determines the oval's width and height (in proper mathe-

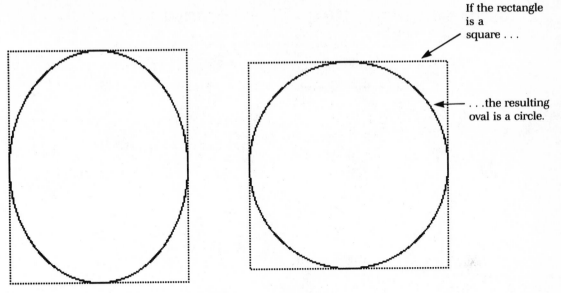

If the rectangle is a square . . .

. . .the resulting oval is a circle.

Figure 5-19 Specifying an oval

matical terms, its major and minor axes); if the rectangle is a perfect square, the resulting oval will be a perfect circle.

Program 5-3 (BigBrother) uses ovals to draw the unblinking eye of Figure 5-20. Just as we did with our stop sign in Program 5-1, we transform the top-left corner of the figure to coordinates (0, 0) and draw the figure in terms of a scale unit whose size is specified as a parameter. We draw the eye by first filling the outermost oval with black, then the next one with white, and finally the innermost with black again. The second oval, representing the inner edge of the eyelids, is derived from the outer one by insetting by one scale unit at the top and bottom; we also inset by 1 pixel at the left and right to leave a thin black outline visible. The innermost oval (actually a circle), representing the pupil of the eye, is inset again from there: two scale units at the left and right, 1 pixel to leave a little white space at the top and bottom. As usual, we carefully restore the port's coordinate system with SetOrigin before exiting.

Rounded Rectangles

In addition to ordinary rectangles, you can draw *rounded rectangles* [5.3.3] with curved corners instead of square ones. To specify a rounded rectangle, you supply the rectangle itself, along

```
procedure BigBrother (figureTop  : INTEGER          {Top edge of figure in local coordinates}
                      figureLeft : INTEGER;          {Left edge of figure in local coordinates}
                      scale      : INTEGER);         {Size of scale unit in pixels}


   { Example of simple shape drawing using ovals.  }


var
   currentPort : GrafPtr;                            {Pointer to current port [4.2.2]}
   oldOrigin   : Point;                              {Origin of port rectangle on entry [4.1.1]}
   ovalRect    : Rect;                               {Rectangle for defining ovals [4.1.2]}


begin  {BigBrother}

   GetPort (currentPort);                            {Get pointer to current port [4.3.3]}
   oldOrigin := currentPort^.portRect.topLeft;       {Save old origin of port rectangle [4.2.2, 4.1.2]}
   with oldOrigin do
      SetOrigin (h - figureLeft, v - figureTop);     {Offset to origin of figure [4.3.4]}

   SetRect (ovalRect, 0, 0, 8 * scale, 6 * scale);   {Set rectangle defining the outer oval [4.1.2]}
   FillOval (ovalRect, Black);                        {Fill outer oval with solid black [5.3.4, 5.1.2]}

   InsetRect (ovalRect, 1, scale);                   {Inset 1 pixel horizontally, 1 scale unit vertically}
   FillOval (ovalRect, White);                        {Fill inner oval with solid white [5.3.4, 5.1.2]}

   InsetRect (ovalRect, 2 * scale, 1);               {Inset 2 scale units horizontally, 1 pixel vertically}
   FillOval (ovalRect, Black);                        {Fill pupil with solid black [5.3.4, 5.1.2]}

   with oldOrigin do
      SetOrigin (h, v)                               {Restore old origin [4.3.4]}

end;   {BigBrother}
```

Program 5-3 Drawing with ovals

with the width and height of the ovals forming the corners (sometimes called the "diameters of curvature"). Each corner will be a quarter of an oval with the given dimensions (see Figure 5-21). QuickDraw won't allow the corner width or height to exceed those of the rectangle itself, even if you try to make them bigger.

Figure 5-20 Output of procedure BigBrother

Arcs and Wedges

There's also a set of routines for drawing arcs or wedges of an oval [5.3.5]. You supply a rectangle defining the oval, along with a pair of angles that tell where the arc begins and how far it extends. The angles can be any whole number of degrees, measured clockwise from the oval's center, with 0 degrees at the top, 90 at the right, 180 at the bottom, and 270 at the left. Negative angles are measured counterclockwise, with −90 degrees at the left and −270 at the right. The arc in Figure 5-22, for instance, could be specified with either a starting angle of 135 degrees and an arc angle of 90, or a starting angle of 225 (or −135) and an arc angle of −90.

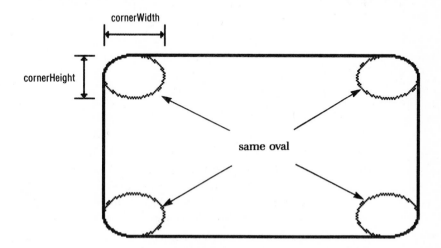

Figure 5-21 Specifying a rounded rectangle

FrameArc (r, 135, 90)

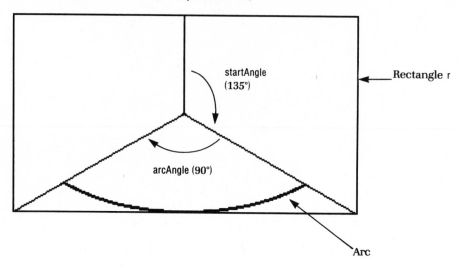

startAngle
(135°)

Rectangle r

arcAngle (90°)

Arc

Figure 5-22 Framing an arc

An important point to notice is that the angles defining an arc aren't necessarily expressed in true circular degrees; they're measured relative to the oval's defining rectangle. The rectangle's top-right corner, for instance, always corresponds to an angle of 45 degrees, whether the rectangle (and hence the oval) is tall and skinny or short and fat. Only if the rectangle is a perfect square (and the oval a circle) will the angles be true.

FrameArc just draws the specified arc of the oval, as in Figure 5-22. All the remaining drawing operations, though they're called PaintArc and so on, actually draw a *wedge* (Figure 5-23) bounded by the arc itself and a pair of lines running from its endpoints to the center of the oval. (Sort of a slice of pi.)

A related utility routine is PtToAngle [5.3.5], which measures the angle of a given point from the center of a rectangle in the same kind of rectangle-relative degrees described above. In Figure 5-24, for example, the value of PtToAngle(thePoint) would be 135.

PaintArc (r, 135, 90)

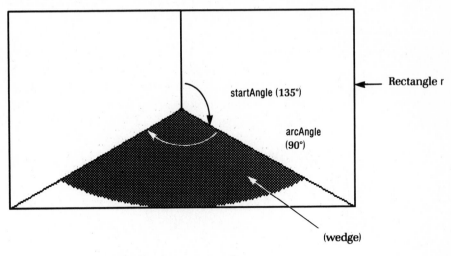

Figure 5-23 Painting a wedge

PtToAngle (r, p, angle)

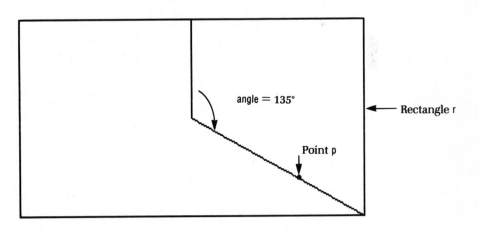

Figure 5-24 Point to angle

Polygons

As we mentioned in Chapter 4, you define the shape of a polygon by drawing its outline with the line-drawing operations Line and LineTo [5.2.4]. First you have to open the polygon definition by calling OpenPoly [4.1.4]. This allocates a new Polygon data structure [4.1.3] from the heap and returns a handle you can use to refer to it. While the polygon is open, all your line-drawing operations will be accumulated into the polygon definition. (OpenPoly automatically hides the graphics pen, so that the lines defining the polygon won't be drawn into the current port.)

When you're finished defining the polygon, you close it with ClosePoly [4.1.4], which reshows the pen, calculates the polygon's bounding box, and stores it into the polyBBox field of the Polygon record [4.1.3]. For example, you can define the polygon shown in Figure 5-25 with the following statements:

```
thePolygon := OpenPoly;

    MoveTo ( 150,   50);
    Line     (−100,   0);
    Line     (   0, 100);
    Line     ( 100,   0);
    Line     ( −50, −50);
    Line     (  50, −50);

ClosePoly
```

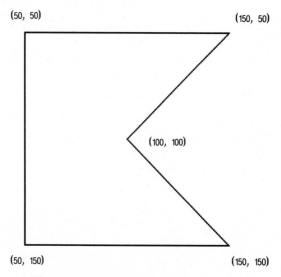

Figure 5-25 Defining a polygon

Once a polygon is defined, you can draw it into the current port with FramePoly, PaintPoly, and so on [5.3.6]. When you're completely through with the polygon, use KillPoly [4.1.4] to destroy it.

In framing a polygon, QuickDraw makes no adjustment for the current pen size; it simply traces the outline of the polygon, from vertex to vertex, with the top-left corner of the graphics pen. This means that the outline that gets drawn will extend beyond the polygon's edges at the right and bottom by the pen's width and height. As mentioned earlier, this is the one exception to the rule that shape-drawing operations never go outside the boundaries of the shape being drawn.

Program 5-4 (StopPoly) shows a version of our earlier stop sign procedure that illustrates how to define and use a polygon. Instead of just drawing the octagonal outline of the stop sign directly, we define it as a polygon by enclosing our line-drawing operations between calls to OpenPoly and ClosePoly. This prevents the lines from being drawn immediately, and accumulates them into the polygon definition instead.

Since we're now treating the octagon as a shape instead of a simple line drawing, we can use a fill pattern to produce the fancier version of the stop sign shown in Figure 5-26. First we use FillPoly to fill the entire octagon with gray; then we draw in its border with FramePoly. Next, to create the white background area around the letters, we define a rectangle representing the area, fill it with solid white, and frame it. Finally we use line-drawing operations to draw the letters, just as before.

Regions

Defining a region is similar to defining a polygon, but differs in a few details. Unlike OpenPoly, the analogous routine OpenRgn [4.1.6] doesn't create the Region data structure for you; you have to do that for yourself first with NewRgn [4.1.6]. OpenRgn simply begins a new, anonymous region definition in the current port and starts collecting your drawing operations into it. In addition to line-drawing operations, a region definition can also include shape-framing operations such as FrameRect, FrameOval, and so on; these operations add the boundary of the framed shape to the boundary

```
procedure StopPoly (figureTop  : INTEGER          {Top edge of figure in local coordinates}
                    figureLeft : INTEGER;         {Left edge of figure in local coordinates}
                    scale      : INTEGER);        {Size of scale unit in pixels}


{ Example showing definition and use of a polygon.  }


var
   currentPort : GrafPtr;                         {Pointer to current port [4.2.2]}
   oldOrigin   : Point;                           {Origin of port rectangle on entry [4.1.1]}
   theOctagon  : PolyHandle;                      {Handle to polygon defining outline of sign [4.1.3]}
   theRect     : Rect;                            {Rectangle surrounding letters [4.1.2]}


begin {StopPoly}

   GetPort (currentPort);                         {Get pointer to current port [4.3.3]}
   oldOrigin := currentPort^.portRect.topLeft;   {Save old origin of port rectangle [4.2.2, 4.1.2]}
   with oldOrigin do
      SetOrigin (h - figureLeft, v - figureTop); {Offset to origin of figure [4.3.4]}

   theOctagon := OpenPoly;                        {Open polygon definition [4.1.4]}
      MoveTo ( 5 $ scale, 0          );          {Draw the octagon [5.2.4]}
      Line   ( 8 $ scale, 0          );
      Line   ( 5 $ scale, 5 $ scale);
      Line   ( 0        , 8 $ scale);
      Line   (-5 $ scale, 5 $ scale);
      Line   (-8 $ scale, 0          );
      Line   (-5 $ scale, -5 $ scale);
      Line   ( 0        , -8 $ scale);
      Line   ( 5 $ scale, -5 $ scale);
   ClosePoly;                                     {Close polygon definition [4.1.4]}

   FillPoly  (theOctagon, Gray);                  {Fill polygon with gray [5.3.6]}
   FramePoly (theOctagon);                        {Outline the polygon [5.3.6]}
   KillPoly  (theOctagon);                        {Dispose of polygon record [4.1.4]}

   SetRect (theRect, 0, 5 $ scale, 18 $ scale, 13 $ scale);
                                                  {Define rectangle surrounding letters [4.1.2]}
   FillRect  (theRect, White);                    {Clear rectangle to white [5.3.2]}
   FrameRect (theRect);                           {Outline the rectangle [5.3.2]}
```

Program 5-4 Defining and drawing a polygon

```
MoveTo ( 4 * scale,  7 * scale);              {Draw the "S" [5.2.4]}
Line   (-2 * scale,  0        );
Line   ( 0       ,  2 * scale);
Line   ( 2 * scale,  0        );
Line   ( 0       ,  2 * scale);
Line   (-2 * scale,  0        );

MoveTo ( 7 * scale,  7 * scale);              {Draw the "T" [5.2.4]}
Line   ( 0       ,  4 * scale);
Move   (-1 * scale, -4 * scale);
Line   ( 2 * scale,  0        );

MoveTo (10 * scale,  7 * scale);              {Draw the "O" [5.2.4]}
Line   ( 2 * scale,  0        );
Line   ( 0       ,  4 * scale);
Line   (-2 * scale,  0        );
Line   ( 0       , -4 * scale);

MoveTo (14 * scale,  7 * scale);              {Draw the "P" [5.2.4]}
Line   ( 0       ,  4 * scale);
Move   ( 0       , -4 * scale);
Line   ( 2 * scale,  0        );
Line   ( 0       ,  2 * scale);
Line   (-2 * scale,  0        );

with oldOrigin do
   SetOrigin (h, v)                           {Restore old origin [4.3.4]}

end; {StopPoly}
```

Program 5-4 *(continued)*

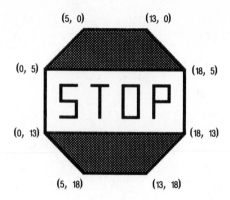

All coordinates are
expressed in scale units.

Figure 5-26 Output of procedure StopPoly

of the region. When you close the region definition with CloseRgn
[4.1.6], you supply the region handle you received from NewRgn and
QuickDraw sets it to the shape you've specified. The region shown
in Figure 5-27 might be defined with the statements

```
theRegion := NewRgn;

OpenRgn;

   SetRect      (theRect, 25, 50, 125, 150);
   FrameOval    (theRect);
   SetRect      (theRect, 75, 50, 175, 150);
   FrameOval    (theRect);

CloseRgn (theRegion)
```

and then drawn with FrameRgn, PaintRgn, and so on [5.3.7].

> A given port can have only one polygon or region definition open
> at a time. Always be sure to close one definition (with ClosePoly or
> CloseRgn) before opening another.

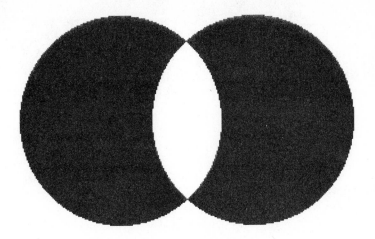

Shaded area is the region.

Figure 5-27 Defining a region

There are special routines, RectRgn and SetRectRgn [4.1.7], for the common case of creating rectangular regions; one accepts a rectangle as an argument, the other accepts four separate integer coordinates. You can also copy one region to another with CopyRgn [4.1.7] or set a region to empty (erasing its existing structure, if any) with SetEmptyRgn [4.1.7]. All these routines merely set the shape of an existing region; you always have to create the region for yourself first with NewRgn. To destroy a region when you're finished with it, use DisposeRgn [4.1.6].

Program 5-5 uses a region to define and draw Big Brother's watchful eye, shown earlier in Figure 5-20. The logic is essentially the same as in Program 5-3, except that the drawing operations that define the eye are enclosed within a region definition delimited by calls to OpenRgn and CloseRgn. Notice that we must draw the ovals with FrameOval instead of FillOval as in the earlier program, since framing is the only operation that accumulates a shape into the open region definition. After the definition is complete, a single drawing operation (in this case FillRgn) draws the entire region at once, even if it has holes and separate pieces like this one.

One use for region definitions is for setting a port's *clipping region*, one of the clipping boundaries we discussed in Chapter 4.

```
procedure BigBrother (figureTop  : INTEGER        {Top edge of figure in local coordinates}
                      figureLeft : INTEGER;       {Left edge of figure in local coordinates}
                      scale      : INTEGER);      {Size of scale unit in pixels}


   { Example showing definition and use of a region.  }



var
   currentPort : GrafPtr;                          {Pointer to current port [4.2.2]}
   oldOrigin   : Point;                            {Origin of port rectangle on entry [4.1.1]}
   ovalRect    : Rect;                             {Rectangle for defining ovals [4.1.2]}
   theEye      : RgnHandle;                         {Handle to region defining the figure [4.1.5]}


begin {BigBrother}

   GetPort (currentPort);                           {Get pointer to current port [4.3.3]}
   oldOrigin := currentPort^.portRect.topLeft;      {Save old origin of port rectangle [4.2.2, 4.1.2]}
   with oldOrigin do
      SetOrigin (h - figureLeft, v - figureTop);    {Offset to origin of figure [4.3.4]}

   theEye := NewRgn;                                {Create a new region [4.1.6]}
   OpenRgn;                                         {Open region definition [4.1.6]}

      SetRect (ovalRect, 0, 0, 8 * scale, 6 * scale); {Set rectangle defining the outer oval [4.1.2]}
      FrameOval (ovalRect);                          {Draw outer oval [5.3.4]}

      InsetRect (ovalRect, 1, scale);                {Inset 1 pixel horizontally, 1 scale unit vertically}
      FrameOval (ovalRect);                          {Draw inner oval [5.3.4]}

      InsetRect (ovalRect, 2 * scale, 1);            {Inset 2 scale units horizontally, 1 pixel vertically}
      FrameOval (ovalRect);                          {Draw pupil [5.3.4]}

   CloseRgn (theEye);                               {Close region definition [4.1.6]}

   FillRgn    (theEye, Black);                      {Fill region with solid black [5.3.7]}
   DisposeRgn (theEye);                             {Dispose of region record [4.1.6]}


   with oldOrigin do
      SetOrigin (h, v)                              {Restore old origin [4.3.4]}

end; {BigBrother}
```

Program 5-5 Defining and drawing a region

Recall that the clipping region is a general-purpose clipping boundary that's available for you to use in any way you need. As an example, Program 5-6 uses the clipping region to draw the globe shown in Figure 5-28. Since the routine will change the current port's coordinate origin, pen width, and clipping region, we begin by saving the old values so we can restore them again later. Then we define a region globeRgn consisting of the globe's circular outline and install it as the port's clipping region with SetClip [4.3.6].

```
procedure Globe (figureTop  : INTEGER        {Top edge of figure in local coordinates}
                 figureLeft : INTEGER;        {Left edge of figure in local coordinates}
                 diameter   : INTEGER;        {Diameter of figure in pixels}
                 edgeWidth  : INTEGER;        {Pen width for drawing figure outline}
                 gridWidth  : INTEGER;        {Pen width for drawing grid lines}
                 nSteps     : INTEGER);       {Number of divisions in grid}


{ Example showing use of a port's clipping region. }


var
    currentPort : GrafPtr;                    {Pointer to current port [4.2.2]}
    oldOrigin   : Point;                      {Origin of port rectangle on entry [4.1.1]}
    oldState    : PenState;                   {State of graphics pen on entry [5.2.1]}
    oldClip     : RgnHandle;                  {Handle to old clipping region [4.1.5]}
    globeRgn    : RgnHandle;                  {Handle to region defining figure outline [4.1.5]}
    ovalRect    : Rect;                       {Rectangle for defining ovals [4.1.2]}
    radius      : INTEGER;                    {Radius of figure in pixels}
    stepNumber  : INTEGER;                    {Counter for drawing grid}
    stepSize    : INTEGER;                    {Size of grid unit in pixels}
    offset      : INTEGER;                    {Offset from center for drawing grid lines}


begin {Globe}

    GetPort (currentPort);                    {Get pointer to current port [4.3.3]}
    oldOrigin := currentPort^.portRect.topLeft;   {Save old origin of port rectangle [4.2.2, 4.1.2]}
    with oldOrigin do
        SetOrigin (h - figureLeft, v - figureTop);   {Offset to origin of figure [4.3.4]}

    GetPenState (oldState);                   {Save old pen state [5.2.1]}
    SetClip     (oldClip);                    {Save old clipping region [4.2.2]}
```

Program 5-6 Using the clipping region

```
globeRgn := NewRgn;                              {Create a new region [4.1.6]}
OpenRgn;                                         {Open region definition [4.1.6]}
   SetRect (ovalRect, 0, 0, diameter, diameter); {Set rectangle defining the outer oval [4.1.2]}
   FrameOval (ovalRect);                         {Draw outline of figure [5.3.4]}
CloseRgn (globeRgn);                             {Close region definition [4.1.6]}
SetClip  (globeRgn);                             {Set port's clipping region [4.3.6]}

PenSize  (edgeWidth, edgeWidth);                 {Set pen size for figure outline [5.2.2]}
FrameRgn (globeRgn);                             {Draw outline of figure [5.3.7]}

radius   := diameter div 2;                      {Find radius}
stepSize := diameter div nSteps;                 {Find size of grid unit}
PenSize (gridWidth, gridWidth);                  {Set pen size for grid [5.2.2]}

for stepNumber := 0 to (nSteps div 2) do         {Draw parallels of latitude}
   begin
      offset := stepNumber * stepSize;           {Find offset from center}

      MoveTo ( 0   , radius - offset);           {Draw parallel north of equator [5.2.4]}
      Line   (diameter,      0   );

      MoveTo ( 0   , radius + offset);           {Draw parallel south of equator [5.2.4]}
      Line   (diameter,      0   )
   end;

for stepNumber := (nSteps div 2) downto 0 do     {Draw meridians of longitude}
   begin
      offset := stepNumber * stepSize;           {Find offset from center}
      SetRect (ovalRect,                         {Set rectangle defining oval [4.1.2]: }
                  radius - offset,               {   from west of prime meridian     }
                  0,                             {       at north pole                }
                  radius + offset,               {   to east of prime meridian        }
                  diameter);                     {       at south pole                }
      FrameOval (ovalRect)                        {Draw the meridians [5.3.4]}
   end;
MoveTo (radius,   0   );                          {Draw prime meridian from north}
Line   ( 0   , diameter);                         {   to south pole [5.2.4]       }

SetClip     (oldClip);                            {Restore old clipping region [4.3.6]}
SetPenState (oldState);                           {Restore old pen state [5.2.1]}
with oldOrigin do
   SetOrigin (h, v);                              {Restore old origin [4.3.4]}

DisposeRgn  (globeRgn)                            {Dispose of region record [4.1.6]}

end;  {Globe}
```

Program 5-6 *(continued)*

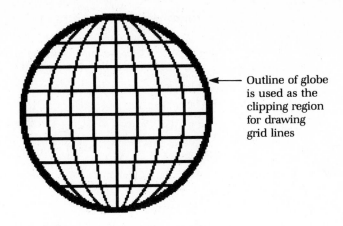

Outline of globe
is used as the
clipping region
for drawing
grid lines

Figure 5-28 Output of procedure Globe

After drawing the outline on the screen with FrameRgn [5.3.7], we proceed to draw in the parallels of latitude. This is where the circular clipping region comes in handy. Instead of calculating the endpoints where each parallel meets the circumference of the globe, we simply draw a series of horizontal lines straight across the full width of the figure, letting QuickDraw clip them to the right lengths for us. For the meridians of longitude, we use a series of ovals of decreasing widths running from north pole to south. A final straight line drawn vertically between the poles marks the prime meridian; then all that remains is to restore the port's original clipping region, pen size, and coordinate origin and dispose of the region globeRgn.

Pictures

Pictures are a very powerful, general mechanism for defining and using graphical images of arbitrary complexity. A picture is like a tape recording of a sequence of QuickDraw calls. Once you've defined it, you can "play back" the recording at any time, duplicating the original sequence of calls and redrawing the picture.

Like a polygon or a region, a picture is represented by a variable-length data structure (in this case, a record of type Picture [5.4.1]). It consists of a picSize field giving the overall length of the structure in bytes, a picFrame rectangle analogous to the polygon's or region's bounding box, and an indefinite amount of additional data defining the picture's contents. A picture differs conceptually from a polygon or region, however, in that it represents a dynamic sequence of QuickDraw operations, not just a static shape on the coordinate grid.

Defining a picture is similar to defining a polygon. You open the definition by calling OpenPicture [5.4.2], supplying a rectangle for the picture frame and getting back a handle to the new picture record. You can then proceed to draw the picture, using any QuickDraw operations you need. All of your calls will be recorded for posterity in the picture definition. When you're finished drawing the picture, call ClosePicture [5.4.2] to close the definition. To "play back" the calls later, use DrawPicture [5.4.3], specifying a rectangle in the current port where you want the picture drawn; it will be stretched or shrunk, if necessary, to make its frame coincide with the given rectangle.

One of the handiest things about pictures is that they allow graphical images to be passed around from one program to another by way of resource files (Chapter 6) or the desk scrap (Chapter 7). The program drawing the picture doesn't have to know anything about its contents, where it came from, or what it represents; all that's necessary is to pass it to DrawPicture and the picture will "draw itself." This is what enables you to copy Mac-Paint pictures to the Scrapbook or paste them into a MacWrite document.

Nuts and Bolts

The Macintosh Plus version of the Toolbox includes a pair of new QuickDraw routines. CalcMask and SeedFill [5.1.6], for performing specialized MacPaint-style drawing operations. Both routines operate on an existing bit image and use it to calculate a mask for the new bit-transfer routine CopyMask [5.1.4]. The image to be operated on is defined by a rectangular portion of an existing bit map; the mask is generated in a rectangle of the same size in another bit map.

CalcMask works like the MacPaint "lasso," finding the largest closed boundary that lies entirely within the given rectangle. It produces a mask with black pixels (1 bits) corresponding to the boundary and its interior; you can use this mask to copy the "lassoed" image with CopyMask (see Figure 5-29). SeedFill finds the smallest closed boundary surrounding a specified "seed" point in

Source bit map

Mask bit map

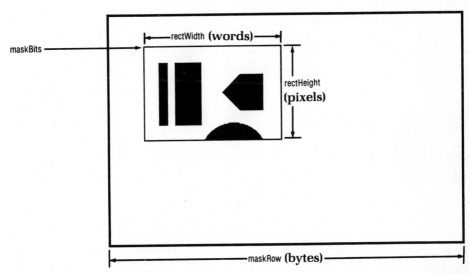

Figure 5-29 Operation of CalcMask

Source bit map

Mask bit map

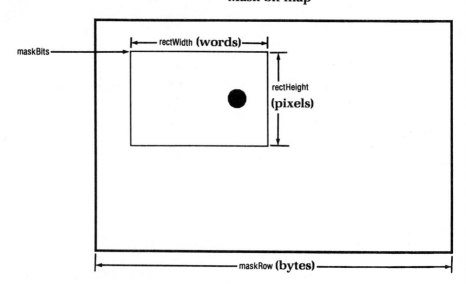

Figure 5-30 Operation of SeedFill

the bit image, representing the area to be filled by clicking at that point with MacPaint's "paint bucket" tool (Figure 5-30). To implement the paint bucket, you can then use CopyMask to fill this area with a pattern. (Since CopyMask doesn't take a pattern parameter, you'll first have to set up a dummy bit map to copy from, filled with the desired pattern.)

The calling conventions for CalcMask and SeedFill have been cleverly devised for your mystification and entertainment. Here are some things to watch out for:

- The pointers you pass for the sourceBits and maskBits parameters point directly to the first byte of data within the rectangle to be operated on—*not* to the beginning of the bit map in which the rectangle is embedded.

- The coordinates of the starting point for SeedFill are given as offsets relative to the origin of the source rectangle itself, *not* in the local coordinate system of its enclosing bit map.

- The dimensions of the source and mask bit maps and the relevant rectangles within them are specified in three different units: the bit map's row width in bytes, the width of the rectangle in words, and the height of the rectangle in bits (pixels).

- All of these conventions differ from those for the related routine CopyMask, which takes each of its three operands (source, mask, and destination) as a normal bit map together with a rectangle expressed in pixels, in local coordinates.

The programmer who thought all this up has been nominated for an Apple Hero medal for imaginative software design.

REFERENCE

5.1 Drawing Fundamentals

5.1.1 Patterns

```
type
    PatHandle  = ^PatPtr;
    PatPtr     = ^Pattern;

    Pattern    = packed array [0..7] of 0..255;        {8 rows of 8 bits each}

    GrafPort   = record

                   . . . . ;
                   bkPat  : Pattern;                    {Background pattern}
                   fillPat : Pattern;                   {Fill pattern for shape drawing}
                   . . . . ;
                   pnPat  : Pattern;                    {Pen pattern for line drawing [5.2.1]}
                   . . .
                 end;

procedure BackPat
            (newPattern : Pattern);                     {New background pattern}

function  GetPattern
            (patternID : INTEGER)                       {Resource ID of desired pattern}
              : PatHandle;                              {Handle to pattern in memory}

procedure GetIndPattern
            (var thePattern : Pattern;                  {Returns desired pattern}
             patListID      : INTEGER;                  {Resource ID of pattern list}
             patIndex       : INTEGER);                 {Index of pattern within list}
```

232

Notes

1. A pattern is an 8-by-8-bit "tile" that can be repeated indefinitely to draw lines or fill areas in a graphical image.

2. When drawn in a graphics port, a pattern is aligned with the coordinates of the port rectangle, so that adjacent patterned areas will blend continuously without creating "seams."

3. Use StuffHex [2.2.4] to fill in the bits defining a pattern, or read it from a resource file with GetPattern or GetIndPattern (notes 9-13, below).

4. Three patterns are associated with each graphics port [4.2.2]:

   - A *pen pattern* (pnPat) for drawing lines and shapes
   - A *fill pattern* (fillPat) for filling areas
   - A *background pattern* (bkPat) for erasing areas

5. The pen and fill patterns are initially solid black, the background pattern solid white.

6. BackPat sets the current port's background pattern.

7. To set a port's pen pattern, use PenPat [5.2.2].

8. The fill pattern is used privately by QuickDraw for shape-filling operations [5.3.1]. Don't store into a port's fillPat field yourself.

9. GetPattern gets a pattern from a resource file (Chapter 6), reads it into memory if necessary, and returns a handle to it.

10. patternID is the resource ID of the desired pattern; its resource type is 'PAT ' [5.5.1].

11. GetIndPattern gets a pattern from a pattern list in a resource file (Chapter 6).

12. patListID is the resource ID of the pattern list (resource type 'PAT#' [5.5.2]); patIndex is the index of the desired pattern within the list.

13. The pattern itself (not a handle) is returned via the variable parameter thePattern.

14. GetIndPattern is part of the Pascal Toolbox interface, not part of the Toolbox itself. It doesn't reside in ROM and can't be called from assembly language via the trap mechanism.

15. A set of standard patterns are available in the system resource file and as QuickDraw global variables: see [5.1.2].

Assembly Language Information

Field offsets in a graphics port:

(Pascal) Field name	(Assembly) Offset name	Offset in bytes
bkPat	bkPat	32
fillPat	fillPat	40
pnPat	pnPat	58

Trap macros:

(Pascal) Routine name	(Assembly) Trap macro	Trap word
BackPat	_BackPat	$A87C
GetPattern	_GetPattern	$A9B8

5.1.2   Standard Patterns

Standard pattern list

Definitions

```
var
    White   : Pattern;      {Solid white}
    LtGray  : Pattern;      {Light gray}
    Gray    : Pattern;      {Medium gray}
    DkGray  : Pattern;      {Dark gray}
    Black   : Pattern;      {Solid black}
const
    SysPatList =  0;        {Resource ID of standard pattern list}
    DeskPatID  = 16;        {Resource ID of screen background pattern}
```

Notes

1. The Toolbox provides five standard patterns for fill tones ranging from solid white to solid black.

2. The standard fill tones are available in the QuickDraw global variables White, LtGray, Gray, DkGray, and Black.

3. SysPatListID is the resource ID of the standard pattern list (see figure) in the system resource file; its recourse type is 'PAT#' [5.5.2]. Use GetIndPattern [5.1.1] to access individual patterns in this list.

4. DeskPatID is the resource ID of the screen background pattern (resource type 'PAT ' [5.5.1]). The pattern itself is held in the assembly-language global variable DeskPattern.

5. To access the variables containing the standard fill tones in assembly language, find the pointer to QuickDraw's globals at the address contained in register A5, then locate the desired variable relative to that pointer using the offset constants given below. See Chapter 3 and [4.3.1, note 4] for further discussion.

Assembly Language Information

Assembly-language constant:

Name	Value	Meaning
DeskPatID	16	Resource ID of screen background pattern

Assembly-language global variable:

Name	Address	Meaning
DeskPattern	$A3C	Screen background pattern

QuickDraw global variables:

Name	Offset in bytes	Meaning
White	−8	Solid white pattern
Black	−16	Solid black pattern
Gray	−24	Medium gray pattern
LtGray	−32	Light gray pattern
DkGray	−40	Dark gray pattern

5.1.3 **Transfer Modes**

Overlay
pattern

Existing
pattern

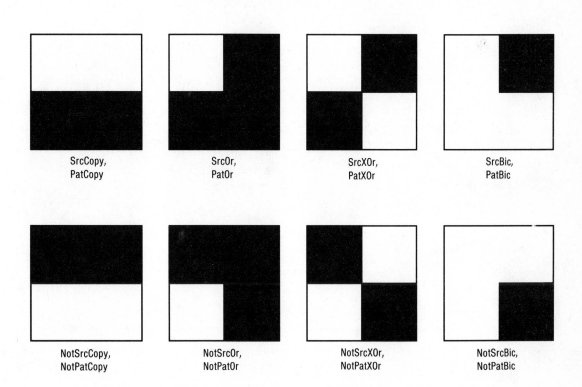

SrcCopy,
PatCopy

SrcOr,
PatOr

SrcXOr,
PatXOr

SrcBic,
PatBic

NotSrcCopy,
NotPatCopy

NotSrcOr,
NotPatOr

NotSrcXOr,
NotPatXOr

NotSrcBic,
NotPatBic

Definitions

```
GrafPort = record
          . . . ;
          pnMode : INTEGER;    {Transfer mode for graphics pen [5.2.1]}
          . . . ;
          txMode : INTEGER;    {Transfer mode for text [8.3.1]}
          . . .
       end;
const
   SrcCopy     =  0;    {Copy source to destination}
   SrcOr       =  1;    {Set selected bits to black}
   SrcXOr      =  2;    {Invert selected bits}
   SrcBic      =  3;    {Clear selected bits to white}
   NotSrcCopy  =  4;    {Copy inverted source to destination}
   NotSrcOr    =  5;    {Leave selected bits alone, set others to black}
   NotSrcXOr   =  6;    {Leave selected bits alone, invert others}
   NotSrcBic   =  7;    {Leave selected bits alone, clear others to white}

   PatCopy     =  8;    {Copy pattern to destination}
   PatOr       =  9;    {Set selected bits to black}
   PatXOr      = 10;    {Invert selected bits}
   PatBic      = 11;    {Clear selected bits to white}
   NotPatCopy  = 12;    {Copy inverted pattern to destination}
   NotPatOr    = 13;    {Leave selected bits alone, set others to black}
   NotPatXOr   = 14;    {Leave selected bits alone, invert others}
   NotPatBic   = 15;    {Leave selected bits alone, clear others to white}
```

Notes

1. Transfer modes control the transfer of pixels between bit maps, or between a pattern and a bit map.

2. The source transfer modes (SrcCopy to NotSrcBic) are used for transfers from one bit map to another with CopyBits [5.1.4] and for drawing text characters into a bit map [8.3.3].

3. The pattern transfer modes (PatCopy to NotPatBic) are used for drawing lines and shapes and filling areas with a pattern [5.1.1].

4. Each transfer mode denotes a way of combining pixels from the source (bit map, character, or pattern) with the corresponding pixels from the destination bit map. The resulting pixels are then stored back into the destination.

5. SrcCopy and PatCopy copy pixels directly from the source to the destination, replacing whatever was there before. Black pixels in the source are set to black in the destination, white pixels to white:

Source pixel	Destination pixel	Result pixel
black	black	black
black	white	black
white	black	white
white	white	white

6. SrcOr and PatOr set selected pixels of the destination to black. Black pixels in the source select the destination pixels to be set; white source pixels leave the corresponding destination pixels unchanged:

Source pixel	Destination pixel	Result pixel
black	black	black
black	white	black
white	black	black
white	white	white

7. SrcXOr and PatXOr invert selected pixels of the destination, from white to black and vice versa. Black pixels in the source select the destination pixels to be inverted; white source pixels leave the corresponding destination pixels unchanged:

Source pixel	Destination pixel	Result pixel
black	black	white
black	white	black
white	black	black
white	white	white

8. SrcBic and PatBic ("bit clear") clear selected pixels of the destination to white. Black pixels in the source select the destination pixels to be cleared; white source pixels leave the corresponding destination pixels unchanged:

Source pixel	Destination pixel	Result pixel
black	black	white
black	white	white
white	black	black
white	white	white

9. The NotSrc and NotPat series of modes reverse the roles of black and white source pixels in the tables above.

10. Two transfer modes are associated with each graphics port [4.2.2]:

- A *pen mode* (pnMode) for drawing lines and shapes [5.2.1]
- A *text mode* (txMode) for drawing text characters [8.3.1]

11. The pen mode should be one of the pattern transfer modes, the text mode one of the source transfer modes.

12. To set a port's pen mode, use PenMode [5.2.2]; to set the text mode, use TextMode [8.3.2].

Assembly Language Information

Field offsets in a graphics port:

(Pascal) Field name	(Assembly) Offset name	Offset in bytes
pnMode	pnMode	56
txMode	txMode	72

Assembly-language constants:

Name	Value	Meaning
SrcCopy	0	Copy source to destination
SrcOr	1	Set selected bits to black
SrcXOr	2	Invert selected bits
SrcBic	3	Clear selected bits to white
NotSrcCopy	4	Copy inverted source to destination
NotSrcOr	5	Leave selected bits alone, set others to black
NotSrcXOr	6	Leave selected bits alone, invert others
NotSrcBic	7	Leave selected bits alone, clear others to white
PatCopy	8	Copy pattern to destination
PatOr	9	Set selected bits to black
PatXOr	10	Invert selected bits
PatBic	11	Clear selected bits to white
NotPatCopy	12	Copy inverted pattern to destination
NotPatOr	13	Leave selected bits alone, set others to black
NotPatXOr	14	Leave selected bits alone, invert others
NotPatBic	15	Leave selected bits alone, clear others to white

5.1.4   Low-Level Bit Transfer

Definitions

```
procedure  CopyBits
            (fromBitMap : BitMap;        {Bit map to copy from}
             toBitMap   : BitMap;        {Bit map to copy to}
             fromRect   : Rect;          {Rectangle to copy from}
             toRect     : Rect;          {Rectangle to copy to}
             mode       : INTEGER;       {Transfer mode}
             clipTo     : RgnHandle);    {Region to clip to}

procedure  CopyMask
            (sourceMap  : BitMap;        {Bit map to copy from}
             maskMap    : BitMap;        {Bit map containing mask}
             destMap    : BitMap;        {Bit map to copy to}
             sourceRect : Rect;          {Rectangle to copy from}
             maskRect   : Rect;          {Rectangle containing mask}
             destRect   : Rect);         {Rectangle to copy to}
```

Notes

1. CopyBits transfers pixels from one bit map to another, in any transfer mode and with any specified scaling and clipping.

2. fromBitMap is the source bit map for the transfer, toBitMap the destination.

3. mode specifies the transfer mode, and should be one of the eight source transfer modes [5.1.3].

4. fromRect tells which pixels of the source bit map to transfer; toRect tells where in the destination bit map to transfer them to.

5. Each of the two rectangles is expressed in the local coordinate system of the corresponding bit map.

6. If the dimensions of the two rectangles don't match, the contents of the source rectangle are scaled to the width and height of the destination rectangle.

7. The transfer operation is clipped to the destination bit map's boundary rectangle. If the destination is the bit map belonging to the current port, the transfer is clipped to the port rectangle and the port's visible and clipping regions as well.

8. clipTo is an additional clipping region to be used for this transfer only, expressed in the destination bit map's coordinate system. If clipTo = NIL, no additional clipping region will be used.

9. CopyMask is an alternate transfer routine that transfers pixels from one bit map to another under the control of a mask.

10. The source, mask, and destination are each specified by a bit map and a rectangle within it.

11. Each rectangle is expressed in the local coordinates of its own bit map.

12. No scaling is performed: all three rectangles must have the same dimensions.

13. The source and destination bit maps may be the same, but the rectangles must not overlap. There is no error checking for this condition; the transfer simply will not work correctly.

14. The transfer mode is always SrcCopy [5.1.3].

15. Like CopyBits, CopyMask clips to the boundary rectangle of the destination bit map and, if it's the bit map belonging to the current port, to the port's port rectangle, visible region, and clipping region.

16. Calls to CopyMask are not recorded in picture definitions [5.4.2].

17. CopyMask is useful for drawing icons, particularly those that are stored with their masks in resources of type 'ICN#' [5.5.4, 7.5.3]. It can also be used in conjunction with CalcMask and SeedFill [5.1.6] to implement the MacPaint "lasso" and "paint bucket" tools.

18. CopyMask is available only on the Macintosh Plus.

Assembly Language Information

Trap macros:

(Pascal) Routine name	(Assembly) Trap macro	Trap word
CopyBits	_CopyBits	$A8EC
CopyMask	_CopyMask	$A817

5.1.5   Scrolling in a Bit Map

Definitions

```
procedure ScrollRect
         (theRect   : Rect;          {Rectangle to be scrolled}
          hScroll   : INTEGER;       {Horizontal scroll distance in pixels}
          vScroll   : INTEGER;       {Vertical scroll distance in pixels}
          updateRgn : RgnHandle);    {Region scrolled into rectangle}
```

Notes

1. ScrollRect shifts pixels horizontally and vertically within the bit map of the current port.

2. theRect is a rectangle in the local coordinate system of the current port. The pixels affected will be those within the intersection of this rectangle with the port's boundary rectangle, port rectangle, visible region, and clipping region.

3. Pixels scrolled out of this region are lost irretrievably; the new space scrolled in at the other end is filled with the port's background pattern (bkPat [5.1.1]).

4. hScroll and vScroll give the horizontal and vertical scrolling distance, in pixels.

5. Positive values of hScroll scroll to the right, negative to the left; positive vScroll values scroll downward, negative values scroll upward.

6. Scrolling doesn't affect the port's coordinate system; it simply shifts the scrolled pixels to new coordinates within the port. To restore the pixels to their previous coordinates, follow ScrollRect with SetOrigin [4.3.4] to adjust the port's coordinate system.

7. The coordinates of the port's graphics pen [5.2.1] aren't affected by scrolling, so it remains at the same position in the port while the image scrolls away from it. Adjusting the coordinate system with SetOrigin will bring the pen back to its previous position relative to the image.

8. The region handle updateRgn is set to the area cleared to the background pattern as a result of scrolling. If the port is a window on the screen, this region can be added to the window's update region with InvalRgn [II:3.4.2], forcing the contents of the scrolled-in area to be drawn on the screen.

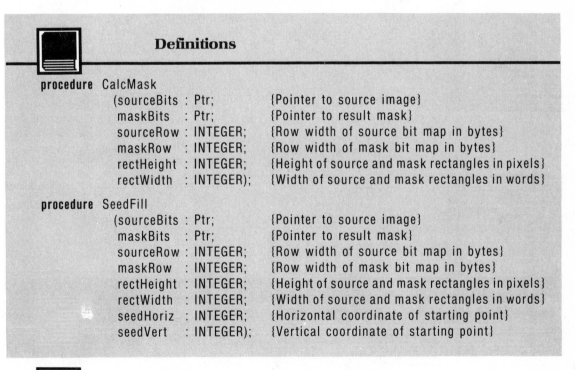

Assembly Language Information

Trap macros:

(Pascal) Routine name	(Assembly) Trap macro	Trap word
ScrollRect	_ScrollRect	$A8EF

5.1.6 Special Operations

Definitions

procedure CalcMask
    (sourceBits : Ptr;   {Pointer to source image}
    maskBits : Ptr;   {Pointer to result mask}
    sourceRow : INTEGER;   {Row width of source bit map in bytes}
    maskRow : INTEGER;   {Row width of mask bit map in bytes}
    rectHeight : INTEGER;   {Height of source and mask rectangles in pixels}
    rectWidth : INTEGER);   {Width of source and mask rectangles in words}

procedure SeedFill
    (sourceBits : Ptr;   {Pointer to source image}
    maskBits : Ptr;   {Pointer to result mask}
    sourceRow : INTEGER;   {Row width of source bit map in bytes}
    maskRow : INTEGER;   {Row width of mask bit map in bytes}
    rectHeight : INTEGER;   {Height of source and mask rectangles in pixels}
    rectWidth : INTEGER;   {Width of source and mask rectangles in words}
    seedHoriz : INTEGER;   {Horizontal coordinate of starting point}
    seedVert : INTEGER);   {Vertical coordinate of starting point}

Notes

1. These routines help implement specialized MacPaint-style drawing operations.

2. Both routines operate on an existing bit image and produce a mask to be passed to the bit-transfer routine CopyMask [5.1.4]. The source image and the resulting mask are each contained within a specified rectangle embedded in an enclosing bit map.

3. CalcMask finds the largest closed boundary lying entirely within the given rectangle (like the MacPaint "lasso") and produces a mask representing the area inside this boundary; SeedFill does the same for the smallest closed boundary surrounding a given starting point, like the MacPaint "paint bucket."

4. For both routines, sourceBits is a pointer directly to the first byte of data in the source rectangle—*not* to the beginning of the bit map in which the rectangle is embedded. Similarly, maskBits points directly to the beginning of the rectangle in which the mask is to be stored, not to the enclosing bit map.

5. sourceRow and maskRow are the row widths, in bytes, of the bit maps in which the source and mask are embedded.

6. The source and mask rectangles are both the same size. The rectWidth parameter gives their width in words, rectHeight their height in pixels.

7. seedHoriz and seedVert give the coordinates of the starting point for SeedFill. The coordinates are expressed relative to the origin of the source rectangle—*not* in the local coordinate system of its enclosing bit map.

8. The source and mask may be embedded in the same bit map, but the corresponding rectangles must not overlap. There is no error checking for this condition; the operation simply will not work correctly.

9. No clipping is performed to either bit map's boundary rectangle or to the current port's port rectangle, visible region, or clipping region.

10. Calls to these routines are not recorded in picture definitions [5.4.2].

11. These routines are available only on the Macintosh Plus.

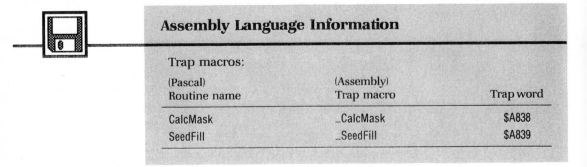

Assembly Language Information

Trap macros:

(Pascal) Routine name	(Assembly) Trap macro	Trap word
CalcMask	_CalcMask	$A838
SeedFill	_SeedFill	$A839

5.2 Line Drawing

5.2.1 Pen Characteristics

Definitions

```
type
  GrafPort = record
              . . . ;
              pnLoc  : Point;      {Current location of graphics pen in local coordinates}
              pnSize : Point;      {Dimensions of graphics pen}
              pnMode : INTEGER;    {Transfer mode for graphics pen [5.1.3]}
              pnPat  : Pattern;    {Pen pattern for line drawing [5.1.1]}
              pnVis  : INTEGER;    {Pen level [5.2.3]}

              . . .
            end;

  PenState = record
              pnLoc  : Point;      {Location of pen in bit map}
              pnSize : Point;      {Width and height of pen in pixels}
              pnMode : INTEGER;    {Transfer mode for line drawing and area fill}
              pnPat  : Pattern     {Pen pattern}
            end;

procedure GetPenState
            (var curState : PenState);  {Returns current pen characteristics}

procedure SetPenState
            (newState : PenState);      {New pen characteristics}
```

Notes

1. Each port has its own graphics pen, used for drawing lines and text characters.

2. The pen has a location, size, transfer mode, drawing pattern, and visibility level, kept in the pnLoc, pnSize, pnMode, pnPat, and pnVis fields of the graphics port [4.2.2].

3. pnLoc is the pen's location, a point on the coordinate grid expressed in the port's local coordinate system. The pen is a rectangle with its top-left corner at this point.

4. pnSize is a point whose horizontal and vertical coordinates define the width and height of the pen in pixels. If either coordinate is zero or negative, the pen shrinks to nothing and will not draw.

5. pnMode is the pen's transfer mode, which should be one of the eight pattern transfer modes [5.1.3].

6. pnPat is the pen pattern [5.1.1], used for drawing lines and outlining shapes.

7. pnVis is the pen's visibility level, which controls whether the pen is visible or hidden; see [5.2.3] for further information.

8. The pen is initially 1 pixel wide by 1 high, located at coordinates (0, 0), with transfer mode PatCopy and a solid black pen pattern, and is initially visible (visibility level = 0).

9. A pen state record summarizes the pen's characteristics. It's used solely for manipulating the state of the pen with GetPenState and SetPenState.

10. GetPenState returns a pen state record describing the current pen characteristics of the current port.

11. SetPenState sets the current port's text characteristics as specified by a pen state record.

12. These routines are useful for saving and restoring the pen's characteristics to make a routine "transparent" to the state of the pen.

Assembly Language Information

Field offsets in a graphics port:

(Pascal) Field name	(Assembly) Offset name	Offset in bytes
pnLoc	pnLoc	48
pnSize	pnSize	52
pnMode	pnMode	56
pnPat	pnPat	58
pnVis	pnVis	66

Field offsets in a pen state record:

(Pascal) Field name	(Assembly) Offset name	Offset in bytes
pnLoc	psLoc	0
pnSize	psSize	4
pnMode	psMode	8
pnPat	psPat	10

Assembly-language constant:

Name	Value	Meaning
PSRec	18	Size of pen state record in bytes

Trap macros:

(Pascal) Routine name	(Assembly) Trap macro	Trap word
GetPenState	_GetPenState	$A898
SetPenState	_SetPenState	$A899

5.2.2   Setting Pen Characteristics

Definitions

```
procedure  PenSize
              (newWidth  : INTEGER;      {New pen width}
               newHeight : INTEGER);     {New pen height}

procedure  PenPat
              (newPat : Pattern);        {New pen pattern}

procedure  PenMode
              (newMode : INTEGER);       {New pen transfer mode}

procedure  PenNormal;
```

Notes

1. These routines set the pen characteristics of the current port.
2. PenSize, PenPat, and PenMode control individual pen characteristics.
3. The current pen size, pattern, and mode can be read from the pnSize, pnPat, and pnMode fields of the graphics port record [4.2.2].
4. If either newWidth or newHeight is zero or negative, both the pen's width and height are set to 0; the pen will not draw in this state.
5. newMode should be one of the eight pattern transfer modes [5.1.3].
6. PenNormal resets the pen to its initial state: 1 pixel wide by 1 high, with a solid black pattern and transfer mode PatCopy [5.1.3].
7. None of these routines affects the pen's location.

Assembly Language Information

Trap macros:

(Pascal) Routine name	(Assembly) Trap macro	Trap word
PenSize	_PenSize	$A89B
PenPat	_PenPat	$A89D
PenMode	_PenMode	$A89C
PenNormal	_PenNormal	$A89E

5.2.3 Hiding and Showing the Pen

Definitions

```
type
    GrafPort = record
            . . . ;
                pnVis : INTEGER;    {Pen visibility level}
            . . .
            end;

procedure HidePen;

procedure ShowPen;
```

Notes

1. These routines control the visibility of the current port's graphics pen by manipulating the *pen level,* an integer kept in the port's pnVis field [4.2.2].

2. The pen is visible if the pen level is zero or positive, hidden if it's negative.

3. Drawing operations have no effect when the pen is hidden.

4. The pen level is initialized to 0 (visible) by OpenPort or InitPort [4.3.2].

5. HidePen makes the pen invisible and decrements the pen level by 1.

6. ShowPen undoes the effects of HidePen and restores the pen's visibility to its previous state. It increments the pen level by 1; if the result is 0, the pen becomes visible again.

7. Calls to HidePen and ShowPen may be nested to any depth. Every call to HidePen should be balanced by a corresponding call to ShowPen.

8. The QuickDraw routines OpenPoly [4.1.4], OpenRgn [4.1.6], and OpenPicture [5.4.2] call HidePen to prevent the drawing operations used to define a polygon, region, or picture from affecting the screen. When the definition is complete, ClosePoly [4.1.4], CloseRgn [4.1.6], and ClosePicture [5.4.2] restore the pen's previous visibility with ShowPen.

Assembly Language Information

Field offsets in a graphics port:

(Pascal) Field name	(Assembly) Offset name	Offset in bytes
pnVis	pnVis	66

Trap macros:

(Pascal) Routine name	(Assembly) Trap macro	Trap word
HidePen	_HidePen	$A896
ShowPen	_ShowPen	$A897

5.2.4 Drawing Lines

Definitions

```
procedure GetPen
          (var penLoc : Point);   {Returns current pen location}
procedure Move
          (horiz : INTEGER;       {Horizontal distance to move, in pixels}
           vert  : INTEGER);      {Vertical distance to move, in pixels}
procedure MoveTo
          (horiz : INTEGER;       {Horizontal coordinate to move to, in pixels}
           vert  : INTEGER);      {Vertical coordinate to move to, in pixels}
procedure Line
          (horiz : INTEGER;       {Horizontal distance to draw, in pixels}
           vert  : INTEGER);      {Vertical distance to draw, in pixels}
procedure LineTo
          (horiz : INTEGER;       {Horizontal coordinate to draw to, in pixels}
           vert  : INTEGER);      {Vertical coordinate to draw to, in pixels}
```

Notes

1. GetPen returns the current port's pen location, a point expressed in the port's local coordinate system.

2. The current pen location is kept in the pnVis field of the graphics port [4.2.2, 5.2.1].

3. Move and MoveTo move the current port's pen to a new location without drawing anything.

4. Line and LineTo move the pen and draw a straight line from the old pen location to the new one.

5. The thickness and appearance of the line are determined by the port's current pen size, pattern, and mode.

6. All drawing in a port is clipped to the intersection of its boundary rectangle, port rectangle, clipping region, and visible region. The pen can move freely outside these boundaries, but only those portions of lines that fall within the clipping boundaries will actually be drawn.

7. Drawing operations have no effect when the pen is hidden.

8. MoveTo and LineTo move the pen to a given absolute location, expressed in the local coordinate system of the current port.

9. Move and Line move the pen a given horizontal and vertical distance from its current location.

10. Positive values of horiz move the pen to the right, negative to the left; positive vert values move it downward, negative values move it upward.

Assembly Language Information

Trap macros:

(Pascal) Routine name	(Assembly) Trap macro	Trap word
GetPen	_GetPen	$A89A
Move	_Move	$A894
MoveTo	_MoveTo	$A893
Line	_Line	$A892
LineTo	_LineTo	$A891

5.3   Drawing Shapes

5.3.1   Basic Drawing Operations

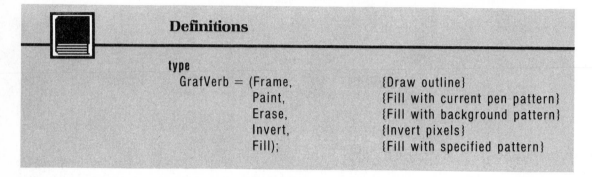

Definitions

```
type
  GrafVerb = (Frame,        {Draw outline}
              Paint,        {Fill with current pen pattern}
              Erase,        {Fill with background pattern}
              Invert,       {Invert pixels}
              Fill);        {Fill with specified pattern}
```

Notes

1. The enumerated type GrafVerb represents the five basic shape-drawing operations. Its only actual use in a program is for customizing QuickDraw operations: see Volume Three for details.

2. Any of the five operations can be applied to rectangles [5.3.2], rounded rectangles [5.3.3], ovals [5.3.4], arcs and wedges [5.3.5], polygons [5.3.6], or regions [5.3.7].

3. Drawing always takes place in the current graphics port, and all shapes are defined in that port's local coordinate system.

4. *Framing* a shape draws its outline, using the port's current pen size, pattern, and mode [5.2.1]. Pixels in the shape's interior are left unchanged.

5. If a region definition [4.1.6] is open, framing any shape adds the shape's outline to the boundary of the region. (*Exception:* Arcs [5.3.5] aren't added to the region definition when framed.)

6. *Painting* a shape fills it completely with the current port's pen pattern, using the current pen mode.

7. *Filling* a shape fills it completely with a specified pattern; the transfer mode is always PatCopy [5.1.3]. The current port's pen pattern and mode are unaffected.

8. *Erasing* a shape fills it completely with the current port's background pattern. The transfer mode is always PatCopy [5.1.3].

9. *Inverting* a shape reverses all pixels it encloses, from white to black and vice versa.

10. The location of the graphics pen is not changed by any shape-drawing operation; however, drawing operations have no effect if the pen is hidden.

11. All drawing operations are clipped to the intersection of the current port's boundary rectangle, port rectangle, clipping region, and visible region. Only those portions of shapes that fall within all of these boundaries will actually be drawn.

12. Drawing operations never affect pixels outside the boundaries of the shape being drawn. (*Exception:* Framing a polygon will draw outside the polygon's boundary; see [5.3.6].)

Assembly Language Information

Assembly-language constants:

Name	Value	Meaning
Frame	0	Draw outline
Paint	1	Fill with current pen pattern
Erase	2	Fill with background pattern
Invert	3	Invert pixels
Fill	4	Fill with specified pattern

5.3.2   Drawing Rectangles

Definitions

```
procedure FrameRect
          (theRect : Rect);        {Rectangle to be framed}

procedure PaintRect
          (theRect : Rect);        {Rectangle to be painted}

procedure FillRect
          (theRect : Rect;         {Rectangle to be filled}
           fillPat : Pattern);     {Pattern to fill it with}

procedure EraseRect
          (theRect : Rect);        {Rectangle to be erased}

procedure InvertRect
          (theRect : Rect);        {Rectangle to be inverted}
```

Notes

1. These routines perform the five basic drawing operations [5.3.1] on rectangles.

2. The trap macro for InvertRect is spelled _InverRect.

Assembly Language Information

Trap macros:

(Pascal) Routine name	(Assembly) Trap macro	Trap word
FrameRect	_FrameRect	$A8A1
PaintRect	_PaintRect	$A8A2
FillRect	_FillRect	$A8A5
EraseRect	_EraseRect	$A8A3
InvertRect	_InverRect	$A8A4

5.3.3   Drawing Rounded Rectangles

Rounded rectangle

Definitions

```
procedure  FrameRoundRect
              (theRect      : Rect;        {Body of rectangle}
               cornerWidth  : INTEGER;     {Width of corner oval}
               cornerHeight : INTEGER);    {Height of corner oval}

procedure  PaintRoundRect
              (theRect      : Rect;        {Body of rectangle}
               cornerWidth  : INTEGER;     {Width of corner oval}
               cornerHeight : INTEGER);    {Height of corner oval}

procedure  FillRoundRect
              (theRect      : Rect;        {Body of rectangle}
               cornerWidth  : INTEGER;     {Width of corner oval}
               cornerHeight : INTEGER;     {Height of corner oval}
               fillPat      : Pattern);    {Pattern to fill with}

procedure  EraseRoundRect
              (theRect      : Rect;        {Body of rectangle}
               cornerWidth  : INTEGER;     {Width of corner oval}
               cornerHeight : INTEGER);    {Height of corner oval}

procedure  InvertRoundRect
              (theRect      : Rect;        {Body of rectangle}
               cornerWidth  : INTEGER;     {Width of corner oval}
               cornerHeight : INTEGER);    {Height of corner oval}
```

Notes

1. These routines perform the five basic drawing operations [5.3.1] on rounded rectangles.

2. cornerWidth and cornerHeight give the *diameters of curvature*, the horizontal and vertical axes of the oval to be used for the rounded corners. Each corner will be a quarter of this oval (see figure).

3. cornerWidth and cornerHeight can never exceed the width and height of the body rectangle theRect, even if the values supplied are larger.

4. The trap macro for InvertRoundRect is spelled _InverRoundRect.

Assembly Language Information

Trap macros:

(Pascal) Routine name	(Assembly) Trap macro	Trap word
FrameRoundRect	_FrameRoundRect	$A8B0
PaintRoundRect	_PaintRoundRect	$A8B1
FillRoundRect	_FillRoundRect	$A8B4
EraseRoundRect	_EraseRoundRect	$A8B2
InvertRoundRect	_InverRoundRect	$A8B3

5.3.4   Drawing Ovals

inRect

Oval

Definitions

procedure FrameOval
         (inRect : Rect);   {Rectangle defining oval}

procedure PaintOval
         (inRect : Rect);   {Rectangle defining oval}

procedure FillOval
         (inRect : Rect;   {Rectangle defining oval}
          fillPat : Pattern);   {Pattern to fill with}

procedure EraseOval
         (inRect : Rect);   {Rectangle defining oval}

procedure InvertOval
         (inRect : Rect);   {Rectangle defining oval}

Notes

1. These routines perform the five basic drawing operations [5.3.1] on ovals.
2. The oval is inscribed in rectangle inRect.
3. If the specified rectangle is a square, the resulting oval will be a circle.

Assembly Language Information

Trap macros:

(Pascal) Routine name	(Assembly) Trap macro	Trap word
FrameOval	_FrameOval	$A8B7
PaintOval	_PaintOval	$A8B8
FillOval	_FillOval	$A8BB
EraseOval	_EraseOval	$A8B9
InvertOval	_InvertOval	$A8BA

5.3.5   Drawing Arcs and Wedges

Definitions

```
procedure  FrameArc
           (inRect      : Rect;        {Rectangle defining oval}
            startAngle  : INTEGER;     {Starting angle}
            arcAngle    : INTEGER);    {Extent of arc}

procedure  PaintArc
           (inRect      : Rect;        {Rectangle defining oval}
            startAngle  : INTEGER;     {Starting angle}
            arcAngle    : INTEGER);    {Extent of arc}

procedure  FillArc
           (inRect      : Rect;        {Rectangle defining oval}
            startAngle  : INTEGER;     {Starting angle}
            arcAngle    : INTEGER;     {Extent of arc}
            fillPat     : Pattern);    {Pattern to fill with}

procedure  EraseArc
           (inRect      : Rect;        {Rectangle defining oval}
            startAngle  : INTEGER;     {Starting angle}
            arcAngle    : INTEGER);    {Extent of arc}

procedure  InvertArc
           (inRect      : Rect;        {Rectangle defining oval}
            startAngle  : INTEGER;     {Starting angle}
            arcAngle    : INTEGER);    {Extent of arc}

procedure  PtToAngle
           (inRect        : Rect;      {Rectangle to measure in}
            thePoint      : Point;     {Point to be measured}
            var theAngle  : INTEGER);  {Returns angle of point, in degrees}
```

Notes

1. These routines perform the five basic drawing operations [5.3.1] on arcs and wedges.

2. The arc is a portion of the oval inscribed in rectangle inRect.

3. startAngle gives the angle at which the arc begins; arcAngle is the arc's angular extent (see figure).

4. All angles are expressed in degrees, modulo 360.

5. Angles are measured from the center of the oval, with 0 degrees at the top.

6. Positive angles are measured clockwise, negative ones counterclockwise.

7. All angles are measured relative to the given rectangle: for instance, 45 degrees designates the rectangle's top-right corner. Unless the rectangle is square, the angles will not be in true circular degrees.

8. FrameArc just draws the specified arc, using the current pen size, pattern, and mode. All other drawing operations draw a wedge bounded by the arc itself and the radii joining its two endpoints to the center of the oval.

9. Unlike other framing operations, FrameArc doesn't add what it draws to any open region definition.

10. PtToAngle calculates the angle corresponding to a given point with respect to a given rectangle, according to the same conventions just given for specifying arcs.

11. The resulting angle is always between 0 and 359, measured clockwise from 0 at the top.

Assembly Language Information

Trap macros:

(Pascal) Routine name	(Assembly) Trap macro	Trap word
FrameArc	_FrameArc	$A8BE
PaintArc	_PaintArc	$A8BF
FillArc	_FillArc	$A8C2
EraseArc	_EraseArc	$A8C0
InvertArc	_InvertArc	$A8C1
PtToAngle	_PtToAngle	$A8C3

5.3.6 Drawing Polygons

Definitions

```
procedure FramePoly
        (thePolygon : PolyHandle);      {Handle to polygon to be framed}

procedure PaintPoly
        (thePolygon : PolyHandle);      {Handle to polygon to be painted}

procedure FillPoly
        (thePolygon : PolyHandle;       {Handle to polygon to be filled}
         fillPat    : Pattern);         {Pattern to fill it with}

procedure ErasePoly
        (thePolygon : PolyHandle);      {Handle to polygon to be erased}

procedure InvertPoly
        (thePolygon : PolyHandle);      {Handle to polygon to be inverted}
```

Notes

1. These routines perform the five basic drawing operations [5.3.1] on polygons.

2. FramePoly uses the standard line-drawing operations [5.2.4] to draw the polygon's outline. This causes it to draw outside the actual outline at the right and bottom by the width and height of the graphics pen. This is the only shape-drawing operation that ever draws outside the boundary of a shape.

Assembly Language Information

Trap macros:

(Pascal) Routine name	(Assembly) Trap macro	Trap word
FramePoly	_FramePoly	$A8C6
PaintPoly	_PaintPoly	$A8C7
FillPoly	_FillPoly	$A8CA
ErasePoly	_ErasePoly	$A8C8
InvertPoly	_InvertPoly	$A8C9

5.3.7   Drawing Regions

Definitions

procedure FrameRgn
(theRegion : RgnHandle);   {Handle to region to be framed}

procedure PaintRgn
(theRegion : RgnHandle);   {Handle to region to be painted}

procedure FillRgn
(theRegion : RgnHandle;   {Handle to region to be filled}
fillPat   : Pattern);   {Pattern to fill it with}

procedure EraseRgn
(theRegion : RgnHandle);   {Handle to region to be erased}

procedure InvertRgn
(theRegion : RgnHandle);   {Handle to region to be inverted}

Notes

1. These routines perform the five basic drawing operations [5.3.1] on regions.

2. A region should always be drawn in the same graphics port in which it was defined.

3. The trap macro for InvertRgn is spelled _InverRgn.

Assembly Language Information

Trap macros:

(Pascal) Routine name	(Assembly) Trap macro	Trap word
FrameRgn	_FrameRgn	$A8D2
PaintRgn	_PaintRgn	$A8D3
FillRgn	_FillRgn	$A8D6
EraseRgn	_EraseRgn	$A8D4
InvertRgn	_InverRgn	$A8D5

5.4   Pictures and Icons

5.4.1   Picture Records

Definitions

```
type
    PicHandle = ^PicPtr;
    PicPtr    = ^Picture;

    Picture = record
                 picSize   : INTEGER;   {Length of this data structure in bytes}
                 picFrame  : Rect;      {Smallest rectangle enclosing the picture}
                 {additional data defining contents of picture}
              end;
```

Notes

1. A Picture is a variable-length data structure representing an arbitrary sequence of QuickDraw operations for drawing an image.

2. At the end of the Picture record is variable-length data (not directly accessible in Pascal) describing in compact, encoded form the operations needed to draw the picture. The Toolbox maintains this data for you—you'll never need to access or store into it yourself.

3. picSize is the overall length of this Picture data structure in bytes, including the variable-length data describing the drawing operations.

4. The Macintosh Plus can accommodate pictures up to 4 gigabytes (2^{32} bytes) long, with sizes expressed as long integers instead of plain integers. To get the true size of a picture, use GetHandleSize [3.2.3] instead of looking in the picSize field of the picture record. picSize holds the low-order 16 bits of the true size, so it's still correct for pictures of up to 32,767 bytes.

5. picFrame is the *picture frame*, the rectangle within which the picture is drawn.

Assembly Language Information

Field offsets in a picture record:

(Pascal) Field name	(Assembly) Offset name	Offset in bytes
picSize	picSize	0
picFrame	picFrame	2
————	picData	10

5.4.2 Defining Pictures

Definitions

```
function   OpenPicture
             (picFrame : Rect)        {Frame for new picture}
               : PicHandle;           {Handle to new picture}

procedure  ClosePicture;

function   GetPicture
             (pictureID : INTEGER)    {Resource ID of desired picture}
               : PicHandle;           {Handle to picture in memory}

procedure  KillPicture
             (thePicture : PicHandle); {Handle to picture to be destroyed}
```

Notes

1. OpenPicture creates a new Picture record [5.4.1], opens it for definition, and returns a handle to it.

2. picFrame is the frame for the new picture.

3. Subsequent drawing operations will be accumulated into the picture definition.

4. The graphics pen [5.2.1] is hidden while a picture is open; the drawing operations that define the picture will not appear on the screen.

5. Only one picture may be open for definition at a time; don't attempt to open another without closing the one that's already open.

6. ClosePicture closes the picture currently open for definition, if any.

7. The graphics pen is redisplayed on the screen; subsequent drawing operations will appear on the screen instead of being accumulated into the picture definition.

8. GetPicture gets a picture from a resource file (Chapter 6), reads it into memory if necessary, and returns a handle to it.

9. pictureID is the resource ID of the desired picture; its resource type is 'PICT' [5.5.5].

10. KillPicture destroys a Picture record and deallocates the memory space it occupies. The picture is no longer usable after this operation.

11. To dispose of a picture that has been read in as a resource [5.5.5], use ReleaseResource [6.3.2] instead of KillPicture.

Assembly Language Information

Trap macros:

(Pascal) Routine name	(Assembly) Trap macro	Trap word
OpenPicture	_OpenPicture	$A8F3
ClosePicture	_ClosePicture	$A8F4
GetPicture	_GetPicture	$A9BC
KillPicture	_KillPicture	$A8F5

5.4.3 Drawing Pictures

Definitions

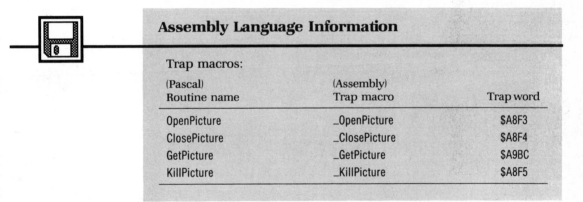

```
procedure DrawPicture
          (thePicture : PicHandle;     {Picture to be drawn}
           inRect     : Rect);         {Rectangle to draw it in}
```

Notes

1. DrawPicture draws a specified picture in the current graphics port.
2. The picture will be scaled so that its picture frame coincides with the given rectangle inRect.

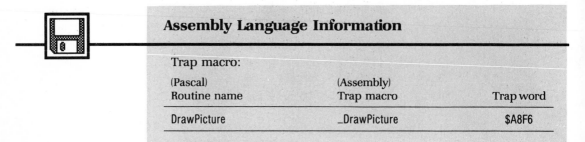

Assembly Language Information

Trap macro:

(Pascal) Routine name	(Assembly) Trap macro	Trap word
DrawPicture	_DrawPicture	$A8F6

5.4.4   Icons

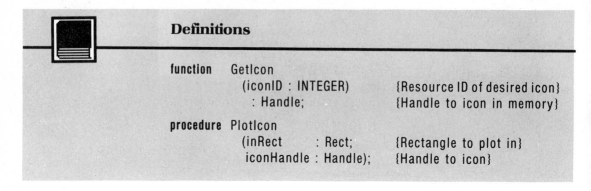

Definitions

```
function   GetIcon
              (iconID : INTEGER)        {Resource ID of desired icon}
                : Handle;               {Handle to icon in memory}

procedure  PlotIcon
              (inRect    : Rect;        {Rectangle to plot in}
               iconHandle : Handle);    {Handle to icon}
```

Notes

1. An icon is a 32-by-32 bit image, commonly (but not necessarily) used to represent an object on the screen.
2. Icons reside in the heap and are referred to by handles.
3. There is no defined data type representing an icon. If you have to create one in your program, you can use an

   `array [1..32] of LONGINT`
4. Icons are usually stored in resource files and read in as resources (Chapter 6).

5. GetIcon gets an icon from a resource file (Chapter 6), reads it into memory if necessary, and returns a handle to it.

6. IconID is the resource ID of the desired icon; its resource type is 'ICON' [5.5.3].

7. PlotIcon draws an icon in the current graphics port, scaled to a specified rectangle.

8. The rectangle inRect is expressed in the local coordinate system of the current port.

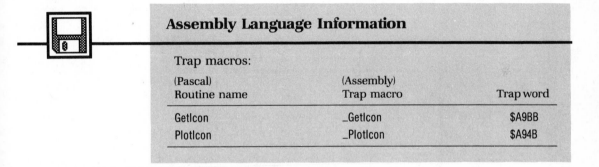

Assembly Language Information

Trap macros:

(Pascal) Routine name	(Assembly) Trap macro	Trap word
GetIcon	_GetIcon	$A9BB
PlotIcon	_PlotIcon	$A94B

5.5   QuickDraw-Related Resources

5.5.1   Resource Type 'PAT '

Notes

1. A resource of type 'PAT ' contains a QuickDraw pattern.
2. The space in 'PAT ' is required.
3. The resource data consists of the bits (pixels) of the pattern, 8 rows of 8 bits (1 byte) each.
4. Use GetPattern [5.1.1] to load a resource of this type.

5.5.2 Resource Type 'PAT#'

Notes

1. A resource of type 'PAT#' contains a list of QuickDraw patterns.

2. The resource data consists of a 2-byte integer giving the number of patterns in the list, followed by the patterns themselves (8 bytes each, as described under 'PAT ' [5.5.1]).

3. Use GetIndPattern [5.1.1] to access individual patterns in a pattern list.

4. The system resource file includes a standard pattern list [5.1.2] containing the 38 patterns in MacPaint's standard pattern palette. The resource ID for this standard pattern list is 0.

5.5.3 Resource Type 'ICON'

Notes

1. A resource of type 'ICON' contains an icon to be displayed on the screen.

2. The resource data consists of the bits (pixels) of the icon, 32 rows of 32 bits (4 bytes) each.

3. Use GetIcon [5.4.4] to load a resource of this type.

5.5.4   Resource Type 'ICN#'

Any number of icons

   Notes

1. A resource of type 'ICN#' contains a list of icons.

2. The resource data consists of any number of icons, 128 bytes each (32 rows of 4 bytes, as described under 'ICON' [5.5.3]).

3. Resources of this type are commonly used to hold a file icon and its mask for use by the Finder [7.5.3].

5.5.5   Resource Type 'PICT'

   Notes

1. A resource of type 'PICT' contains a QuickDraw picture.

2. The resource data consists of a QuickDraw picture record [5.4.1], with a 2-byte picSize field and an 8-byte picFrame rectangle, followed by any number of bytes of the picture definition.

3. Use GetPicture [5.4.2] to load a resource of this type.

4. When you're finished with the picture, use ReleaseResource [6.3.2] (not KillPicture [5.4.2]) to dispose of it.

CHAPTER

6

Summoning Your Resources

Oone of the brightest of the bright ideas in the Macintosh Toolbox is the concept of *resources*. A program's resources can include all the little odds and ends it needs to do its job: the menus it offers in the menu bar, the icons and character fonts it uses to display information on the screen, the layout and contents of its dialog and alert boxes. Even the code of the program itself consists of one or more *code segments*, each of which is a resource. Looked at in a certain way, a Macintosh program is nothing but a bundle of resources.

Resources were originally invented to help convert (the in word is "localize") Macintosh software for use in foreign countries. From the start, Apple designed the Macintosh to be an international product. The idea behind resources was to isolate those aspects of a program's behavior that could vary from one country to another. That way you could translate all the menus and error messages into Dutch, or reconfigure the keyboard to the standard French layout, or display text in a Japanese Katakana font, without having to change the underlying program itself. By making proper use of resources, you could write programs that would work just as well in Brussels or Buenos Aires as they would in Boston or Boise.

Resources were soon recognized, though, as a powerful and general mechanism that could be useful for much more than just

275

foreign localization. Separating the text of menus and dialogs from the rest of the program makes it easy to correct misspellings or change terminology. By making the code that draws windows on the screen a resource, you can experiment with windows of different shapes and styles without affecting either the code of a particular program or the general window-management code built into the Macintosh ROM. Not only application programs, but the individual data files they work on can have resources of their own, so that a text document, for instance, can carry its own font information and illustrations with it even when it's copied from one disk to another.

Resources have another important advantage as well: they allow descriptive information about a program's behavior to be separated into bite-sized "chunks" rather than embedded in the code of the program itself. Because they're identified as separate entities, not all the "chunks" have to be kept in memory at once. They can be read in from the disk on demand and then purged from memory when no longer needed. This allows great flexibility in managing the program's memory space. In particular, it provides a natural mechanism for breaking up the code itself into segments that can be loaded into memory as needed and "swapped out" when they're not actually being executed. We'll be coming back to this subject in the next chapter.

In fact, resources are so useful that they've become a pervasive part of the whole Macintosh software design. Just about every part of the Toolbox uses them in one way or another, and they'll be coming up again and again in the course of our discussions. Any program you write will make extensive use of resources through the Toolbox, even if you never explicitly refer to them yourself.

Although this chapter tells how to use resources in a program, there's still the problem of creating the resources in the first place. Historically, this has been done with a utility program named RMaker, a "resource compiler" that reads a coded text file describing the desired resources and produces an equivalent resource file. RMaker is included with many of the most popular software development systems, such as TML's MacLanguage Series Pascal, Borland's Turbo Pascal for the Mac, and Consulair's Macintosh Development System (MDS).

RMaker's main drawback is that its text format for describing a program's resources amounts to yet another language for you to learn. Another utility, a "resource editor" named ResEdit, takes a more convenient approach. Instead of compiling your resources from a coded text description, ResEdit allows you to define and modify them directly on your Macintosh screen with the mouse and keyboard. (This, in fact, is how the resources were created for our example program MiniEdit in Volume Two.)

ResEdit is included as part of Apple's Macintosh Programmer's Workshop (MPW), and is also widely available in the public domain through Macintosh clubs, user groups, and "bulletin boards." MPW also includes its own resource compiler and decompiler, named Rez and DeRez. In addition, there's a growing array of specialized tools for handling specific types of resources, such as font editors, menu editors, and Apple's own Font/DA Mover for copying existing fonts and desk accessories from one resource file to another. For special needs that aren't covered by any of these existing tools, you'll have to write your own *ad hoc* programs to create the resources you need, using the Toolbox facilities described in this chapter, the information on resource formats given in the rest of the book, and your own ingenuity.

Identifying Resources

Every resource has a *resource type* and a *resource ID*. The resource type is a four-character string denoting the kind of information the resource represents, such as 'ICON' or 'MENU'. The resource ID is an identifying number to distinguish one resource from another of the same type. Together, the resource type and resource ID make up a *resource specification* that uniquely identifies a particular resource.

A resource's type determines what kind of information it contains (the *resource data*) and how that information is structured internally. The name of a resource type can be any four characters at all. The contents and structure of resources of that type can follow any conventions agreed on between the program that creates them and the one that uses them (which may or may not be the same program). Certain standard resource types are built into the Toolbox [6.1.1]; you can also invent your own resource types, provided that their four-character names don't conflict with any of the standard ones.

> The name of a resource type must always be exactly four characters long. If it's shorter, it must include trailing spaces to fill it out to four characters, as in 'STR ' or 'PAT '. Upper- and lowercase letters are distinguished, so 'BLOB', 'Blob', and 'blob' would be considered three different resource types. Notice also that the Pascal string quotes (') enclosing the type name are merely delimiters, not part of the name itself.

A resource ID can be any 16-bit signed integer, as long as it doesn't conflict with another resource of the same type. (It's OK for resources of different types to have the same ID number. In fact, this can be a convenient way of indicating that the resources are related in some way—such as a font resource of type 'FONT' [8.4.5] and the corresponding character-width table of type 'FWID' [8.4.6].) However, all negative ID numbers and positive ones up to 127 are reserved for system use. Resources that you create for yourself must have positive IDs between 128 and 32767.

In addition to a type and an ID number, a resource may also have a *resource name*, which can be any string up to 255 characters long. Resource names are optional, and are generally used only for resources that will be listed on a menu, such as fonts or desk accessories. A named resource can be identified by type and name instead of type and ID number. To make sure the identification is unique, resources of the same type must always have different names. (Again, it's OK—although not necessarily advisable—to have two distinct resources with the same name, as long as they're of different types.)

Resource Files

Resources reside in *resource files* on the disk. A single resource file can contain any number of resources of any types. The file's contents are summarized in a table called the *resource map*, stored as part of the file itself. Each entry in the resource map holds all the pertinent information about one resource in the file: its type, ID number, name (if any), attributes, and the location of its data within the resource file (see Figure 6-1). The resource map is read into memory from the disk when you open the file, and remains in memory for as long as the file remains open.

Resources reside in *resource files* on the disk.

Figure 6-1 Resource map

Strictly, speaking, there's really no such thing as a resource file as such. Or, to look at it another way, every file on the disk is (at least potentially) a resource file. Each file has two parts, or "forks": a *data fork* and a *resource fork*. It's almost as if there were two distinct files with the same name, which are inseparably linked and always travel together as a unit (for instance, when copied from one disk to another with the Finder). To read or write a file's data fork, you use the ordinary input/output operations that we'll be discussing in Volume Two, Chapter 8; to read or write the resource fork, you use the resource operations described in this chapter. The term "resource file" is just a convenient fiction: when we speak of a resource file named, say, Rumpelstiltskin, what we're really referring to is the resource fork of the file by that name.

For a file containing a document of some sort, the document's contents are kept in the data fork, while the resource fork can hold document-specific resources such as fonts and icons. For a file containing an application program, the data fork is usually empty. (Remember, the code of the program is just another resource like anything else.) Of course, a program can store into its own data fork if it wants to—this can be a convenient place, for instance, to stash global information that needs to be remembered from one run of the program to the next.

The most important resource file of all is the *system resource file*, which contains shared resources available to all programs. These include such things as the standard fonts, icons, cursors, and gray patterns; the standard keyboard layout; definition routines for the standard window, control, and menu types; and the code of desk accessories such as the Calculator, Alarm Clock, and Scrapbook. The system resource file is actually the resource fork of the file named System, which must be present on every startup disk. (This file's data fork contains RAM-based system and Toolbox routines to be loaded into memory when the system is started up—typically to correct errors in the ROM versions of the routines.) The file is opened automatically when the system is started up, and normally just remains open continuously.

On the Macintosh Plus, some of the most commonly used system resources actually reside in ROM, rather than in the System file on the disk. See [6.6.3] for more information.

Another important resource file is the *application resource file*, which is the resource fork of the file containing the application program itself. This is where a program normally keeps its own private resources (including the actual code of the program). The application resource file is opened automatically when a program is started up, so there's no need for the program to open it explicitly.

In addition to the system and application resource files, you can open any other resource files you need by calling OpenResFile [6.2.1]. You designate the file to be opened by name; OpenResFile gives you back a *file reference number*, which you use from then on whenever you need to identify the file. (We'll learn more about file reference numbers when we talk about files in Volume Two.)

All resource-related Toolbox routines that deal with file reference numbers interpret a reference number of 0 to denote the system resource file. This is merely a convention, however; the file actually has a true reference number different from 0.

All the open resource files are kept in a list, linked together through a field of their resource maps in memory. When a new file is opened, it's linked to the front of this list. So the files are listed in reverse order chronologically, with the most recently opened resource file first in the list, and the system resource file last.

When you ask for a resource, the Toolbox searches each file in the list until it finds a resource with the specified type and ID (or type and name). The search always begins with the *current resource file* and proceeds from there to the end of the list (see Figure 6-2). Opening a new resource file makes it current, so normally the current file is the first one in the list. If necessary, you can change this by calling UseResFile or find out which file is current with CurResFile [6.2.2]. Changing the current resource file just causes some files at the beginning of the list to be bypassed; you can't change the order of the list itself.

Closing a resource file removes it from the list and deallocates the space occupied by its resource map. It also deallocates any of the file's resources that may have been read into memory. All open resource files (except the system file) are closed automatically

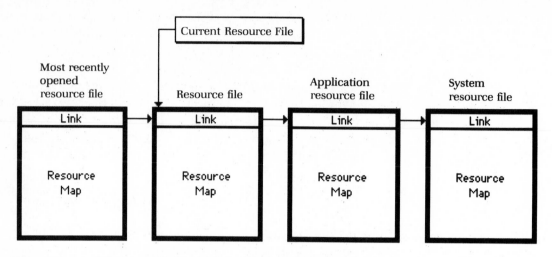

When a resource file is opened, the map is read into memory, but the resource data remains on the disk. The open resource files are linked through a field of their resource maps.

Figure 6-2 Current resource file

when a program terminates, but if you're pressed for space you may want to close a file explicitly while your program is still running. You can do this by calling CloseResFile [6.2.1], giving the reference number of the file you want to close.

> Closing the system resource file automatically closes all other open resource files as well. This isn't something you'd normally want to do, since other parts of the system depend on the system resource file.

Access to Resources

To use a resource, you first have to read it into memory from its resource file. The usual way of doing this is with GetResource [6.3.1], identifying the resource by its type and ID number. For resources with names, you can use GetNamedResource, giving a type and name instead of a type and ID. Both routines search the list of resource files beginning with the current file, as described in the preceding section. When they find the resource you asked for, they allocate space in the heap for the resource's data, read the data in from the file, and return a handle to it. You can then use this handle to do whatever you need to do with the data. A copy of the handle is also saved in the file's resource map in memory. If the resource is still in memory the next time you ask for it, you'll just get back this same handle; the resource won't have to be read in again from the disk.

One of the new features of the Macintosh Plus Toolbox is a collection of "one-deep" resource routines that apply only to the current resource file, instead of the entire list of open resource files. The new routines Get1Resource and Get1NamedResource [6.3.1] are analogous to GetResource and GetNamedResource, but look for a requested resource in the current resource file only. If they don't find it there, they simply abandon the search and report an error instead of going on to the next file in the list. These routines can make some of your resource operations more efficient—but bear in mind that they aren't available if you're running on an older-model Macintosh.

Like any other relocatable block, a resource in the heap can be locked or unlocked, purgeable or unpurgeable. The resource's attributes (discussed in the next section) determine the initial settings of these properties when the resource is first read in from the disk. After that, you can change them as needed with HLock and HUnlock, HPurge and HNoPurge [3.2.4].

If you make a resource purgeable, of course, then each time you use it you have to check first to make sure it's still in memory. The best way to do this is to call LoadResource [6.3.4] before each use of the resource's handle. If the handle is empty (the resource has been purged), LoadResource will reload the resource from the disk; if it isn't empty (the resource is still in memory), LoadResource does nothing. You might then want to make the resource temporarily unpurgeable while it's in use (see Program 6-1).

```
{ Skeleton code showing the use of a purgeable resource. }

var
   theHandle  : Handle;
   thePointer : Ptr;

begin

   . . . ;

   LoadResource (theHandle);              {Make sure resource is in memory [6.3.4]}

   HLock (theHandle);                     {Lock before dereferencing [3.2.4]}
      thePointer := theHandle^;           {Dereference handle}
      ...thePointer^...;                  {Use simple pointer}
   HUnlock (theHandle);                   {Unlock when through [3.2.4]}

   . . .

end
```

Program 6-1 Using a purgeable resource

> Whether to make a given resource purgeable or unpurgeable depends on a number of factors, including the size of the resource, how often you'll be referring to it, and how desperate you are for heap space. In general, you'll probably want to make larger resources (such as fonts) purgeable and smaller ones (such as patterns) unpurgeable.

When you're all through with a resource, you can free the memory space it occupies with ReleaseResource [6.3.2]. As usual, this makes all handles to the resource invalid; it also sets the resource's handle in the resource map to NIL, so that the resource will be reloaded from the disk the next time you ask for it. All the resources in a resource file are released automatically when you close the file.

Sometimes, though, you may want to hold onto a resource even after the file it came from is closed. For instance, suppose you need a single resource from a particular resource file. Once you have the resource, there's no need to keep the file open, with its resource map taking up space in memory. To keep the resource from being deallocated when you close the file, you can *detach* it first with DetachResource [6.3.2]. This clears the resource's handle in the resource map but doesn't deallocate the resource itself. The resource isn't removed from the file; your copy of it in memory is just decoupled from the file's resource map, so that it won't go away when you close the file (see Figure 6-3). Even after the file is

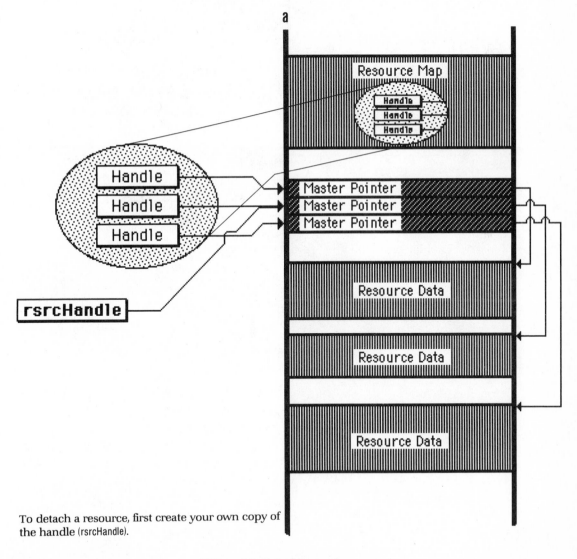

To detach a resource, first create your own copy of the handle (rsrcHandle).

Figure 6-3 Detaching a resource

DetachResource (rsrcHandle)

Note this handle set to NIL

Procedure DetachResource sets the original handle to NIL.

Figure 6-3 (*continued*)

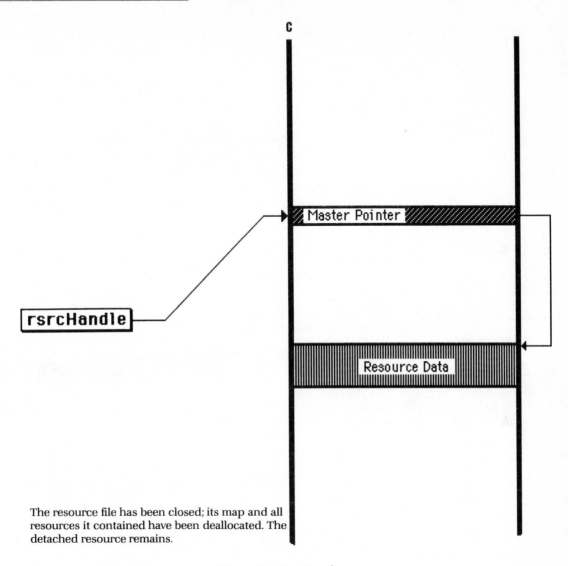

The resource file has been closed; its map and all resources it contained have been deallocated. The detached resource remains.

Figure 6-3 (*continued*)

closed, your own copy of the resource's handle remains valid and you can continue to use it to refer to the resource data, as in Program 6-2.

You may sometimes want to perform some operation on all available resources of a given type, or of every type. Program 6-3 shows how. The function CountTypes [6.3.3] returns the total number of distinct resource types contained in all open resource files. You can then call GetIndType [6.3.3] once for each value of its index parameter from 1 up to the number of types. Each time it will return a different resource type. For each of these types, CountResources [6.3.3] will return the total number of available resources of that type in all open files; you can get each of the resources in turn by calling GetIndResource [6.3.3] once for each value from 1 to the number of resources. We'll see a further example of this technique in Chapter 8.

```
{ Skeleton code to get one single resource from a resource file. }

const
    blobID = 128;                               {Resource ID of desired 'BLOB' resource}

var
    theFile : INTEGER;                          {Reference number of the resource file}
    theBlob : Handle;                           {Handle to the resource}

begin

    . . . ;

    theFile := OpenResFile ('Rumpelstiltskin');  {Open the file [6.2.1]}
    theBlob := GetResource ('BLOB', blobID);     {Get the resource [6.3.1]}
    DetachResource (theBlob);                    {Detach the resource [6.3.2]}
    CloseResFile   (theFile);                    {Close the file [6.2.1]}

    ...theBlob...;                               {Use the resource}

    . . .

end
```

Program 6-2 Detaching a resource

```
{ Skeleton code to generate all available resources. }

var
   typeIndex  : INTEGER;                              {Index of resource type}
   rsrcIndex  : INTEGER;                              {Index of individual resource}
   theType    : ResType;                              {Resource type}
   rsrcHandle : Handle;                               {Handle to resource}

begin

   ... ;

   for typeIndex := 1 to CountTypes do                {Loop over all resource types [6.3.3]}
      begin
         GetIndType (theType, typeIndex);             {Get next type [6.3.3]}
         for rsrcIndex := 1 to CountResources (theType) do  {Loop over all resources of this type [6.3.3]}
            begin
               rsrcHandle := GetIndResource (theType, rsrcIndex);  {Get handle to next resource [6.3.3]}
               ...rsrcHandle...                       {Use the handle}
            end
      end;

   ...

end
```

Program 6-3 Generating all resources

Notice that these routines always operate on *all* open resource files, no matter which one happens to be current. On the Macintosh Plus, you can limit your operations to just one particular resource file by making that file current with UseResFile [6.2.2], then using the new one-deep routines Count1Types, Get1IndType, Count1Resources, and Get1Ind-Resource [6.3.3] to generate the resources. On older machines, where the one-deep routines aren't available, you can achieve the same effect by generating all available resources with the old routines and testing each one with HomeResFile [6.4.3] to see if it belongs to the file of interest. This method is much slower than using the one-deep routines, however.

Resource Attributes

Besides its resource data, every resource has some additional items of information associated with it. These additional items are kept in the resource's entry in its file's resource map. They fall into two categories: identifying information and resource attributes.

The *identifying information* for a resource consists of its resource type, ID number, and (optional) name. Given a handle to the resource, you can find out its identifying information with GetResInfo or change it with SetResInfo [6.4.1]. (You can't change a resource's type, just its ID and name.) To find out the size of a resource's data, in bytes, use SizeResource [6.4.3].

If speed is more important than absolute accuracy, you can save some time (on the Macintosh Plus only) by using the new routine MaxSizeRsrc [6.4.3] rather than SizeResource. Instead of examining the resource itself (which may have to be read from the disk if it isn't already in memory), MaxSizeRsrc just looks in the resource map and finds the number of bytes between the beginning of this resource's data and that of the next resource following it in the file. This is a quick operation, since the resource map is always immediately available in memory—but the result may not accurately reflect the true size of the resource. If the resource has been shortened while in memory, there may be some extra, unused space following it that won't be closed up until the file is written back out to the disk. Thus the resource can never be larger than the value reported by MaxSizeRsrc, but it may be smaller. If you really need the exact size, use SizeResource instead.

A resource's *attributes* are a set of 1-bit flags describing various properties of the resource. They're collected in a single "attribute byte" of the resource map entry, with the format shown in Figure 6-4. The Toolbox provides the routines GetResAttrs and SetResAttrs [6.4.2] for reading and changing a resource's attributes, as well as constants for referring to each of the individual attribute bits. In every case, the constant's name tells the meaning of the corresponding attribute bit when set to 1; a bit value of 0 has the opposite meaning. (For instance, a resource is protected if its ResProtected bit is set to 1, unprotected if it's 0.)

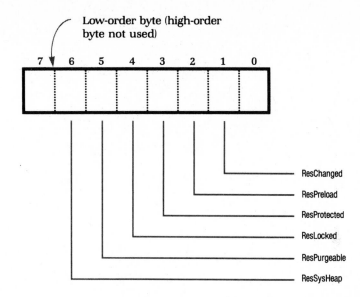

Figure 6-4 Resource attributes

You can use these attribute constants along with the bit-manipulation routines BitAnd, BitOr, BitXOr, and BitNot [2.2.2] to operate on the individual attribute bits of a resource. For example, if theResource is a handle to a resource, you might turn on its ResProtected attribute as follows:

```
attrs := GetResAttrs (theResource);
attrs := BitOr (attrs, ResProtected);
SetResAttrs (theResource, attrs)
```

The ResSysHeap attribute tells whether the space for a resource's data is allocated from the system heap or the application heap. ResLocked and ResPurgeable control whether the resource is initially locked and made purgeable when it's loaded from the disk. Changing these attributes does *not* immediately lock or unlock the resource or change its purgeability—you still have to do that in the usual way, with HLock and HUnlock, HPurge and HNoPurge [3.2.4]. Changing the ResLocked and ResPurgeable attributes only affects what will happen the next time the resource is read in from the disk.

The ResProtected attribute prevents you from removing a resource from its resource file or changing its name or ID. (You can still change the resource's attributes, however—if you couldn't, there would be no way to turn off the ResProtected attribute itself!) ResPreload causes the resource to be read into memory immediately when its resource file is opened, instead of waiting for you to get or load it explicitly. Finally, ResChanged means that the resource has been changed since the last time it was read in from the disk, and must be written back out before the file is closed. (We'll have more to say about this process in the next section.) The first and last bits of the attribute byte are reserved for private use by the Toolbox.

Not only individual resources, but whole resource files have attributes of their own, which you can access and change with GetResFileAttrs and SetResFileAttrs [6.6.2]. You'll rarely have to deal with resource file attributes, but there are a few cases when they're useful. Some examples are given in the "Nuts and Bolts" section at the end of this chapter.

Modifying Resources

So far, we've assumed that all you want to do is read and use existing resources from existing resource files. In most applications that's all you'll need, but occasionally you may want to add new resources to a resource file, remove old ones, change existing ones, or even create whole new resource files.

When you change a resource, you have to take special measures if you want the change to be incorporated permanently on the disk. Simply changing the resource in memory isn't enough—you also have to mark it as changed by setting its ResChanged attribute. When the file is later *updated*, all resources that have been marked as changed will be written out to the disk. A resource file is automatically updated when it's closed (and recall that all except the system resource file are closed automatically when your program terminates). If for some reason you want to update a resource file without closing it, use UpdateResFile [6.5.4].

You can add resources to the current resource file with AddResource and remove them with RmveResource [6.5.3]. Both of these routines make the appropriate changes in the resource map of the current file; AddResource also marks the new resource as changed, so it will automatically be written out to the disk when the file is updated. When you add a resource, you can use UniqueID [6.5.3] to make sure the ID number you give it doesn't conflict with another resource of the same type. To create a brand-new resource file, use CreateResFile [6.5.1] and then add whatever resources the new file is to contain.

When you make any change in the data of an existing resource in memory (or change its resource map information with SetResInfo or SetResAttrs [6.4.2]), you can choose whether to make the change permanently on the disk, or just temporarily for as long as the resource remains in memory. To make the change permanent, you have to call ChangedResource [6.5.2] to mark the resource as changed. This ensures that it'll be written out when the resource file is updated. (Always use ChangedResource for this purpose; never directly manipulate a resource's ResChanged attribute yourself!)

> If any single resource in a file is marked as changed, the entire resource map will always be written out when the file is updated. This means that changes in some other resource's identifying information or attributes may be written back to the disk even though you haven't marked that specific resource as changed. If you want such a change to be temporary, it's up to you to undo the change before the file is updated.

The situation is especially tricky when the resource you're modifying is purgeable. First of all, you have to make sure the resource isn't purged from the heap while you're in the middle of changing it. To prevent this, always use HNoPurge to make the resource temporarily unpurgeable while you're modifying it, then HPurge to make it purgeable again when you're through. But even if you take this precaution, there's still the danger that the resource may be purged after you've changed it and before its resource file is updated. In that case your changes will be lost, and empty (zero-length) data will be written to the file for that resource.

One way to make sure your changes aren't accidentally lost is to write the resource out explicitly with WriteResource [6.5.4] as soon as you finish changing it, and before you make it purgeable again. Another way to do it is with SetResPurge [6.5.5]. The call

    SetResPurge(TRUE)

tells the Toolbox to check every time it purges a block from the heap, to see if the block is a changed resource. If it is, the Toolbox will write it out to its resource file before purging it. This guarantees that all your changes will be saved eventually, although you have no control over exactly when.

    SetResPurge(FALSE)

turns off this feature, so that blocks are again purged from the heap without any checking. Automatic purge checking is initially off, so you have to turn it on explicitly with SetResPurge if you want it.

Error Reporting

The routines dealing with resources use an error-reporting mechanism similar to the one used in memory management, which we discussed in Chapter 3. The function ResError [6.6.1] is analogous to MemError [3.1.3]: after a call to any resource-related routine, this function returns an integer result code. A code of 0 (NoErr) means that all is well; a nonzero code reports an error of some kind. If the routine reporting the error is a function, it generally returns some special value, such as NIL or —1, to alert you that an error has occurred; if it's a procedure, it typically just posts the error and returns without doing anything.

> In assembly language, you can find the result code from the last resource-related operation in the global variable ResErr.

The list given in [6.6.1] includes only those error codes that deal specifically with resources. It's also possible for ResError to return error codes related to other parts of the Toolbox. For instance, you may get a code of MemFullErr [3.1.2] if you try to load a resource from the disk when there isn't enough room for it in the heap. See Appendix E for a complete list of possible error codes.

Nuts and Bolts

Since a resource's identifying information and attributes reside in the resource map, it isn't necessary to load the resource into memory to work with them. A routine called SetResLoad [6.3.4] allows you to get a handle to a resource without loading its data from the resource file. The call

```
SetResLoad(FALSE)
```

turns off the automatic loading of resources by GetResource [6.3.1], GetNamedResource [6.3.1], and GetIndResource [6.3.3] (and their one-deep counterparts). If the resource you ask for is already in memory, these routines will still return a handle to it, as usual; but if it isn't, they'll give you back an empty handle instead of loading the resource from the file. This empty handle identifies the resource well enough for those routines that operate on its resource map entry (GetResInfo and SetResInfo [6.4.1], GetResAttrs and SetResAttrs [6.4.2], HomeResFile and MaxSizeRsrc [6.4.3]). If you later need to refer to the resource's data, you can read it in explicitly with LoadResource [6.3.4].

Be careful, though! Turning off automatic resource loading is tricky, and can lead to a number of subtle problems if you don't watch your step. For one thing, some parts of the Toolbox rely on automatic loading and won't work properly without it. So if you do turn it off, be sure to turn it back on again as soon as possible with

```
SetResLoad(TRUE)
```

It's especially crucial to turn automatic loading back on before terminating your program and exiting back to the Finder. Don't forget that the code of the Finder, like that of any other program (including your own), is stored on the disk as a resource. If you leave automatic loading turned off, the Toolbox will be unable to load the Finder into memory for execution, and will crash the system instead.

For another thing, recall that if any one resource in a resource file is marked as changed, the entire resource map will be written out when the file is updated. Changes you make to a resource's identifying information or attributes in the resource map (even if you intend them to be temporary) may accidentally be incorporated into the permanent disk copy of the file because of changes made to other resources. If you've made any other changes, you have to be careful to undo the temporary ones and restore the resource's map entry to its original state before the file is updated.

Yet another trap awaits you if you *do* want your changes to be permanent. SetResInfo and SetResAttrs don't automatically mark the affected resource as changed; to make sure your changes are written out when the file is updated, you have to mark the resource explicitly with ChangedResource [6.5.2]. But if you've turned off automatic resource loading with SetResLoad, to get a handle to a resource without loading its data from the disk, the resource map will now contain an empty handle for that resource. When the file is updated, the empty handle will cause the existing resource data to be replaced with empty (zero-length) data.

One way to prevent this from happening is to turn on the resource file's MapChanged attribute with SetResFileAttrs [6.6.2] instead of marking the resource itself with ChangedResource. This will cause the resource map to be written out when the file is updated (making your changes permanent), but since the resource itself isn't marked as changed, the empty handle in the resource map won't replace the existing resource data in the file with empty data.

Another occasional use for SetResFileAttrs has to do with the file's MapCompact attribute. Certain changes that you make in a resource file create "holes" in the file: areas of the file's contents that are no longer in use and can be closed up by compaction when the file is written back to the disk. The MapCompact attribute tells the Toolbox to compact the file's contents the next time it's updated.

Some operations that create holes in the file, such as RmveResource [6.5.3], cause this attribute to be set automatically. Similarly, if you increase the length of a resource's data, the new data has to be written at the end when the file is updated, since it will no longer fit at its original location within the file. This leaves a hole where the resource used to be. So again, the file's

MapCompact attribute is set automatically whenever you lengthen the data of any resource. For some reason, however, MapCompact is *not* set automatically when you *shorten* a resource, even though this also creates a hole that could be closed up by compaction. So in this case you can use SetResFileAttrs to turn on the MapCompact attribute yourself and force a compaction when the file is updated.

This problem has been corrected on the Macintosh Plus: any operation that creates a hole in the resource file correctly sets the file's MapCompact attribute.

One final use for SetResFileAttrs is to "protect" a resource file by turning on its MapReadOnly attribute. This prevents the file from being updated at all, ensuring that any and all changes you make will be temporary and will never be written out to the disk.

REFERENCE

6.1   Resource Types

6.1.1   Resource Types

Definitions

```
type
    ResType = packed array [1..4] of CHAR;    {Resource type}
```

Resource type	Description	See section
'PAT '	QuickDraw pattern	[5.5.1]
'PAT#'	Pattern list	[5.5.2]
'ICON'	Icon	[5.5.3]
'ICN#'	Icon list	[5.5.4]
'PICT'	QuickDraw picture	[5.5.5]
'CODE'	Code segment	[7.5.1]
'PACK'	Package	[7.5.2]
'FREF'	Finder file reference	[7.5.3]
'BNDL'	Finder bundle	[7.5.4]
'DRVR'	I/O driver (including desk accessories)	[7.5.5]
'TEXT'	Any text	[8.4.1]
'STR '	Pascal-format string	[8.4.2]
'STR#'	String list	[8.4.3]
'INIT'	Initialization resource (including keyboard configurations)	[8.4.4]
'FONT'	Font	[8.4.5]
'NFNT'	Non-menu font	[8.4.5]
'FWID'	Font width table	[8.4.6]
'FRSV'	Reserved font list	[8.4.7]
'CURS'	Cursor	[II:2.9.1]
'FKEY'	Low-level keyboard routine	[II:2.9.2]
'WIND'	Window template	[II:3.7.1]
'MENU'	Menu	[II:4.8.1]
'MBAR'	Menu bar	[II:4.8.2]
'CNTL'	Control template	[II:6.6.1]
'ALRT'	Alert template	[II:7.6.1]
'DLOG'	Dialog template	[II:7.6.2]
'DITL'	Dialog or alert item list	[II:7.6.3]
'MACS'	Macintosh system autograph	
'FOND'	Font family definition	
'WDEF'	Window definition function	
'MDEF'	Menu definition procedure	
'CDEF'	Control definition function	
'LDEF'	List definition procedure	

'PDEF'	Printing code
'PREC'	Print record
'SERD'	Serial driver
'INTL'	International localization resource
'DSAT'	"Dire straits" alert table
'CACH'	RAM cache code
'FMTR'	Disk formatting code
'PTCH'	System patch code
'ROvr'	ROM override code
'ROv#'	ROM override list
'APPL'	Finder application table
'FDIR'	Finder directory
'FOBJ'	Finder object
'FCMT'	Finder comment
'LAYO'	Finder folder layout
'MINI'	MiniFinder resource
'FBTN'	File button (MiniFinder)
'NBPC'	Name-Binding Protocol code (AppleTalk)
'PAPA'	Printer Access Protocol address (AppleTalk)
'RDEV'	Remote device (Chooser)
'PRER'	Printer remote (Chooser)
'PRES'	Printer serial (Chooser)
'SIZE'	Partition size (Switcher)
'TMPL'	Resource type template (ResEdit)

Notes

1. Names of resource types are always exactly four characters long.

2. Type names may include any characters without restriction, including letters, digits, spaces, and special characters. Notice that the space is significant (and required) in names such as 'STR ' and 'PAT '.

3. Upper- and lowercase letters are considered distinct: for example, 'BLOB', 'Blob', and 'blob' are three different resource types.

4. Resource types listed in the table above have reserved meanings assigned to them by the Toolbox; those that you invent for your own

use must not conflict with them. In addition, all type names consisting entirely of lowercase letters (such as 'blob') are reserved by Apple for the private use of the Toolbox.

5. Resource types for which no section number is given in the table are not covered in this book; see Volume Three or Apple's *Inside Macintosh* manual for information. (However, some of these are private to the Toolbox and are not documented even in *Inside Macintosh*.)

6.2   Resource Files

6.2.1   Opening and Closing Resource Files

Definitions

```
function   OpenResFile
             (fileName : Str255)    {Name of resource file to be opened}
               : INTEGER;           {Reference number of file}

procedure  CloseResFile
             (refNum : INTEGER);    {Reference number of resource file to be closed}
```

Notes

1. OpenResFile opens a resource file; CloseResFile closes it.

2. OpenResFile accepts the name of the resource file to be opened and returns the file's reference number. Thereafter, the reference number is used whenever you want to refer to the file.

3. The file's resource map is read into memory and remains there for as long as the file remains open.

4. The designated file becomes the current resource file.

5. If the designated resource file is already open, OpenResFile just returns its reference number.

6. In case of an error opening the file, OpenResFile returns −1.

7. The system resource file is opened automatically at system startup and the application resource file when the application is started. These files need not be explicitly opened within the program itself.

8. CloseResFile releases the space occupied by the file's resource map and all its resources.

9. If the file or any of its resources have been changed, the file is updated on the disk before closing.

10. A reference number of 0 denotes the system resource file.

11. Closing the system resource file causes all other open resource files to be closed as well.

12. All open resource files except the system resource file are closed automatically when a program terminates.

Assembly Language Information

Trap macros:

(Pascal) Routine name	(Assembly) Trap macro	Trap word
OpenResFile	_OpenResFile	$A997
CloseResFile	_CloseResFile	$A99A

6.2.2 Current Resource File

Definitions

```
function   CurResFile
             : INTEGER;           {Reference number of current resource file}
procedure  UseResFile
             (refNum : INTEGER);  {Reference number of resource file to be made current}
```

Notes

1. CurResFile returns the reference number of the current resource file; UseResFile makes a designated file the current resource file.

2. The search for a requested resource begins with the current resource file and proceeds backward chronologically through all resource files opened earlier.

3. A reference number of 0 denotes the system resource file.

4. The reference number of the current resource file is available in assembly language in the global variable CurMap.

5. On the Macintosh Plus, ROM-based resources are searched *before* the current resource file; see [6.6.3] for details.

Assembly Language Information

Trap macros:

(Pascal) Routine name	(Assembly) Trap macro	Trap word
CurResFile	_CurResFile	$A994
UseResFile	_UseResFile	$A998

Assembly-language global variables:

Name	Address	Meaning
CurMap	$A5A	Reference number of current resource file
CurApRefNum	$900	Reference number of application resource file
SysMap	$A58	True reference number (not 0) of system resource file
SysResName	$AD8	Name of system resource file (string, maximum 19 characters)
SysMapHndl	$A54	Handle to resource map of system resource file
TopMapHndl	$A50	Handle to resource map of most recently opened (not necessarily current) resource file

6.3   Access to Resources

6.3.1   Getting Resources

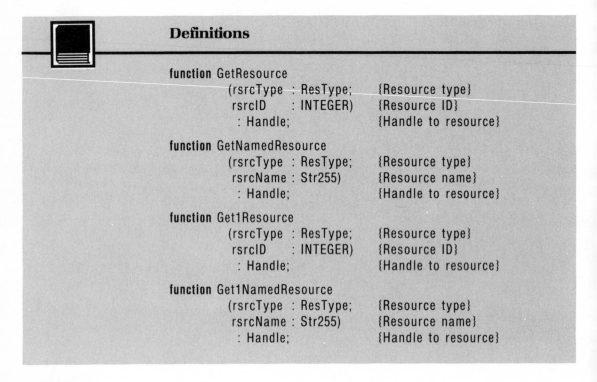

Definitions

```
function GetResource
        (rsrcType : ResType;      {Resource type}
         rsrcID   : INTEGER)      {Resource ID}
         : Handle;                {Handle to resource}

function GetNamedResource
        (rsrcType : ResType;      {Resource type}
         rsrcName : Str255)       {Resource name}
         : Handle;                {Handle to resource}

function Get1Resource
        (rsrcType : ResType;      {Resource type}
         rsrcID   : INTEGER)      {Resource ID}
         : Handle;                {Handle to resource}

function Get1NamedResource
        (rsrcType : ResType;      {Resource type}
         rsrcName : Str255)       {Resource name}
         : Handle;                {Handle to resource}
```

Notes

1. These routines search the list of open resource files for a designated resource, read it into memory if necessary, and return a handle to it.

2. The resource is identified by type and ID number (GetResource, Get1Resource) or type and name (GetNamedResource, Get1NamedResource).

3. GetResource and GetNamedResource begin with the current resource file [6.2.2] and search backward chronologically through all resource files opened earlier. The "one-deep" operations Get1Resource and Get1Named-Resource search the current resource file only.

4. The resource's handle is saved in the file's resource map in memory for future use.

5. If the resource is already in memory, its existing handle is returned.

6. In case of an error, the handle returned is NIL.

7. Automatic loading of resources into memory can be suppressed with SetResLoad [6.3.4]. In this case, an empty handle is returned if the requested resource isn't already in memory. This empty handle is sufficient to identify the resource for routines that operate only on the resource map, such as GetResInfo and SetResInfo [6.4.1], GetResAttrs and SetResAttrs [6.4.2], HomeResFile and MaxSizeRsrc [6.4.3]. It can also be used to load the resource into memory later with LoadResource [6.3.4].

8. If ROMMapInsert [6.6.3] is set, GetResource and GetNamedResource search ROM-based resources before the current resource file; Get1Resource and Get1NamedResource search ROM-based resources only.

9. Get1Resource and Get1NamedResource are available only on the Macintosh Plus.

Assembly Language Information

Trap macros:

(Pascal) Routine name	(Assembly) Trap macro	Trap word
GetResource	_GetResource	$A9A0
GetNamedResource	_GetNamedResource	$A9A1
Get1Resource	_Get1Resource	$A81F
Get1NamedResource	_Get1NamedResource	$A820

6.3.2 Disposing of Resources

Definitions

procedure ReleaseResource
                (theResource : Handle);   {Resource to be released}

procedure DetachResource
                (theResource : Handle);   {Resource to be detached}

Notes

1. ReleaseResource deallocates the space occupied by a resource and removes its handle from its file's resource map in memory. All existing handles to the resource become invalid.

2. DetachResource removes the resource's handle from the resource map, but doesn't deallocate the resource itself. Existing handles remain valid, but are no longer recognized as referring to a resource.

3. In both cases, later attempts to get the resource with GetResource [6.3.1], GetNamedResource [6.3.1], or GetIndResource [6.3.3] (or the corresponding "one-deep routines" Get1Resource [6.3.1], Get1NamedResource [6.3.1], or Get1IndResource [6.3.3]) will cause it to be reread into memory from its resource file and a new handle allocated.

4. Detaching a resource prevents it from being deallocated when its resource file is closed.

5. A resource may not be detached if its ResChanged attribute [6.4.2] is set. Attempting to do so results in the error ResErrAttr [6.6.1].

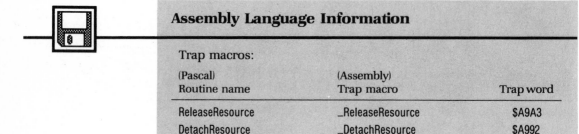

Assembly Language Information

Trap macros:

(Pascal) Routine name	(Assembly) Trap macro	Trap word
ReleaseResource	_ReleaseResource	$A9A3
DetachResource	_DetachResource	$A992

6.3.3   Generating All Resources

Definitions

```
function   CountTypes
             : INTEGER;                        {Total number of resource types}

procedure  GetIndType
             (var rsrcType : ResType;          {Returns next resource type}
              index        : INTEGER);          {Index of desired resource type}

function   CountResources
             (rsrcType : ResType)              {Resource type}
             : INTEGER;                        {Total number of resources of this type}

function   GetIndResource
             (rsrcType : ResType;              {Resource type}
              index    : INTEGER)              {Index (not ID) of desired resource}
             : Handle;                         {Handle to resource}

function   Count1Types
             : INTEGER;                        {Total number of resource types}

procedure  Get1IndType
             (var rsrcType : ResType;          {Returns next resource type}
              index        : INTEGER);          {Index of desired resource type}

function   Count1Resources
             (rsrcType : ResType)              {Resource type}
             : INTEGER;                        {Total number of resources of this type}

function   Get1IndResource
             (rsrcType : ResType;              {Resource type}
              index    : INTEGER)              {Index (not ID) of desired resource}
             : Handle;                         {Handle to resource}
```

Notes

1. These routines are used to iterate through all available resources of a given type or of all types.

2. CountTypes returns the total number of distinct resource types contained in all open resource files. For each value of index from 1 up to this count, GetIndType returns a different resource type in the variable parameter rsrcType.

3. CountResources returns the total number of resources of a given type contained in all open resource files. For each value of index from 1 up to this count, GetIndResource returns a different resource of the designated type.

4. In case of an error, GetIndResource returns NIL.

5. These routines always operate on *all* open resource files, regardless of which one is current.

6. If ROMMapInsert [6.6.3] is set, these routines include ROM-based resources as well as those that reside in open resource files.

7. Count1Types, Get1IndType, Count1Resources, and Get1IndResource work the same way as the first four routines, but apply to the current resource file only (or only to ROM-based resources if ROMMapInsert is set).

8. Count1Types, Get1IndType, Count1Resources, and Get1IndResource are available only on the Macintosh Plus.

9. The trap macros for Get1IndType and Get1IndResource are spelled _Get1IxType and _Get1IxResource.

Assembly Language Information

Trap macros:

(Pascal) Routine name	(Assembly) Trap macro	Trap word
CountTypes	_CountTypes	$A99E
GetIndType	_GetIndType	$A99F
CountResources	_CountResources	$A99C
GetIndResource	_GetIndResource	$A99D
Count1Types	_Count1Types	$A81C
Get1IndType	_Get1IxType	$A80F
Count1Resources	_Count1Resources	$A80D
Get1IndResource	_Get1IxResource	$A80E

6.3.4 Loading Resources

Definitions

```
procedure  SetResLoad
              (onOrOff : BOOLEAN);        {Turn automatic loading on or off?}
procedure  LoadResource
              (theResource : Handle);     {Resource to be loaded}
```

Notes

1. SetResLoad controls whether resources are automatically loaded into memory from their resource files by GetResource [6.3.1], GetNamedResource [6.3.1], and GetIndResource [6.3.3] (or the corresponding "one-deep" routines Get1Resource [6.3.1], Get1NamedResource [6.3.1], and Get1IndResource [6.3.3]).

2. When automatic loading of resources is on, the "get" routines automatically load any requested resource into memory if it isn't already there. When automatic loading is off, they just return an empty handle if the requested resource isn't already in memory.

3. Automatic loading is initially off.

4. Automatic loading overrides the ResPreload attribute of an individual resource [6.4.2]; it forces all resources to be preloaded when their resource file is opened, regardless of whether this attribute is on or off.

5. The flag that controls automatic loading is accessible in machine language as the global variable ResLoad. Set this flag to $FF to turn automatic loading on, $00 to turn it off.

6. Don't turn off automatic loading for any longer than is absolutely necessary, since some parts of the Toolbox depend on it. In particular, make sure you turn it back on before your program terminates, or the Toolbox will be unable to load the code of the program you're exiting to (normally the Finder).

7. LoadResource accepts an empty handle to a resource and loads the resource into memory from its resource file. If the handle isn't empty, LoadResource does nothing.

8. The empty handle may have been returned by GetResource, Get-NamedResource, or GetIndResource (or Get1Resource, Get1NamedResource, or

Get1IndResource) when automatic loading was off, or it may have become empty because the resource it refers to was purged from memory.

9. Call LoadResource before using any handle to a purgeable resource, to make sure the resource is in memory.

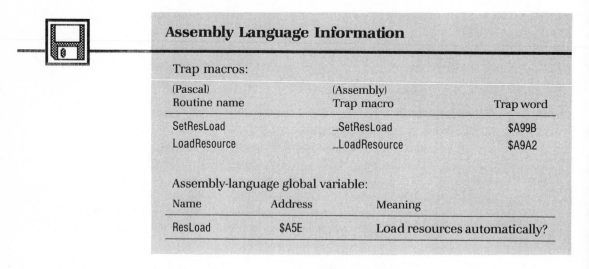

Assembly Language Information

Trap macros:

(Pascal) Routine name	(Assembly) Trap macro	Trap word
SetResLoad	_SetResLoad	$A99B
LoadResource	_LoadResource	$A9A2

Assembly-language global variable:

Name	Address	Meaning
ResLoad	$A5E	Load resources automatically?

6.4   Properties of Resources

6.4.1   Identifying Information

Definitions

```
procedure GetResInfo
          (theResource  : Handle;       {Handle to resource}
           var rsrcID    : INTEGER;     {Returns resource ID}
           var rsrcType  : ResType;     {Returns resource type}
           var rsrcName  : Str255);     {Returns resource name}

procedure SetResInfo
          (theResource  : Handle;       {Handle to resource}
           rsrcID        : INTEGER;     {New resource ID}
           rsrcName      : Str255);     {New resource name}
```

Notes

1. GetResInfo returns the identifying information of a resource (resource type, ID number, and name) via its **var** parameters.

2. SetResInfo sets a resource's ID and name; the resource type can't be changed.

3. The identifying information of a protected resource can't be changed.

4. An empty string as the rsrcName parameter to SetResInfo removes the resource's name, if any; a NIL value leaves the existing name unchanged.

5. Changing the name or ID number of a resource in the system resource file is dangerous, since the Toolbox or other programs may depend on them.

Assembly Language Information

Trap macros:

(Pascal) Routine name	(Assembly) Trap macro	Trap word
GetResInfo	_GetResInfo	$A9A8
SetResInfo	_SetResInfo	$A9A9

6.4.2 Resource Attributes

Definitions

```
function   GetResAttrs
              (theResource : Handle)        {Handle to resource}
                 : INTEGER;                 {Current resource attributes}

procedure  SetResAttrs
              (theResource : Handle;        {Handle to resource}
               newAttrs     : INTEGER);     {New resource attributes}

const
  ResSysHeap   = $0040;                     {Resides in system heap}
  ResPurgeable = $0020;                     {Purgeable from heap}
  ResLocked    = $0010;                     {Locked during heap compaction}
  ResProtected = $0008;                     {Protected from change}
  ResPreload   = $0004;                     {Preload when file opened}
  ResChanged   = $0002;                     {Has been changed in memory}
```

Notes

1. GetResAttrs returns the attributes of a resource; SetResAttrs sets them.

2. The constants for the individual attribute bits can be combined with BitAnd, BitOr, BitXOr, and BitNot [2.2.2] to form any combination of attributes you need.

3. The ResSysHeap attribute tells whether the resource data resides in the system (1) or application (0) heap.

4. The ResPurgeable and ResLocked attributes define the initial settings of these properties when the resource is loaded from the disk—*not* their current settings. To change these properties for a resource already in memory, you must use HLock and HUnlock, HPurge and HNoPurge [3.2.4].

5. A protected resource (ResProtected = 1) can't be removed from its resource file or have its identifying information changed. Unlike other attributes, changes in the ResProtected attribute take effect immediately.

6. The ResPreload attribute causes a resource to be loaded into memory immediately when its resource file is opened, instead of waiting to be loaded explicitly with GetResource [6.3.1], GetNamedResource [6.3.1], GetIndResource [6.3.3], or LoadResource [6.3.4] (or the "one-deep" routines Get1Resource [6.3.1], Get1NamedResource [6.3.1], or Get1IndResource [6.3.3]).

7. The ResPreload attribute is overridden by SetResLoad [6.3.4]. Resources are always preloaded when automatic loading is on, regardless of the setting of this attribute.

8. The ResChanged attribute tells whether a resource has been changed in memory and so must be written out to the disk when its resource file is updated.

9. The assembly-language constants ResSysHeap, ResPurgeable, etc. (below) are bit numbers for use with the BTST, BSET, BCLR, and BCHG instructions.

10. Always use ChangedResource [6.5.2] to mark a resource as changed, never SetResAttrs. Make sure all calls to SetResAttrs preserve the existing value of the ResChanged attribute. In assembly language, the constant RCBMask is a mask to be used for this purpose.

Assembly Language Information

Trap macros:

(Pascal) Routine name	(Assembly) Trap macro	Trap word
GetResAttrs	_GetResAttrs	$A9A6
SetResAttrs	_SetResAttrs	$A9A7

Bit numbers of resource attributes:

Name	Value	Meaning
ResSysHeap	6	Resides in system heap
ResPurgeable	5	Purgeable from heap
ResLocked	4	Locked during compaction
ResProtected	3	Protected from change
ResPreload	2	Preload when file opened
ResChanged	1	Has been changed in memory

Assembly-language constant:

Name	Value	Meaning
RCBMask	$FD	Mask for ResChanged bit

6.4.3   Other Properties

Definitions

```
function SizeResource
        (theResource : Handle)   {Handle to resource}
           : LONGINT;            {Size of resource data, in bytes}

function MaxSizeRsrc
        (theResource : Handle)   {Handle to resource}
           : LONGINT;            {Approximate size of resource data, in bytes}

function HomeResFile
        (theResource : Handle)   {Handle to resource}
           : INTEGER;            {Reference number of home resource file}
```

Notes

1. SizeResource returns the size of a resource's data, in bytes.

2. The resource need not be in memory; its size will be read from the resource file if necessary.

3. The trap macro for SizeResource is spelled _SizeRsrc.

4. MaxSizeRsrc quickly finds the approximate size of a resource's data.

5. The value returned is the number of bytes between the beginning of this resource's data and the beginning of the next resource following it in the resource file. Since the needed information is found in the file's resource map (which is always immediately available in memory), MaxSizeRsrc is often faster than SizeResource (which may have to read in the resource itself from the disk).

6. The true size of the resource may be smaller than the value returned by MaxSizeRsrc, but can never be bigger. If absolute accuracy is essential, use SizeResource instead.

7. MaxSizeRsrc is available only on the Macintosh Plus.

8. HomeResFile returns the reference number of the resource file that contains a given resource.

9. A reference number of 0 denotes the system resource file; 1 denotes a ROM-based resource [6.6.3].

10. In case of an error, all three functions return −1.

Assembly Language Information

Trap macros:

(Pascal) Routine name	(Assembly) Trap macro	Trap word
SizeResource	_SizeRsrc	$A9A5
MaxSizeRsrc	_MaxSizeRsrc	$A821
HomeResFile	_HomeResFile	$A9A4

6.5 Modifying Resources

6.5.1 Creating Resource Files

Definitions

```
procedure  CreateResFile
              (fileName : Str255);     {Name of resource file to be created}
```

Notes

1. CreateResFile creates a new, empty resource file with the given name.
2. The new file is not opened and no reference number is returned; call OpenResFile [6.2.1] to get a reference number for the file.
3. If no file of the specified name exists, a new one is created with both its data and resource forks empty.
4. If there's already a file of this name with no resource fork, it is given one.
5. If there's already a file of this name with a nonempty resource fork, an error is posted.

Assembly Language Information

Trap macro:

(Pascal) Routine name	(Assembly) Trap macro	Trap word
CreateResFile	_CreateResFile	$A9B1

6.5.2   Marking Changed Resources

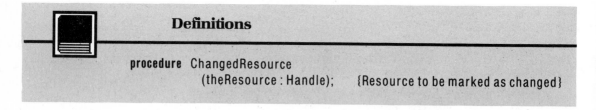

Definitions

```
procedure  ChangedResource
              (theResource : Handle);    {Resource to be marked as changed}
```

Notes

1. ChangedResource marks a resource as changed, so that it will be written out to its resource file the next time the file is updated.

2. Always use ChangedResource to mark a resource as changed; never change the ResChanged attribute yourself with SetResAttrs [6.4.2].

3. ChangedResource checks to see whether there's enough disk space to write out the new version of the resource to its file. If not, it will post the error code DskFulErr [6.6.1] and will *not* set the resource's ResChanged attribute. Consequently, when the resource file is later updated, the resource will not be written out; no error will be reported at that time. To detect this problem, you must check for an error at the time you mark the resource as changed, by following ChangedResource with a call to ResError [6.6.1].

Assembly Language Information

Trap macro:

(Pascal) Routine name	(Assembly) Trap macro	Trap word
ChangedResource	_ChangedResource	$A9AA

6.5.3 Adding and Removing Resources

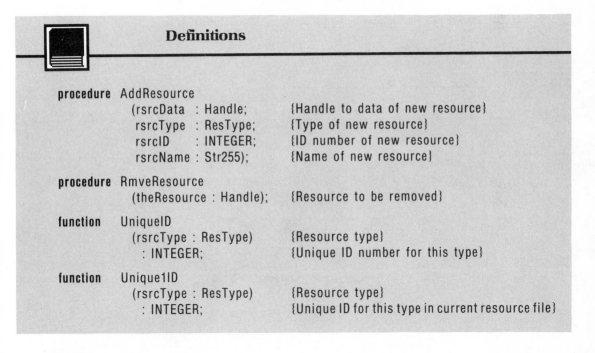

Definitions

```
procedure AddResource
        (rsrcData  : Handle;        {Handle to data of new resource}
         rsrcType  : ResType;       {Type of new resource}
         rsrcID    : INTEGER;       {ID number of new resource}
         rsrcName : Str255);        {Name of new resource}

procedure RmveResource
        (theResource : Handle);     {Resource to be removed}

function UniqueID
        (rsrcType : ResType)        {Resource type}
          : INTEGER;                {Unique ID number for this type}

function Unique1ID
        (rsrcType : ResType)        {Resource type}
          : INTEGER;                {Unique ID for this type in current resource file}
```

Notes

1. AddResource adds a new resource to the current resource file; RmveResource removes an existing resource.

2. The resource affected is automatically marked as changed, so that the change will be incorporated permanently on the disk the next time the resource file is updated.

3. RmveResource doesn't deallocate the resource's data from the heap; do it yourself with DisposHandle [3.2.2].

4. AddResource adds a new resource to the current resource file, with the resource data given by rsrcData and the identifying information given by rsrcType, rsrcID, and rsrcName. It's an error if rsrcData is already a handle to an existing resource.

5. RmveResource removes an existing resource from the current resource file. It's an error if theResource doesn't belong to the current file.

6. Removing a resource from the system resource file is dangerous, since other programs and parts of the Toolbox may depend on it.

7. UniqueID returns a positive ID number for a new resource that doesn't conflict with that of any existing resource of the given type in any open resource file. Unique1ID returns an ID number that's unique with respect to the current resource file [6.2.2] only.

8. Unique1ID is available only on the Macintosh Plus.

Assembly Language Information

Trap macros:

(Pascal) Routine name	(Assembly) Trap macro	Trap word
AddResource	_AddResource	$A9AB
RmveResource	_RmveResource	$A9AD
UniqueID	_UniqueID	$A9C1
Unique1ID	_Unique1ID	$A810

6.5.4   Updating Resource Files

Definitions

```
procedure  UpdateResFile
              (refNum : INTEGER);        {Reference number of resource file to be updated}
procedure  WriteResource
              (theResource : Handle);    {Resource to be written out}
```

Notes

1. UpdateResFile writes out a new version of the designated resource file on the disk, incorporating all changes since the file was last opened or updated.

2. All resources marked as changed (ResChanged = 1) are written out.

3. If at least one resource is marked as changed, the file's entire resource map is written out.

4. The updated version of the file is compacted to remove any empty space resulting from changes in the file.

5. If the file's MapReadOnly attribute [6.6.2] is set, UpdateResFile will post the error code MapReadErr [6.6.1].

6. A reference number of 0 designates the system resource file.

7. Closing a resource file updates it automatically.

8. WriteResource writes out a single resource to the disk if the resource has been changed.

9. If the resource's ResChanged attribute [6.4.2] is 1, the resource data is written to its file and ResChanged is cleared to 0; if ResChanged is already 0, WriteResource does nothing.

10. Protected resources are never written out to the disk by either UpdateResFile or WriteResource.

11. If a resource to be written out by either UpdateResFile or WriteResource has been purged, the resource data written to the file will be empty (zero-length).

Assembly Language Information

Trap macros:

(Pascal) Routine name	(Assembly) Trap macro	Trap word
UpdateResFile	_UpdateResFile	$A999
WriteResource	_WriteResource	$A9B0

6.5.5   Purge Checking

Definitions

```
procedure  SetResPurge
               (onOrOff : BOOLEAN);    {Turn purge checking on or off?}
```

Notes

1. SetResPurge is used to turn purge checking on or off.

2. When purge checking is on, any block about to be purged from the heap is checked to see if it's a changed resource; if so, it's written out to its resource file before being purged.

3. When purge checking is off, no special checking is performed when a block is purged.

4. Purge checking is initially off.

Assembly Language Information

Trap macro:

(Pascal) Routine name	(Assembly) Trap macro	Trap word
SetResPurge	_SetResPurge	$A993

6.6 Nuts and Bolts

6.6.1 Error Reporting

Definitions

```
function ResError
       : INTEGER;          {Result code from last resource-related operation}

const
  NoErr         =     0;   {No error; all is well}
  ResNotFound   = −192;    {Resource not found}
  ResFNotFound  = −193;    {Resource file not found}
  AddResFailed  = −194;    {AddResource failed}
  RmvResFailed  = −196;    {RmveResource failed}
  ResErrAttr    = −198;    {Operation prohibited by resource attribute}
  MapReadErr    = −199;    {Error reading resource map}
  DskFulErr     = −34;     {Disk full}
```

Notes

1. ResError returns the result code from the last resource-related procedure or function call.

2. The result code returned in the normal case is 0 (NoErr). Any nonzero result code denotes an error.

3. Error codes listed here are only those directly related to resources. Errors from other parts of the Toolbox can also occur in the course of resource-related operations, and will be reported by ResError.

4. In assembly language, the result code is also available in the global variable ResErr.

Assembly Language Information

Trap macro:

(Pascal) Routine name	(Assembly) Trap macro	Trap word
ResError	_ResError	$A9AF

Result codes:

Name	Value	Meaning
NoErr	0	No error; all is well
ResNotFound	−192	Resource not found
ResFNotFound	−193	Resource file not found
AddResFailed	−194	AddResource failed
RmvResFailed	−196	RmveResource failed
ResErrAttr	−198	Operation prohibited by resource attribute
MapReadErr	−199	Error reading resource map
DskFulErr	−34	Disk full

Assembly-language global variable:

Name	Address	Meaning
ResErr	$A60	Result code from last resource-related call

6.6.2 Resource File Attributes

Definitions

```
function   GetResFileAttrs
              (refNum : INTEGER)      {Reference number of resource file}
              : INTEGER;              {Current resource file attributes}

procedure  SetResFileAttrs
              (refNum   : INTEGER;    {Reference number of resource file}
              newAttrs : INTEGER);    {New resource file attributes}

const
   MapReadOnly = 128;                 {No changes allowed}
   MapCompact  = 64;                  {Compact file when updated}
   MapChanged  = 32;                  {Write resource map when updated}
```

Notes

1. GetResFileAttrs returns the current attributes of a resource file; SetResFileAttrs changes them.

2. The MapReadOnly attribute prevents the file from being updated. No changes made to the file or its resources in memory will be written out to the disk.

3. MapCompact tells the Toolbox to compact the file when it's updated, in order to squeeze out unused space.

4. The MapCompact attribute is set automatically when a resource is removed from the file or when the data of a resource is lengthened, but not when it's shortened.

5. MapChanged tells the Toolbox to write out the file's resource map when the file is updated.

6. The MapChanged attribute is set automatically when a resource is added to or removed from the file or when any resource is marked as changed.

7. The assembly-language constants MapReadOnly, MapCompact, and Map-Changed (below) are bit numbers for use with the BTST, BSET, BCLR, and BCHG instructions.

Assembly Language Information

Trap macros:

(Pascal) Routine name	(Assembly) Trap macro	Trap word
GetResFileAttrs	_GetResFileAttrs	$A9F6
SetResFileAttrs	_SetResFileAttrs	$A9F7

Bit numbers of resource file attributes:

Name	Value	Meaning
MapReadOnly	7	No changes allowed
MapCompact	6	Compact file when updated
MapChanged	5	Write resource map when updated

6.6.3 ROM-Based Resources

Resource Type	Resource ID	Description
'CURS'	1	I-beam cursor [II:2.5.2, II:2.9.1]
	2	Cross cursor [II:2.5.2, II:2.9.1]
	3	Plus-sign cursor [II:2.5.2, II:2.9.1]
	4	Wristwatch cursor [II:2.5.2, II:2.9.1]
'FONT'	0	Name of system font [8.2.1, 8.4.5]
	12	System font [8.2.1, 8.4.5]
'WDEF'	0	Standard window definition function
'MDEF'	0	Standard menu definition procedure
'PACK'	4	Floating-Point Arithmetic Package [7.2.1, 7.5.2]
	5	Transcendental Functions Package [7.2.1, 7.5.2]
	7	Binary/Decimal Conversion Package [7.2.1, 7.5.2]
'DRVR'	2	Printer driver shell (.Print) [7.5.5]
	3	Sound driver (.Sound) [7.5.5]
	4	Disk driver (.Sony) [7.5.5]
	9	AppleTalk driver, Macintosh Packet Protocol (.MPP) [7.5.5]
	10	AppleTalk driver, AppleTalk Transaction Protocol (.ATP) [7.5.5]
'SERD'	0	Serial drivers (.AIn, .AOut, .BIn, .BOut) [7.5.5]

Notes

1. On a Macintosh Plus, the standard system resources listed in the table reside in ROM, rather than in the disk-based system resource file.

2. The assembly-language global flag ROMMapInsert controls whether the ROM-based resources are to be included in the next resource-related operation. If this flag is TRUE ($FF), the operation applies first to the ROM-based resources, then to the list of open resource files, beginning with the current resource file [6.2.2]. If the flag is FALSE ($00), the ROM-based resources are skipped and the operation begins with the current resource file.

3. One-deep routines (Get1Resource, Get1NamedResource [6.3.1], Count1Types, Get1IndType, Count1Resources, Get1IndResource [6.3.3], and Unique1ID [6.5.3]) apply only to the ROM-based resources if ROMMapInsert is TRUE. If the flag is FALSE, these routines skip the ROM-based resources and apply to the current resource file instead.

4. When ROMMapInsert is TRUE, the assembly-language flag TmpResLoad controls automatic resource loading for the next operation only, overriding the global ResLoad flag [6.3.4]. The previous ResLoad setting is restored after the operation.

5. If ROMMapInsert is FALSE, TmpResLoad is ignored.

6. Both ROMMapInsert and TmpResLoad are "one-shot" flags: they're automatically cleared to FALSE ($00) after each resource operation, and must be explicitly set again before the next operation if they are to remain in effect.

7. Both flags are one byte in length.

8. The Toolbox always sets ROMMapInsert and TmpResLoad to TRUE before performing any resource operation on its own behalf; on operations requested by your program, both flags are normally FALSE. In assembly language, you can set the flags for yourself if you wish before the operation. (There is no straightforward way to set these flags in Pascal.)

9. The foregoing notes apply to the Macintosh Plus only. On earlier models, all system resources reside in the system resource file on the disk; there are no ROM-based resources and no ROMMapInsert and TmpResLoad flags. Attempting to store into these locations on an earlier-model Macintosh will destroy information in the system heap, with unpredictable but predictably catastrophic results.

Assembly Language Information

Assembly-language global variables (Macintosh Plus only):

Name	Address	Meaning
ROMMapInsert	$B9E	Include ROM-based resources in search? (1 byte)
TmpResLoad	$B9F	Load resources automatically just this once? (1 byte)

CHAPTER

7

Getting Loaded

Now that we know something about resources, we're ready to discuss the way programs are started up and how code is loaded into memory for execution. Most of the information in this chapter is offered strictly for purposes of "curriculum enrichment"; you don't really need to know it in order to write small, straightforward application programs. You'll find it useful, however, if you want to produce "stand-alone" programs that can be started directly from the Finder, or define your own icons to stand for your program and its files on the Finder desktop, or support cut-and-paste editing between your program and other programs or desk accessories. If you're in a hurry and want to skip most of this chapter, you should at least read the section on packages, since you'll need it to understand certain other topics discussed elsewhere in the book, such as the Standard File Package (Volume Two, Chapter 8).

Code Segments

We mentioned in the last chapter that the code of an application program is stored in the application's own resource file. The resources containing it are called *code segments*, and have resource type 'CODE' [7.5.1]. Their resource data consists mainly of executable machine-language code, ready to be loaded into memory and run. (There's also a short *segment header* that we'll be discussing later.) The entire program can be contained in a single code segment, or it can be divided into as many separate segments as you like.

Code segments are meaningful only for programs that are assembled or compiled directly into executable machine language. If you're doing your programming in an interpreter-based system, the program has no machine code as such, so there aren't any code segments.

The main advantage of code segments is that they allow you to divide a program into separate pieces that don't all have to be in memory at once. Like any resource, a code segment can be read into memory from the disk when needed and then purged when you're finished with it, freeing the space for another use. This means you can isolate seldom-used portions of your program in segments of their own, so that they won't take up precious memory space when they're not actually in use. It also means you can write programs bigger than the Macintosh's available memory, by breaking them into segments that can be "swapped" in and out as needed.

Exactly how you go about breaking your program into segments depends on the language you're writing in; you'll have to consult your language documentation for details. Typically you give each segment a name, and switch from one segment to another with a compilation-time directive of some sort. Code will then be compiled (or assembled) into the segment you name until you switch to another. Such segment names are meaningful only at compilation time, however; the Toolbox just identifies each segment by its resource ID, known as a *segment number*. The compiler will assign a number to correspond to each segment name, then place the segment's code in a 'CODE' resource with that number as its resource ID. (If you never mention segments at all, the whole program will be placed in a single segment by default.)

The Jump Table

Calls from one code segment to another are made through a *jump table* in RAM. The jump table is part of your program's application global space, or "A5 world," which we discussed in Chapter 3. The contents and organization of the application global space are repeated for reference in Figure 7-1.

The information needed to set up the application global space is stored in a special 'CODE' resource with ID number 0, created automatically by the language software when the program is compiled or assembled. Every stand-alone program must have a

Low memory addresses

Figure 7-1 Application global space

Figure 7-2 Contents of segment 0

segment 0 in addition to the one or more segments holding the actual code. Figure 7-2 shows the format of this special segment, which includes the following information:

- The "above A5" size: the total number of bytes to be reserved between the beginning of the screen buffer (or the alternate sound buffer) and the base address in register A5, including both the application parameters and the jump table
- The "below A5" size: the number of bytes to be reserved for application globals between the A5 address and the base of the stack
- The length of the jump table in bytes
- The length of the application parameters (normally 32 bytes), which is also the offset from the A5 address to the beginning of the jump table
- The contents of the jump table

When a program is started up, the Toolbox reads in this information from segment 0 and uses it to reserve the memory needed for the application global space, set up the jump table, initialize register A5, and position the base of the stack.

The jump table handles routine calls from one segment to another. It contains one 8-byte entry for every routine in the program that can be called from a segment other than the one it's in; routines that are called only from within the same segment are not included. The first entry in the table corresponds to the program's *main entry point*, where execution begins when the program is first started up. Initially only the segment containing this main entry point (the *main segment*) is loaded into memory; other segments will be read in only when they're actually needed.

When a segment is not in memory, the jump table entry for each of its routines has the form shown in Figure 7-3a. The first 2 bytes give the relative location of the routine's entry point within the segment, as an offset from the beginning of the segment's

a. Unloaded state

| Offset from beginning of segment
(2 bytes) |
| Machine instruction to push
segment number onto stack
(4 bytes) |
| LoadSeg trap
(2 bytes) |

b. Loaded state

| Segment number
(2 bytes) |
| Machine instruction to jump
to routine in memory

(6 bytes) |

Figure 7-3 Jump table entry

code. This is followed by 6 bytes of actual machine instructions that push the segment number onto the stack as a parameter and then trap to the Toolbox routine LoadSeg [7.1.2]. Each "external reference" to this routine from another segment will be represented in machine code by a subroutine jump to these instructions in the jump table entry. They in turn call LoadSeg, which reads in the code segment containing the routine from the application resource file and locks it into the heap. Then it uses the offset in the first 2 bytes of the table entry to locate the routine within the segment and jump to it.

Once the segment has been loaded into memory, there's no need to load it again the next time. So before jumping to the routine, LoadSeg "patches" the jump table entries for all routines in the segment into the form shown in Figure 7-3b. Here the first 2 bytes of the entry hold the segment number and the last 6 contain a direct jump instruction to the beginning of the routine in memory. Subsequent calls to any routine in the segment will thus be directed straight to the proper memory address, bypassing the LoadSeg call.

The information about which entries in the jump table belong to a given segment (and so must be patched when the segment is loaded) is found in a 4-byte *segment header* at the beginning of the segment itself (see Figure 7-4). The first 2 bytes of the header give the offset in bytes from the start of the jump table to the first entry for this segment; the last 2 bytes give the number of entries belonging to the segment.

```
Jump table offset of first routine in segment
                   ( 2 bytes)
Number of jump table entries for segment
                   ( 2 bytes)
```

Figure 7-4 Segment header

When a segment is no longer needed in memory, you release it by calling UnloadSeg [7.1.2]. You identify the segment by passing a pointer to any of its routines; UnloadSeg marks the segment purgeable to free the heap space it occupies, and patches its jump table entries back to the original "unloaded" state of Figure 7-3a. The next time you call one of the segment's routines, LoadSeg will again be called to load it back into memory from the resource file.

> Notice that you have to call UnloadSeg for yourself, whereas LoadSeg is always called implicitly, by way of the instructions in a jump table entry, when you try to call a routine in an unloaded segment. In fact, LoadSeg won't work properly *unless* it's called through the jump table; you should never try to call it explicitly from within your own program.

Packages

Another kind of code-containing resource, similar in some ways to a code segment, is a *package*. Like a code segment, a package is a collection of routines grouped together as a unit, which reside in a resource file and are loaded into memory only when needed. It differs from a code segment, however, in that it isn't a part of any particular program: it's a set of general-purpose routines that are available for any program to use, and normally resides in the system resource file (or in ROM on a Macintosh Plus) rather than in a program's own application resource file.

The Toolbox can accommodate as many as eight separate packages, referred to by *package numbers* from 0 to 7. (The Macintosh Plus Toolbox can handle up to sixteen packages, numbered 0 to 15.) The package number is simply the resource ID of the package in the system resource file; its resource type is 'PACK' [7.5.2]. The standard System file found on Macintosh software disks includes the following standard packages:

- The *List Manager Package* (package number 0) displays scrollable lists of items from which the user can choose with the mouse (like the one used in selecting files to be read from the disk).

- The *Disk Initialization Package* (package number 2) takes corrective action when an unreadable disk is inserted into the disk drive, usually by initializing the disk.

- The *Standard File Package* (package number 3) provides a convenient, standard way for the user to supply file names for input/output operations.

- The *Floating-Point Arithmetic Package* (package number 4) performs arithmetic on floating-point numbers in accordance with the "IEEE standard" published by the Institute of Electrical and Electronic Engineers, using the Standard Apple Numeric Environment (SANE).

- The *Transcendental Functions Package* (package number 5) calculates various transcendental functions on floating-point numbers, such as logarithms, exponentials, trigonometric functions, compound interest, and discounted value.

- The *International Utilities Package* (package number 6) helps a program conform to the prevailing conventions of different countries in such matters as formatting of numbers, dates, times, and currency; use of metric units; and alphabetization of foreign-language accents, diacriticals, and ligatures.

- The *Binary/Decimal Conversion Package* (package number 7) converts numbers between their internal binary format and their external representation as strings of decimal digits.

Only the Disk Initialization [II:8.4], Standard File [II:8.3], and Binary/Decimal Conversion [2.3.7] packages are covered in Volumes One and Two of this book. For information on the List Manager Package, see Volume Three; for the others, see Apple's *Inside Macintosh* manual. Package numbers 1 and 8–15 are reserved for future expansion.

> The List Manager Package (number 0) was introduced at the same time as the Macintosh Plus, and is available only in versions 3.0 or greater of the System file. Also, on the Plus, the Floating-Point Arithmetic, Transcendental Functions, and Binary/Decimal Conversion packages (numbers 4, 5, and 7) reside in ROM instead of the System file.

At the machine-language level, packages are called via the Toolbox "package traps," _Pack0 to _Pack15 [7.2.1]. To call a routine that belongs to a package, you push the routine's parameters onto the stack, then push an integer *routine selector* to identify the particular routine you want within the package, and finally execute the trap corresponding to the package the routine belongs to (for instance, _Pack7 for the Binary/Decimal Conversion Package). If the package isn't already in memory, the Toolbox reads it in from the resource file and locks it into the heap. Then it jumps to the routine, using the routine selector to look up its address within the package in a small table at the beginning of the package itself.

Ordinarily, though, you needn't worry about routine selectors and package traps. The Pascal interface to the Toolbox includes a unit named PackIntf for calling the routines in the standard packages. This unit contains "glue routines" to convert your Pascal calls into the proper low-level trap sequences, as described above. By including PackIntf in your program with a **uses** declaration (or a $i directive, or whatever method your particular Pascal System requires), you can call all the package routines in the normal way, as if they were part of the Toolbox proper. Thus you needn't ever think about whether a given routine resides in ROM or in a package on the disk. Similarly in assembly language, the interface file PackMacs defines macros for calling all the standard package routines. You simply push the routine's parameters onto the stack and execute the macro for that routine; the macro pushes the routine selector and executes the package trap for you.

Signatures and File Types

The normal way for a user to start up an application program is to open a file in the Finder, either by selecting the file's icon with the mouse and choosing the Open command from the Finder's File menu, or by the equivalent shortcut of double-clicking the icon. At this point one of three things may happen:

- If the selected file contains an application program, the Finder starts up the program.
- If the file contains a document belonging to some application program, the Finder starts up that program.
- If the file isn't identified as belonging to a particular application program, or if the program it belongs to isn't available on the disk, the Finder displays an alert message: An application can't be found for this document.

The Finder decides what to do by looking at two special pieces of information that are associated with every file on the disk, the *file type* and *creator signature* [7.3.1]. Both of these are four-character strings, just like a resource type. Whenever a program creates a new file, it must supply a file type and creator signature.

The Finder keeps track of each file's type and creator (along with other items such as the location of the file's icon on the screen) in a special *desktop file* for each disk. The desktop file is invisible to the user: the Finder never displays an icon for it on the screen, so there's no danger of the user's destroying or damaging it. The Toolbox routine GetFInfo [7.3.3] returns all the Finder information associated with a given file, summarized in a *Finder information record* [7.3.2]. SetFInfo [7.3.3] accepts a Finder information record as a parameter and sets the file's Finder information accordingly.

The creator signature attached to a file tells the Finder what program the file belongs to, so it can start up that program when the user opens the file. Every application program has its own four-character signature: for example, the signature of the Mac-Paint graphics editor is 'MPNT'. If you were writing an interactive music editor named Allegro, you might give it the signature 'BRIO'.

A program ordinarily puts its own signature on any file it creates, but in some cases you may want to use another program's signature instead. For instance, a program that creates a MacPaint drawing should put MacPaint's signature on it, so that the Finder will start up MacPaint when the user opens the file. A file that is not to be opened at all from the Finder should carry the creator signature '????'.

The data files that a program works on are called *document files*, or simply *documents*. Most programs just deal with one particular type of document, although it's possible to support several distinct document types in the same program, containing different kinds of information to be used for different purposes. Each kind of document is identified by its own four-character file type. For instance, MacPaint documents have file type 'PNTG' (for "painting"); a document produced by our hypothetical music editor Allegro, representing a musical score, might have file type 'SCOR'. In Volume Two, we'll learn how to use the Standard File Package to offer the user a scrollable list of files from which to select with the mouse. In doing this, you can designate one or more specific file types to be listed. Thus you can use different file types to restrict the user's choice to only those files that are appropriate in a given situation.

To avoid conflicts, all "serious" Macintosh applications are supposed to be registered with Apple's Macintosh Technical Support group so they can be assigned unique signatures and file types. Unless you're a professional software developer, you probably won't want to go to this extreme—but you should still take care not to use a signature or file type that's already used by another program or that conflicts with an existing resource type.

There are two standard file types of particular interest. A file containing a stand-alone program to be started from the Finder should be of type 'APPL' (for "application") and carry the program's own signature as its creator. File type 'TEXT' identifies a *text file* consisting of a stream of "raw" text characters, without any additional formatting or other information. This type of file is useful for exchanging pure text between different programs: for instance, MacWrite writes a text file when it's asked to save a document with the Text Only option, and will accept text files written by another program.

Finder Startup Information

When the user selects and opens one or more document files, the Finder examines their creator signatures to find out what application program they belong to. If the signatures aren't all the same, it just puts up an alert message (Please open only documents of the same kind); otherwise it starts up the designated application, passing it a handle to a table of *startup information* [7.3.4] identifying which documents were selected. Recall from Chapter 3 that this *startup handle* is one of the program's application parameters, located at address 16(A5) in the application global space (that is, at an offset of 16 bytes from the base address kept in register A5). The program can then use the startup handle to find out which document files to open on first starting up.

One way to access the startup information is with the Toolbox routine GetAppParms [7.3.4]. This returns a copy of the startup handle, along with the name and file reference number of your program's application resource file. However, you're then faced with the problem of deciphering the startup information to find out which documents to open—an awkward task in Pascal, since the startup information is a variable-length data structure that can't be properly described in a Pascal type declaration.

It's generally more convenient to use CountAppFiles and GetApp-Files, letting the Toolbox parse the startup information for you. CountAppFiles [7.3.4] tells you the number of document files to be opened. It also returns an integer "message" telling whether the user chose the Finder's Open command after selecting the documents (in which case you should open them for work in the usual way) or whether they were opened with the Finder's Print command (in which case you should just print each of the selected documents and then exit back to the Finder). The subject of printing is covered in Volume Three.

Once you know how many documents there are, you use GetAppFiles [7.3.4] to find out their names. GetAppFiles accepts an index number as a parameter, ranging from 1 up to the number of documents reported by CountAppFiles. For each index value, it returns an information record of type AppFile [7.3.4] giving the document's file name, file type, and other identifying information. After opening (or printing) each file, you should call ClrAppFiles [7.3.4] to notify the Finder that the file has been duly processed. Putting all this together, your startup code should run something like this:

```
CountAppFiles (openOrPrint, nFiles);
for index := 1 to nFiles do
  begin
    GetAppFiles (index, infoRecord);
    if openOrPrint = AppOpen then
      with infoRecord do
        {Open document for work}
    else
      with infoRecord do
        {Open and print document};
    ClrAppFiles (index)
  end;
if openOrPrint = AppPrint then
  ExitToShell
```

(ExitToShell [7.1.3] terminates the program and starts up the Finder in its place. This routine is needed only for taking an immediate exit from somewhere in the middle of the program, as in this example; there's no need to call it when the program terminates in the normal way, by "falling out the bottom" of its main program body.)

Finder Resources

A program can provide its own icons to stand for its files on the Finder desktop. There can be a separate icon for each distinct file type the program works with, as well as one for the application file (file type 'APPL') containing the program itself. The icons and their association with the various file types are defined by a set of *Finder resources* in the program's application resource file. If a program doesn't provide its own file icons, the Finder will use the standard ones shown in Figure 7-5 for the application file and its documents.

Every stand-alone program, whether it defines its own file icons or not, must have a special resource called an *autograph* in its resource file. The resource type of the autograph is always the same as the program's own signature; by convention, its resource ID should be 0. Whenever the program is copied from one disk to

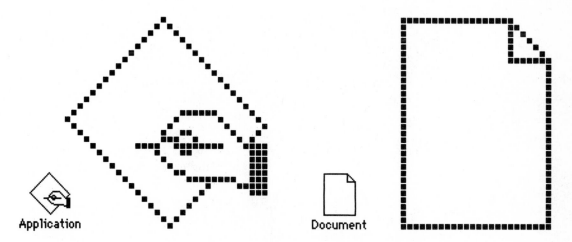

Figure 7-5 Standard file icons

another, the Finder will copy its autograph resource into the desktop file on the new disk. The sole purpose of the autograph is to serve as the program's representative in the desktop file.

The Finder never looks at the autograph's resource data, so you can use it for any purpose you like. Typically it's used to hold a string identifying the version of the program, such as

Allegro version 2.0, 8 November 1984

(For this reason, the autograph is sometimes referred to as the program's "version data" resource.) Notice that an autograph resource is *required* for every stand-alone application file; the rest of the Finder resources discussed in this section are optional.

Every file icon that a program defines is represented in the application resource file by an *icon list* resource of type 'ICN#' [5.5.4]. The icon list must contain exactly two icons of 32 by 32 bits each. The first is the file icon itself and the second is a mask telling the Finder how to draw the icon against the existing background on the screen. A white (0) bit in the mask means to leave the background pixel unchanged at that position; a black (1) bit means to replace it with the corresponding pixel of the file icon. The mask usually just consists of the icon's outline, filled in with solid black: for example, Figure 7-6 shows a possible application and document icon and their masks for our music editor.

The connection between a file type and its icon is established by a *file reference* resource of type 'FREF' [7.5.3]. The resource data consists of the four-character file type and the resource ID of the corresponding icon list. (For the icon representing the application file itself, the file type would of course be 'APPL').

Actually, the ID number of the icon list as given in a file reference isn't necessarily the same as its true resource ID in the application resource file. The translation from this "local ID" to the actual resource ID is given by yet another Finder resource called a *bundle* (resource type 'BNDL' [7.5.4]). Any program that defines its own file icons must include a bundle resource to tie all of its other Finder resources together. The bundle gives the program's signature and the ID number of its autograph resource, then goes on to define a series of correspondences between local and actual resource IDs for any number of resource types. The other Finder resources can then refer to each other by their local IDs; the bundle tells the Finder the actual IDs under which to look for them in the application file.

Application icon

Application mask

Document icon

Document mask

Figure 7-6 File icons and masks

When a program is copied from one disk to another, its Finder-related resources have to travel along with it. The program's *bundle bit* tells the Finder whether there are any such resources that need to be copied (other than the autograph, which must always be present). The bundle bit is one of the bits in the fdFlags field of the Finder information record [7.3.2]. If it's set, the Finder will copy the program's bundle resource to the desktop file on the new disk, along with any other Finder resources that are identified in the bundle. If the bundle bit isn't set, none of the program's Finder resources will be installed in the new disk's desktop file.

Using local IDs allows the Finder to resolve ("arbitrate") conflicts among different programs. If two programs use the same IDs for their file icons or other Finder resources, the Finder can avoid a conflict by changing the actual IDs for one of the programs when it copies the resources to a disk's desktop file. It can then adjust the actual IDs given in the bundle resource to reflect the change, without affecting the local IDs that the resources use to refer to one another.

The format of a bundle resource is general enough to define local IDs for any number of resource types. At present, bundles are useful only for file references ('FREF') and icon lists ('ICN#'), but the same mechanism may eventually be used for other purposes as well.

As an example, recall that our music editor Allegro has the signature 'BRIO' and that it works with document files of type 'SCOR'. The program might then have the following Finder resources in its application resource file:

- An autograph resource (resource type 'BRIO', ID 0) containing a string identifying the program version and date
- Two file references (resource type 'FREF', IDs 1000 and 1001) associating file types 'APPL' and 'SCOR' with icon lists 0 and 1, respectively
- Two icon lists (resource type 'ICN#', IDs 1000 and 1001) containing the icons and associated masks for the two file types
- A bundle (resource type 'BNDL', ID 0) giving the type and ID of the autograph resource ('BRIO', 0) and associating the local icon-list IDs 0 and 1 with actual IDs 1000 and 1001

Drivers and Desk Accessories

The Macintosh can communicate with a variety of input/output devices, some of them built in (screen, speaker, disk drive), others peripheral and connected via cables (printer, modem, hard disk). Since each device has its own characteristics and peculiarities, a certain amount of specialized knowledge is needed to communicate with it. This "expertise" about a particular device is isolated in a piece of low-level software called a *device driver*. Each different kind of I/O device has its own driver; the rest of the system communicates with the device through the driver.

The drivers for devices that are built into the Macintosh are stored permanently in ROM, where they're always available. These include the *sound driver*, the *disk driver* for the standard Sony disk drive, and the *serial driver* for communicating through the serial ports on the back of the machine. Other drivers are stored in resource files under resource type 'DRVR' [7.5.5], and are loaded into RAM only when needed; one important example of such a RAM-based driver is the *printer driver*.

> The Macintosh Plus also has drivers in ROM for the AppleTalk network, as well as a built-in "shell" for the printer driver. (The shell in turn calls the actual printer driver, which is still loaded from the disk as before. This allows it to be changed easily to configure the system for different types of printer, such as the ImageWriter or LaserWriter.)

Every driver, whether ROM- or RAM-based, has a name, which conventionally begins with a period (.), and a *unit number* from 0 to 31. For drivers that reside in resource files, the driver name and unit number are also the resource name and resource ID. When a driver is opened for use, it is also given a *driver reference number* by which it is always referred to. The driver reference number is always a negative number from −1 to −32, and is derived from the unit number by the formula

    refNum = −(unitNum + 1)

For example, the sound driver has a unit number of 3 and a reference number of -4. The names and numbers of the standard device drivers are summarized in [7.5.5].

A very important special class of drivers are *desk accessories* like the Calculator, Scrapbook, and Control Panel. These behave like device drivers from the Toolbox's point of view, but they're actually "mini-applications" that can coexist on the screen with an ordinary application program (and with each other). Desk accessories are stored under resource type 'DRVR', just like bona fide device drivers, and are supposed to have unit numbers (resource IDs) of 12 and above.

> Unlike the names of ordinary drivers, those of desk accessories *don't* begin with a period. We'll see in Volume Two that this allows them to be listed by name on a menu; ordinary drivers begin with a period precisely so that they will be suppressed from the menu.

The Toolbox includes all the facilities you need to give the user access to desk accessories while running your program. The program itself doesn't need to know what accessories are available, what they do, or how they work. In Volume Two we'll learn how to offer a menu of available desk accessories for the user to choose from, how to open, close, and manipulate the system windows they appear in, and how to pass them the user's mouse and keyboard actions for processing. See Volume Three if you're interested in writing desk accessories of your own.

The Desk Scrap

The *desk scrap* is what allows the user to cut and paste between application programs, between a program and a desk accessory, or between accessories. It corresponds to what Macintosh user manuals call the Clipboard: the place to which the standard editing commands Cut and Copy transfer information, and from which Paste retrieves it. When you cut or copy a picture from MacPaint and paste it into a MacWrite document, or transfer text from MacWrite to MacPaint, the information travels by way of the desk scrap. Similarly pictures can be moved to or from the Scrapbook desk accessory, and text to or from the Scrapbook, Note Pad,

Key Caps, or even the Calculator. In each case the desk scrap serves as the intermediary vehicle for transferring the information from one program or accessory to another.

> In a program that performs any sort of cut-and-paste editing, it's up to you to make sure the contents of the desk scrap are properly maintained. Normally this just means copying information directly to the scrap whenever the user issues a Cut or Copy command, and back from the scrap on a Paste command. As we'll see in Volume Two, however, the Toolbox text editing routines maintain an internal text scrap of their own, separate from the desk scrap. If you're using these routines and want to be able to exchange information with other programs, you have to arrange to transfer the information between this Toolbox internal scrap and the desk scrap at the appropriate times: on entry and exit, and whenever control passes to or from a desk accessory. We'll see how to do this when we take up text editing in Volume Two, Chapter 5.

Conceptually, the scrap always holds a single item, the last to be cut or copied. In reality, it may contain several different items representing the same underlying information in different forms [7.4.1]. This allows the contents of the scrap to be handled in different ways depending on what program they're passed to. Each separate representation is stored as a resource of some kind; if there are more than one, they should all be of different resource types.

Two resource types in particular are considered standard: 'TEXT' [8.4.1], consisting of straight ASCII text characters, and 'PICT' [5.5.5], containing a QuickDraw picture definition. These standard types serve as a "lingua franca" for exchanging text and graphics among programs. Every application or desk accessory that uses the desk scrap is expected to deliver at least one of the standard types as output, and to accept at least one, and preferably both, as input. In addition, a program may use the desk scrap for any other type of data it likes. For instance, our music editor might write the same musical fragment to the scrap both in its own private data format and also as a QuickDraw picture for displaying the notes graphically on the screen or printing them in a hard copy.

The contents of the desk scrap normally reside in the application heap, and are located through a handle kept in a system global named ScrapHandle. You can get a copy of this handle by calling the Toolbox function InfoScrap [7.4.2]. This returns a *scrap information record* that includes the scrap handle, the current size of the scrap in bytes, and other descriptive information.

Usually, though, you'll want to use GetScrap [7.4.3] to access the scrap's contents. You specify the particular resource type you're interested in, and supply a handle (normally empty) to be filled with an item from the scrap. Like most of the Toolbox routines dealing with the scrap, GetScrap is a function that returns an Operating System result code, similar to those we discussed in Chapters 3 and 6 on memory management and resources. If the scrap contains an item of the requested type, GetScrap will make a *copy* of the item's resource data and set the handle you supply to point to the copy; if there's no such item, GetScrap will return the result code NoTypeErr.

To transfer an item *to* the desk scrap, use PutScrap [7.4.3]. You supply a *pointer* (not a handle) to the item's resource data, along with its resource type and length in bytes. PutScrap simply adds the new item to the existing contents of the scrap; it doesn't delete any other items already there. It's up to you to make sure the scrap doesn't already contain an item of the same resource type. To completely replace the contents of the scrap, clear the old contents with ZeroScrap [7.4.3] before storing the new contents with PutScrap.

Any call to ZeroScrap also changes the value of the *scrap count*. This is an integer maintained by the Toolbox, whose value is always available as one of the fields in the information record returned by InfoScrap [7.4.2]. The numerical value of the scrap count has no intrinsic meaning; its sole purpose is to tell you when the scrap's contents have been changed. When the user activates a system window (one that contains a desk accessory), you can save the old value of the scrap count before passing control to the accessory, then compare it with the new value when control returns to your program. If the scrap count has changed, then the accessory must have called ZeroScrap, and has presumably replaced the previous contents of the scrap. You can then copy the desk scrap to the internal Toolbox scrap, or take whatever other action is appropriate. If the scrap count is the same on return from the accessory as it was before, then the scrap hasn't changed and no special action is needed. Again, we'll see an example of how this works in the chapter on text editing in Volume Two.

The contents of the desk scrap normally reside in the application heap. However, if heap space is scarce or the scrap is large, you may want to keep it in a disk file instead. The Toolbox routines LoadScrap and UnloadScrap [7.4.4] transfer the scrap between a file and the heap. The usual name of the scrap file, if there is one, is Clipboard File. The Toolbox keeps a pointer to this file name in the system global ScrapName; in assembly language, you can change the name of the scrap file by storing a new string pointer into this global. There's no way to change the scrap file name in Pascal, but you can find out the current name via the ScrapName field of the information record returned by InfoScrap [7.4.2].

Nuts and Bolts

The Toolbox routine that the Finder uses to start up an application program is called Launch [7.1.1]. This routine reinitializes the application heap, the application global space, and the stack for the new program, destroying their previous contents. (However, it leaves the system heap intact from one application to the next.) It opens the new program's application resource file and reads in the contents of segment 0, which it then uses to allocate the application global space, set up the program's jump table, and initialize register A5. Finally, it starts up the program by transferring control to its main entry point through the first entry in the jump table.

The only thing in the old application heap that gets preserved across the launch of a new program is, of course, the desk scrap. The Launch routine locates the scrap by means of the system scrap handle in low memory and copies it temporarily into the stack. Then, after reinitializing the application heap, it retrieves the scrap from the stack, reinstalls it in the new heap, and fixes the system scrap handle to point to it at its new location. Thus the scrap is preserved even though everything else in the heap is lost.

Ordinarily the Finder is the only program that should ever call the Launch routine; however, there's a related routine named Chain [7.1.1] that you may sometimes find useful. Like Launch, Chain terminates the program that called it and starts up another in its place. The difference is that Chain doesn't reinitialize the application heap; it leaves it intact, so that the first program can leave information there for the second program to use. Neither Launch nor Chain can be called through the Pascal interface to the Toolbox; they're available only from assembly language via the trap mechanism. See [7.1.1] for details.

REFERENCE

7.1 Starting and Ending a Program

7.1.1 Starting a Program

Definitions

procedure Launch	{Assembly language only}
procedure Chain	{Assembly language only}

Notes

1. Both of these routines start up a new application program.

2. The previous program's application resource file is closed and the new one's is opened.

3. The information given in segment 0 in the application resource file is used to allocate the program's application global space, set up its segment jump table, initialize register A5, and position the base of the stack.

4. Launch reinitializes the application heap, destroying its previous contents, before starting the new program.

349

5. The contents of the desk scrap [7.4] are preserved by copying them temporarily to the stack. After initialization, the scrap is retrieved from the stack and reinstalled in the new heap, and the global scrap handle is updated to point to it.

6. Launch is normally used only by the Finder, not by a running program.

7. Chain leaves the entire application heap intact, and can be used to pass information from one application program to the next.

8. Both routines can be called from assembly language only, via the trap macros _Launch and _Chain.

9. On entry to either routine, register A0 contains the address of a 4-byte pointer, which in turn points to a string giving the name of the file containing the application program to be started.

10. Following the file name pointer in memory is a 2-byte integer telling which screen and sound buffers the program will use:

Value	Screen buffer	Sound buffer
Zero	Main	Main
Positive	Main	Alternate
Negative	Alternate	Alternate

The value passed for this integer is kept in the assembly-language global CurPageOption.

Assembly Language Information

Trap macros:

(Assembly) Trap macro	Trap word
_Launch	$A9F2
_Chain	$A9F3

Register usage:

Routine	Register	Contents
Launch	A0.L (in)	Pointer to parameter block:
	0(A0)	Pointer to name of application file
	4(A0)	Coded integer specifying screen and sound buffers (see note 10)
Chain	A0.L (in)	Pointer to parameter block:
	0(A0)	Pointer to name of application file
	4(A0)	Coded integer specifying screen and sound buffers (see note 10)

Assembly-language global variable:

Name	Address	Meaning
CurPageOption	$936	Integer specifying screen and sound buffers

7.1.2   Loading and Unloading Segments

Definitions

```
procedure  LoadSeg                    {Assembly language only}
procedure  UnloadSeg
           (anyRoutine : Ptr);        {Pointer to any routine in the segment}
```

Notes

1. LoadSeg loads a code segment from the application resource file on the disk and locks it into the application heap.

2. The segment isn't reloaded if it's already in memory.

3. The segment to be loaded is identified by a segment number passed on the stack.

4. After the segment is loaded, all of its jump table entries are patched to jump directly to the corresponding routines in memory.

5. LoadSeg can be called only at the machine-language level, and only from within a jump table entry. It will not work properly if called from within the body of a program.

6. UnloadSeg unloads a segment from memory, freeing its space for some other purpose.

7. The parameter anyRoutine is a pointer to any routine in the segment. The segment number is obtained from the jump table entry for this routine.

8. The unloaded segment is made purgeable, but is not immediately purged from the heap.

9. All jump entries for the segment are restored to the "unloaded" state, so that they will reload the segment the next time it's needed.

Assembly Language Information

Trap macros:

(Pascal) Routine name	(Assembly) Trap macro	Trap word
	_LoadSeg	$A9F0
UnloadSeg	_UnloadSeg	$A9F1

7.1.3 Ending a Program

Definitions

procedure ExitToShell;

procedure Restart;

Notes

1. ExitToShell terminates a program and immediately returns control to the Finder.

2. The application heap is reinitialized, destroying its previous contents.

3. The contents of the desk scrap [7.4] are preserved. After initialization, the scrap is reinstalled in the new heap and the global scrap handle is updated to point to it.

4. A Pascal program need not call ExitToShell when it terminates in the normal way, by "falling out" of its main program body.

5. Restart restarts the entire system, just as if the power had been turned off and back on.

6. Restart is part of the Pascal Toolbox interface, not part of the Toolbox itself. It doesn't reside in ROM and can't be called from assembly language via the trap mechanism.

7. To restart the system in assembly language, jump to the memory address ten bytes past the beginning of ROM (that is, to the address $0A greater than that contained in the system global ROMBase [3.1.3]).

8. *BEWARE:* Restarting the system unexpectedly or without proper precautions can cause the user to lose valuable information.

Assembly Language Information

Trap macro:

(Pascal) Routine name	(Assembly) Trap macro	Trap word
ExitToShell	_ExitToShell	$A9F4

Assembly-language global variable:

Name	Address	Meaning
FinderName	$2E0	Name of program to exit to (maximum 15 characters)

7.2   Packages

7.2.1   Standard Packages

Definitions

```
const
    ListMgr = 0;     {List Manager Package}
    DskInit = 2;     {Disk Initialization Package}
    StdFile = 3;     {Standard File Package}
    FlPoint = 4;     {Floating-Point Arithmetic Package}
    TrFunc  = 5;     {Transcendental Functions Package}
    IntUtil = 6;     {International Utilities Package}
    BDConv  = 7;     {Binary/Decimal Conversion Package}
```

Notes

1. Code packages are stored as resources of type 'PACK' [7.5.2].

2. The resource ID is the same as the *package number*, which must be between 0 and 7. The Toolbox can accommodate no more than eight packages at a time, including the standard ones. (The Macintosh Plus Toolbox can handle up to sixteen packages, numbered 0 to 15.)

3. The standard packages are included in the system resource file provided on Macintosh software disks. (On the Macintosh Plus, the Floating-Point Arithmetic, Transcendental Functions, and Binary/Decimal Conversion packages, numbers 4, 5, and 7, reside in ROM instead [6.6.3].)

4. Package numbers 1 and 8–15 are reserved for future expansion.

5. The List Manager Package displays scrollable lists of items from which the user can choose with the mouse (like the one used in selecting files to be read from the disk). This package was introduced at the same time as the Macintosh Plus, and is available only in versions of the System file numbered 3.0 or higher. See Volume Three for details.

6. The Disk Initialization Package [II:8.4] takes corrective action when an unreadable disk is inserted into the disk drive, usually by initializing the disk.

7. The Standard File Package [II:8.3] provides a convenient, standard way for the user to supply file names for input/output operations.

8. The Floating-Point Arithmetic Package performs arithmetic on floating-point numbers in accordance with the "IEEE standard" published by the Institute of Electrical and Electronic Engineers, using the Standard Apple Numeric Environment (SANE). See *Inside Macintosh* for details.

9. The Transcendental Functions Package calculates various transcendental functions on floating-point numbers, such as logarithms, exponentials, trigonometric functions, compound interest, and discounted value. See *Inside Macintosh* for details.

10. The International Utilities Package helps a program conform to the prevailing conventions of different countries in such matters as formatting of numbers, dates, times, and currency; use of metric units; and alphabetization of foreign-language accents, diacriticals, and ligatures. See [2.4.4] and *Inside Macintosh* for more information.

11. The Binary/Decimal Conversion Package [2.3.7] converts numbers between their internal binary format and their external representation as strings of decimal digits.

12. Each routine within a package is identified by an integer *routine selector;* see the sections on individual routines for specific values. To call such a routine in assembly language, push the selector onto the stack and execute the appropriate trap (_Pack0 to _Pack15) for the package it belongs to. The Pascal interface routines in unit PackIntf and the assembly-language macros in file PackMacs do this automatically for all routines in the standard packages.

Assembly Language Information

Trap macros:

(Assembly) Trap macro	Trap word
_Pack0	$A9E7
_Pack1	$A9E8
_Pack2	$A9E9
_Pack3	$A9EA
_Pack4	$A9EB
_Pack5	$A9EC
_Pack6	$A9ED
_Pack7	$A9EE
_Pack8	$A816
_Pack9	$A82B
_Pack10	$A82C
_Pack11	$A82D
_Pack12	$A82E
_Pack13	$A82F
_Pack14	$A830
_Pack15	$A831

Standard package numbers:

Name	Number	Meaning
ListMgr	0	List Manager Package (System file 3.0 or later)
DskInit	2	Disk Initialization Package
StdFile	3	Standard File Package
FlPoint	4	Floating-Point Arithmetic Package
TrFunc	5	Transcendental Functions Package
IntUtil	6	International Utilities Package
BDConv	7	Binary/Decimal Conversion Package

7.2.2   Initializing Packages

Definitions

procedure InitPack
          (packNumber : INTEGER);   {Package number}

procedure InitAllPacks;

Notes

1. These routines initialize the standard packages, making them available for use in a program.

2. InitPack initializes a single package; InitAllPacks initializes all of the standard packages at once.

3. InitAllPacks is called automatically at program startup; there's normally no need to call either of these routines from within a running program.

Assembly Language Information

Trap macros:

(Pascal) Routine name	(Assembly) Trap macro	Trap word
InitPack	_InitPack	$A9E5
InitAllPacks	_InitAllPacks	$A9E6

7.3   Finder Information

7.3.1   Signatures and File Types

Definitions

```
type
   OSType = packed array [1..4] of CHAR;   {Creator signature or file type}
```

Notes

1. Every file has a *file type* and a *creator signature*, assigned when the file is first created [II:8.2.1].

2. The creator signature identifies the application program to be started up when the file is opened from the Finder.

3. The signature '????' denotes a file that is not to be opened from the Finder.

4. The file type determines the icon the Finder uses to represent the file on the screen, and controls the user's access to the file via the Standard File Package [II:8.3.2].

5. File type 'APPL' identifies a file containing an application program to be run from the Finder. Such a file should carry the program's own signature as its creator.

6. File type 'TEXT' denotes a file consisting of pure text characters, with no additional formatting or other information.

7. Serious commercial applications should have their signatures and associated file types registered for uniqueness with Apple's Macintosh Technical Support.

7.3.2   Finder Information Records

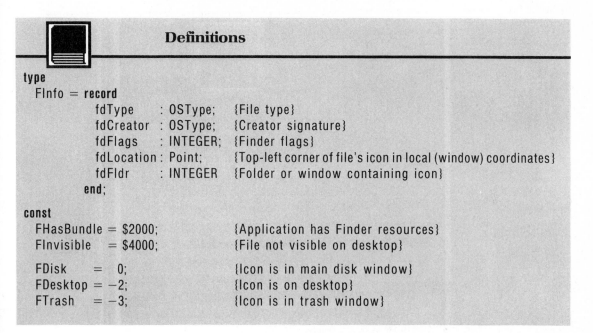

Definitions

```
type
  FInfo = record
            fdType    : OSType;    {File type}
            fdCreator : OSType;    {Creator signature}
            fdFlags   : INTEGER;   {Finder flags}
            fdLocation: Point;     {Top-left corner of file's icon in local (window) coordinates}
            fdFldr    : INTEGER    {Folder or window containing icon}
          end;

const
  FHasBundle = $2000;              {Application has Finder resources}
  FInvisible = $4000;              {File not visible on desktop}

  FDisk    =  0;                   {Icon is in main disk window}
  FDesktop = -2;                   {Icon is on desktop}
  FTrash   = -3;                   {Icon is in trash window}
```

Notes

1. A Finder information record summarizes a file's Finder-related properties.

2. fdType and fdCreator are the file type and creator signature [7.3.1], respectively.

3. fdFlags is a word of flags representing Finder-related attributes of the file.

4. Bit 15 (the high-order bit) of the flag word is the *lock bit*. A 1 in this bit prevents the file from being deleted, renamed, or replaced.

5. Bit 14 of the flag word is the *invisible bit*. A 1 in this bit means that the file's icon is not to be displayed on the screen by the Finder. The constant FInvisible is a mask for manipulating this bit.

6. Bit 13 of the flag word is the *bundle bit*. A 1 in this bit means that the file has a "bundle" of Finder-related resources [7.5.4] to be installed in the Finder's desktop file. The constant FHasBundle is a mask for manipulating this bit.

7. Bit 12 of the flag word is the *system bit*. A 1 in this bit means that the file is needed by the system for proper operation.

8. Bit 11 of the flag word is the *bozo bit* (named for the Apple programmer who invented it). A 1 in this bit prevents the file from being copied: a protection scheme so feeble that only a bozo would think of it. Recent versions of the Finder (version 5.0 or greater) don't even pay any attention to this bit.

9. Bit 10 of the flag word is the *busy bit*. A 1 in this bit means that the file is currently in use—that is, it has been opened and not yet closed.

10. Bit 9 of the flag word is the *change bit*. A 1 in this bit means that the file's contents have been changed and must be updated on the disk.

11. Bit 8 of the flag word is the *init bit*. A 1 in this bit means that the file's Finder-related resources [7.5.4] have been installed in the desktop file.

12. The low-order byte of the flag word (bits 7-0) is reserved for private use by the Finder.

13. fdFldr specifies the location of the file's icon on the Finder screen. Common locations are the main window for the disk the file resides on (FDisk), out on the desktop (FDesktop), or in the trash window (FTrash). Any positive, nonzero value is a *folder number* assigned by the Finder to designate a subsidiary folder on the disk.

14. fdLocation gives the position of the top-left corner of the file's icon, in the local coordinate system of the window designated by fdFldr.

15. If the icon is on the desktop (fdFldr = FDesktop), fdLocation is in global (screen) coordinates.

16. The fdFldr field is unused under the new Hierarchical File System (see Volume Two, Chapter 8).

Assembly Language Information

Field offsets in a Finder information record:

(Pascal) Field name	(Assembly) Offset name	Offset in bytes
fdType	fdType	0
fdCreator	fdCreator	4
fdFlags	fdFlags	8
fdLocation	fdLocation	10
fdFldr	fdFldr	14

Assembly-language constants:

Name	Value	Meaning
FHasBundle	$2000	Mask for bundle bit
FInvisible	$4000	Mask for invisible bit

7.3.3 Accessing Finder Properties

Definitions

```
function GetFInfo
        (fName        : Str255;        {File name}
         vRefNum      : INTEGER;       {Volume or directory}
         var finderInfo : FInfo)       {Returns current Finder information [7.3.2]}
         : OSErr;                      {Result code}

function SetFInfo
        (fName        : Str255;        {File name}
         vRefNum      : INTEGER;       {Volume or directory}
         finderInfo   : FInfo)         {New Finder information [7.3.2]}
         : OSErr;                      {Result code}
```

Notes

1. These routines return or change a file's Finder-related properties [7.3.2].

2. The file is identified by its name and the reference number of the volume or directory it resides in. Volumes, directories, and their reference numbers are discussed in Volume Two, Chapter 8.

3. A file needn't be open in order to get or set its Finder information.

4. These routines are part of the high-level file system and are not directly available from assembly language. The trap macros correspond to the low-level file routines PBGetFInfo and PBSetFInfo. (See Volume Two, Chapter 8 for the distinction between high- and low-level file systems, and *Inside Macintosh* for details on PBGetFInfo and PBSet-FInfo.)

5. The trap macros are spelled _GetFileInfo and _SetFileInfo.

Assembly Language Information

Trap macros:

(Pascal) Routine name	(Assembly) Trap macro	Trap word
PBGetFInfo	_GetFileInfo	$A00C
PBSetFInfo	_SetFileInfo	$A00D

7.3.4 Startup Information

0 = Open file
1 = Print file

Message (2 bytes)

Number of files (2 bytes)

First volume reference number (2 bytes)

File type
(4 bytes)

Version number (1 byte) | Not used

Length of file name (1 byte)

File name
(indefinite length)

Last volume reference number (2 bytes)

File type
(4 bytes)

Version number (1 byte) | Not used

Length of file name (1 byte)

File name
(indefinite length)

Any number of files

Definitions

```
procedure CountAppFiles
          (var message : INTEGER;        {Open or print?}
           var count   : INTEGER);       {Returns number of files selected}

procedure GetAppFiles
          (index       : INTEGER;        {Index number of desired file}
           var theFile : AppFile);       {Returns identifying information about file}

procedure ClrAppFiles
          (index : INTEGER);             {Index number of file to be cleared}

procedure GetAppParms
          (var appName     : Str255;     {Returns name of application file}
           var appResFile  : INTEGER;    {Returns reference number of application resource file}
           var startHandle : Handle);    {Returns handle to startup information}

const
  AppOpen = 0;                           {Open document file}
  AppPrint = 1;                          {Print document file}

type
  AppFile = record
            vRefNum : INTEGER;           {Volume or directory}
            fType   : OSType;            {File type}
            versNum : INTEGER;           {Version number}
            fName   : Str255             {Name of file}
          end;
```

Notes

1. These routines are used for accessing a program's Finder startup information, which identifies the document files the user selected in the Finder when starting up the program.

2. CountAppFiles returns the number of documents selected by the user.

3. The value returned in the message parameter tells whether the documents are to be opened for work (AppOpen) or for printing (AppPrint). See Volume Three for information on printing.

4. GetAppFiles returns identifying information for one of the documents selected by the user.

5. The index parameter is an integer ranging from 1 to the count value returned by CountAppFiles.

6. The identifying information is returned as a record of type AppFile, giving the volume or directory reference number, file name, file type [7.3.1], and version number. Volume and directory reference numbers and version numbers are discussed in Volume Two, Chapter 8.

7. After opening or printing a document identified by GetAppFiles, call ClrAppFiles to notify the Finder that the document has been processed.

8. These routines are not available in assembly language via the trap mechanism. Instead, you can access the Finder startup information directly via the *startup handle* at address 16(A5) in the application global space; a copy of the startup handle is also kept in the system global variable AppParmHandle. The internal structure of the startup information is shown in the figure.

9. GetAppParms returns the name of the program's application file, the reference number of its application resource file, and a handle to its "raw" startup information.

10. In assembly language, the same information is available directly in the system globals CurApName, CurApRefNum, and AppParmHandle.

Assembly Language Information

Trap macro:

(Pascal) Routine name	(Assembly) Trap macro	Trap word
GetAppParms	_GetAppParms	$A9F5

Assembly-language global variables:

Name	Address	Meaning
CurApName	$910	Name of current application (maximum 31 characters)
CurApRefNum	$900	Reference number of application resource file
AppParmHandle	$AEC	Handle to Finder startup information

7.4   Desk Scrap

7.4.1   Scrap Format

Format of desk scrap

Notes

1. The desk scrap may contain any number of separate items, each of which is a single resource of any type. They should all represent the same underlying information in different forms.

2. For each item, the scrap contains a four-character resource type and a long integer giving the length of the resource data in bytes, followed by the actual resource data.

3. The data must physically consist of an even number of bytes. If the specified length count is odd, there must be an extra byte of "padding" at the end to keep the physical length to a whole number of 16-bit words.

4. Two resource types are considered standard for the scrap: 'TEXT' [8.4.1], consisting of plain, unformatted ASCII text, and 'PICT' [5.5.5], representing a QuickDraw picture. Any program that uses the scrap at all should deliver at least one of these types to the scrap, and should be able to accept at least one and preferably both.

7.4.2 Scrap Information

Definitions

```
type
  PScrapStuff = ^ScrapStuff;

  ScrapStuff  = record
                  scrapSize    : LONGINT;    {Overall size of scrap in bytes}
                  scrapHandle  : Handle;     {Handle to scrap in memory}
                  scrapCount   : INTEGER;    {Current scrap count}
                  scrapState   : INTEGER;    {Is scrap in memory?}
                  scrapName    : StringPtr   {Pointer to name of scrap file}
                end;

function InfoScrap
          : PScrapStuff;                     {Pointer to current scrap information}
```

Notes

1. InfoScrap returns a *scrap information record* summarizing the current contents and properties of the desk scrap.

2. scrapSize is the overall length of the scrap in bytes, including all items.

3. scrapHandle is a handle to the contents of the scrap in memory. If the scrap is on the disk, this field is NIL.

4. scrapCount is the current value of the scrap count, which is changed whenever ZeroScrap [7.4.3] is called. This number has no intrinsic meaning; its sole purpose is to enable a program to tell whether the scrap's contents have been changed on regaining control from a desk accessory.

5. scrapState is zero if the scrap currently resides on the disk, nonzero if it's in memory.

6. scrapName is a pointer to the name of the scrap file.

7. The scrap file is normally named Clipboard File, and resides on the startup volume. If the startup volume is hierarchical, the scrap file resides in the system folder. (Hierarchical volumes are discussed in Volume Two, Chapter 8.)

8. In assembly language, the contents of the scrap information record are accessible directly in the global variables listed below.

Assembly Language Information

Trap macro:

(Pascal) Routine name	(Assembly) Trap macro	Trap word
InfoScrap	_InfoScrap	$A9F9

Assembly-language global variables:

Name	Address	Meaning
ScrapSize	$960	Current scrap size
ScrapHandle	$964	Handle to scrap contents
ScrapCount	$968	Current scrap count
ScrapState	$96A	Current scrap state
ScrapName	$96C	Pointer to scrap file name

7.4.3   Reading and Writing the Scrap

Definitions

```
function GetScrap
        (theItem    : Handle;        {Handle to be set to requested item}
         itemType   : ResType;       {Resource type of desired item}
     var offset     : LONGINT)       {Returns byte offset of item data within scrap contents}
         : LONGINT;                  {Length of item data in bytes, or error code}

function PutScrap
        (itemLength : LONGINT;       {Length of item data in bytes}
         itemType   : ResType;       {Resource type of item}
         theItem    : Ptr)           {Pointer to item data}
         : LONGINT;                  {Result code}

function ZeroScrap
         : LONGINT;                  {Result code}

const
   NoScrapErr = −100;                {Desk scrap not initialized}
   NoTypeErr  = −102;                {No item of requested type}
```

Notes

1. GetScrap reads an item from the desk scrap; PutScrap writes one; ZeroScrap empties the scrap.

2. The itemType parameter to GetScrap identifies the resource type of the desired item.

3. If the scrap contains an item of the requested type, a copy of the item is made and the handle theItem is set to point to the copy. The offset parameter returns the offset in bytes from the beginning of the scrap to the beginning of the item's data; the function result gives the (logical) length of the item's data in bytes.

4. If the scrap doesn't contain an item of the requested type, GetScrap returns the error code NoTypeErr. theItem and offset are undefined.

5. Pass NIL for theItem to get an item's length and offset, but no handle to its data. This allows you to check whether an item of a given type is present, or find out its length, without making a copy of the item itself.

6. PutScrap doesn't replace the existing contents of the scrap; it merely *adds* an item. To replace the scrap completely, call ZeroScrap first, to clear its previous contents.

7. PutScrap doesn't check for an existing item of the same type you're adding. It's up to you to avoid placing two items of the same type in the scrap.

8. Notice that PutScrap accepts a *pointer* to the data of the new item, not a handle.

9. In addition to emptying the scrap, ZeroScrap changes the value of the scrap count [7.4.2]. This enables you to detect when the scrap's contents have been changed by a desk accessory.

Assembly Language Information

Trap macros:

(Pascal) Routine name	(Assembly) Trap macro	Trap word
GetScrap	_GetScrap	$A9FD
PutScrap	_PutScrap	$A9FE
ZeroScrap	_ZeroScrap	$A9FC

7.4.4   Loading and Unloading the Scrap

Definitions

```
function LoadScrap
        : LONGINT;          {Result code}

function UnloadScrap
        : LONGINT;          {Result code}
```

Notes

1. These routines transfer the desk scrap between memory and the disk. LoadScrap reads the scrap into memory from the scrap file; UnloadScrap writes the scrap out to the scrap file.

2. A pointer to the name of the scrap file is kept in the system global ScrapName, and is accessible via the InfoScrap routine [7.4.2].

3. The scrap file is normally named Clipboard File, and resides on the startup volume. If the startup volume is hierarchical, the scrap file resides in the system folder. (Hierarchical volumes are discussed in Volume Two, Chapter 8.)

4. The trap macros are spelled _LodeScrap and _UnlodeScrap.

Assembly Language Information

Trap macros:

(Pascal) Routine name	(Assembly) Trap macro	Trap word
LoadScrap	_LodeScrap	$A9FB
UnloadScrap	_UnlodeScrap	$A9FA

7.5 Resource Formats

7.5.1 Resource Type 'CODE'

Format of segment 0

Notes

1. A resource of type 'CODE' contains executable machine-language code.

2. The resource ID is called the *segment number*.

3. The resource data begins with a 4-byte *segment header* identifying which entries in the jump table belong to this segment; this is followed by the code of the segment itself.

4. The first 2 bytes of the segment header give the offset in bytes from the beginning of the jump table to the first entry belonging to this segment. The last 2 bytes give the number of jump table entries belonging to this segment.

5. Every application program has one special segment, resource ID 0, containing information needed to initialize the program's application global space and jump table. The format of segment 0 is shown in the second figure above.

7.5.2   Resource Type 'PACK'

Notes

1. A resource of type 'PACK' contains a *package* of predefined machine-language routines.

2. The resource data begins with a header used internally by the Toolbox to find the starting addresses of routines within the package; this is followed by the code of the routines themselves.

3. Resource IDs of packages, called *package numbers*, must be between 0 and 15.

4. The standard packages [7.2.1] are included in the system resource file. (On the Macintosh Plus, the Floating-Point Arithmetic, Transcendental Functions, and Binary/Decimal Conversion packages, numbers 4, 5, and 7, reside in ROM instead [6.6.3].)

7.5.3   Resource Type 'FREF'

Notes

1. A resource of type 'FREF' ("file reference") establishes a correspondence between a file type associated with an application program and the icon to be used by the Finder to represent files of that type on the screen.

2. The icon is defined by an *icon list* of resource type 'ICN#' [5.5.4]. The list contains two icon definitions: the first representing the actual icon, the second a mask to be used for drawing it on the screen. The mask is normally just the outline of the icon, filled in with solid black.

3. The resource data of a file reference consists of the four-character file type [7.3.1], followed by the "local ID" of the corresponding icon list. The translation from this local ID to the true resource ID is defined by a bundle resource [7.5.4].

7.5.4   **Resource Type 'BNDL'**

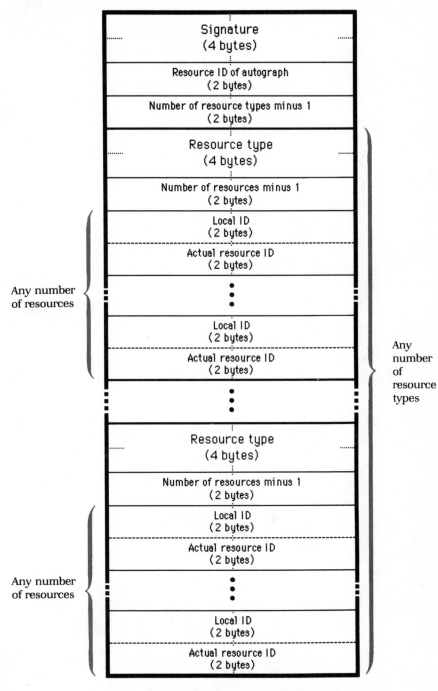

Format of resource type '**BNDL**'

Notes

1. A resource of type 'BNDL' ("bundle") identifies all of the Finder-related resources associated with an application program.

2. The resource data begins by defining the program's signature [7.3.1] and the resource ID of its autograph resource (note 6). This is followed by bundle entries for any number of resource types.

3. For any given resource type, the bundle may contain any number of individual resources. Each resource has a *local ID* by which other resources in the bundle refer to it. The bundle defines the correspondence between these local IDs and the true IDs under which the resources are actually stored.

4. At present, the only resource types in a bundle that are meaningful to the Finder are 'FREF' [7.5.3] and 'ICN#' [5.5.4], in addition to the program's autograph (note 6). In the future, bundles may also be used for other purposes and may contain other resource types as well.

5. Any program with a bundle should have the bundle bit set in the fdFlags field of its Finder information record [7.3.2]. This tells the Finder to install the resources contained in the bundle into the desktop file when copying the program to another disk.

6. Any program with a bundle must also have an *autograph* resource. The resource type of the autograph is the same as the program's signature; its resource ID is defined in the program's bundle, and is conventionally 0.

7. The autograph can have any information at all as its resource data. Typically it contains a text string identifying the program and version.

7.5.5 Resource Type 'DRVR'

Unit number	Reference number	Driver name	Description
2	−3	.Print	Printer driver
3	−4	.Sound	Sound driver
4	−5	.Sony	Sony disk driver
5	−6	.AIn	Serial driver, port A (modem port) in
6	−7	.AOut	Serial driver, port A (modem port) out
7	−8	.BIn	Serial driver, port B (printer port) in
8	−9	.BOut	Serial driver, port B (printer port) out
9	−10	.MPP	Network driver (Macintosh Packet Protocol)
10	−11	.ATP	Network driver (AppleTalk Transaction Protocol)
12	−13	Calculator	Calculator desk accessory
13	−14	Alarm Clock	Alarm Clock desk accessory
14	−15	Key Caps	Key Caps desk accessory
15	−16	Puzzle	Puzzle desk accessory
16	−17	Note Pad	Note Pad desk accessory
17	−18	Scrapbook	Scrapbook desk accessory
18	−19	Control Panel	Control Panel desk accessory
19	−20	Chooser	Chooser desk accessory

Notes

1. A resource of type 'DRVR' contains the code of an input/output device driver or a desk accessory.

2. A driver's resource ID is the same as its *unit number*, and must be between 0 and 31.

3. The unit number also determines the *driver reference number*, by the formula

$$refNum = -(unitNum + 1)$$

4. Every driver resource must have a resource name as well as a resource ID. For true device drivers, the name begins with a period (.); for desk accessories, it must not.

5. The table lists the standard device drivers and desk accessories. The sound, disk, and serial drivers (and the network drivers on the Macintosh Plus) are permanently resident in ROM. The printer driver and desk accessories are resources included in the system resource file.

6. The unit and reference numbers shown in the table may differ in some versions of the System file.

7. See Volume Three for further information on devices and drivers.

CHAPTER

8

Upstanding Characters

The Macintosh can display text on the screen in an almost endless variety of typefaces, sizes, and styles. In this chapter we'll learn how text is represented internally and how to display it and control its appearance on the screen.

The Macintosh Character Set

Every text character is represented by an 8-bit *character code* [8.1.1]. The Macintosh character set is based on the 7-bit ASCII code (American Standard Code for Information Interchange) widely used throughout the computer industry. Character codes from 0 to 127 ($7F) correspond to the standard ASCII characters; the remaining 128 codes are used for additional, non-ASCII characters available only on the Macintosh.

In the standard ASCII character set, the first 32 character codes, from 0 to 31 ($1F), along with 127 ($7F), stand for "control characters" with no direct visual representation. These were devised in early medieval times (circa 1940) to control teletype transmission, and many have outmoded or arcane meanings such as "end of tape," "negative acknowledge," and "synchronous idle." The Macintosh has no use for most of them; in fact, there isn't even any way to type them, since the Macintosh keyboard doesn't have the Control key found on most other computers. The only

379

control characters that have their standard meanings on the Macintosh are backspace (ASCII code $08), tab ($09), and carriage return ($0D). A few more can be typed from the Macintosh keyboard or keypad but have nonstandard meanings: the Enter key produces the ASCII Control-C or "end-of-text" character ($03), and others are generated by the Clear and arrow keys [8.1.1].

There are also a few control characters that can't be typed from the keyboard but have special graphical representations on the Macintosh screen, including the "cloverleaf" command symbol, the check mark for marking menu items, and the Apple symbol used for the title of the menu of desk accessories. The character codes for these screen-only characters are defined as Toolbox constants for use in your programs [8.1.1]. For instance, you can refer to the Apple character as CHR(AppleMark).

Character codes of 128 ($80) and above denote extra characters added to the Macintosh character set for business and scientific purposes, as well as accents and other special characters used in foreign languages. Most of these special characters can be typed from the keyboard by holding down the Option key in combination with some other character. If you happen to be proficient in Dutch or Italian, Norwegian or Portuguese (or Albanian, Basque, or Rhaeto-Romansch, for that matter), you'll find the Macintosh provides all the characters you need to type your grocery list in those languages; if you haven't a clue what some of these characters are good for, don't lose any sleep over it.

As we learned in Chapter 2, the Toolbox uses an internal format for character strings consisting of a 1-byte character count followed by a series of bytes containing the character codes themselves. Strings of this form can be stored in resource files under resource type 'STR ' [8.4.2] or 'STR#' [8.4.3], and read into memory with GetString or GetIndString [8.1.2]. (Notice that the space in 'STR ' is required.) There are also utility routines [8.1.2] for copying strings within the heap: NewString simply returns a brand-new handle to the copy, while SetString accepts an existing handle and sets it to point to the copy.

Notice, though, that since the character count for such "Pascal-format" strings is limited to 1 byte, they can be no more than 255 characters long. For longer blocks of text there's resource type 'TEXT' [8.4.1], which has no count byte and unlimited length. (You can find out its length with SizeResource [6.4.3].) It's recommended that you use string and text resources for all text your program displays on the screen, such as window titles and error or prompting messages. This makes it easy to reword messages, change terminology, correct misspellings, or translate your messages into alien tongues (such as English) without having to change the program itself.

Keyboard Configurations

Not only is the Macintosh character set designed for international use, but even the physical arrangement of characters on the keyboard can be tailored to the needs of different countries. The Macintosh keyboard is *configurable* to any desired layout. The correspondence between physical keys and the characters they stand for is defined by a *keyboard configuration* that's read from the system resource file (under resource type 'INIT' [8.4.4]) each time the system is started up. On software disks for use in a foreign country, the system file will include that country's preferred keyboard configuration. Starting the machine with such a disk transforms the keyboard into a German QWERTZ or a French AZERTY instead of the familiar American QWERTY layout. Fans of the more efficient Dvorak arrangement can reconfigure their keyboards that way if they prefer. (Of course, they'll have to rearrange the physical keycaps for themselves!)

When reporting the user's keystrokes to your program, the Toolbox gives both a *key code* and a *character code*. A program that uses this information properly will work the same way no matter how the user's keyboard is laid out. The key code [8.1.3] identifies the physical key that was pressed, and is unaffected by the keyboard configuration in effect; the character code [8.1.1] tells what character the key stands for, as determined by the keyboard configuration. The Shift, Caps Lock, Option, and Command keys are *modifier keys* that don't generate any characters of their own, but may change the meanings of the remaining *character keys*. (For instance, the Shift key normally changes lowercase letters to capitals.) Exactly what effect the modifier keys have on the characters keys is determined by the keyboard configuration; for details on the standard American configuration, see [8.1.4].

You'll probably never have occasion to define your own keyboard configuration, but if you do—or if you're just curious about how the mechanism works—you'll find further information in [8.4.4] and in the "Nuts and Bolts" section at the end of this chapter.

Graphical Representation of Text

You can control the appearance of text on the screen by specifying its typeface, size, and style. The term *typeface* (or just "face") refers to the overall form or design of the characters, independent of size or style. Macintosh typefaces are conventionally named after world cities, such as New York, Geneva, or Athens. The type size is theoretically measured in printer's points; 72 points equal approximately one inch. (In practice this is more of a fiction than a reality: the actual type sizes aren't exact enough to satisfy a professional typographer, but nevertheless they're often called "point sizes.") *Type style* (or "text style" or "character style") refers to variations in the basic form of the characters such as bold, italic, underline, outline, or shadow. Together, the typeface, size, and style determine the exact form of a character as it appears on the screen.

What we're calling typefaces are commonly referred to as "fonts," but that term also has another, more restricted meaning, as we'll see later. This unfortunate double use of the same term leads to a certain amount of confusion in terminology. To try to minimize the ambiguity, we'll use *typeface* as defined here and reserve *font* for the second meaning to be introduced later.

The graphical representation of a character on the screen (or on a printer or other output device) is an array of pixels called a *character image* (Figure 8-1). The image is defined relative to a reference line called the *baseline* and a point on the baseline called the *character origin*. The character origin marks the position of the QuickDraw graphics pen when the character is drawn; the *character width* tells QuickDraw how far to advance the pen after drawing the character.

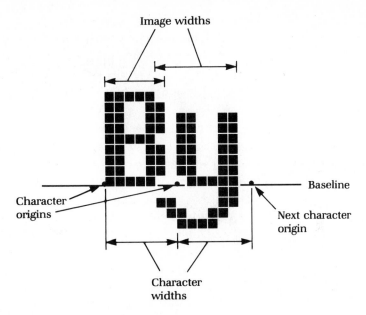

Figure 8-1 Character images

The character image isn't confined to these boundaries, however. The second character in Figure 8-1, for example, extends to the left of the character origin, causing it to jut slightly below the preceding character. In printer's lingo this is known as a *kern*— in this case, a backward kern. A character can also kern forward, if its image extends beyond the character width to the right. The actual width of the character image, in pixels, is called the *image width*. The character's *ascent* and *descent* measure how far it extends above and below the baseline.

Notice that the character width and the image width aren't the same thing. The character width controls the positioning of the graphics pen as text is drawn, and is always measured from the origin of one character to that of the next. It includes not only the width of the character itself, but also the extra space separating it from the next character. The image width measures the actual width of the character image itself. Either of the two may be 0: a space character, for instance, has a zero image width but a nonzero character width. A zero character width produces a "dead" character that doesn't advance the pen, such as an accent that combines with the letter following it.

Fonts and Font Numbers

The collection of all the character images of a given typeface and size is called a *font*. Fonts are kept in resource files and are read into memory as needed; their resource type, reasonably enough, is 'FONT' [8.4.5]. You don't normally have to deal with fonts directly: you just specify the typeface, size, and style you want and let the Toolbox take care of the details. Before it can do so, though, you have to initialize it for font handling with InitFonts [8.2.4]. Always make sure you call this routine at the beginning of your program, after calling InitGraf [4.3.1] and before InitWindows [II:3.2.1].

You identify a font by giving a *font number* [8.2.1] and a type size. The font number should really be called a "face number," since it designates a particular typeface independent of size. Legal font numbers run from 0 to 255, and type sizes can range from 1 to 127 points. The 8-bit font number combines with the 7-bit size to form a 15-bit resource ID for the corresponding font. This is equivalent to multiplying the font number by 128 and adding the size: for example, font number 3 stands for the Geneva typeface, so the resource ID for the 12-point Geneva font would be 3*128 + 12, or 396.

Font number 0 stands for the *system font*. (It should really be the "system face.") This is the typeface the Toolbox uses for all text it displays on the screen, such as window titles and menu items. The standard system font for American use is named Chicago, and the Toolbox always uses it in a standard size of 12 points. A program can also have its own *application font*, denoted by font number 1. There is no actual typeface with this number; it refers to some other existing face whose true font number is found in the system global ApFontID. The application font is initialized to Geneva each time a new application program is started up, but you can change it to any other typeface you wish in assembly language, anyway by storing the desired font number into this variable. (There's no easy way to change the application font in a high-level language like Pascal.)

Font numbers from 2 to 127 are reserved for typefaces provided by Apple itself. So far there are 15 such faces available in addition to the Chicago system font, five of which are designed specifically for use with the new LaserWriter printer. The font numbers for these standard typefaces are included in the Toolbox interface as predefined constants [8.2.1]. Licensed Macintosh software developers can register their own typefaces with Apple and have them assigned font numbers from 128 to 255.

The Toolbox routines GetFontName and GetFNum [8.2.5] convert between a font number and the corresponding typeface name. The Toolbox finds the name by looking for a font resource with the given font number and a point size of 0. The resource name of this resource gives the name of the typeface: for example, font resource number 384 (3∗128 + 0) has the resource name 'Geneva'. This "0-point" font has no resource data; it exists solely to carry the name of the typeface. The real fonts, those with nonzero point sizes, have no resource names.

The Macintosh Plus version of the Toolbox uses a more elaborate scheme of font identification based on a new data structure, the *family record*. There's one family record for each typeface, stored on the disk as a resource of type 'FOND' ("font definition"). The internal structure of the family record is too complex to discuss here; it's described in detail in the Macintosh Plus supplement (Volume IV) of Apple's *Inside Macintosh* manual. Among other things, it includes a table giving the resource IDs of the available font resources for various sizes and styles of a typeface.

Under the new scheme, the name and font number (now called a "family number") of each typeface are given by the resource name and ID of its 'FOND' resource. However, the original version of the Toolbox knows nothing of family records, and pays no attention to 'FOND' resources. Although the new Toolbox can deal with family (font) numbers from −32768 to +32767, the old one only recognizes those between 0 and 255. To maintain compatibility with older machines, all fonts falling within this range must still follow the old numbering and naming conventions described above.

Not every point size actually exists for a given typeface. If you ask to use a face and size that can't be found in any open resource file, the Toolbox will automatically choose a suitable existing font in that typeface and scale it to the requested size. The results aren't always pleasing to the eye, however—as you can see by looking at, say, 12-point Athens in MacWrite or MacPaint. To find out if a given combination actually exists, use the Toolbox routine RealFont [8.2.5].

On the Macintosh Plus, you also have the option of turning off automatic font scaling with a new routine named SetFScaleDisable [8.2.8]. Instead of scaling an existing font to the requested (nonexistent) point size, the Toolbox will simply use the next smaller available size but space the characters farther apart, as if they were in the size you asked for. This method is both faster and more readable than scaling, and gives a truer approximation to the proper word placements, line breaks, and so forth. Font scaling is initially turned on, for backward compatibility with existing applications, but you'll probably want to turn it off if you're running on a Macintosh Plus.

Structure of a Font

The complete definition of a font is contained in a *font record* [8.2.2]. This is a complex data structure that includes the character images themselves, along with additional information about the font's overall characteristics. The Toolbox normally handles font records for you, so you don't really need to know their internal structure. The following discussion is intended purely for your background understanding, and you can safely skip it if you're in a hurry.

Do keep in mind, though, that font records are large objects and take up a lot of space in memory or on the disk. It takes a great many bits to define all those character images, and since the images are two-dimensional, they grow with the square of the point size. Besides the actual character images, there's also a sizable fixed overhead for every font record. A typical 9-point font occupies about 2K bytes, an 18-point font about 5K, and a 24-point font about 8K. Fonts intended for use with the LaserWriter printer can be twice these sizes or even larger.

A program that uses many fonts will find that it can't keep them all in memory at once, particularly on machines with smaller memory capacities. Such a program tends to become "disk-bound," spending most of its time waiting for fonts to be read in from the disk. To see this effect for yourself, try making up a MacWrite document that uses ten or twelve different fonts on the same line of text, and listen to the disk spin when you try to select an insertion point on that line with the mouse.

Figure 8-2 shows some of the font characteristics that are defined in the font record. If all the individual character images in the font are superimposed with their character origins coinciding, the *font rectangle* is the smallest rectangle, relative to the baseline and character origin, that encloses them all. Its width, fRectWidth, encloses the image widths of all the characters. (Don't forget that the image width isn't the same as the character width; the font's maximum character width, from character origin to character origin, is given by the widMax field.) The maximum ascent and descent for any individual character determine the overall ascent and descent of the font, and thus establish its *ascent line* and *descent line* with respect to the baseline. Together, the ascent and descent give the *font height*, the overall height of the font rectangle from ascent line to descent line. *Leading* (rhymes with "heading," not "heeding") is the amount of extra vertical space between lines of text, from the descent line of one to the ascent line of the next.

The heart of the font record is the *font image* [8.2.3], which defines the appearance of every character. This is a rectangular bit image made up of all the individual character images laid end to end in one long horizontal row, often called a "strike" of the

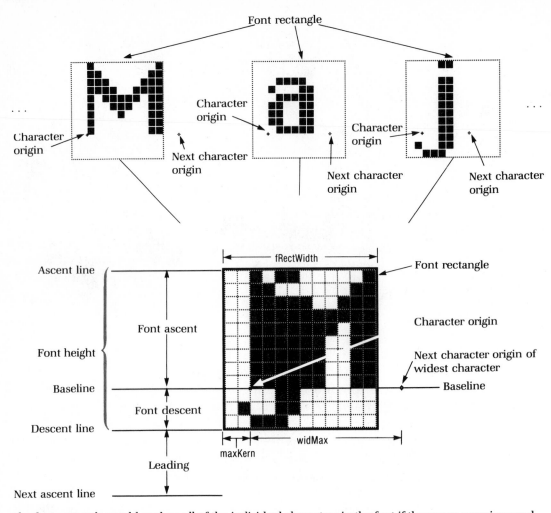

The font rectangle would enclose all of the individual characters in the font if they were superimposed with their character origins coinciding. fRectMax, the width of the font rectangle, is the font's maximum image width; widMax is the maximum character width.

Figure 8-2 Font characteristics

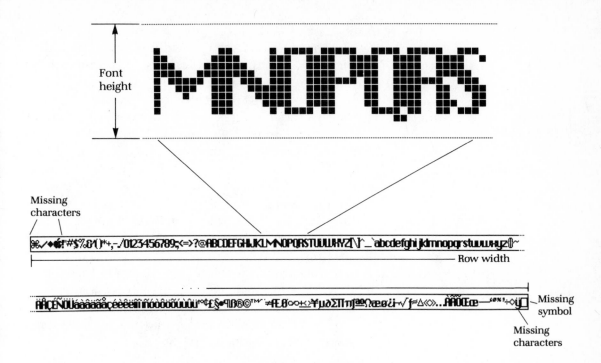

Figure 8-3 A font image

font (see Figure 8-3). The height of the font image is simply the font height; its row width is given by the rowWords field of the font record. (Notice that the row width is given in *words*, not in bytes as in a QuickDraw bit map [4.2.1].)

The character images are arranged within the strike by ascending character code. There needn't be an image for every possible character; characters that aren't included in the strike are said to be *missing* from the font. Every font includes a special *missing symbol* (typically a hollow square) to be used in place of all missing characters. The missing symbol is always the last character image in the strike. The font record's firstChar and lastChar fields give the character codes of the first and last character actually defined. Characters outside this range are understood to be missing, and some of those within the range may be missing as well.

To locate each individual character within the strike, there's a *location table* [8.2.3] with an entry for each character from firstChar to lastChar. The location table entry gives the horizontal offset, in pixels, from the beginning of the strike to the left edge of the character. The character's image width is found by subtracting this offset from that of the next character, taken from the next entry in the location table. (Notice that for this arrangement to work properly, the location table entry for a missing character must always be the same as that of the next defined character.) At the end of the location table are two extra entries, one for the missing symbol and another to mark the end of the strike; this last entry is simply the total width of the strike in pixels.

Following the location table is the *offset/width table* [8.2.3], which controls the positioning of the graphics pen as text is drawn. Like the location table, the offset/width table is indexed from firstChar to lastChar + 2. An entry of −1 in this table marks a character as missing. Otherwise, the second byte of the 2-byte table entry gives the character width, the distance the pen advances after drawing the character. The first byte positions the character image with respect to the character origin (which marks the pen position when the character is drawn). This positioning is done in a somewhat roundabout way, which we'll discuss in a minute. After the entry for lastChar is one for the missing symbol, then a final entry of −1 marking the end of the table.

> Because the font image, location table, and offset/width table all vary in length from one font to another, they can't be included in a valid Pascal declaration for the font record. (Notice that they're shown in comment brackets in [8.2.2].) The Toolbox has no trouble accessing them, of course, since it's written in assembly language; they can even be reached in Pascal if you're willing to do some (ugh!) pointer arithmetic. The owTLoc field of the font record serves as a guidepost by giving the distance in words (not bytes!) from itself to the beginning of the offset/width table.

Returning to the font rectangle shown in Figure 8-2, notice that it extends to the left of the character origin by an amount equal to the font's maxKern field, the maximum leftward kern of any character in the font. Because it's measured from right to left, maxKern always has a negative (or zero) value; in the figure, it would be −2. Now suppose that a given character kerns by less than the maximum—say by one pixel instead of two (see Figure 8-4). Then

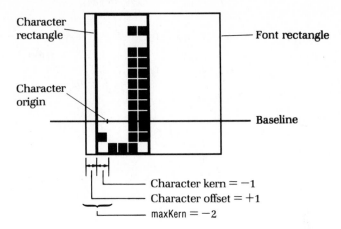

Character rectangle

Font rectangle

Character origin

Baseline

Character kern = −1
Character offset = +1
maxKern = −2

Figure 8-4 Character offset

the left edge of the character lies one pixel in from the left edge of the overall font rectangle. This *character offset* is what's kept in the high-order byte of an offset/width table entry. Adding the character offset (+1 in the figure) to the font's maximum kern (−2) gives the kern for the individual character (−1). For a character with no kern at all, the character offset is the negative of maxKern (+2 in the example), so when they're added together they cancel and produce a character kern of 0.

Kerning is more flexible on the Macintosh Plus: the size of a character's kern can vary depending on the character preceding or following it. The kerning information for each typeface is given by a *kerning table* in the family record; see *Inside Macintosh*, Volume IV, for details.

To take advantage of high-resolution devices such as the LaserWriter printer, the Macintosh Plus Toolbox allows the character widths for a font to be expressed as fixed-point fractions instead of integers. The Toolbox will automatically round such fractional character widths to a whole number of dots at whatever resolution is available on a given device (for example, 72 dots per inch for the screen, 144 for the ImageWriter printer, or 300 for the LaserWriter). The use of this feature is optional, and is controlled by a global flag named FractEnable. For compatibility with older applications, fractional widths are disabled by default; all character placements are calculated in whole pixels at screen resolution, as they were under the original Toolbox. If you wish, you can enable fractional widths with the Pascal interface routine SetFractEnable [8.2.8], or by storing directly into the global variable FractEnable in assembly language.

To support fractional character widths, two extra tables are added at the end of the font record, following the offset/width table. The new tables are not required, and old fonts are still usable without them; they simply improve the speed and accuracy with which text is drawn. If present, they're the same length as the location and offset/width tables: 2 bytes per entry, indexed from firstChar to lastChar + 2. The fontType field of the font record [8.2.2] tells whether they're included.

The *character-width table* gives the width of each character in fixed-point form, with an 8-bit integer part and an 8-bit fraction. If it's omitted, the integer character widths found in the offset/width table will be used instead. The only penalty is less accurate character placement on the LaserWriter or other high-resolution devices.

The *image-height table* gives the true height of each character image, relative to the overall font height defined by the font's ascent and descent lines. The first byte of each entry tells how many rows of empty white space to skip from the ascent line to the first pixel of the character; the second gives the number of nonwhite rows in the actual character image. If this table is missing, the Toolbox can construct one for itself when it reads the font in from the disk, using the information already present in the font image and location table. Including an image-height table in the font resource just speeds things up a bit; most fonts don't have one.

QuickDraw Text Characteristics

Like anything else you put on the screen, text gets drawn through the medium of a QuickDraw graphics port. The GrafPort record includes six fields that control the way text is drawn in that port [8.3.1]. The QuickDraw routines to set these fields, as well as those that draw and measure text, operate implicitly on the current port—so before using them you have to "get into" the right port with SetPort [4.3.3].

> Unfortunately, the names of the port's text-related fields suffer from the inconsistent terminology mentioned earlier. The txFont field doesn't really identify a font, but a typeface (that is, a "font number"); the field named txFace doesn't refer to the typeface at all, but to what we're calling the character style, such as bold or italic. Please make the appropriate mental annotations on your conceptual map.

A newly created graphics port is initially set up to display text in the system font (font number 0) at the standard size of 12 points, with plain character style. You can change the typeface for the current port with TextFont, the point size with TextSize, the character style with TextFace, or the transfer mode used for drawing text with TextMode [8.3.2]. Character styles are expressed as Pascal sets containing values of the enumerated type StyleItem [8.3.1]. For instance, the set [Underline] denotes underlining, [Bold, Underline] denotes bold and underline in combination, and the empty set [ ] stands for plain character style, with none of the fancy variations. You can do "set arithmetic" to turn individual style variations on or off without affecting the others: for example, the statement

```
TextFace (ThePort^.txFace + [Underline])
```

turns on underlining without affecting the remaining settings, and

```
TextFace (ThePort^.txFace - [Underline])
```

turns it off.

QuickDraw ordinarily produces these style variations by applying transformations to the character images it gets from the font. For instance, it produces boldface by thickening the character horizontally a suitable number of pixels, and italic by skewing the pixels horizontally depending on their height above or below the baseline. In the original Toolbox, such style transformations aren't normally reflected in the font itself.

On the Macintosh Plus, however, there can be separate font definitions for such variations as bold and italic, producing better-looking results than those obtained by applying mechanical transformations to the plain-text font. The family record for each typeface includes the resource IDs of any such variant fonts that may be available. To keep them from showing up in menus and font lists, they're stored under resource type 'NFNT' ("non-menu font"), which has exactly the same structure as 'FONT' [8.4.5]. The sole purpose of 'NFNT' is to provide an alternative form of font resource that won't be included when you ask for a menu of available resources of type 'FONT'. 'NFNT' resources are meaningless to the old Toolbox; it will ignore them and continue to produce its style variations the old way, by mechanically transforming the characters of the plain font.

The spExtra field of the graphics port (set with SpaceExtra [8.3.2] is useful mainly for justifying text to both a left and a right margin at the same time. This field holds a fixed-point number [2.3.1] with a 16-bit integer part and a 16-bit fraction. When drawing text, QuickDraw uses this information to widen the space characters so as to make the text come out even at both margins. To find the proper spExtra value for a line of text, divide the excess line width (the width between margins minus the measured width of the text) by the number of spaces in the line, using the utility function FixRatio [2.3.2] to produce a fixed-point result.

Finally, there's a device field that tells what output device the port is intended to draw on, such as the screen or a printer. The Toolbox uses this information to select the appropriate fonts for that particular device. When you create a port, its device field is initialized to 0, representing the Macintosh screen, and for most ordinary purposes you'll just want to leave this setting alone.

Drawing and Measuring Text

To draw text in the current graphics port, you use the QuickDraw routines DrawChar, DrawString, and DrawText [8.3.3]. DrawChar is the basic routine, which just draws a single character; the other two routines call it repeatedly to draw the text a character at a time. DrawString accepts a Pascal string, which is expected to begin with a 1-byte character count. DrawText accepts a pointer to an arbitrary data structure, which *doesn't* start with a character count; the text to be drawn can be any specified sequence of bytes from within the structure.

> DrawText is useful for displaying the contents of 'TEXT' resources [8.4.1], but notice that you have to convert the handle you get from GetResource [6.3.1] into a simple pointer to pass to DrawText. To be safe, you'd better lock the text into the heap before dereferencing the handle—and don't forget to unlock it again when you're through drawing it!

Text is always drawn in the port's current typeface, size, style, and text mode. Each character is drawn with its character origin at the port's current pen position (pnLoc [5.2.1]); the pen then advances to the right by the character width, adjusted for style variations if necessary. The operation leaves the pen positioned on the baseline just after the last character drawn. ASCII control characters such as carriage return, line feed, tab, and backspace have no special meaning to QuickDraw; if you want to use these characters for formatting purposes, you have to test for them and reposition the pen yourself with Move or MoveTo [5.2.4].

Program 8-1 (ShowFonts) shows an example of text drawing. This routine finds every available font in all open resource files and displays a sample of each in the current graphics port, as in Figure 8-5. (Of course, if the current port is a window on the screen, it may not have room to display this much text all at once. In that case, some of the text will fall outside the window's port rectangle and won't be drawn: QuickDraw will suppress it automatically, as it always does when you try to draw anything outside a port's clipping boundaries.)

```
procedure ShowFonts;


   { Display samples of all available fonts.  }



   const
      leftMargin = 10;                            {Margin from left edge of window, in pixels}
      topMargin  = 10;                            {Margin from top edge of window, in pixels}


   var
      currentPort : GrafPtr;                      {Pointer to current port [4.2.2]}

      oldOrigin   : Point;                        {Previous origin of port rectangle [4.1.1]}
      oldPenLoc   : Point;                        {Previous position of graphics pen [4.1.1]}

      oldFont     : INTEGER;                      {Previous typeface ("font number") [8.3.1]}
      oldSize     : INTEGER;                      {Previous point size [8.3.1]}
      oldFace     : Style;                        {Previous text style ("face") [8.3.1]}

      baseline    : INTEGER;                      {Vertical position of baseline in pixels}

      nFonts      : INTEGER;                      {Total number of font resources available}
      thisFont    : INTEGER;                      {Index for accessing individual fonts}

      rsrcHandle  : Handle;                       {Handle to font resource [3.1.1]}
      rsrcID      : INTEGER;                      {Resource ID of font}
      rsrcType    : ResType;                      {Resource type of font [6.1.1]}
      rsrcName    : Str255;                       {Resource name of font [2.1.1]}

      faceNumber  : INTEGER;                      {"Font number" for typeface}
      faceName    : Str255;                       {Name of typeface [2.1.1]}

      pointSize   : INTEGER;                      {Type size in points}
      pointString : Str255;                       {Type size as character string [2.1.1]}

      theInfo     : FontInfo;                     {Font information record [8.2.6]}


   begin {ShowFonts}

      GetPort (currentPort);                      {Get pointer to current port [4.3.3]}
      with currentPort^ do
         begin
            oldOrigin := portRect.topLeft;        {Save old origin of port rectangle [4.2.2, 4.1.2]}
            GetPen (oldPenLoc);                   {Save old pen position [5.2.4]}
```

Program 8-1 Display available fonts

```
        oldFont    := txFont;                    {Save old typeface ("font number") [8.3.1]}
        oldSize    := txSize;                    {Save old point size [8.3.1]}
        oldFace    := txFace                     {Save old text style ("face") [8.3.1]}
    end;

SetOrigin (-leftMargin, -topMargin);            {Offset to origin of text [4.3.4]}
baseline := 0;                                   {Start text at top margin}
TextFace ([ ]);                                  {Use plain text style [8.3.2]}

nFonts := CountResources ('FONT');               {Get total number of available fonts [6.3.3]}
for thisFont := 1 to nFonts do                   {Iterate through available fonts}
  begin

        rsrcHandle := GetIndResource ('FONT', thisFont);      {Get next font [6.3.3]}
        GetResInfo (rsrcHandle, rsrcID, rsrcType, rsrcName);  {Get resource information [6.4.1]}

        faceNumber := rsrcID div 128;            {Isolate typeface number}
        pointSize  := rsrcID mod 128;            {   and point size      }

        if pointSize <> 0 then                   {Ignore dummy "font name" resources}
          begin

                TextFont (faceNumber);           {Set port's typeface [8.3.2]}
                TextSize (pointSize);            {Set port's type size [8.3.2]}

                GetFontInfo (theInfo);           {Get font measurements [8.2.6]}
                baseline := baseline + theInfo.ascent;   {Advance baseline by font ascent [8.2.6]}
                MoveTo (0, baseline);            {Position pen at start of line [5.2.4]}

                GetFontName (faceNumber, faceName);   {Get name of typeface [8.2.5]}
                DrawString  (faceName);          {Display typeface name [8.3.3]}
                DrawChar    (' ');               {Insert space character for separation [8.3.3]}

                NumToString (pointSize, pointString); {Convert type size to string [2.3.7]}
                DrawString  (pointString);       {Display type size [8.3.3]}

                with theInfo do                  {Advance to next ascent line [8.2.6]}
                    baseline := baseline + descent + leading

        end {if}

  end; {for}
```

Program 8-1 *(continued)*

```
TextFont (oldFont);                    {Restore previous typeface ("font number") [8.3.2]}
TextSize (oldSize);                    {Restore previous point size [8.3.2]}
TextFace (oldFace);                    {Restore previous text style ("face") [8.3.2]}

with oldOrigin do
    SetOrigin (h, v);                  {Restore previous origin [4.3.4]}

with oldPenLoc do
    MoveTo (h, v)                      {Restore previous pen position [5.2.4]}

end;   {ShowFonts}
```

Program 8-1 (*continued*)

We begin by saving various properties of the current port that we'll be changing within the routine (the coordinate origin, pen position, typeface, type size, and type style), so we can restore their previous settings before returning. For convenience, we transform the coordinate origin to the top-left corner of the area where the font samples will be displayed, as defined by the pair of constants leftMargin and topMargin. The baseline for text drawing is initialized to the very top of this area; we'll be advancing it downward by the appropriate distance as we draw each line of text.

After setting the port's type style with TextFace [8.3.2] to plain text (no bold, italic, or other variations), we're ready to start generating the available font resources, using the Toolbox routines CountResources and GetIndResource [6.3.3]. As we learned in Chapter 6, CountResources tells how many resources there are of a given type (in this case 'FONT') in all open resource files. By calling GetIndResource with an index number (thisFont) ranging from 1 up to this total number, we can get a handle to each individual font resource in turn.

For each font resource, we call GetResInfo [6.4.1] to find out the resource ID, which we then break down with the Pascal **div** and **mod** operators into an 8-bit typeface number and a 7-bit point size. Remember, though, that some of the fonts in a resource file are "dummy" fonts with a point size of 0, which exist solely to carry the typeface name; these "0-point" fonts have no character images to display text with, so we just ignore them. For every font with a nonzero point size, we set the current port's text characteristics to the font's typeface and size with TextFont and TextSize [8.3.2], then

Chicago 12
Geneva 9
Geneva 10
Geneva 12
Geneva 14
Geneva 18
Geneva 20
Geneva 24
New York 9
New York 10
New York 12
New York 14
New York 18
New York 20
New York 24
Monaco 9
Monaco 12
Venice 14
𝕷𝖔𝖓𝖉𝖔𝖓 18
Athens 18

Figure 8-5 Output of procedure ShowFonts

call GetFontInfo [8.2.6] to get the font's ascent, descent, and leading measurements.

The ascent value tells us how far to lower our baseline to position it for the line of text we're about to display. Then we move the graphics pen to the beginning of the new baseline to get ready to display the characters. We get the name of the font's typeface by calling GetFontName [8.2.5] and display it with DrawString [8.3.3]. (Notice that we can't simply use the resource name we received earlier from GetResInfo, since only the dummy "0-point" fonts have resource names; the resource representing a "real" font has no name of its own.) Following the typeface name, we insert a space character with DrawChar [8.3.3] to separate it from the point size; then we convert the point size from an integer to a character string with NumToString [2.3.7] and use DrawString again to display the result. Finally we advance the baseline by the font's descent and leading, to prepare for the next line of text, and repeat the loop.

After all available fonts have been generated, we restore the port's original typeface, size, style, pen position, and coordinate origin, then exit from the routine. Notice that at the beginning of the routine we saved the pen position *before* adjusting the port's coordinate origin. When we get to the end of the routine, we have to be careful to restore the original pen position *after* the coordinate origin, so that it's expressed in the same system of coordinates in which it was originally reported.

Sometimes you just want to measure how wide a piece of text would be *if* you drew it, but without actually drawing it. (For instance, you might be calculating how much extra space you need between words to justify a line of text to the left and right margins.) For this, you can use CharWidth, StringWidth, and TextWidth [8.3.4]. These routines measure the width of the specified text in pixels, using the text characteristics of the current graphics port. No text is actually drawn and the pen is not moved.

> The Macintosh Plus has a new routine named MeasureText [8.3.4] that measures all sequences of characters up to a given maximum length, beginning at a designated position in a piece of text. (That is, it measures the width of the first character at that position, the first two characters, the first three, and so on, up to the specified maximum.) This information is particularly useful for finding line breaks: it tells you which character in a line exceeds the maximum width, so you can decide where to break the line and start a new one.

QuickDraw doesn't need a font's actual character images to measure text, just the character widths given in the font's offset/width table. So to conserve heap space, there's a special, abbreviated form of font record especially for measuring text, called a *font width table*. It's identified by the constant FontWid in the font's fontType field [8.2.2], and contains no font image, location table, or rowWords field. Width tables are stored in resource files under resource type 'FWID' [8.4.6]; the resource ID is the same as for the corresponding font. If such a resource is available for a given font, the Toolbox will use it for text-measuring operations. If no 'FWID' resource is available, the full font is used instead. (Font width tables are used only by the original version of the Toolbox; they're ignored on the Macintosh Plus.)

Nuts and Bolts

"Dead" Characters

Some of the accented foreign letters in the Macintosh character set have no direct keyboard equivalents, even using the Option key. Instead, they're typed as two-character sequences: first the accent, followed by the letter it applies to. For instance, to type a circumflex "e" (ê, character code $90), you have to type the circumflex (ˆ) first, then the letter e.

The Macintosh keyboard driver—the part of the system software that reads characters typed from the keyboard and feeds them to the running program by way of the Toolbox—automatically detects such sequences and converts them into the corresponding accented letters. By the time the program sees them, it receives the single accented letter instead of the two-character sequence that was actually typed. In effect, the accents (acute, grave, circumflex, umlaut, and tilde) function as "dead keys": typing them doesn't advance the insertion point, so the next letter is combined with the accent instead of following it separately.

Actually, the accents combine with the following letter only if the resulting combination exists as a distinct single character in the Macintosh character set. Otherwise, the accent and the letter remain two separate characters. For instance, although the circumflex accent combines with a following e to form the character ê ($90) as described above, a circumflex followed by an f would remain two separate characters.

Notice, also, that three of the accents are included in the standard ASCII character set, with character codes below $7F: grave (`, code $60), circumflex (^, $5E), and tilde (~, $7E). Each of these characters can be typed in two different ways, on different keys, one with and one without the Option key. When typed without Option, the accent always stands alone as a separate character. With Option, it becomes a "dead" character and will combine with the following letter if appropriate (for instance, the tilde will combine with a following n). If you find all this a little hard to follow, try experimenting for yourself with the Key Caps desk accessory.

Details of Keyboard Configurations

The job of translating the "raw" keystrokes typed by the user into characters to be sent to the program is performed by a pair of low-level machine language routines, one for the keyboard and another for the numeric keypad. Pointers to these routines are kept in the system globals Key1Trans and Key2Trans. The configuration routines are loaded from the system resource file each time the system is started up; they have resource type 'INIT' [8.4.4] and resource IDs 1 (keyboard) and 2 (keypad). The resource data is simply the machine-language code of the routine.

The configuration routines receive their arguments and return their results directly in the processor's registers, so they can only be written in and called from assembly language. They receive a key code in register D2 and a word giving the state of the modifier keys in D1, and return a character code in D0 (or 0 for no character). See [8.4.4] for further details.

REFERENCE

8.1 Keys and Characters

8.1.1 Character Set

Definitions

```
const
  CommandMark = $11;    {Character code of command mark}
  CheckMark   = $12;    {Character code of check mark}
  DiamondMark = $13;    {Character code of diamond mark}
  AppleMark   = $14;    {Character code of Apple mark}
```

First hex digit

	$0	$1	$2	$3	$4	$5	$6	$7	$8	$9	$A	$B	$C	$D	$E	$F
0	NUL	□	space	0	@	P	`	p	Ä	ê	†	∞	¿	–	‡	(apple)
1	□	⌘	!	1	A	Q	a	q	Å	ë	°	±	¡	—	·	Ò
2	□	✓	"	2	B	R	b	r	Ç	í	¢	≤	¬	"	‚	Ú
3	□	◆	#	3	C	S	c	s	É	ì	£	≥	√	"	„	Û
4	□	(apple)	$	4	D	T	d	t	Ñ	î	§	¥	ƒ	'	‰	Ù
5	□	□	%	5	E	U	e	u	Ö	ï	•	µ	≈	'	Â	ı
6	□	□	&	6	F	V	f	v	Ü	ñ	¶	∂	∆	÷	Ê	^
7	□	□	'	7	G	W	g	w	á	ó	ß	Σ	«	◊	Á	~
8	□	□	(	8	H	X	h	x	à	ò	®	Π	»	ÿ	Ë	¯
9	TAB	□	)	9	I	Y	i	y	â	ô	©	π	…	Ÿ	È	˘
A	□	□	*	:	J	Z	j	z	ä	ö	™	∫	non-break space	/	Í	˙
B	□	□	+	;	K	[	k	{	ã	õ	´	ª	Â	¤	Î	°
C	□	□	,	<	L	\	l	|	å	ú	¨	º	Ã	‹	Ï	¸
D	CR	□	–	=	M	]	m	}	ç	ù	≠	Ω	Õ	›	Ì	˝
E	□	□	.	>	N	^	n	~	é	û	Æ	æ	Œ	fi	Ó	˛
F	□	□	/	?	O	_	o		è	ü	Ø	ø	œ	fl	Ô	□

Second hex digit

Characters with shading are typed as two-character combinations

Character codes

Notes

1. Character codes stand for the characters themselves, not the keys that produce them. The character produced by a given key depends on which modifier keys were held down along with it and on the keyboard configuration in effect.

2. Character codes from $00 to $7F follow the standard ASCII character set (American Standard Code for Information Interchange).

3. Most ASCII control characters (character codes $00 to $1F, as well as $7F) can't be generated from the Macintosh keyboard or keypad. Exceptions are:

Character code	Key
$03	Enter
$08	Backspace
$09	Tab
$0D	Return
$1B	Clear
$1C	Left arrow
$1D	Right arrow
$1E	Up arrow
$1F	Down arrow

The original-model keyboard doesn't include the Clear and arrow keys; these are available only on the optional numeric keypad. The Macintosh Plus keyboard has the keypad built in.

4. The following ASCII control characters are redefined as special symbols for use on the Macintosh screen:

Character code	Symbol	Name
$11	⌘	Command mark
$12	✓	Check mark
$13	◆	Diamond mark
$14		Apple mark

These characters are intended only for display on the screen, and can't be typed from the keyboard.

5. The command mark is used for displaying Command-key equivalents of items on a menu; the check mark for marking menu items [II:4.6.4]; the Apple mark for the title of the menu of desk accessories.

6. The diamond mark is a vestige of earlier versions of the Macintosh user interface and no longer has any specific use.

7. Character codes of $80 and above denote special characters added to the Macintosh character set for international, business, and scientific use. Those beginning with $D9 are included for use on the LaserWriter printer, and are generally available only in fonts designed specifically for the LaserWriter [8.2.1].

8. Characters shaded in the figure aren't generated directly from the keyboard. Instead they're typed as two-character combinations, a diacritical (accent) mark followed by the letter it is combined with. The Toolbox automatically converts such two-character combinations into the corresponding single accented characters.

Assembly Language Information

Assembly language constants:

Name	Value	Meaning
CommandMark	$11	Character code of command mark
CheckMark	$12	Character code of check mark
DiamondMark	$13	Character code of diamond mark
AppleMark	$14	Character code of Applemark

8.1.2 Character Strings

Definitions

```
type
    StringPtr    = ^Str255;              {Pointer to a string}
    StringHandle = ^StringPtr;           {Handle to a string}

function    NewString
                (oldString : Str255)     {String to be copied}
                : StringHandle;          {Handle to copy}

function    GetString
                (stringID : INTEGER)     {Resource ID of desired string}
                : StringHandle;          {Handle to string in memory}

procedure   GetIndString
                (var theString : Str255; {Returns requested string}
                stringListID   : INTEGER;   {Resource ID of string list}
                stringIndex    : INTEGER);  {Index of string within list}

procedure   SetString
                (theString : StringHandle;  {Handle to be set}
                setTo      : Str255);       {String to set it to}
```

Notes

1. StringPtr and StringHandle are a pointer and a handle to a string, respectively.

2. NewString allocates heap space for a new, relocatable copy of a given string and returns a handle to the copy.

3. GetString gets a string from a resource file, reads it into memory if necessary, and returns a handle to it.

4. stringID is the resource ID of the desired string; its resource type is 'STR ' [8.4.2].

5. GetIndString reads a string from a string list stored in a resource file and returns a copy of it in the variable parameter theString.

6. stringListID is the resource ID of the string list; its resource type is 'STR#' [8.4.3]. stringIndex is the index of the desired string within the list.

7. If the specified string list doesn't exist or the index is out of range, the empty string is returned.

8. GetIndString is part of the Pascal interface to the Toolbox, not part of the Toolbox itself. It doesn't reside in ROM and can't be called from assembly language via the trap mechanism.

9. SetString makes a copy of a given string and sets an existing string handle to point to the copy.

Assembly Language Information

Trap macros:

(Pascal) Routine name	(Assembly) Trap macro	Trap word
NewString	_NewString	$A906
GetString	_GetString	$A9BA
SetString	_SetString	$A907

8.1.3 Key Codes

Notes

1. Key codes stand for physical keys on the Macintosh keyboard or keypad, not the characters the keys represent. They're independent of any particular keyboard configuration and are not affected by modifier keys.

2. The modifier keys (Shift, Caps Lock, Option, Command) have no key codes, since they don't generate characters by themselves.

Original keyboard

Original keypad

Key codes

$32 `	$12 1	$13 2	$14 3	$15 4	$17 5	$16 6	$1A 7	$1C 8	$19 9	$1D 0	$1B −	$18 =	$33 Back-space
$30 Tab	$0C Q	$0D W	$0E E	$0F R	$11 T	$10 Y	$20 U	$22 I	$1F O	$23 P	$21 [	$1E]	
$39 Caps Lock	$00 A	$01 S	$02 D	$03 F	$05 G	$04 H	$26 J	$28 K	$25 L	$29 ;	$27 '	$24 Return	
$38 Shift	$06 Z	$07 X	$08 C	$09 V	$0B B	$2D N	$2E M	$2B ,	$2F .	$2C /	$38 Shift	$4D ↑	
$3A Option	$37 ⌘	$31								$2A \	$46 ←	$42 →	$48 ↓

Macintosh Plus keyboard

$47 Clear	$48 =	$4D /	$42 *
$59 7	$5B 8	$5C 9	$4E −
$56 4	$57 5	$58 6	$46 +
$53 1	$54 2	$55 3	$4C
$52 0		$41 .	Enter

Macintosh Plus keypad

8.1.4   Standard Keyboard Layout

Standard keyboard layout (unshifted)

Standard keyboard layout (with Shift)

Standard keyboard layout (with Option)

Standard keyboard layout (with Option-Shift)

Macintosh Plus keyboard layout (unshifted)

Macintosh Plus keyboard layout (with Shift)

Macintosh Plus keyboard layout (with Option)

Macintosh Plus keyboard layout (with Option-Shift)

Notes

1. The keyboard layouts shown are for the standard (American) keyboard configuration.

2. Keys left blank in the diagrams have no character assignment for that modifier combination.

3. The Caps Lock key has the same effect as Shift, but for letter keys only; it has no effect on other keys.

8.2 Fonts

8.2.1 Standard Font Numbers

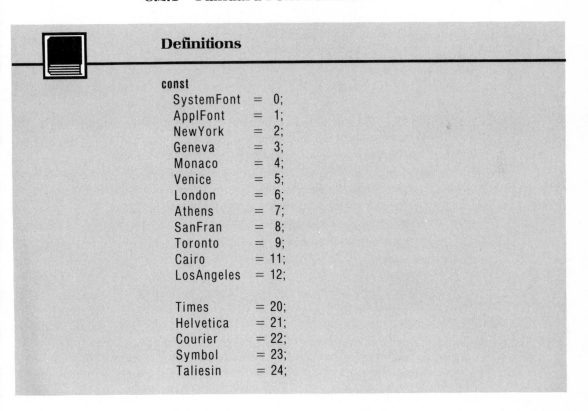

Definitions

```
const
    SystemFont   =  0;
    ApplFont     =  1;
    NewYork      =  2;
    Geneva       =  3;
    Monaco       =  4;
    Venice       =  5;
    London       =  6;
    Athens       =  7;
    SanFran      =  8;
    Toronto      =  9;
    Cairo        = 11;
    LosAngeles   = 12;

    Times        = 20;
    Helvetica    = 21;
    Courier      = 22;
    Symbol       = 23;
    Taliesin     = 24;
```

Notes

1. A font number identifies a typeface, independent of size or style.

2. Font numbers must not exceed 255.

3. To get the resource ID of the font for a given typeface and size, multiply the font number by 128 and add the type size in points.

4. Font number 0 refers to the *system font,* used for menu items, window titles, and other text displayed on the screen by the system.

5. The system font is named Chicago, and is always displayed in a standard size of 12 points. The system font cannot be changed.

6. The assembly-language global variable ROMFont0 holds a handle to the font record [8.2.2] for the system font.

7. Font number 1 refers to the *application font,* which is always some other existing typeface with a (true) font number of its own. There is no actual typeface with this number.

8. By default, the application font is set to Geneva each time a new application program is started up. The font number of this default application font is kept in the global variable SPFont.

9. To change the application font in assembly language, store the desired font number into the global variable ApFontID. There is no straightforward way to change this setting in Pascal.

10. The Times, Helvetica, Courier, and Symbol typefaces (font numbers 20–23) are designed specifically for use with the LaserWriter printer.

11. Font numbers from 2 to 127 are reserved for Apple's own typefaces, 128 to 255 for those formally registered with Apple by licensed Macintosh software developers.

12. Font numbers on the Macintosh Plus are called *family numbers,* and can range from −32768 to +32767. Fonts belonging to a given typeface are identified by means of a *family record* of resource type 'FOND' ("font definition"), rather than by the numbering convention described in note 3, above. However, since the original Toolbox recognizes font numbers between 0 and 255 only, all typefaces within this range must still follow the old numbering convention for compatibility. Typefaces outside the original range are unavailable under the old Toolbox.

Assembly Language Information

Standard font numbers:

Name	Value
SysFont	0
ApplFont	1
NewYork	2
Geneva	3
Monaco	4
Venice	5
London	6
Athens	7
SanFran	8
Toronto	9
Cairo	11
LosAngeles	12
Times	20
Helvetica	21
Courier	22
Symbol	23
Taliesin	24

Assembly-language global variables:

Name	Address	Meaning
ROMFont0	$980	Handle to system font
ApFontID	$984	True font number of current application font
SPFont	$204	True font number of default application font

8.2.2   Font Records

Definitions

```
type
  FontRecord = record
                 fontType     : INTEGER; {Font type (proportional or fixed-width)}
                 firstChar    : INTEGER; {Character code of first defined character}
                 lastChar     : INTEGER; {Character code of last defined character}
                 widMax       : INTEGER; {Maximum character width in pixels}
                 kernMax      : INTEGER; {Maximum backward kern in pixels}
                 nDescent     : INTEGER; {Negative of descent in pixels}
                 fRectWidth   : INTEGER; {Width of font rectangle in pixels}
                 fRectHeight  : INTEGER; {Height of font rectangle in pixels}
                 owTLoc       : INTEGER; {Offset to owTable in words}
                 ascent       : INTEGER; {Ascent in pixels}
                 descent      : INTEGER; {Descent in pixels}
                 leading      : INTEGER; {Leading in pixels}
                 rowWords     : INTEGER; {Row width of bitImage in words}
                 {bitImage    : array [1..rowWords, 1..fRectHeight] of INTEGER;}
                                         {Font image [8.2.3]}
                 {locTable    : array [firstChar..lastChar+2] of INTEGER;}
                                         {Location table [8.2.3]}
                 {owTable     : array [firstChar..lastchar+2] of INTEGER;}
                                         {Offset/width table [8.2.3]}
                 {widthTab    : array [firstChar..lastChar+2] of INTEGER;}
                                         {Character-width table (optional)}
                 {heightTab   : array [firstChar..lastChar+2] of INTEGER}
                                         {Image-height table (optional)}
               end;

const
  PropFont  = $9000;      {Font type for proportional font}
  PrpFntH   = $9001;      {   Proportional font with height table [8.2.3]}
  PrpFntW   = $9002;      {   Proportional font with width table [8.2.3]}
  PrpFntHW  = $9003;      {   Proportional font with height and width tables [8.2.3]}

  FixedFont = $B000;      {Font type for fixed-width font}
  FxdFntH   = $B001;      {   Fixed-width font with height table [8.2.3]}
  FxdFntW   = $B002;      {   Fixed-width font with width table [8.2.3]}
  FxdFntHW  = $B003;      {   Fixed-width font with height and width tables [8.2.3]}

  FontWid   = $ACB0;      {Font type for font width table}
```

Notes

1. A font record defines the character images and other characteristics of a single font.

2. Font records are used internally by the Toolbox; there's normally no need for an application program to refer to them directly.

3. Font records are stored in resource files under resource types 'FONT' and 'NFNT' [8.4.5] and read into the heap with GetResource [6.3.1].

4. fontType identifies the font as a proportional font (character widths vary), a fixed-width font (all characters the same width), or a font width table [8.4.6].

5. A font width table has no rowWords, bitImage, and locTable fields.

6. firstChar and lastChar are the character codes of the first and last characters defined in this font.

7. fRectWidth and fRectHeight give the dimensions of the *font rectangle*. If all the individual character images in the font are superimposed with their character origins coinciding, the font rectangle is the smallest rectangle enclosing them all. (In older versions of the Toolbox interface, the fRectWidth and fRectHeight fields are named fRectMax and chHeight.)

8. widMax is the maximum *character width* for any single character in the font; fRectWidth is the width of the font rectangle, enclosing all the individual *image widths*.

9. ascent and descent define the font's vertical extent relative to the baseline. Their sum gives the overall font height, fRectHeight.

10. nDescent should always equal the negative of descent.

11. kernMax is the maximum negative (leftward) kern of any character in the font, and should never be greater than 0. This value determines the position of the character origin within the font rectangle.

12. leading is the amount of extra vertical space in pixels between lines of text, from the descent line of one to the ascent line of the next.

13. The leading value given in the font record is merely recommended, and is not binding on the application program. Some parts of the Toolbox—notably the TextEdit routines for cut-and-paste editing (Volume Two, Chapter 5)—will use this value by default, but you can override it to produce whatever vertical spacing you like.

14. The remaining fields (owTLoc, rowWords, bitImage, locTable, owTable, widthTab, heightTab) are discussed in [8.2.3].

15. Older and more recent versions of the assembly-language Toolbox interface define different names for the field offsets within a font record. The table below shows both sets of names.

Assembly Language Information

Field offsets in a font record:

(Pascal) Field name	(Assembly) Offset name	Old offset name	Offset in bytes
fontType	fFontType	fFormat	0
firstChar	fFirstChar	fMinChar	2
lastChar	fLastChar	fMaxChar	4
widMax	fWidMax	fMaxWd	6
kernMax	fKernMax	fBBOX	8
nDescent	fNDescent	fBBOY	10
fRectWidth	fFRectWidth	fBBDX	12
fRectHeight	fFRectHeight	fBBDY	14
owTLoc	fOWTLoc	fLength	16
ascent	fAscent	fAscent	18
descent	fDescent	fDescent	20
leading	fLeading	fLeading	22
rowWords	fRowWords	fRaster	24

Assembly-language constants:

Name	Value	Meaning
PropFont	$9000	Font type for proportional font
PrpFntH	$9001	Proportional font with height table
PrpFntW	$9002	Proportional font with width table
PrpFntHW	$9003	Proportional font with height and width tables
FixedFont	$B000	Font type for fixed-width font
FxdFntH	$B001	Fixed-width font with height table
FxdFntW	$B002	Fixed-width font with width table
FxdFntHW	$B003	Fixed-width font with height and width tables
FontWid	$ACB0	Font type for font width table

8.2.3 The Font Image

Font image

Image Width

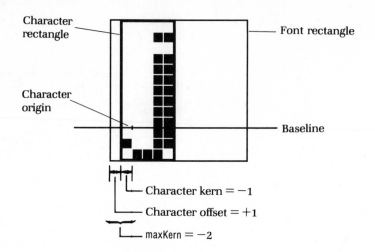

Character rectangle

Font rectangle

Character origin

Baseline

Character kern = −1

Character offset = +1

maxKern = −2

Character offset

Notes

1. The font image, location table, and offset/width table for a font are the last three required fields of its font record [8.2.2]. There are also two more optional fields, the character-width and image-height tables. These are all variable-length structures and can't be included (except as comments) in a valid Pascal type declaration for the font record. They're accessible in assembly language, or in Pascal via pointer manipulation with POINTER, ORD, and @ (Chapter 2).

2. The *font image* (bitImage) is a bit image containing all the font's character images arranged consecutively in a single horizontal "strike."

3. The row width of the font image (rowWords) is given in *words*, not in bytes as in a QuickDraw bit map [4.2.1].

4. Every font has a *missing symbol* to be used for drawing characters that are missing from the font. The missing symbol is always the last character in the font image, following the last defined character.

5. A character is considered missing if its character code is less than firstChar or greater than lastChar [8.2.2], or if its entry in the offset/width table is −1.

6. The ASCII null character (character code $00), horizontal tab ($09), and carriage return ($0D) must not be missing; they must be defined in the font image, even if only with zero image width. The tab character, in particular, is commonly defined to be equivalent to an ordinary space.

7. The *location table* (locTable) gives the horizontal offset, in pixels, from the beginning of the font image to the beginning of each character image.

8. A character's image width is found by subtracting its location table entry from that of the next character. The entry for a missing character should be the same as that of the next defined character in the font.

9. The next-to-last entry in the location table, locTable[lastChar+1], gives the location of the missing symbol within the font image. The last entry, locTable[lastChar+2], contains the total width of the font image (strike) in pixels.

10. The *offset/width table* (owTable) is located within the font record by means of the owTLoc field, which gives the offset in words from itself to the beginning of the table.

11. The low-order byte of an offset/width table entry gives the character width in pixels.

12. The high-order byte gives the *character offset*, the difference between this character's leftward kern and maxKern. This determines the position of the character rectangle relative to the overall font rectangle, and thus locates the character origin (QuickDraw pen position) within the character image.

13. Missing characters have an offset/width table entry of −1.

14. The next-to-last entry in the offset/width table, owTable[lastChar+1], gives the offset and width of the font's missing symbol. The last entry, owTable[lastChar+2], is always −1.

15. The character-width and image-height tables are optional fields used only by the Macintosh Plus version of the Toolbox. The fontType field of the font record [8.2.2] tells whether either or both of these tables are present.

16. Both tables are indexed from firstChar to lastChar+2, the same as the location and offset/width tables.

17. The *character-width table* (widthTab) gives the width of each character in fixed-point form, for use with the new fractional character width feature [8.2.8]. Although nominally declared as an array of integers, this table actually contains fixed-point values with an 8-bit integer part and an 8-bit fraction.

18. For a font with no character-width table, the integer character widths given in the offset/width table are used instead. Such a font is still usable, but character positioning is less precise, particularly on high-resolution devices such as the LaserWriter printer.

19. The *image-height table* (heightTab) gives the true height of each character image in pixels, for faster text drawing. The first byte of each entry is the number of empty rows between the font's overall ascent line and the first pixel of the character image; the second is the number of nonempty rows in the image.

20. Most fonts don't include an image-height table, since the Toolbox can construct one for itself from the information in the font image and location table.

8.2.4 Initializing the Toolbox for Fonts

Definitions

procedure InitFonts;

Notes

1. InitFonts must be called before any other operation involving fonts directly (such as drawing or measuring text [8.3.3, 8.3.4]) or indirectly (such as displaying windows, menus, and so forth).

2. It initializes the Toolbox's font-related data structures, reads the system font into memory if necessary, and initializes the application font to its default setting [8.2.1].

3. InitFonts should be called after InitGraf [4.3.1] and before InitWindows [II:3.2.1].

Assembly Language Information

Trap macro:

(Pascal) Routine name	(Assembly) Trap macro	Trap word
InitFonts	_InitFonts	$A8FE

8.2.5   Access to Fonts

Definitions

```
procedure  GetFontName
              (fontNumber : INTEGER;      {Font number}
               var name   : Str255);      {Returns name of typeface}

procedure  GetFNum
              (name            : Str255;        {Name of typeface}
               var fontNumber : INTEGER);       {Returns font number}

function   RealFont
              (fontNumber : INTEGER;      {Desired font number}
               pointSize  : INTEGER)      {Desired point size}
                 : BOOLEAN;               {Does font exist?}
```

Notes

1. GetFontName returns the name of the typeface with a given font number; GetFNum returns the font number of the face with a given name.
2. If no such typeface exists, GetFontName returns the empty string and GetFNum returns 0.
3. RealFont returns a Boolean result telling whether a 'FONT' resource exists for a given combination of typeface (font number) and point size. If this result is FALSE, requests to draw or measure text in that face and size will be carried out by substituting (and possibly scaling) a suitable existing font; see [8.2.8] and [8.3.1, note 4].
4. The trap macro for GetFontName is spelled _GetFName.

Assembly Language Information

Trap macros:

(Pascal) Routine name	(Assembly) Trap macro	Trap word
GetFontName	_GetFName	$A8FF
GetFNum	_GetFNum	$A900
RealFont	_RealFont	$A902

8.2.6   Requesting Font Information

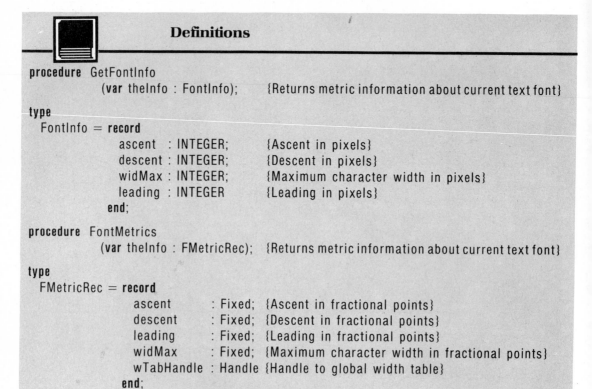

Definitions

```
procedure  GetFontInfo
           (var theInfo : FontInfo);       {Returns metric information about current text font}
type
  FontInfo = record
           ascent   : INTEGER;      {Ascent in pixels}
           descent  : INTEGER;      {Descent in pixels}
           widMax   : INTEGER;      {Maximum character width in pixels}
           leading  : INTEGER       {Leading in pixels}
         end;
procedure  FontMetrics
           (var theInfo : FMetricRec);  {Returns metric information about current text font}
type
  FMetricRec = record
           ascent      : Fixed;  {Ascent in fractional points}
           descent     : Fixed;  {Descent in fractional points}
           leading     : Fixed;  {Leading in fractional points}
           widMax      : Fixed;  {Maximum character width in fractional points}
           wTabHandle  : Handle  {Handle to global width table}
         end;
```

Notes

1. These routines return information on the metric characteristics of a font.

2. The information returned is for the font identified by the txFont and txSize fields [8.3.1] of the current graphics port, and is adjusted for the character style specified in the txFace field.

3. GetFontInfo returns the metrics in integer form; FontMetrics gives them in more precise fixed-point form.

4. The metric information returned by FontMetrics is expressed in device-independent printer's points, 72 points to the inch.

5. FontMetrics is available only on the Macintosh Plus.

6. The wTabHandle field of the font metric record is a handle to the font's *global width table*, which holds the individual fixed-point character

widths and other low-level data about the font. The global width table is of interest mainly to the Toolbox itself; if you can't live without knowing the contents of this enthralling data structure, see the Macintosh Plus supplement (Volume IV) of *Inside Macintosh*.

7. In assembly language, the global variable WidthTabHandle holds a handle to the global width table for the current font. This variable exists only on the Macintosh Plus.

8. Notice that FontInfo and FMetricRec have their widMax and leading fields in opposite orders, just to see if you're paying attention.

Assembly Language Information

Trap macros:

(Pascal) Routine name	(Assembly) Trap macro	Trap word
GetFontInfo	_GetFontInfo	$A88B
FontMetrics	_FontMetrics	$A835

Field offsets in a font information record:

(Pascal) Field name	(Assembly) Offset name	Offset in bytes
ascent	ascent	0
descent	descent	2
widMax	widMax	4
leading	leading	6

Field offsets in a font metric record:

(Pascal) Field name	(Assembly) Offset name	Offset in bytes
ascent	fmAscent	0
descent	fmDescent	4
leading	fmLeading	8
widMax	fmWidMax	12
wTabHandle	fmWTabHandle	16

Assembly-language global variable (Macintosh Plus only):

Name	Address	Meaning
WidthTabHandle	$B2A	Handle to global width table for current font

8.2.7   Locking a Font

Definitions

procedure SetFontLock
             (lock : BOOLEAN);   {Lock or unlock?}

Notes

1. SetFontLock locks or unlocks a font in the heap.
2. A locked font can't be moved or purged.
3. The font affected is the last one used in any text-drawing operation [8.3.3].
4. Fonts are normally unlocked by default.

Assembly Language Information

Trap macro:

(Pascal) Routine name	(Assembly) Trap macro	Trap word
SetFontLock	_SetFontLock	$A903

8.2.8   Nuts and Bolts

Definitions

procedure SetFractEnable
             (useFracts : BOOLEAN);   {Use fractional character widths?}

procedure SetFScaleDisable
             (noScaling : BOOLEAN);   {Turn off font scaling?}

Notes

1. SetFractEnable controls the use of fractional character widths for drawing text.

2. When fractional widths are enabled, all character placements will be rounded to the nearest integer at the available resolution of the device they're drawn on. This results in more accurate text positioning on high-resolution devices such as the LaserWriter printer.

3. If fractional widths are disabled or are unavailable for a particular font, the integer widths given in the font's offset/width table [8.2.3] will be used instead.

4. Fractional character widths are available only on the Macintosh Plus; the original Toolbox always uses integer widths.

5. SetFractEnable is part of the Pascal interface to the Toolbox, not part of the Toolbox itself. It doesn't reside in ROM and can't be called from assembly language via the trap mechanism.

6. To control the use of fractional character widths in assembly language, just set the byte-length global flag FractEnable for yourself: $FF (TRUE) to enable fractional widths, $00 (FALSE) to disable.

7. *BEWARE:* The FractEnable flag exists only on the Macintosh Plus. Attempting to set it on earlier models will destroy other, unrelated information in the system heap.

8. SetFScaleDisable controls the method of font substitution to be used when a requested font is unavailable.

9. When font scaling is enabled, an existing font in the requested typeface will be enlarged or reduced to the specified size. If possible, an even multiple or submultiple (such as double or half) of the requested size will be used. If no such multiple is available, some other size will be used instead, producing ugly or unreadable results.

10. When font scaling is disabled on the Macintosh Plus, the next smaller available size of the requested typeface will be used, but with the characters spaced farther apart, according to the character widths of the size requested. The results are faster and more readable, and more closely approximate the proper character placements and line breaks for the requested type size.

11. When font scaling is disabled under the original Toolbox, the substituted font may be either larger or smaller than the size requested. In either case, the characters will be positioned according to their own character widths rather than those of the requested size.

12. Font scaling is controlled by the byte-length global flag FScaleDisable: $00 (FALSE) for scaling, $FF (TRUE) for no scaling.

13. Scaling is initially enabled by default.

14. On the Macintosh Plus, always use the Toolbox routine SetFScaleDisable to turn font scaling on or off; merely setting the global flag is not sufficient. On earlier models, you can simply set the flag for yourself in assembly language, but there is no straightforward way to set it from Pascal: the SetFScaleDisable routine is available only on the Macintosh Plus.

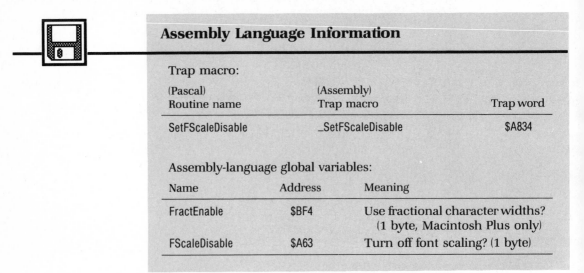

Assembly Language Information

Trap macro:

(Pascal) Routine name	(Assembly) Trap macro	Trap word
SetFScaleDisable	_SetFScaleDisable	$A834

Assembly-language global variables:

Name	Address	Meaning
FractEnable	$BF4	Use fractional character widths? (1 byte, Macintosh Plus only)
FScaleDisable	$A63	Turn off font scaling? (1 byte)

8.3   Text and QuickDraw

8.3.1   QuickDraw Text Characteristics

Definitions

```
type
  GrafPort = record
              device  : INTEGER;   {Device code (see notes 10-12)}
              . . . ;
              txFont  : INTEGER;   {Font number of typeface}
              txFace  : Style;     {Type style}
              txMode  : INTEGER;   {Transfer mode for text}
              txSize  : INTEGER;   {Type size in points}
              spExtra : Fixed;     {Extra space between words, in pixels}
              . . .
            end;

  StyleItem = (Bold, Italic, Underline, Outline, Shadow, Condense, Extend);

  Style     = set of StyleItem;
```

Notes

1. These fields of the GrafPort record [4.2.2] pertain to the drawing of text in a given graphics port.

2. txFont is a font number identifying the typeface to be used; 0 designates the system font.

3. txSize is the type size in points; 0 specifies the standard size of 12 points.

4. If no font exists for the requested combination of typeface and size, another size of the same face will be substituted. If the requested typeface isn't available in any size, the application font [8.2.1] will be used; if the application font isn't available in any size, the system font [8.2.1] will be used. If font scaling [8.2.8] is enabled, the substituted font will be scaled to the size requested.

5. txFace identifies the text style as a Pascal set of type Style. The set can include any combination of individual style properties of type StyleItem.

6. The assembly-language constants BoldBit, ItalicBit, etc. (below) are bit numbers within the byte representing a Style set, for use with the BTST, BSET, BCLR, and BCHG instructions.

7. txMode is the transfer mode for text in this graphics port, and should be one of the eight source transfer modes [5.1.3].

8. Under the original Toolbox, only the SrcOr, SrcXOr, and SrcBic modes can be used for text drawing. The Macintosh Plus supports all eight modes.

9. spExtra is a fixed-point number [2.3.1] consisting of a 16-bit integer part and a 16-bit fraction. It specifies the amount of extra space, in pixels, to be added to each space character for text justification.

10. device identifies the output device on which text will be drawn. This information is used in choosing the appropriate fonts for use on the device.

11. The high-order byte of the device code is the reference number of the device driver, which is always negative; the low-order byte is a device-dependent modifier controlling the way the device is to be used (for example, the dot resolution on a printer with a choice of resolutions).

12. A device code of 0 denotes the Macintosh screen.

13. A newly created graphics port is initialized to draw text on the screen, using the system font at the standard size of 12 points, with a transfer mode of SrcOr [5.1.3], plain character style, and no extra width for spaces.

Assembly Language Information

Field offsets in a graphics port:

(Pascal) Field name	(Assembly) Offset name	Offset in bytes
device	device	0
txFont	txFont	68
txFace	txFace	70
txMode	txMode	72
txSize	txSize	74
spExtra	spExtra	76

Bit numbers in a Style byte:

Name	Bit Number	Meaning
BoldBit	0	Bold
ItalicBit	1	Italic
UlineBit	2	Underline
OutlineBit	3	Outline
ShadowBit	4	Shadow
CondenseBit	5	Condense
ExtendBit	6	Extend

8.3.2 Setting Text Characteristics

Definitions

```
procedure GrafDevice
            (deviceCode : INTEGER);    {Device code [8.3.1]}

procedure TextFont
            (fontNumber : INTEGER);    {Font number of desired typeface [8.2.1]}

procedure TextSize
            (pointSize : INTEGER);     {Type size in points}

procedure TextFace
            (typeStyle : Style);       {Type style [8.3.1]}

procedure TextMode
            (mode : INTEGER);          {Transfer mode for text [5.1.3]}

procedure SpaceExtra
            (extraSpace : Fixed);      {Extra space between words, in pixels [2.3.1]}
```

Notes

1. These routines set the text characteristics of the current graphics port [8.3.1]. All subsequent text will be drawn with the specified characteristics.

2. If the point size specified to TextSize isn't available in the current typeface, another size will be substituted (and possibly scaled) to match; see [8.2.8] and [8.3.1, note 4].

3. mode should be one of the eight source transfer modes [5.1.3]. (Under the orignal Toolbox, it must be one of the three modes SrcOr, SrcXOr, or SrcBic.)

4. extraSpace is a fixed-point number [2.3.1] consisting of a 16-bit integer part and a 16-bit fraction, specifying the amount of extra space to be added between words.

5. To obtain the proper value of extraSpace for a line of justified text, use FixRatio [2.3.2] to divide the excess line width in pixels by the number of spaces in the line.

Assembly Language Information

Trap macros:

(Pascal) Routine name	(Assembly) Trap macro	Trap word
GrafDevice	_GrafDevice	$A872
TextFont	_TextFont	$A887
TextSize	_TextSize	$A88A
TextFace	_TextFace	$A888
TextMode	_TextMode	$A889
SpaceExtra	_SpaceExtra	$A88E

8.3.3 Drawing Text

Definitions

```
procedure  DrawChar
        (theChar : CHAR);          {Character to be drawn}

procedure  DrawString
        (theString : Str255);      {String to be drawn}

procedure  DrawText
        (theText    : Ptr;         {Pointer to text to be drawn}
         firstChar  : INTEGER;     {Index of first character within text}
         charCount : INTEGER);     {Number of characters to be drawn}
```

Notes

1. These routines draw text in the current graphics port, using the port's current typeface, size, style, and other text characteristics [8.3.1].

2. Each character is drawn with its character origin at the current pen position; the pen is then advanced to the right by the character width.

3. Characters not defined in the port's current font are replaced with the font's missing symbol.

4. Space characters include any extra space called for by the port's spExtra field [8.3.1].

5. ASCII control characters such as carriage return, line feed, tab, and backspace have no special meaning; if these characters are to be used for formatting, their effects must be simulated by explicitly moving the pen with Move and MoveTo [5.2.4].

6. The pen is left positioned beyond the last character drawn, ready for the next drawing operation.

Assembly Language Information

Trap macros:

(Pascal) Routine name	(Assembly) Trap macro	Trap word
DrawChar	_DrawChar	$A883
DrawString	_DrawString	$A884
DrawText	_DrawText	$A885

8.3.4   Measuring Text

Definitions

```
function   CharWidth
           (theChar : CHAR)           {Character to be measured}
             : INTEGER;               {Width of character}

function   StringWidth
           (theString : Str255)       {String to be measured}
             : INTEGER;               {Width of string}

function   TextWidth
           (theText    : Ptr;         {Pointer to text to be measured}
            firstChar  : INTEGER;     {Index of first character within text}
            charCount  : INTEGER)     {Number of characters to be measured}
             : INTEGER;               {Width of text}

procedure  MeasureText
           (charCount  : INTEGER;     {Number of characters to be measured}
            theText    : Ptr;         {Pointer to text to be measured}
            widthTable : Ptr);        {Pointer to table of text widths}
```

Notes

1. These routines measure the width of the specified text without drawing it.

2. The result is the distance in pixels that the pen would be advanced if the text were drawn in the current graphics port, using the port's current typeface, size, style, and other text characteristics [8.3.1].

3. Characters not defined in the port's current font are considered to have the same width as the font's missing symbol.

4. Space characters include any extra space called for by the port's spExtra field [8.3.1].

5. ASCII control characters such as carriage return, line feed, tab, and backspace have no special meaning, but are just treated as ordinary characters.

6. The port's graphics pen is not moved from its previous position.

7. MeasureText measures the width of the first character in the designated text, the first two characters, the first three, and so on up to the specified character count. The results are equivalent to calling TextWidth repeatedly for each text length from 1 to charCount.

8. This operation is particularly useful for finding line breaks in a text passage to be displayed on the screen.

9. The widthTable parameter should point to an array of type

    array [0..charCount] **of** INTEGER

    Each element i of this array will be filled with the width of the first i characters of theText. (Element 0 will always contain the value 0.)

10. *BEWARE:* No type or range checking is performed. To avoid destroying other information, make sure widthTable points to an array of at least charCount + 1 words.

11. MeasureText is available only on the Macintosh Plus.

Assembly Language Information

Trap macros:

(Pascal) Routine name	(Assembly) Trap macro	Trap word
CharWidth	_CharWidth	$A88D
StringWidth	_StringWidth	$A88C
TextWidth	_TextWidth	$A886
MeasureText	_MeasureText	$A837

8.4   Text-Related Resources

8.4.1   Resource Type 'TEXT'

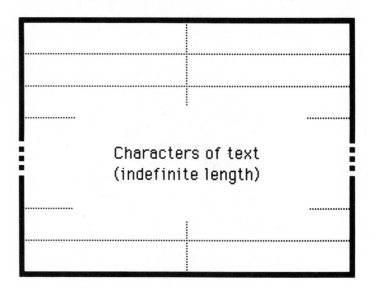

Characters of text
(indefinite length)

A 'TEXT' resource does not begin with a length byte.

Notes

1. A resource of type 'TEXT' contains any number of characters of "raw" text.

2. The resource data doesn't include a character count. The length of the text can be found with SizeResource [6.4.3].

8.4.2   Resource Type 'STR '

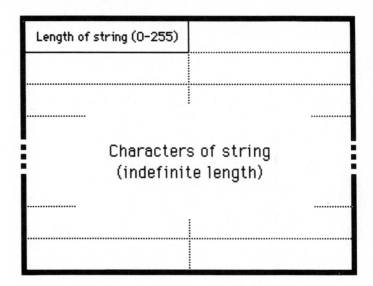

The maximum length of a 'STR ' resource is 255 characters.

Notes

1. A resource of type 'STR ' contains a character string in internal Pascal format.

2. The space in 'STR ' is required.

3. The first byte of resource data gives the length of the string, which cannot exceed 255 characters. The rest of the data consists of the characters themselves.

8.4.3   Resource Type 'STR#'

Notes

1. A resource of type 'STR#' contains a list of character strings.

2. The resource data consists of a 2-byte integer giving the number of strings in the list, followed by the strings themselves in internal Pascal format (1-byte character count, 0 to 255 characters), as described under 'STR ' [8.4.2].

3. Use GetIndString [8.1.2] to retrieve individual strings from a resource of this type.

8.4.4   Resource Type 'INIT'

Register D1 contains the fourth word of the system key map which includes the state of the four modifier keys.

Modifier bits for configuration routines

Notes

1. Resources of type 'INIT' contain system initialization routines. Whenever the Macintosh system is started up (such as when the power is turned on), all resources of this type found in the system resource file are executed.

2. The resource data is simply the machine-language code of the initialization routine. Its entry point must be at the beginning.

3. The order in which 'INIT' resources are executed is unpredictable.

4. Versions 3.0 and later of the system resource file (System) contain a special 'INIT' resource (ID 31) that searches the system folder on the startup disk for files with a file type [7.3.1] of 'INIT'. It then executes any 'INIT' resources that these files in turn contain. This allows a program to define initialization routines of its own and have them executed at system startup, without installing them in the system resource file itself.

5. The 'INIT' resources with IDs 1 and 2 are used to install pointers to the *keyboard configuration routines* into the system globals Key1Trans and Key2Trans. These routines are then used by the low-level keyboard driver to translate the user's keystrokes into corresponding characters to be passed to the running program.

6. 'INIT' resource 1 installs the configuration routine for the keyboard, resource 2 the one for the numeric keypad. These two routines are separate even on the Macintosh Plus, which has the keypad physically built into the keyboard unit.

7. The configuration routines must be written in assembly language, since they accept their arguments and return their results directly in the processor's registers.

8. On entry to the configuration routine, register D2 contains the key code [8.1.3] for the key to be translated. D1 contains the fourth word of the system key map [II:2.6.1], which includes the state of the four modifier keys (see figure). The routine can use this modifier information in any way it wishes.

9. The routine returns the character code corresponding to the given key and modifiers in the low-order byte of register D0.

10. The routine should preserve the contents of all registers except D0.

Assembly Language Information

Assembly-language global variables:

Name	Address	Meaning
Key1Trans	$29E	Pointer to keyboard configuration routine
Key2Trans	$2A2	Pointer to keypad configuration routine

8.4.5 Resource Type 'FONT'

Notes

1. A resource of type 'FONT' contains a complete font record [8.2.2], including the variable-length fields bitImage, locTable, and owTable [8.2.3].

2. The resource ID for a font consists of an 8-bit font number [8.2.1] identifying the typeface, followed by a 7-bit point size. Thus the resource ID is equal to the font number times 128, plus the point size.

3. For each typeface, the 'FONT' resource corresponding to a point size of 0 is a dummy resource with no data, which exists solely to carry the name of the typeface as its resource name. "Real" fonts with nonzero point sizes have no resource name.

4. On the Macintosh Plus, fonts belonging to a typeface are identified by means of a *family record* stored as a resource of type 'FOND' ("font definition"). See *Inside Macintosh*, Volume IV, for the structure of a family record.

5. For compatibility with older versions of the Toolbox, all typefaces with font numbers between 0 and 255 must still follow the numbering and naming conventions described in notes 2 and 3 above.

6. The Macintosh Plus Toolbox also recognizes font resources of type 'NFNT' ("non-menu font"), with the same structure shown here. The sole purpose of 'NFNT' is to provide an alternative form of font resource that won't be included when you create a menu of available resources of type 'FONT', using the Toolbox routines AddResMenu or InsertResMenu [II:4.3.3].

7. The original Toolbox ignores resources of types 'FOND' and 'NFNT'.

fontType (2 bytes)
firstChar (2 bytes)
lastChar (2 bytes)
widMax (2 bytes)
kernMax (2 bytes)
nDescent (2 bytes)
fRectWidth (2 bytes)
fRectHeight (2 bytes)
owTloc (2 bytes)
ascent (2 bytes)
descent (2 bytes)
leading (2 bytes)
rowWords (2 bytes)
bitImage (indefinite length)
locTable (indefinite length)
owTable (indefinite length)

Resource ID of a font

8.4.6   Resource Type 'FWID'

fontType (2 bytes)
firstChar (2 bytes)
lastChar (2 bytes)
widMax (2 bytes)
kernMax (2 bytes)
nDescent (2 bytes)
fRectWidth (2 bytes)
fRectHeight (2 bytes)
owTloc (2 bytes)
ascent (2 bytes)
descent (2 bytes)
leading (2 bytes)
owTable (indefinite length)

Notes

1. A resource of type 'FWID' contains a font width table.
2. The resource data consists of an abbreviated font record [8.2.2] with no rowWords, bitImage, and locTable fields [8.2.3].
3. The fontType field always contains the constant FontWid [8.2.2].
4. The owTLoc field is always set to 4.
5. The resource ID for a font width table is the same as for the corresponding font [8.4.5].
6. Font width tables are not used on the Macintosh Plus; all resources of type 'FWID' are ignored.

8.4.7   Resource Type 'FRSV'

Notes

1. A resource of type 'FRSV' identifies one or more reserved fonts that are needed by the Toolbox for proper operation.
2. The fonts are identified by resource ID, under resource type 'FONT' [8.4.5].
3. There should be exactly one 'FRSV' resource in the system resource file, with an ID of 1. Fonts designated by this resource must be present in the system resource file for the Toolbox to function properly.
4. Apple's Font/DA Mover utility program examines 'FRSV' resource number 1 and will refuse to delete any of the designated fonts from the System file.

Volume One
Toolbox Summary

Chapter 2   General Utilities

2.1   Elementary Data Structures

2.1.1   Strings and Procedures

```
type
  Str255  = STRING[255];            {Any text string, maximum 255 characters}

  ProcPtr = Ptr;                    {Pointer to a procedure or function}
```

2.1.2   String Operations

```
function   EqualString
             (string1      : Str255;      {First string to be compared}
              string2      : Str255;      {Second string to be compared}
              caseCounts   : BOOLEAN;     {Distinguish upper- and lowercase?}
              marksCount   : BOOLEAN)     {Include diacritical marks?}
               : BOOLEAN;                 {Are the two strings equivalent?}
```

```
function   RelString
              (string1      : Str255;        {First string to be compared}
               string2      : Str255;        {Second string to be compared}
               caseCounts   : BOOLEAN;       {Distinguish upper- and lowercase?}
               marksCount   : BOOLEAN)       {Include diacritical marks?}
               : INTEGER;                    {Which string comes first?}

procedure UprString
              (var theString : Str255;       {String to be converted}
               stripMarks    : BOOLEAN);     {Eliminate diacritical marks?}

const
  SortsBefore = −1;                          {First string precedes second}
  SortsEqual  =  0;                          {Strings are equivalent}
  SortsAfter  = +1;                          {First string follows second}
```

2.2   Bit-Level Operations

2.2.1   Single Bit Access

```
procedure BitSet
              (bitsPtr    : Ptr;             {Pointer to bits}
               bitNumber : LONGINT);         {Number of bit to be set to 1}

procedure BitClr
              (bitsPtr    : Ptr;             {Pointer to bits}
               bitNumber : LONGINT);         {Number of bit to be cleared to 0}

function   BitTst
              (bitsPtr    : Ptr;             {Pointer to bits}
               bitNumber : LONGINT)          {Number of bit to be tested}
               : BOOLEAN;                    {Is bit set to 1?}
```

2.2.2   Logical Operations

```
function BitAnd
              (bits1 : LONGINT;              {First operand}
               bits2 : LONGINT)             {Second operand}
               : LONGINT;                    {Bitwise "and"}

function BitOr
              (bits1 : LONGINT:              {First operand}
               bits2 : LONGINT)             {Second operand}
               : LONGINT;                    {Bitwise "or"}
```

```
function BitXOr
          (bits1 : LONGINT;              {First operand}
           bits2 : LONGINT)             {Second operand}
           : LONGINT;                   {Bitwise "exclusive or"}

function BitNot
          (bits : LONGINT)              {Bits to be complemented}
           : LONGINT;                   {Bitwise complement}

function BitShift
          (bits       : LONGINT;        {Bits to be shifted}
           shiftCount : INTEGER)        {Number of places to shift}
           : LONGINT;                   {Result of shift}
```

2.2.3 Word Access

```
function HiWord
          (longWord : LONGINT)          {32-bit operand}
           : INTEGER;                   {High-order 16 bits}

function LoWord
          (longWord : LONGINT)          {32-bit operand}
           : INTEGER;                   {Low-order 16 bits}
```

2.2.4 Direct Storage

```
procedure StuffHex
          (destPtr   : Ptr;            {Pointer to data structure to be stuffed}
           hexString : Str255);        {String representing data in hexadecimal}
```

2.3 Arithmetic Operations

2.3.1 Fixed-Point Numbers

```
type
  Fixed = LONGINT;                      {Fixed-point number}

function Long2Fix
          (theNumber : LONGINT)         {Long integer to be converted}
           : Fixed;                     {Fixed-point equivalent}

function Fix2Long
          (theNumber : Fixed)           {Fixed-point number to be converted}
           : LONGINT;                   {Long-integer equivalent}

function FixRound
          (theNumber : Fixed)           {Fixed-point number to be rounded}
           : INTEGER;                   {Number rounded to an integer}
```

2.3.2   Fixed-Point Arithmetic

function FixMul
        (number1 : Fixed;   {First fixed-point operand}
         number2 : Fixed)   {Second fixed-point operand}
         : Fixed;   {Fixed-point product}

function FixDiv
        (dividend : Fixed;   {Fixed-point dividend}
         divisor   : Fixed)   {Fixed-point divisor}
         : Fixed;   {Fixed-point quotient}

function FixRatio
        (numerator   : INTEGER;   {Integer numerator}
        denominator : INTEGER)   {Integer denominator}
         : Fixed;   {Fixed-point quotient}

2.3.3   Fractions

type
  Fract = LONGINT;

function Fix2Frac
        (theNumber: Fixed)   {Fixed-point number to be converted}
         : Fract;   {Fraction equivalent}

function Frac2Fix
        (theNumber: Fract)   {Fraction to be converted}
         : Fixed;   {Fixed-point equivalent}

2.3.4   Fraction Arithmetic

function FracMul
        (fraction1 : Fract;   {First fractional operand}
         fraction2 : Fract)   {Second fractional operand}
         : Fract;   {Fractional product}

function FracDiv
        (dividend : Fract;   {Fractional dividend}
         divisor   : Fract)   {Fractional divisor}
         : Fract;   {Fractional quotient}

function FracSqrt
        (theNumber : Fract)   {Fractional operand}
         : Fract;   {Fractional square root}

2.3.5 Long Multiplication

```
type
  Int64Bit = record
                hiLong : LONGINT;          {High-order 32 bits}
                loLong : LONGINT           {Low-order 32 bits}
             end;

procedure LongMul
            (number1    : LONGINT;          {First 32-bit operand}
             number2    : LONGINT;          {Second 32-bit operand}
             var product : Int64Bit);       {Returns 64-bit product}
```

2.3.6 Trigonometric Functions

```
function FracSin
            (theAngle : Fixed)             {Fixed-point angle in radians}
             : Fract;                      {Fractional sine}

function FracCos
            (theAngle : Fixed)             {Fixed-point angle in radians}
             : Fract;                      {Fractional cosine}

function FixATan2
            (denominator : LONGINT;        {Denominator of tangent}
             numerator    : LONGINT)       {Numerator of tangent}
             : Fixed;                      {Fixed-point arc tangent in radians}
```

2.3.7 Binary/Decimal Conversion

```
procedure NumToString
            (theNumber  : LONGINT;         {Number to be converted}
             var theString : Str255);      {Returns equivalent string}

procedure StringToNum
            (theString    : Str255;        {String to be converted}
             var theNumber : LONGINT);      {Returns equivalent number}
```

2.3.8 Random Numbers

```
function Random
             : INTEGER;                    {Random number}

var
  RandSeed : LONGINT;                      {"Seed" for random number generation}
```

2.4 Date and Time

2.4.1 Date and Time in Seconds

procedure GetDateTime
        (**var** seconds : LONGINT);   {Returns current date and time in "raw" seconds}

function SetDateTime
        (seconds : LONGINT)   {New date and time in "raw" seconds}
         : OSErr;   {Result code}

const
  ClkRdErr = −85;   {Unable to read clock}
  ClkWrErr = −86;   {Clock not written correctly}

2.4.2 Date and Time Records

type
  DateTimeRec = **record**
        year   : INTEGER;   {Year}
        month   : INTEGER;   {Month: 1 (January) to 12 (December)}
        day   : INTEGER;   {Day of month: 1 to 31}
        hour   : INTEGER;   {Hour: 0 to 23}
        minute   : INTEGER;   {Minute: 0 to 59}
        second   : INTEGER;   {Second: 0 to 59}
        dayOfWeek : INTEGER   {Day of week: 1 (Sunday) to 7 (Saturday)}
      end;

procedure GetTime
        (**var** dateAndTime : DateTimeRec);   {Returns current date and time}

procedure SetTime
        (dateAndTime : DateTimeRec);   {Current date and time}

2.4.3 Date and Time Conversion

procedure Secs2Date
        (seconds   : LONGINT;   {Date and time in "raw" seconds}
         var dateAndTime : DateTimeRec);   {Returns equivalent date and time record}

procedure Date2Secs
        (dateAndTime : DateTimeRec;   {Date and time record}
         var seconds : LONGINT);   {Returns equivalent in "raw" seconds}

2.4.4   Date and Time Strings

type
```
DateForm = (ShortDate, LongDate, AbbrevDate);
```

procedure IUDateString
```
          (seconds      : LONGINT;        {Date and time in "raw" seconds}
           format       : DateForm;       {Format desired for date}
           var theString : Str255);        {Returns equivalent character string}
```

procedure IUTimeString
```
          (seconds      : LONGINT;        {Date and time in "raw" seconds}
           withSeconds  : BOOLEAN;        {Include seconds in string?}
           var theString : Str255);        {Returns equivalent character string}
```

Chapter 3   Memory

3.1   Memory Basics

3.1.1   Elementary Data Types

type
```
  Byte       =    0..255;          {Any byte in memory}
  SignedByte = −128..127;          {Any byte in memory}

  Ptr        = ^SignedByte;        {General pointer}
  Handle     = ^Ptr;               {General handle}

  Size       = LONGINT;            {Size of a heap block in bytes}
```

3.1.2   Error Reporting

type
```
  OSErr        = INTEGER;          {Operating System result (error) code}
```

const
```
  NoErr        =    0;             {No error; all is well}
  MemFullErr   = −108;             {No room; heap is full}
  NilHandleErr = −109;             {Illegal operation on empty handle}
  MemWZErr     = −111;             {Illegal operation on free block}
  MemPurErr    = −112;             {Illegal operation on locked block}
  MemLockedErr = −117;             {Attempt to move locked block}
```

function MemError
```
         : OSErr;                  {Result code of last memory operation}
```

3.1.3 Machine Configuration

```
procedure Environs
          (var romVersion  : INTEGER;     {Version number of installed ROM}
           var machineType : INTEGER);    {Type of machine}

function TopMem
          : Ptr;                          {Pointer to end of memory}

const
   MacXLMachine = 0;                      {Macintosh XL (Lisa)}
   MacMachine   = 1;                      {Skinny Mac, Fat Mac, or Mac Plus}
```

3.2 Heap Allocation

3.2.1 Allocating Blocks

```
function NewHandle
          (blockSize : Size)              {Size of needed block in bytes}
           : Handle;                      {Handle to new relocatable block}

function NewPtr
          (blockSize : Size)              {Size of needed block in bytes}
           : Ptr;                         {Pointer to new nonrelocatable block}

function NewEmptyHandle
          : Handle;                       {New empty handle}

function RecoverHandle
          (masterPtr : Ptr)               {Master pointer to relocatable block}
           : Handle;                      {Handle to block}
```

3.2.2 Releasing Blocks

```
procedure DisposHandle
          (theHandle : Handle);           {Handle to relocatable block to be deallocated}

procedure DisposPtr
          (thePtr : Ptr);                 {Pointer to nonrelocatable block to be deallocated}
```

3.2.3 Size of Blocks

```
function   GetHandleSize
          (theHandle : Handle)            {Handle to a relocatable block}
           : Size;                        {Size of block in bytes}

function   GetPtrSize
          (thePtr : Ptr)                  {Pointer to a nonrelocatable block}
           : Size;                        {Size of block in bytes}
```

```
procedure  SetHandleSize
             (theHandle : Handle;        {Handle to a relocatable block}
              newSize   : Size);         {New size of block in bytes}

procedure  SetPtrSize
             (thePtr   : Ptr;            {Pointer to a nonrelocatable block}
              newSize : Size);           {New size of block in bytes}
```

3.2.4   Properties of Blocks

```
procedure  HLock
             (theHandle : Handle);       {Handle to a relocatable block}

procedure  HUnlock
             (theHandle : Handle);       {Handle to a relocatable block}

procedure  HPurge
             (theHandle : Handle);       {Handle to a relocatable block}

procedure  HNoPurge
             (theHandle : Handle);       {Handle to a relocatable block}

procedure  HSetRBit
             (theHandle : Handle);       {Handle to a relocatable block}

procedure  HClrRBit
             (theHandle : Handle);       {Handle to a relocatable block}

function   HGetState
             (theHandle : Handle)        {Handle to a relocatable block}
              : SignedByte;              {Current properties of block}

procedure  HSetState
             (theHandle : Handle;        {Handle to a relocatable block}
              properties : SignedByte);  {New properties of block}
```

3.2.5   Block Location

```
procedure  ResrvMem
             (blockSize : Size);         {Size of needed block in bytes}

procedure  MoveHHi
             (theHandle : Handle);       {Handle to a relocatable block}

procedure  MoreMasters;
```

3.2.6   Copying Blocks

```
function   HandToHand
             (var theHandle : Handle)    {Handle to relocatable block to be copied}
              : OSErr;                   {Result code}
```

function	PtrToHand		
	(fromPtr	: Ptr;	{Pointer to nonrelocatable block to be copied}
	var toHandle	: Handle;	{Returns handle to relocatable copy}
	byteCount	: LONGINT)	{Number of bytes to be copied}
	: OSErr;		{Result code}

function	PtrToXHand		
	(fromPtr	: Ptr;	{Pointer to nonrelocatable block to be copied}
	toHandle	: Handle;	{Handle to be set to relocatable copy}
	byteCount	: LONGINT)	{Number of bytes to be copied}
	: OSErr;		{Result code}

procedure	BlockMove		
	(fromPtr	: Ptr;	{Pointer to data to be copied}
	toPtr	: Ptr;	{Pointer to destination location}
	byteCount	: Size);	{Number of bytes to be copied}

3.2.7 Combining Blocks

function	HandAndHand		
	(appendHandle	: Handle;	{Handle to relocatable block to be appended}
	afterHandle	: Handle)	{Handle to relocatable block to append to}
	: OSErr;		{Result code}

function	PtrAndHand		
	(appendPtr	: Ptr;	{Pointer to nonrelocatable block to be appended}
	afterHandle	: Handle;	{Handle to relocatable block to append to}
	byteCount	: LONGINT)	{Number of bytes to append}
	: OSErr;		{Result code}

3.3 Heap Management

3.3.1 Available Space

function	FreeMem		
	: LONGINT;		{Total free bytes in the heap}

function	MaxBlock		
	: LONGINT;		{Largest contiguous block obtainable by compaction}

procedure	PurgeSpace		
	(**var** totalBytes	: LONGINT;	{Total free bytes obtainable by purging}
	var contigBytes	: LONGINT);	{Largest contiguous block obtainable by purging}

3.3.2 Reclaiming Free Space

function   CompactMem
        (sizeNeeded : Size)   {Size of needed block in bytes}
        : Size;   {Size of largest free block after compaction}

procedure PurgeMem
        (sizeNeeded : Size);   {Size of needed block in bytes}

function   MaxMem
        (**var** growBytes : Size)   {Returns maximum bytes by which heap can expand}
        : Size;   {Size of largest free block in heap}

3.3.3 Purging Blocks

procedure EmptyHandle
        (theHandle : Handle);   {Handle to relocatable block to be purged}

procedure ReallocHandle
        (theHandle : Handle;   {Empty handle to be reallocated}
        sizeNeeded : Size);   {Size of block to be allocated in bytes}

3.3.4 Heap Expansion

procedure SetApplLimit
        (newLimit : Ptr);   {Pointer to new application heap limit}

function   GetApplLimit
        : Ptr;   {Current application heap limit}

procedure MaxApplZone;

function   StackSpace
        : LONGINT;   {Amount stack can grow}

Chapter 4   QuickDraw Fundamentals

4.1   Mathematical Foundations

4.1.1   Points

```
type
  VHSelect = (V, H);                                    {Selector for coordinates of a point}

  Point    = record
                case INTEGER of

                   0: (v : INTEGER;                     {Vertical coordinate}
                       h : INTEGER);                     {Horizontal coordinate}

                   1: (vh : array [VHSelect] of INTEGER) {Coordinates as a two-element array}

                 end;

procedure  SetPt
             (var thePoint : Point;                     {Point to be set}
              hCoord       : INTEGER;                    {Horizontal coordinate}
              vCoord       : INTEGER);                   {Vertical coordinate}
```

4.1.2   Rectangles

```
type
  Rect = record
            case INTEGER of

               0: (top    : INTEGER;                     {Top coordinate}
                   left   : INTEGER;                      {Left coordinate}
                   bottom : INTEGER;                      {Bottom coordinate}
                   right  : INTEGER);                     {Right coordinate}

               1: (topLeft  : Point;                      {Top-left corner}
                   botRight : Point)                       {Bottom-right corner}
             end;

procedure  SetRect
             (var theRect : Rect;                         {Rectangle to be set}
              left        : INTEGER;                      {Left coordinate}
              top         : INTEGER;                      {Top coordinate}
              right       : INTEGER;                      {Right coordinate}
              bottom      : INTEGER);                     {Bottom coordinate}
```

```
procedure  Pt2Rect
              (point1    : Point;                   {First corner}
               point2    : Point;                   {Diagonally opposite corner}
               var theRect : Rect);                 {Rectangle to be set}
```

4.1.3 Polygons

```
type
  PolyHandle = ^PolyPtr;
  PolyPtr    = ^Polygon;

  Polygon    = record
                  polySize   : INTEGER;             {Length of this data structure in bytes}
                  polyBBox   : Rect;                {Bounding box}
                  polyPoints : array [0..0] of Point  {Variable-length array of vertices}
               end;
```

4.1.4 Defining Polygons

```
function   OpenPoly
              : PolyHandle;                         {Handle to new polygon}

procedure  ClosePoly;

procedure  KillPoly
              (thePolygon : PolyHandle);            {Handle to polygon to be destroyed}
```

4.1.5 Regions

```
type
  RgnHandle = ^RgnPtr;
  RgnPtr    = ^Region;

  Region    = record
                 rgnSize  : INTEGER;                {Length of this data structure in bytes}
                 rgnBBox  : Rect;                   {Bounding box}
                 {additional data defining shape of region}
              end;
```

4.1.6 Defining Regions

```
function   NewRgn
              : RgnHandle;                          {Handle to new region}

procedure  OpenRgn;

procedure  CloseRgn
              (theRegion : RgnHandle);              {Handle to be set to defined region}
```

procedure DisposeRgn
     (theRegion : RgnHandle);   {Handle to region to be destroyed}

4.1.7   Setting Regions

procedure SetEmptyRgn
     (theRegion : RgnHandle);   {Handle to region to be set empty}

procedure RectRgn
     (theRegion : RgnHandle;   {Handle to region to be set}
     theRect   : Rect);   {Rectangle to set it to}

procedure SetRectRgn
     (theRegion : RgnHandle;   {Handle to region to be set}
     left   : INTEGER;   {Left coordinate of rectangle to set it to}
     top   : INTEGER;   {Top coordinate of rectangle to set it to}
     right   : INTEGER;   {Right coordinate of rectangle to set it to}
     bottom : INTEGER);   {Bottom coordinate of rectangle to set it to}

procedure CopyRgn
     (fromRegion : RgnHandle;   {Region to be copied}
     toRegion   : RgnHandle);   {Region to copy it to}

4.2   Graphical Foundations

4.2.1   Bit Maps

BitMap = **record**
     baseAddr : Ptr;   {Pointer to bit image}
     rowBytes : INTEGER;   {Row width in bytes}
     bounds   : Rect   {Boundary rectangle}
    end;

var
  ScreenBits : BitMap;   {Bit map for Macintosh screen}

4.2.2   Graphics Ports

type
```
  GrafPtr  = ^GrafPort;
```

```
  GrafPort = record
```
device	: INTEGER;	{Device code for font selection}
portBits	: BitMap;	{Bit map for this port}
portRect	: Rect;	{Port rectangle}
visRgn	: RgnHandle;	{Visible region}
clipRgn	: RgnHandle;	{Clipping region}
bkPat	: Pattern;	{Background pattern}
fillPat	: Pattern;	{Fill pattern for shape drawing}
pnLoc	: Point;	{Current pen location in local coordinates}
pnSize	: Point;	{Dimensions of graphics pen}
pnMode	: INTEGER;	{Transfer mode for graphics pen}
pnPat	: Pattern;	{Pen pattern for line drawing}
pnVis	: INTEGER;	{Pen visibility level}
txFont	: INTEGER;	{Font number for text}
txFace	: Style;	{Type style for text}
txMode	: INTEGER;	{Transfer mode for text}
txSize	: INTEGER;	{Type size for text}
spExtra	: Fixed;	{Extra space between words}
fgColor	: LONGINT;	{Foreground color}
bkColor	: LONGINT;	{Background color}
colrBit	: INTEGER;	{Color plane}
patStretch	: INTEGER;	{Private}
picSave	: Handle;	{Private}
rgnSave	: Handle;	{Private}
polySave	: Handle;	{Private}
grafProcs	: QDProcsPtr	{Pointer to bottleneck procedures}

```
           end;
```

4.2.3   Pixel Access

function GetPixel

(hCoord	: INTEGER;	{Horizontal coordinate of pixel}
vCoord	: INTEGER)	{Vertical coordinate of pixel}
	: BOOLEAN;	{Is it a black pixel?}

4.3 Operations on Graphics Ports

4.3.1 Initializing QuickDraw

```
procedure  InitGraf
              (globalVars : Ptr);          {Pointer to QuickDraw global variables}

var
  ThePort    : GrafPtr;                     {Pointer to current port}
  White      : Pattern;                     {Solid white pattern}
  Black      : Pattern;                     {Solid black pattern}
  Gray       : Pattern;                     {Medium gray pattern}
  LtGray     : Pattern;                     {Light gray pattern}
  DkGray     : Pattern;                     {Dark gray pattern}
  Arrow      : Cursor;                      {Standard arrow cursor}
  ScreenBits : BitMap;                      {Bit map for Macintosh screen}
  RandSeed   : LONGINT;                     {Seed for random number generation}
```

4.3.2 Creating and Destroying Ports

```
procedure  OpenPort
              (whichPort : GrafPtr);        {Pointer to port to open}

procedure  InitPort
              (whichPort : GrafPtr);        {Pointer to port to initialize}

procedure  ClosePort
              (whichPort : GrafPtr);        {Pointer to port to close}
```

4.3.3 Current Port

```
procedure  SetPort
              (newPort : GrafPtr);          {Pointer to port to be made current}

procedure  GetPort
              (var curPort : GrafPtr);      {Returns pointer to current port}

var
  ThePort : GrafPtr;                        {Pointer to current port}
```

4.3.4 Bit Map and Coordinate System

```
procedure  SetPortBits
              (theBits : BitMap);           {New bit map for current port}

procedure  SetOrigin
              (hOrigin : INTEGER;           {New horizontal coordinate of port rectangle}
               vOrigin : INTEGER);          {New vertical coordinate of port rectangle}
```

4.3.5   Port Rectangle

procedure MovePortTo
            (leftGlobal : INTEGER;   {New left edge of port rectangle in global coordinates}
             topGlobal : INTEGER);   {New top edge of port rectangle in global coordinates}

procedure PortSize
            (portWidth : INTEGER;   {New width of port rectangle}
             portHeight : INTEGER);   {New height of port rectangle}

4.3.6   Clipping Region

procedure SetClip
            (newClip : RgnHandle);   {Handle to new clipping region}

procedure ClipRect
            (newClip : Rect);   {Rectangle defining new clipping region}

procedure GetClip
            (curClip : RgnHandle);   {Handle to current clipping region}

4.4   Calculations on Graphical Entities

4.4.1   Calculations on Points

procedure AddPt
            (addPoint   : Point;   {Point to be added}
             var toPoint : Point);   {Point to add it to}

procedure SubPt
            (subPoint   : Point;   {Point to be subtracted}
             var fromPoint : Point);   {Point to subtract it from}

function   DeltaPoint
            (fromPoint : Point;   {Point to subtract from}
             subPoint : Point)   {Point to be subtracted}
             : LONGINT;   {Difference between points}

function   EqualPt
            (point1 : Point;   {First point to be compared}
             point2 : Point)   {Second point to be compared}
             : BOOLEAN;   {Are they equal?}

4.4.2   Coordinate Conversion

procedure LocalToGlobal
            (**var** thePoint : Point);   {Point to be converted}

procedure GlobalToLocal
            (**var** thePoint : Point);   {Point to be converted}

4.4.3   Testing for Inclusion

```
function PtInRect
        (thePoint : Point;              {Point to be tested}
         theRect  : Rect)              {Rectangle to test it against}
         : BOOLEAN;                    {Is the point in the rectangle?}

function PtInRgn
        (thePoint   : Point;          {Point to be tested}
         theRegion : RgnHandle)        {Handle to region to test it against}
         : BOOLEAN;                    {Is the point in the region?}

function RectInRgn
        (theRect   : Rect;            {Rectangle to be tested}
         theRegion : RgnHandle)        {Handle to region to test it against}
         : BOOLEAN;                    {Does the rectangle intersect the region?}

function PinRect
        (theRect  : Rect;             {Rectangle to pin to}
         thePoint : Point)            {Point to be pinned}
         : LONGINT;                   {Point pinned to rectangle}
```

4.4.4   Calculations on One Rectangle

```
procedure OffsetRect
        (var theRect : Rect;          {Rectangle to be offset}
         hOffset     : INTEGER;       {Horizontal offset in pixels}
         vOffset     : INTEGER);      {Vertical offset in pixels}

procedure InsetRect
        (var theRect : Rect;          {Rectangle to be inset}
         hInset      : INTEGER;       {Horizontal inset in pixels}
         vInset      : INTEGER);      {Vertical inset in pixels}

function   EmptyRect
        (theRect : Rect)              {Rectangle to be tested}
         : BOOLEAN;                   {Is the rectangle empty?}
```

4.4.5   Calculations on Two Rectangles

```
procedure UnionRect
        (rect1          : Rect;       {First rectangle}
         rect2          : Rect;       {Second rectangle}
         var resultRect : Rect);      {Returns union of two rectangles}

function   SectRect
        (rect1          : Rect;       {First rectangle}
         rect2          : Rect;       {Second rectangle}
         var resultRect : Rect)       {Returns intersection of two rectangles}
         : BOOLEAN;                   {Do the rectangles intersect?}
```

function   EqualRect
       (rect1 : Rect;   {First rectangle}
       rect2 : Rect)   {Second rectangle}
        : BOOLEAN;   {Are the rectangles equal?}

4.4.6   Calculations on Polygons

procedure OffsetPoly
       (thePolygon : PolyHandle;   {Polygon to be offset}
       hOffset   : INTEGER;   {Horizontal offset in pixels}
       vOffset   : INTEGER);   {Vertical offset in pixels}

4.4.7   Calculations on One Region

procedure OffsetRgn
       (theRegion : RgnHandle;   {Handle to region to be offset}
       hOffset   : INTEGER;   {Horizontal offset in pixels}
       vOffset   : INTEGER);   {Vertical offset in pixels}

procedure InsetRgn
       (theRegion : RgnHandle;   {Handle to region to be inset}
       hInset   : INTEGER;   {Horizontal inset in pixels}
       vInset   : INTEGER);   {Vertical inset in pixels}

function   EmptyRgn
       (theRegion : RgnHandle)   {Handle to region to be tested}
        : BOOLEAN;   {Is the region empty?}

4.4.8   Calculations on Two Regions

procedure UnionRgn
       (region1   : RgnHandle;   {Handle to first region}
       region2   : RgnHandle;   {Handle to second region}
       resultRegion : RgnHandle);   {Handle to be set to union of two regions}

procedure SectRgn
       (region1   : RgnHandle;   {Handle to first region}
       region2   : RgnHandle;   {Handle to second region}
       resultRegion : RgnHandle);   {Handle to be set to intersection of two regions}

procedure DiffRgn
       (region1   : RgnHandle;   {Handle to region to be subtracted from}
       region2   : RgnHandle;   {Handle to region to subtract from it}
       resultRegion : RgnHandle);   {Handle to be set to difference of two regions}

procedure XOrRgn
       (region1   : RgnHandle;   {Handle to first region}
       region2   : RgnHandle;   {Handle to second region}
       resultRegion : RgnHandle);   {Handle to be set to "exclusive or" of two regions}

```
function   EqualRgn
             (region1 : RgnHandle;          {Handle to first region}
              region2 : RgnHandle)          {Handle to second region}
               : BOOLEAN;                   {Are the regions equal?}
```

4.4.9   Scaling and Mapping

```
procedure  ScalePt
             (var thePoint : Point;         {Point to be scaled}
              fromRect     : Rect;          {Rectangle to scale it from}
              toRect       : Rect);         {Rectangle to scale it to}

procedure  MapPt
             (var thePoint : Point;         {Point to be mapped}
              fromRect     : Rect;          {Rectangle to map it from}
              toRect       : Rect);         {Rectangle to map it to}

procedure  MapRect
             (var theRect : Rect;           {Rectangle to be mapped}
              fromRect    : Rect;           {Rectangle to map it from}
              toRect      : Rect);          {Rectangle to map it to}

procedure  MapPoly
             (thePolygon : PolyHandle;      {Polygon to be mapped}
              fromRect   : Rect;            {Rectangle to map it from}
              toRect     : Rect);           {Rectangle to map it to}

procedure  MapRgn
             (theRegion : RgnHandle;        {Region to be mapped}
              fromRect  : Rect;             {Rectangle to map it from}
              toRect    : Rect);            {Rectangle to map it to}
```

Chapter 5   Drawing

5.1   Drawing Fundamentals

5.1.1   Patterns

```
type
  PatHandle = ^PatPtr;
  PatPtr    = ^Pattern;

  Pattern   = packed array [0..7] of 0..255;    {8 rows of 8 bits each}
```

```
GrafPort = record
        . . . ;
            bkPat  : Pattern;              {Background pattern}
            fillPat : Pattern;             {Fill pattern for shape drawing}
        . . . ;
            pnPat  : Pattern;              {Pen pattern for line drawing}
        . . .
        end;

procedure  BackPat
            (newPattern : Pattern);        {New background pattern}

function   GetPattern
            (patternID : INTEGER)          {Resource ID of desired pattern}
             : PatHandle;                  {Handle to pattern in memory}

procedure  GetIndPattern
            (var thePattern : Pattern;     {Returns desired pattern}
             patListID      : INTEGER;     {Resource ID of pattern list}
             patIndex       : INTEGER);    {Index of pattern within list}
```

5.1.2 Standard Patterns

```
var
  White  : Pattern;                        {Solid white}
  LtGray : Pattern;                        {Light gray}
  Gray   : Pattern;                        {Medium gray}
  DkGray : Pattern;                        {Dark gray}
  Black  : Pattern;                        {Solid black}

const
  SysPatList = 0;                          {Resource ID of standard pattern list}
  DeskPatID = 16;                          {Resource ID of screen background pattern}
```

5.1.3 Transfer Modes

```
GrafPort = record
        . . . ;
            pnMode : INTEGER;              {Transfer mode for graphics pen}
        . . . ;
            txMode : INTEGER;              {Transfer mode for text}
        . . .
        end;
```

```
const
  SrcCopy    = 0;        {Copy source to destination}
  SrcOr      = 1;        {Set selected bits to black}
  SrcXOr     = 2;        {Invert selected bits}
  SrcBic     = 3;        {Clear selected bits to white}
  NotSrcCopy = 4;        {Copy inverted source to destination}
  NotSrcOr   = 5;        {Leave selected bits alone, set others to black}
  NotSrcXOr  = 6;        {Leave selected bits alone, invert others}
  NotSrcBic  = 7;        {Leave selected bits alone, clear others to white}

  PatCopy    = 8;        {Copy pattern to destination}
  PatOr      = 9;        {Set selected bits to black}
  PatXOr     = 10;       {Invert selected bits}
  PatBic     = 11;       {Clear selected bits to white}
  NotPatCopy = 12;       {Copy inverted pattern to destination}
  NotPatOr   = 13;       {Leave selected bits alone, set others to black}
  NotPatXOr  = 14;       {Leave selected bits alone, invert others}
  NotPatBic  = 15;       {Leave selected bits alone, clear others to white}
```

5.1.4   Low-Level Bit Transfer

```
procedure CopyBits
          (fromBitMap : BitMap;      {Bit map to copy from}
           toBitMap   : BitMap;      {Bit map to copy to}
           fromRect   : Rect;        {Rectangle to copy from}
           toRect     : Rect;        {Rectangle to copy to}
           mode       : INTEGER;     {Transfer mode}
           clipTo     : RgnHandle);  {Region to clip to}

procedure CopyMask
          (sourceMap : BitMap;       {Bit map to copy from}
           maskMap   : BitMap;       {Bit map containing mask}
           destMap   : BitMap;       {Bit map to copy to}
           sourceRect : Rect;        {Rectangle to copy from}
           maskRect  : Rect;         {Rectangle containing mask}
           destRect  : Rect);        {Rectangle to copy to}
```

5.1.5   Scrolling in a Bit Map

```
procedure ScrollRect
          (theRect   : Rect;        {Rectangle to be scrolled}
           hScroll   : INTEGER;     {Horizontal scroll distance in pixels}
           vScroll   : INTEGER;     {Vertical scroll distance in pixels}
           updateRgn : RgnHandle);  {Region scrolled into rectangle}
```

5.1.6   Special Operations

procedure CalcMask
```
        (sourceBits : Ptr;          {Pointer to source image}
        maskBits    : Ptr;          {Pointer to result mask}
        sourceRow   : INTEGER;      {Row width of source bit map in bytes}
        maskRow     : INTEGER;      {Row width of mask bit map in bytes}
        rectHeight  : INTEGER;      {Height of source and mask rectangles in pixels}
        rectWidth   : INTEGER);     {Width of source and mask rectangles in words}
```

procedure SeedFill
```
        (sourceBits : Ptr;          {Pointer to source image}
        maskBits    : Ptr;          {Pointer to result mask}
        sourceRow   : INTEGER;      {Row width of source bit map in bytes}
        maskRow     : INTEGER;      {Row width of mask bit map in bytes}
        rectHeight  : INTEGER;      {Height of source and mask rectangles in pixels}
        rectWidth   : INTEGER;      {Width of source and mask rectangles in words}
        seedHoriz   : INTEGER;      {Horizontal coordinate of starting point}
        seedVert    : INTEGER);     {Vertical coordinate of starting point}
```

5.2   Line Drawing

5.2.1   Pen Characteristics

type
```
  GrafPort = record
            . . . ;
            pnLoc  : Point;         {Current location of graphics pen in local coordinates}
            pnSize : Point;         {Dimensions of graphics pen}
            pnMode : INTEGER;       {Transfer mode for graphics pen}
            pnPat  : Pattern;       {Pen pattern for line drawing}
            pnVis  : INTEGER;       {Pen level}

            . . .
        end;

  PenState = record
            pnLoc  : Point;         {Location of pen in bit map}
            pnSize : Point;         {Width and height of pen in pixels}
            pnMode : INTEGER;       {Transfer mode for line drawing and area fill}
            pnPat  : Pattern        {Pen pattern}
        end;
```

procedure GetPenState
```
        (var curState : PenState);  {Returns current pen characteristics}
```

procedure SetPenState
```
        (newState : PenState);      {New pen characteristics}
```

5.2.2   Setting Pen Characteristics

```
procedure  PenSize
              (newWidth  : INTEGER;        {New pen width}
               newHeight : INTEGER);       {New pen height}

procedure  PenPat
              (newPat : Pattern);          {New pen pattern}

procedure  PenMode
              (newMode : INTEGER);         {New pen transfer mode}

procedure  PenNormal;
```

5.2.3   Hiding and Showing the Pen

```
type
   GrafPort = record
                 . . . ;
                 pnVis : INTEGER;          {Pen visibility level}
                 . . .
              end;

procedure  HidePen;

procedure  ShowPen;
```

5.2.4   Drawing Lines

```
procedure  GetPen
              (var penLoc : Point);        {Returns current pen location}

procedure  Move
              (horiz : INTEGER;            {Horizontal distance to move, in pixels}
               vert  : INTEGER);           {Vertical distance to move, in pixels}

procedure  MoveTo
              (horiz : INTEGER;            {Horizontal coordinate to move to, in pixels}
               vert  : INTEGER);           {Vertical coordinate to move to, in pixels}

procedure  Line
              (horiz : INTEGER;            {Horizontal distance to draw, in pixels}
               vert  : INTEGER);           {Vertical distance to draw, in pixels}

procedure  LineTo
              (horiz : INTEGER;            {Horizontal coordinate to draw to, in pixels}
               vert  : INTEGER);           {Vertical coordinate to draw to, in pixels}
```

5.3 Drawing Shapes

5.3.1 Basic Drawing Operations

```
type
  GrafVerb = (Frame,                    {Draw outline}
              Paint,                     {Fill with current pen pattern}
              Erase,                     {Fill with background pattern}
              Invert,                    {Invert pixels}
              Fill);                     {Fill with specified pattern}
```

5.3.2 Drawing Rectangles

```
procedure FrameRect
          (theRect : Rect);             {Rectangle to be framed}

procedure PaintRect
          (theRect : Rect);             {Rectangle to be painted}

procedure FillRect
          (theRect : Rect;              {Rectangle to be filled}
           fillPat : Pattern);          {Pattern to fill it with}

procedure EraseRect
          (theRect : Rect);             {Rectangle to be erased}

procedure InvertRect
          (theRect : Rect);             {Rectangle to be inverted}
```

5.3.3 Drawing Rounded Rectangles

```
procedure FrameRoundRect
          (theRect      : Rect;         {Body of rectangle}
           cornerWidth  : INTEGER;      {Width of corner oval}
           cornerHeight : INTEGER);     {Height of corner oval}

procedure PaintRoundRect
          (theRect      : Rect;         {Body of rectangle}
           cornerWidth  : INTEGER;      {Width of corner oval}
           cornerHeight : INTEGER);     {Height of corner oval}

procedure FillRoundRect
          (theRect      : Rect;         {Body of rectangle}
           cornerWidth  : INTEGER;      {Width of corner oval}
           cornerHeight : INTEGER;      {Height of corner oval}
           fillPat      : Pattern);     {Pattern to fill with}
```

```
procedure  EraseRoundRect
           (theRect      : Rect;        {Body of rectangle}
            cornerWidth  : INTEGER;     {Width of corner oval}
            cornerHeight : INTEGER);    {Height of corner oval}

procedure  InvertRoundRect
           (theRect      : Rect;        {Body of rectangle}
            cornerWidth  : INTEGER;     {Width of corner oval}
            cornerHeight : INTEGER);    {Height of corner oval}
```

5.3.4 Drawing Ovals

```
procedure  FrameOval
           (inRect : Rect);            {Rectangle defining oval}

procedure  PaintOval
           (inRect : Rect);            {Rectangle defining oval}

procedure  FillOval
           (inRect : Rect;             {Rectangle defining oval}
            fillPat : Pattern);        {Pattern to fill with}

procedure  EraseOval
           (inRect : Rect);            {Rectangle defining oval}

procedure  InvertOval
           (inRect : Rect);            {Rectangle defining oval}
```

5.3.5 Drawing Arcs and Wedges

```
procedure  FrameArc
           (inRect     : Rect;         {Rectangle defining oval}
            startAngle : INTEGER;      {Starting angle}
            arcAngle   : INTEGER);     {Extent of arc}

procedure  PaintArc
           (inRect     : Rect;         {Rectangle defining oval}
            startAngle : INTEGER;      {Starting angle}
            arcAngle   : INTEGER);     {Extent of arc}

procedure  FillArc
           (inRect     : Rect;         {Rectangle defining oval}
            startAngle : INTEGER;      {Starting angle}
            arcAngle   : INTEGER;      {Extent of arc}
            fillPat    : Pattern);     {Pattern to fill with}

procedure  EraseArc
           (inRect     : Rect;         {Rectangle defining oval}
            startAngle : INTEGER;      {Starting angle}
            arcAngle   : INTEGER);     {Extent of arc}
```

```
procedure InvertArc
        (inRect     : Rect;          {Rectangle defining oval}
         startAngle : INTEGER;       {Starting angle}
         arcAngle   : INTEGER);      {Extent of arc}

procedure PtToAngle
        (inRect       : Rect;        {Rectangle to measure in}
         thePoint     : Point;       {Point to be measured}
         var theAngle : INTEGER);    {Returns angle of point, in degrees}
```

5.3.6   Drawing Polygons

```
procedure FramePoly
        (thePolygon : PolyHandle);   {Handle to polygon to be framed}

procedure PaintPoly
        (thePolygon : PolyHandle);   {Handle to polygon to be painted}

procedure FillPoly
        (thePolygon : PolyHandle;    {Handle to polygon to be filled}
         fillPat    : Pattern);      {Pattern to fill it with}

procedure ErasePoly
        (thePolygon : PolyHandle);   {Handle to polygon to be erased}

procedure InvertPoly
        (thePolygon : PolyHandle);   {Handle to polygon to be inverted}
```

5.3.7   Drawing Regions

```
procedure FrameRgn
        (theRegion : RgnHandle);     {Handle to region to be framed}

procedure PaintRgn
        (theRegion : RgnHandle);     {Handle to region to be painted}

procedure FillRgn
        (theRegion : RgnHandle;      {Handle to region to be filled}
         fillPat   : Pattern);       {Pattern to fill it with}

procedure EraseRgn
        (theRegion : RgnHandle);     {Handle to region to be erased}

procedure InvertRgn
        (theRegion : RgnHandle);     {Handle to region to be inverted}
```

5.4   Pictures and Icons

5.4.1   Picture Records

```
type
  PicHandle = ^PicPtr;
  PicPtr    = ^Picture;

  Picture = record
              picSize  : INTEGER;     {Length of this data structure in bytes}
              picFrame : Rect;        {Smallest rectangle enclosing the picture}
              {additional data defining contents of picture}
            end;
```

5.4.2   Defining Pictures

```
function   OpenPicture
             (picFrame : Rect)        {Frame for new picture}
               : PicHandle;           {Handle to new picture}

procedure  ClosePicture;

function   GetPicture
             (pictureID : INTEGER)    {Resource ID of desired picture}
               : PicHandle;           {Handle to picture in memory}

procedure  KillPicture
             (thePicture : PicHandle);  {Handle to picture to be destroyed}
```

5.4.3   Drawing Pictures

```
procedure  DrawPicture
             (thePicture : PicHandle;   {Picture to be drawn}
              inRect     : Rect);       {Rectangle to draw it in}
```

5.4.4   Icons

```
function   GetIcon
             (iconID : INTEGER)       {Resource ID of desired icon}
               : Handle;              {Handle to icon in memory}

procedure  PlotIcon
             (inRect     : Rect;      {Rectangle to plot in}
              iconHandle : Handle);   {Handle to icon}
```

Chapter 6   Resources

6.1   Resource Types

6.1.1   Resource Types

type
  ResType = **packed array** [1..4] **of** CHAR;   {Resource type}

6.2   Resource Files

6.2.1   Opening and Closing Resource Files

function   OpenResFile
        (fileName : Str255)   {Name of resource file to be opened}
         : INTEGER;   {Reference number of file}

procedure CloseResFile
        (refNum : INTEGER);   {Reference number of resource file to be closed}

6.2.2   Current Resource File

function   CurResFile
         : INTEGER;   {Reference number of current resource file}

procedure UseResFile
        (refNum : INTEGER);   {Reference number of resource file to be made current}

6.3   Access to Resources

6.3.1   Getting Resources

function GetResource
        (rsrcType : ResType;   {Resource type}
         rsrcID   : INTEGER)   {Resource ID}
         : Handle;   {Handle to resource}

function GetNamedResource
        (rsrcType : ResType;   {Resource type}
         rsrcName : Str255)   {Resource name}
         : Handle;   {Handle to resource}

function Get1Resource
        (rsrcType : ResType;   {Resource type}
         rsrcID   : INTEGER)   {Resource ID}
         : Handle;   {Handle to resource}

```
function Get1NamedResource
        (rsrcType : ResType;          {Resource type}
         rsrcName : Str255)           {Resource name}
          : Handle;                   {Handle to resource}
```

6.3.2   Disposing of Resources

```
procedure ReleaseResource
        (theResource : Handle);       {Resource to be released}

procedure DetachResource
        (theResource : Handle);       {Resource to be detached}
```

6.3.3   Generating All Resources

```
function   CountTypes
            : INTEGER;                {Total number of resource types}

procedure  GetIndType
        (var rsrcType : ResType;      {Returns next resource type}
             index       : INTEGER);  {Index of desired resource type}

function   CountResources
        (rsrcType : ResType)          {Resource type}
          : INTEGER;                  {Total number of resources of this type}

function   GetIndResource
        (rsrcType : ResType;          {Resource type}
         index    : INTEGER)          {Index (not ID) of desired resource}
          : Handle;                   {Handle to resource}

function   Count1Types
            : INTEGER;                {Total number of resource types}

procedure  Get1IndType
        (var rsrcType : ResType;      {Returns next resource type}
             index       : INTEGER);  {Index of desired resource type}

function   Count1Resources
        (rsrcType : ResType)          {Resource type}
          : INTEGER;                  {Total number of resources of this type}

function   Get1IndResource
        (rsrcType : ResType;          {Resource type}
         index    : INTEGER)          {Index (not ID) of desired resource}
          : Handle;                   {Handle to resource}
```

6.3.4   Loading Resources

procedure SetResLoad
            (onOrOff : BOOLEAN);   {Turn automatic loading on or off?}

procedure LoadResource
            (theResource : Handle);   {Resource to be loaded}

6.4   Properties of Resources

6.4.1   Identifying Information

procedure GetResInfo
            (theResource : Handle;   {Handle to resource}
        var rsrcID   : INTEGER;   {Returns resource ID}
        var rsrcType : ResType;   {Returns resource type}
        var rsrcName : Str255);   {Returns resource name}

procedure SetResInfo
            (theResource : Handle;   {Handle to resource}
             rsrcID   : INTEGER;   {New resource ID}
             rsrcName   : Str255);   {New resource name}

6.4.2   Resource Attributes

function   GetResAttrs
            (theResource : Handle)   {Handle to resource}
              : INTEGER;   {Current resource attributes}

procedure SetResAttrs
            (theResource : Handle;   {Handle to resource}
             newAttrs   : INTEGER);   {New resource attributes}

const
  ResSysHeap   = $0040;   {Resides in system heap}
  ResPurgeable = $0020;   {Purgeable from heap}
  ResLocked   = $0010;   {Locked during heap compaction}
  ResProtected = $0008;   {Protected from change}
  ResPreload   = $0004;   {Preload when file opened}
  ResChanged   = $0002;   {Has been changed in memory}

6.4.3   Other Properties

function SizeResource
            (theResource : Handle)   {Handle to resources}
              : LONGINT;   {Size of resource data, in bytes}

```
function MaxSizeRsrc
        (theResource : Handle)        {Handle to resource}
             : LONGINT;               {Approximate size of resource data, in bytes}

function HomeResFile
        (theResource : Handle)        {Handle to resource}
             : INTEGER;               {Reference number of home resource file}
```

6.5   Modifying Resources

6.5.1   Creating Resource Files

```
procedure CreateResFile
        (fileName : Str255);          {Name of resource file to be created}
```

6.5.2   Marking Changed Resources

```
procedure ChangedResource
        (theResource : Handle);       {Resource to be marked as changed}
```

6.5.3   Adding and Removing Resources

```
procedure AddResource
        (rsrcData   : Handle;         {Handle to data of new resource}
         rsrcType   : ResType;        {Type of new resource}
         rsrcID     : INTEGER;        {ID number of new resource}
         rsrcName   : Str255);        {Name of new resource}

procedure RmveResource
        (theResource : Handle);       {Resource to be removed}

function UniqueID
        (rsrcType : ResType);         {Resource type}
             : INTEGER               {Unique ID number for this type}

function Unique1ID
        (rsrcType : ResType)          {Resource type}
             : INTEGER;               {Unique ID for this type in current resource file}
```

6.5.4   Updating Resource Files

```
procedure UpdateResFile
        (refNum : INTEGER);           {Reference number of resource file to be updated}

procedure WriteResource
        (theResource : Handle);       {Resource to be written out}
```

6.5.5   Purge Checking

procedure SetResPurge
        (onOrOff : BOOLEAN);   {Turn purge checking on or off?}

6.6   Nuts and Bolts

6.6.1   Error Reporting

function ResError
        : INTEGER;   {Result code from last resource-related operation}

const
  ResNotFound   = −192;   {Resource not found}
  ResFNotFound = −193;   {Resource file not found}
  AddResFailed = −194;   {AddResource failed}
  RmvResFailed = −196;   {RmveResource failed}
  ResErrAttr   = −198;   {Operation prohibited by resource attribute}
  MapReadErr   = −199;   {Error reading resource map}
  DskFulErr   = − 34;   {Disk full}

6.6.2   Resource File Attributes

function   GetResFileAttrs
        (refNum : INTEGER)   {Reference number of resource file}
        : INTEGER;   {Current resource file attributes}

procedure SetResFileAttrs
        (refNum   : INTEGER;   {Reference number of resource file}
         newAttrs : INTEGER);   {New resource file attributes}

const
  MapReadOnly = 128;   {No changes allowed}
  MapCompact = 64;   {Compact file when updated}
  MapChanged = 32;   {Write resource map when updated}

Chapter 7   Program Startup

7.1   Starting and Ending a Program

7.1.1   Starting a Program

procedure Launch   {Assembly language only}

procedure Chain   {Assembly language only}

7.1.2   Loading and Unloading Segments

procedure LoadSeg   {Assembly language only}

procedure UnloadSeg
      (anyRoutine : Ptr);   {Pointer to any routine in the segment}

7.1.3   Ending a Program

procedure ExitToShell;

procedure Restart;

7.2   Packages

7.2.1   Standard Packages

const
  ListMgr = 0;   {List Manager Package}
  DskInit = 2;   {Disk Initialization Package}
  StdFile = 3;   {Standard File Package}
  FlPoint = 4;   {Floating-Point Arithmetic Package}
  TrFunc   = 5;   {Transcendental Functions Package}
  IntUtil = 6;   {International Utilities Package}
  BDConv   = 7;   {Binary/Decimal Conversion Package}

7.2.2   Initializing Packages

procedure InitPack
      (packNumber : INTEGER);   {Package number}

procedure InitAllPacks;

7.3   Finder Information

7.3.1   Signatures and File Types

type
  OSType = packed array [1..4] of CHAR;   {Creator signature or file type}

7.3.2   Finder Information Records

type
  FInfo = **record**
```
        fdType      : OSType;      {File type}
        fdCreator   : OSType;      {Creator signature}
        fdFlags     : INTEGER;     {Finder flags}
        fdLocation  : Point;       {Top-left corner of file's icon in local (window) coordinates}
        fdFldr      : INTEGER      {Folder or window containing icon}
     end;
```

const
```
  FHasBundle = $2000;            {Application has Finder resources}
  FInvisible  = $4000;           {File not visible on desktop}

  FDisk     =  0;                {Icon is in main disk window}
  FDesktop = −2;                 {Icon is on desktop}
  FTrash    = −3;                {Icon is in trash window}
```

7.3.3   Accessing Finder Properties

function GetFInfo
```
        (fName        : Str255;     {File name}
        vRefNum      : INTEGER;     {Volume or directory}
        var finderInfo : FInfo)     {Returns current Finder information}
         : OSErr;                   {Result code}
```

function SetFInfo
```
        (fName      : Str255;       {File name}
        vRefNum    : INTEGER;       {Volume or directory}
        finderInfo : FInfo)         {New Finder information}
         : OSErr;                   {Result code}
```

7.3.4   Startup Information

procedure CountAppFiles
```
        (var message : INTEGER;     {Open or print?}
        var count    : INTEGER);    {Returns number of files selected}
```

procedure GetAppFiles
```
        (index      : INTEGER;      {Index number of desired file}
        var theFile : AppFile);     {Returns identifying information about file}
```

procedure ClrAppFiles
```
        (index : INTEGER);          {Index number of file to be cleared}
```

procedure GetAppParms
```
        (var appName    : Str255;   {Returns name of application file}
        var appResFile  : INTEGER;  {Returns reference number of application resource file}
        var startHandle : Handle);  {Returns handle to startup information}
```

```
const
  AppOpen = 0;                              {Open document file}
  AppPrint = 1;                             {Print document file}
type
  AppFile = record
              vRefNum : INTEGER;            {Volume or directory}
              fType   : OSType;             {File type}
              versNum : INTEGER;            {Version number}
              fName   : Str255              {Name of file}
            end;
```

7.4   Desk Scrap

7.4.2   Scrap Information

```
type
  PScrapStuff = ^ScrapStuff;

  ScrapStuff = record
                 scrapSize   : LONGINT;     {Overall size of scrap in bytes}
                 scrapHandle : Handle;      {Handle to scrap in memory}
                 scrapCount  : INTEGER;     {Current scrap count}
                 scrapState  : INTEGER;     {Is scrap in memory?}
                 scrapName   : StringPtr    {Pointer to name of scrap file}
               end;

function InfoScrap
           : PScrapStuff;                   {Pointer to current scrap information}
```

7.4.3   Reading and Writing the Scrap

```
function GetScrap
           (theItem   : Handle;             {Handle to be set to requested item}
            itemType  : ResType;            {Resource type of desired item}
            var offset : LONGINT)           {Returns byte offset of item data within scrap contents}
             : LONGINT;                     {Length of item data in bytes, or error code}

function PutScrap
           (itemLength : LONGINT;           {Length of item data in bytes}
            itemType   : ResType;           {Resource type of item}
            theItem    : Ptr)               {Pointer to item data}
             : LONGINT;                     {Result code}

function ZeroScrap
           : LONGINT;                       {Result code}
```

```
const
  NoScrapErr = −100;                    {Desk scrap not initialized}
  NoTypeErr  = −102;                    {No item of requested type}
```

7.4.4   Loading and Unloading the Scrap

```
function LoadScrap
          : LONGINT;                    {Result code}

function UnloadScrap
          : LONGINT;                    {Result code}
```

Chapter 8   Text

8.1   Keys and Characters

8.1.1   Character Set

```
const
  CommandMark  = $11;                   {Character code of command mark}
  CheckMark    = $12;                   {Character code of check mark}
  DiamondMark  = $13;                   {Character code of diamond mark}
  AppleMark    = $14;                   {Character code of Apple mark}
```

8.1.2   Character Strings

```
type
  StringPtr    = ^Str255;               {Pointer to a string}
  StringHandle = ^StringPtr;            {Handle to a string}

function   NewString
              (oldString : Str255)      {String to be copied}
               : StringHandle;          {Handle to copy}

function   GetString
              (stringID : INTEGER)      {Resource ID of desired string}
               : StringHandle;          {Handle to string in memory}

procedure  GetIndString
              (var theString : Str255;  {Returns requested string}
               stringListID  : INTEGER; {Resource ID of string list}
               stringIndex   : INTEGER);{Index of string within list}

procedure  SetString
              (theString : StringHandle;{Handle to be set}
               setTo     : Str255);     {String to set it to}
```

8.2   Fonts

8.2.1   Standard Font Numbers

```
const
  SystemFont  =  0;
  ApplFont    =  1;
  NewYork     =  2;
  Geneva      =  3;
  Monaco      =  4;
  Venice      =  5;
  London      =  6;
  Athens      =  7;
  SanFran     =  8;
  Toronto     =  9;
  Cairo       = 11;
  LosAngles   = 12;

  Times       = 20;
  Helvetica   = 21;
  Courier     = 22;
  Symbol      = 23;
  Taliesin    = 24;
```

8.2.2   Font Records

```
type
  FontRec = record
              fontType    : INTEGER;          {Font type (proportional or fixed-width)}
              firstChar   : INTEGER;          {Character code of first defined character}
              lastChar    : INTEGER;          {Character code of last defined character}
              widMax      : INTEGER;          {Maximum character width in pixels}
              kernMax     : INTEGER;          {Maximum backward kern in pixels}
              nDescent    : INTEGER;          {Negative of descent in pixels}
              fRectWidth  : INTEGER;          {Width of font rectangle in pixels}
              fRectHeight : INTEGER;          {Height of font rectangle in pixels}
              owTLoc      : INTEGER;          {Offset to owTable in words}
              ascent      : INTEGER;          {Ascent in pixels}
              descent     : INTEGER;          {Descent in pixels}
              leading     : INTEGER;          {Leading in pixels}
              rowWords    : INTEGER;          {Row width of bitimage in words}
              {bitImage   : array [1..rowWords, 1..chHeight] of INTEGER;}
                                              {Font image}
              {locTable   : array [firstChar..lastChar+2] of INTEGER;}
                                              {Location table}
```

```
        {owTable    : array [firstChar..lastChar+2] of INTEGER;}
                                {Offset/width table}
        {widthTab   : array [firstChar..lastChar+2] of INTEGER;}
                                {Character-width table (optional)}
        {heightTab  : array [firstChar..lastChar+2] of INTEGER}
                                {Image-height table (optional)}
        end;
const
  PropFont  = $9000;                {Font type for proportional font}
  PrpFntH   = $9001;                {   Proportional font with height table}
  PrpFntW   = $9002;                {   Proportional font with width table}
  PrpFntHW  = $9003;                {   Proportional font with height and width tables}

  FixedFont = $B000;                {Font type for fixed-width font}
  FxdFntH   = $B001;                {   Fixed-width font with height table}
  FxdFntW   = $B002;                {   Fixed-width font with width table}
  FxdFntHW  = $B003;                {   Fixed-width font with height and width tables}

  FontWid   = $ACB0;                {Font type for font width table}
```

8.2.4 Initializing the Toolbox for Fonts

procedure InitFonts;

8.2.5 Access to Fonts

```
procedure  GetFontName
            (fontNumber : INTEGER;      {Font number}
            var name    : Str255);      {Returns name of typeface}

procedure  GetFNum
            (name              : Str255;    {Name of typeface}
            var fontNumber : INTEGER);  {Returns font number}

function   RealFont
            (fontNumber : INTEGER;      {Desired font number}
            pointSize   : INTEGER)      {Desired point size}
            : BOOLEAN;                  {Does font exist?}
```

8.2.6 Requesting Font Information

```
procedure  GetFontInfo
            (var theInfo : FontInfo);   {Returns metric information about current text font}
```

```
type
  FontInfo = record
              ascent  : INTEGER;        {Ascent in pixels}
              descent : INTEGER;        {Descent in pixels}
              widMax  : INTEGER;        {Maximum character width in pixels}
              leading : INTEGER         {Leading in pixels}
            end;

procedure  FontMetrics
            (var theInfo : FMetricRec);   {Returns metric information about current text font}

type
  FMetricRec = record
              ascent     : Fixed;      {Ascent in fractional points}
              descent    : Fixed;      {Descent in fractional points}
              leading    : Fixed;      {Leading in fractional points}
              widMax     : Fixed;      {Maximum character width in fractional points}
              wTabHandle : Handle      {Handle to global width table}
            end;
```

8.2.7 Locking a Font

```
procedure  SetFontLock
            (lock : BOOLEAN);          {Lock or unlock?}
```

8.2.8 Nuts and Bolts

```
procedure  SetFractEnable
            (useFracts : BOOLEAN);     {Use fractional character widths?}

procedure  SetFScaleDisable
            (noScaling : BOOLEAN);     {Turn off font scaling?}
```

8.3   Text and QuickDraw

8.3.1   QuickDraw Text Characteristics

```
type
  GrafPort = record
                device  : INTEGER;      {Device code}
                . . . ;
                txFont  : INTEGER;      {Font number of typeface}
                txFace  : Style;        {Type style}
                txMode  : INTEGER;      {Transfer mode for text}
                txSize  : INTEGER;      {Type size in points}
                spExtra : Fixed;        {Extra space between words, in pixels}
                . . .
           end;

StyleItem = (Bold, Italic, Underline, Outline, Shadow, Condense, Extend);

Style     = set of StyleItem;
```

8.3.2   Setting Text Characteristics

```
procedure GrafDevice
            (deviceCode : INTEGER);     {Device code}

procedure TextFont
            (fontNumber : INTEGER);     {Font number of desired typeface}

procedure TextSize
            (pointSize : INTEGER);      {Type size in points}

procedure TextFace
            (typeStyle : Style);        {Type style}

procedure TextMode
            (mode : INTEGER);           {Transfer mode for text}

procedure SpaceExtra
            (extraSpace : Fixed);       {Extra space between words, in pixels}
```

8.3.3   Drawing Text

```
procedure DrawChar
            (theChar : CHAR);           {Character to be drawn}

procedure DrawString
            (theString : Str255);       {String to be drawn}
```

```
procedure  DrawText
           (theText    : Ptr;            {Pointer to text to be drawn}
            firstChar  : INTEGER;        {Index of first character within text}
            charCount  : INTEGER);       {Number of characters to be drawn}
```

8.3.4 Measuring Text

```
function   CharWidth
           (theChar : CHAR)             {Character to be measured}
             : INTEGER;                 {Width of character}

function   StringWidth
           (theString : Str255)         {String to be measured}
             : INTEGER;                 {Width of string}

function   TextWidth
           (theText    : Ptr;           {Pointer to text to be measured}
            firstChar  : INTEGER;        {Index of first character within text}
            charCount : INTEGER)         {Number of characters to be measured}
             : INTEGER;                 {Width of text}

procedure  MeasureText
           (charCount  : INTEGER;        {Number of characters to be measured}
            theText    : Ptr;            {Pointer to text to be measured}
            widthTable : Ptr);           {Pointer to table of text widths}
```

APPENDIX

B

Resource Formats

Resource Type 'BNDL' [7.5.4]

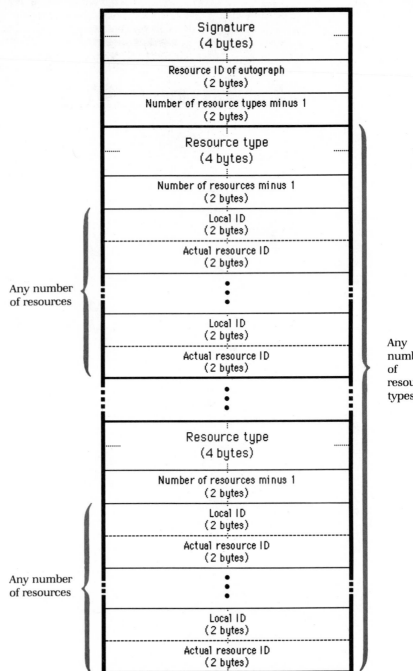

Resource Type 'CODE' [7.5.1]

```
┌─────────────────────────────────────────┐ ⎫
│   Jump table offset of first routine in segment │ ⎬
│              (2 bytes)                    │ ⎪ Segment
├─────────────────────────────────────────┤ ⎬ header
│   Number of jump table entries for segment │ ⎪
│              (2 bytes)                    │ ⎭
├─────────────────────────────────────────┤
│                                          │
│         Code of segment                  │
│                                          │
│         (indefinite length)              │
│                                          │
└─────────────────────────────────────────┘
```

Resource Type 'FONT' [8.4.5]

fontType (2 bytes)
firstChar (2 bytes)
lastChar (2 bytes)
widMax (2 bytes)
kernMax (2 bytes)
nDescent (2 bytes)
fRectWidth (2 bytes)
fRectHeight (2 bytes)
owTloc (2 bytes)
ascent (2 bytes)
descent (2 bytes)
leading (2 bytes)
rowWords (2 bytes)
bitImage (indefinite length)
locTable (indefinite length)
owTable (indefinite length)

Resource Type 'FREF' [7.5.3]

```
┌──────────────────────────────┐
│         File type            │
│         (4 bytes)            │
├──────────────────────────────┤
│ Local ID of icon list (2 bytes) │
└──────────────────────────────┘
```

Resource Type 'FRSV' [8.4.7]

```
┌──────────────────────────────┐
│   Number of fonts (2 bytes)  │
├──────────────────────────────┤
│ Resource ID of first font (2 bytes) │
├──────────────────────────────┤
│                              │
┊                              ┊
│                              │
├──────────────────────────────┤
│ Resource ID of last font (2 bytes) │
└──────────────────────────────┘
```

Resource Type 'FWID' [8.4.6]

```
┌─────────────────────────────┐
│     fontType (2 bytes)      │
├─────────────────────────────┤
│    firstChar (2 bytes)      │
├─────────────────────────────┤
│    lastChar (2 bytes)       │
├─────────────────────────────┤
│     widMax (2 bytes)        │
├─────────────────────────────┤
│     kernMax (2 bytes)       │
├─────────────────────────────┤
│    nDescent (2 bytes)       │
├─────────────────────────────┤
│   fRectWidth (2 bytes)      │
├─────────────────────────────┤
│   fRectHeight (2 bytes)     │
├─────────────────────────────┤
│     owTloc (2 bytes)        │
├─────────────────────────────┤
│     ascent (2 bytes)        │
├─────────────────────────────┤
│    descent (2 bytes)        │
├─────────────────────────────┤
│    leading (2 bytes)        │
├─────────────────────────────┤
│                             │
│         owTable             │
│                             │
│     (indefinite length)     │
│                             │
└─────────────────────────────┘
```

Resource Type 'ICN#' [5.5.4]

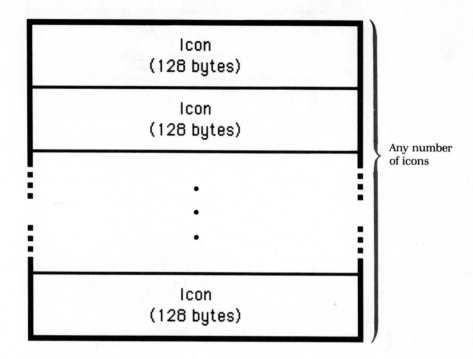

Resource Type 'ICON' [5.5.3]

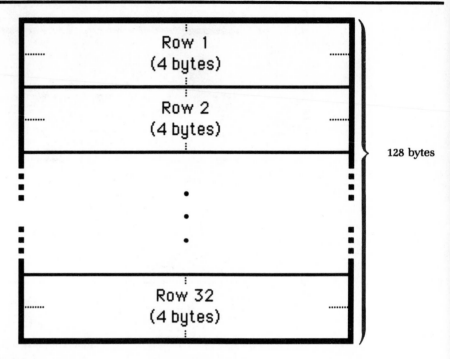

Resource Type 'INIT' [8.4.4]

Resource Type 'NFNT' [8.4.5]

fontType (2 bytes)
firstChar (2 bytes)
lastChar (2 bytes)
widMax (2 bytes)
kernMax (2 bytes)
nDescent (2 bytes)
fRectWidth (2 bytes)
fRectHeight (2 bytes)
owTloc (2 bytes)
ascent (2 bytes)
descent (2 bytes)
leading (2 bytes)
rowWords (2 bytes)
bitImage (indefinite length)
locTable (indefinite length)
owTable (indefinite length)

Resource Type 'PACK' [7.5.2]

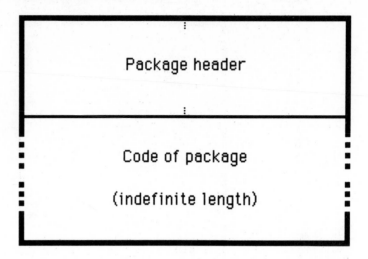

Resource Type 'PAT ' [5.5.1]

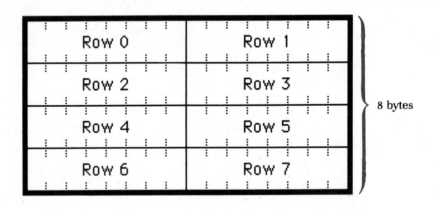

Resource Type 'PAT#' [5.5.2]

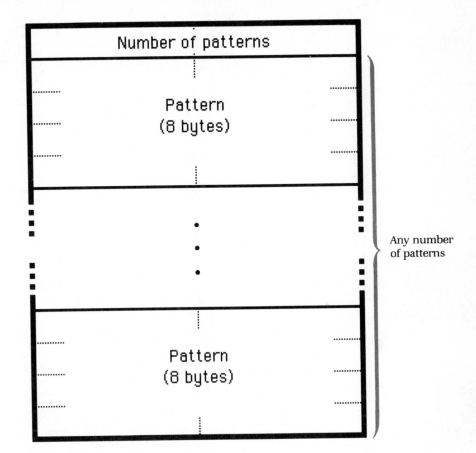

Resource Type 'PICT' [5.5.5]

```
┌────────────────────────────────┐
│        Length in bytes         │
├────────────────────────────────┤
│             Frame              │
│           (8 bytes)            │
├────────────────────────────────┤
│                                │
│     Data defining picture      │
│                                │
│      (indefinite length)       │
│                                │
└────────────────────────────────┘
```

Resource Type 'STR ' [8.4.2]

```
┌─────────────────────────────────────┐
│ Length of string (0-255)            │
│                                      │
│                                      │
│                                      │
│         Characters of string        │
│          (indefinite length)        │
│                                      │
│                                      │
│                                      │
└─────────────────────────────────────┘
```

The maximum length of a 'STR ' resource is 255 characters.

Resource Type 'STR#' [8.4.3]

Resource Type 'TEXT' [8.4.1]

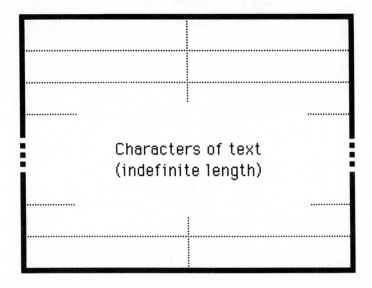

Characters of text
(indefinite length)

A 'TEXT' resource does *not* begin with a length byte.

APPENDIX C

Memory Layouts

128K "Skinny Mac"

128K
Macintosh

$00	Trap Vectors
$100	System Globals
$400	Dispatch Table
$800	System Globals
$B00	System Heap
$4E00	Application Heap
	Stack
	Application Global Space
$1A700	Main Screen Buffer
$1FC7F	
$1FD00	Main Sound Buffer
$1FFE3	
$1FFFF	

KEY

  System Use

↑ Arrows show direction of
growth of stack and
application heap.

505

512K "Fat Mac"

512K
Macintosh

$00	Trap Vectors
$100	System Globals
$400	Dispatch Table
$800	System Globals
$B00	System Heap
$CB00	Application Heap
	Stack
	Application Global Space
$7A700	Main Screen Buffer
$7FC7F	
$7FD00	Main Sound Buffer
$7FFE3	
$7FFFF	

1M Macintosh Plus

512K Macintosh XL (Lisa)

512K
Macintosh XL

Address	Region
$00	Trap Vectors
$100	System Globals
$400	Dispatch Table
$800	System Globals
$B00	System Heap
$CB00	Application Heap
	↓
	↑
	Stack
	Application Global Space
$4EF86	
$78000	Main Screen Buffer
$7FFF8	
$7FFFF	

1M Macintosh XL (Lisa)

A P P E N D I X

Key Codes and Character Codes

Key Codes for the Standard Macintosh Keyboard and Keypad

Original keyboard

Original keypad

Key Codes for the Macintosh Plus Keyboard

$32 `	$12 1	$13 2	$14 3	$15 4	$17 5	$16 6	$1A 7	$1C 8	$19 9	$1D 0	$1B –	$18 =	$33 Back-space
$30 Tab	$0C Q	$0D W	$0E E	$0F R	$11 T	$10 Y	$20 U	$22 I	$1F O	$23 P	$21 [	$1E]	
$39 Caps Lock	$00 A	$01 S	$02 D	$03 F	$05 G	$04 H	$26 J	$28 K	$25 L	$29 ;	$27 '	$24 Return	
$38 Shift	$06 Z	$07 X	$08 C	$09 V	$0B B	$2D N	$2E M	$2B ,	$2F .	$2C /	$38 Shift	$4D ↑	
$3A Option	$37 ⌘	$31								$2A \	$46 ←	$42 →	$48 ↓

Macintosh Plus keyboard

$47 Clear	$48 =	$4D /	$42 *
$59 7	$5B 8	$5C 9	$4E –
$56 4	$57 5	$58 6	$46 +
$53 1	$54 2	$55 3	$4C
$52 0		$41 .	Enter

Macintosh Plus keypad

Standard Keyboard Layouts

Standard keyboard layout (unshifted)

Standard keyboard layout (with Shift)

Standard keyboard layout (with Option)

Standard keyboard layout (with Option-Shift)

Macintosh Plus keyboard layout (unshifted)

Macintosh Plus keyboard layout (with Shift)

Macintosh Plus keyboard layout (with Option)

Macintosh Plus keyboard layout (with Option-Shift)

Character Codes

First hex digit

	$0	$1	$2	$3	$4	$5	$6	$7	$8	$9	$A	$B	$C	$D	$E	$F
0	NUL	□	space	0	@	P	`	p	Ä	ê	†	∞	¿	–	‡	
1	□	⌘	!	1	A	Q	a	q	Å	ë	°	±	¡	—	·	Ò
2	□	✓	"	2	B	R	b	r	Ç	í	¢	≤	¬	"	‚	Ú
3	□	◆	#	3	C	S	c	s	É	ì	£	≥	√	"	„	Û
4	□		$	4	D	T	d	t	Ñ	î	§	¥	ƒ	'	‰	Ù
5	□	□	%	5	E	U	e	u	Ö	ï	•	µ	≈	'	Â	ı
6	□	□	&	6	F	V	f	v	Ü	ñ	¶	∂	∆	÷	Ê	ˆ
7	□	□	'	7	G	W	g	w	á	ó	ß	Σ	«	◊	Á	˜
8	□	□	(	8	H	X	h	x	à	ò	®	∏	»	ÿ	Ë	¯
9	TAB	□	)	9	I	Y	i	y	â	ô	©	π	…	Ÿ	È	˘
A	□	□	*	:	J	Z	j	z	ä	ö	™	∫	non-break space	/	Í	˙
B	□	□	+	;	K	[	k	{	ã	õ	´	ª	À	¤	Î	˚
C	□	□	,	<	L	\	l	|	å	ú	¨	º	Ã	‹	Ï	¸
D	CR	□	–	=	M	]	m	}	ç	ù	≠	Ω	Õ	›	Ì	
E	□	□	.	>	N	^	n	~	é	û	Æ	æ	Œ	fi	Ó	
F	□	□	/	?	O	_	o		è	ü	Ø	ø	œ	fl	Ô	□

Second hex digit

Characters with shading are typed as two-character combinations

APPENDIX

E

Error Codes

Operating System Errors

The following is a complete list of Operating System error codes. Not all are covered in this book, and some of the meanings may be obscure. (I don't know what a bit-slip nybble is either.) For the errors you're most likely to encounter, see reference sections [3.1.2, 6.6.1, II:8.2.8].

Number	Name	Meaning
0	NoErr	No error; all is well
−1	QErr	Queue element not found during deletion
−2	VTypErr	Invalid queue element
−3	CorErr	Trap ("core routine") number out of range
−4	UnimpErr	Unimplemented trap
−8	SENoDB	No debugger installed
−17	ControlErr	Driver error during Control operation
−18	StatusErr	Driver error during Status operation
−19	ReadErr	Driver error during Read operation
−20	WritErr	Driver error during Write operation
−21	BadUnitErr	Bad unit number

Number	Name	Meaning
−22	UnitEmptyErr	No such entry in unit table
−23	OpenErr	Driver error during Open operation
−24	CloseErr	Driver error during Close operation
−25	DRemovErr	Attempt to remove an open driver
−26	DInstErr	Attempt to install nonexistent driver
−27	AbortErr	Driver operation aborted
−28	NotOpenErr	Driver not open
−33	DirFulErr	Directory full
−34	DskFulErr	Disk full
−35	NSVErr	No such volume
−36	IOErr	Disk I/O error
−37	BdNamErr	Bad name
−38	FNOpnErr	File not open
−39	EOFErr	Attempt to read past end of file
−40	PosErr	Attempt to position before start of file
−41	MFulErr	Memory (system heap) full
−42	TMFOErr	Too many files open (more than 12)
−43	FNFErr	File not found
−44	WPrErr	Disk is write-protected
−45	FLckdErr	File locked
−46	VLckdErr	Volume locked
−47	FBsyErr	File busy
−48	DupFNErr	Duplicate file name
−49	OpWrErr	File already open for writing
−50	ParamErr	Invalid parameter list
−51	RfNumErr	Invalid reference number
−52	GFPErr	Error during GetFPos
−53	VolOffLinErr	Volume off-line
−54	PermErr	Permission violation
−55	VolOnLinErr	Volume already on-line
−56	NSDrvErr	No such drive
−57	NoMacDskErr	Non-Macintosh disk
−58	ExtFSErr	External file system
−59	FSRnErr	Unable to rename file
−60	BadMDBErr	Bad master directory block
−61	WrPermErr	No write permission
−64	NoDriveErr	No such drive
−65	OffLinErr	Drive off-line
−66	NoNybErr	Can't find 5 nybbles
−67	NoAdrMkErr	No address mark
−68	DataVerErr	Data read doesn't verify
−69	BadCksmErr	Bad checksum (address mark)
−70	BadBtSlpErr	Bad bit-slip nybbles (address mark)
−71	NoDtaMkErr	No data mark
−72	BadDCksum	Bad checksum (data mark)

Number	Name	Meaning
−73	BadDBtSlp	Bad bit-slip nybbles (data mark)
−74	WrUnderrun	Write underrun
−75	CantStepErr	Can't step disk drive
−76	Tk0BadErr	Track 0 bad
−77	InitIWMErr	Can't initialize disk chip ("Integrated Wozniak Machine")
−78	TwoSideErr	Two-sided operation on one-sided drive
−79	SpdAdjErr	Can't adjust disk speed
−80	SeekErr	Seek to wrong track
−81	SectNFErr	Sector not found
−85	ClkRdErr	Error reading clock
−86	ClkWrErr	Error writing clock
−87	PRWrErr	Error writing parameter RAM
−88	PRInitErr	Parameter RAM uninitialized
−89	RcvrErr	Receiver error (serial communications)
−90	BreakRecd	Break received (serial communications)
−91	DDPSktErr	Socket error (AppleTalk, Datagram Delivery Protocol)
−92	DDPLenErr	Packet too long (AppleTalk, Datagram Delivery Protocol)
−93	NoBridgeErr	No bridge found (AppleTalk)
−94	LAPProtErr	Protocol error (AppleTalk, Link Access Protocol)
−95	ExcessCollsns	Excessive collisions (AppleTalk)
−97	PortInUse	Port already in use (AppleTalk)
−98	PortNotCf	Port not configured for this connection (AppleTalk)
−99	MemROZError	Error in read-only zone
−100	NoScrapErr	No desk scrap
−102	NoTypeErr	No item in scrap of requested type
−108	MemFullErr	No room; heap is full
−109	NilHandleErr	Illegal operation on empty handle
−110	MemAdrErr	Bad memory address
−111	MemWZErr	Illegal operation on free block
−112	MemPurErr	Illegal operation on locked block
−113	MemAZErr	Address not in heap zone
−114	MemPCErr	Pointer check failed
−115	MemBCErr	Block check failed
−116	MemSCErr	Size check failed
−117	MemLockedErr	Attempt to move a locked block
−120	DirNFErr	Directory not found
−121	TMWDOErr	Too many working directories open
−122	BadMovErr	Invalid move operation
−123	WrgVolTypErr	Wrong volume type (not HFS)
−127	FSDSIntErr	Internal file system error

Number	Name	Meaning
−192	ResNotFound	Resource not found
−193	ResFNotFound	Resource file not found
−194	AddResFailed	AddResource failed
−196	RmvResFailed	RmveResource failed
−198	ResErrAttr	Operation prohibited by resource attribute
−199	MapReadErr	Error reading resource map
−1024	NBPBuffOvr	Buffer overflow (AppleTalk, Name-Binding Protocol)
−1025	NBPNoConfirm	Name not confirmed (AppleTalk, Name-Binding Protocol)
−1026	NBPConfDiff	Name confirmed for different socket (AppleTalk, Name-Binding Protocol)
−1027	NBPDuplicate	Name already exists (AppleTalk, Name-Binding Protocol)
−1028	NBPNotFound	Name not found (AppleTalk, Name-Binding Protocol)
−1029	NBPNISErr	Names information socket error (Appletalk, Name-Binding Protocol)
−1096	ReqFailed	Request failed (AppleTalk)
−1097	TooManyReqs	Too many concurrent requests (AppleTalk)
−1098	TooManySkts	Too many responding sockets (AppleTalk)
−1099	BadATPSkt	Bad responding socket (AppleTalk Transaction Protocol)
−1100	BadBuffNum	Bad buffer number (AppleTalk)
−1101	NoRelErr	No release received (AppleTalk)
−1102	CBNotFound	Control block not found (AppleTalk)
−1103	NoSendResp	AddResponse before SendResponse (AppleTalk)
−1104	NoDataArea	Too many outstanding calls (AppleTalk)
−1105	ReqAborted	Request aborted (AppleTalk)
−3101	Buf2SmallErr	Buffer too small (AppleTalk)
−3102	NoMPPError	Driver not installed (AppleTalk, Macintosh Packet Protocol)
−3103	CkSumErr	Bad checksum (AppleTalk)
−3104	ExtractErr	No tuple in buffer (AppleTalk)
−3105	ReadQErr	Invalid socket or protocol type (AppleTalk)
−3106	ATPLenErr	Packet too long (AppleTalk Transaction Protocol)
−3107	ATPBadRsp	Bad response (AppleTalk Transaction Protocol)
−3108	RecNotFnd	No AppleBus record (AppleTalk)
−3109	SktClosedErr	Socket closed (AppleTalk)

"Dire Straits" Errors

The following errors are reported directly to the user—not to the running program—by the "Dire Straits" Manager (officially called the System Error Handler). Errors in this category are considered so serious that recovery is impossible: the Toolbox simply displays a "dire straits" alert box (the one with the bomb icon) on the screen, forcing the user to restart the system. Some people insist that DS really stands for "deep spaghetti," but most Macintosh programmers prefer a more colorful term.

Number	Name	Meaning
1	DSBusErr	Bus error
2	DSAddressErr	Address error
3	DSIllInstErr	Illegal instruction
4	DSZeroDivErr	Attempt to divide by zero
5	DSChkErr	Check trap
6	DSOvflowErr	Overflow trap
7	DSPrivErr	Privilege violation
8	DSTraceErr	Trace trap
9	DSLineAErr	"A emulator" trap
10	DSLineFErr	"F emulator" trap
11	DSMiscErr	Miscellaneous hardware exception
12	DSCoreErr	Unimplemented core routine
13	DSIRQErr	Uninstalled interrupt
14	DSIOCoreErr	I/O core error
15	DSLoadErr	Segment Loader error
16	DSFPErr	Floating-point error
17	DSNoPackErr	Package 0 not present
18	DSNoPk1	Package 1 not present
19	DSNoPk2	Package 2 not present
20	DSNoPk3	Package 3 not present
21	DSNoPk4	Package 4 not present
22	DSNoPk5	Package 5 not present
23	DSNoPk6	Package 6 not present
24	DSNoPk7	Package 7 not present
25	DSMemFullErr	Out of memory
26	DSBadLaunch	Can't launch program
27	DSFSErr	File system error
28	DSStkNHeap	Stack/heap collision
30	DSReinsert	Ask user to reinsert disk
31	DSNotTheOne	Wrong disk inserted
84	MenuPrgErr	Menu purged from heap

APPENDIX

Summary of Trap Macros and Trap Words

Trap Macros

The following is an alphabetical list of assembly-language trap macros covered in this volume, with their corresponding trap words. For routines belonging to the standard packages, the trap word shown is one of the eight package traps (_Pack0 to _Pack7) and is followed by a routine selector in parentheses. Routines marked with an asterisk (*) are available only on the Macintosh Plus.

Trap macro name	Trap word	Reference section
_AddPt	$A87E	[4.4.1]
_AddResource	$A9AB	[6.5.3]
_BackPat	$A87C	[5.1.1]
_BitAnd	$A858	[2.2.2]
_BitClr	$A85F	[2.2.1]
_BitNot	$A85A	[2.2.2]
_BitOr	$A85B	[2.2.2]
_BitSet	$A85E	[2.2.1]
_BitShift	$A85C	[2.2.2]
_BitTst	$A85D	[2.2.1]
_BitXOr	$A859	[2.2.2]
_BlockMove	$A02E	[3.2.6]

Trap macro name	Trap word	Reference section
*_CalcMask	$A838	[5.1.6]
_Chain	$A9F3	[7.1.1]
_ChangedResource	$A9AA	[6.5.2]
_CharWidth	$A88D	[8.3.4]
_ClipRect	$A87B	[4.3.6]
_ClosePgon	$A8CC	[4.1.4]
_ClosePicture	$A8F4	[5.4.2]
_ClosePort	$A87D	[4.3.2]
_CloseResFile	$A99A	[6.2.1]
_CloseRgn	$A8DB	[4.1.6]
_CmpString	$A03C	[2.1.2]
_CompactMem	$A04C	[3.3.2]
_CopyBits	$A8EC	[5.1.2]
*_CopyMask	$A817	[5.1.4]
_CopyRgn	$A8DC	[4.1.7]
_CountResources	$A99C	[6.3.3]
_CountTypes	$A99E	[6.3.3]
*_Count1Resources	$A80D	[6.3.3]
*_Count1Types	$A81C	[6.3.3]
_CreateResFile	$A9B1	[6.5.1]
_CurResFile	$A994	[6.2.2]
_Date2Secs	$A9C7	[2.4.3]
_DeltaPoint	$A94F	[4.4.1]
_DetachResource	$A992	[6.3.2]
_DiffRgn	$A8E6	[4.4.8]
_DisposHandle	$A023	[3.2.2]
_DisposPtr	$A01F	[3.2.2]
_DisposRgn	$A8D9	[4.1.6]
_DrawChar	$A883	[8.3.3]
_DrawPicture	$A8F6	[5.4.3]
_DrawString	$A884	[8.3.3]
_DrawText	$A885	[8.3.3]
_EmptyHandle	$A02B	[3.3.3]
_EmptyRect	$A8AE	[4.4.4]
_EmptyRgn	$A8E2	[4.4.7]
_EqualPt	$A881	[4.4.1]
_EqualRect	$A8A6	[4.4.5]
_EqualRgn	$A8E3	[4.4.8]
_EraseArc	$A8C0	[5.3.5]
_EraseOval	$A8B9	[5.3.4]
_ErasePoly	$A8C8	[5.3.6]
_EraseRect	$A8A3	[5.3.2]
_EraseRgn	$A8D4	[5.3.7]
_EraseRoundRect	$A8B2	[5.3.3]
_ExitToShell	$A9F4	[7.1.3]

Trap macro name	Trap word	Reference section
_FillArc	$A8C2	[5.3.5]
_FillOval	$A8BB	[5.3.4]
_FillPoly	$A8CA	[5.3.6]
_FillRect	$A8A5	[5.3.2]
_FillRgn	$A8D6	[5.3.7]
_FillRoundRect	$A8B4	[5.3.3]
*_FixATan2	$A818	[2.3.6]
*_FixDiv	$A84D	[2.3.2]
_FixMul	$A868	[2.3.2]
_FixRatio	$A869	[2.3.2]
_FixRound	$A86C	[2.3.1]
*_Fix2Frac	$A841	[2.3.3]
*_Fix2Long	$A840	[2.3.1]
*_FontMetrics	$A835	[8.2.6]
*_FracCos	$A847	[2.3.6]
*_FracDiv	$A84B	[2.3.4]
*_FracMul	$A84A	[2.3.4]
*_FracSin	$A848	[2.3.6]
*_FracSqrt	$A849	[2.3.4]
*_Frac2Fix	$A842	[2.3.3]
_FrameArc	$A8BE	[5.3.5]
_FrameOval	$A8B7	[5.3.4]
_FramePoly	$A8C6	[5.3.6]
_FrameRect	$A8A1	[5.3.2]
_FrameRgn	$A8D2	[5.3.7]
_FrameRoundRect	$A8B0	[5.3.3]
_FreeMem	$A01C	[3.3.1]
_GetAppParms	$A9F5	[7.3.4]
_GetClip	$A87A	[4.3.6]
_GetFileInfo	$A00C	[7.3.3]
_GetFName	$A8FF	[8.2.5]
_GetFNum	$A900	[8.2.5]
_GetFontInfo	$A88B	[8.2.6]
_GetHandleSize	$A025	[3.2.3]
_GetIndResource	$A99D	[6.3.3]
_GetIndType	$A99F	[6.3.3]
_GetNamedResource	$A9A1	[6.3.1]
_GetPattern	$A9B8	[5.1.1]
_GetPen	$A89A	[5.2.4]
_GetPenState	$A898	[5.2.1]
_GetPicture	$A9BC	[5.4.2]
_GetPixel	$A865	[4.2.3]
_GetPort	$A874	[4.3.3]
_GetPtrSize	$A021	[3.2.3]
_GetResAttrs	$A9A6	[6.4.2]

Trap macro name	Trap word	Reference section
_GetResFileAttrs	$A9F6	[6.6.2]
_GetResInfo	$A9A8	[6.4.1]
_GetResource	$A9A0	[6.3.1]
_GetScrap	$A9FD	[7.4.3]
_GetString	$A9BA	[8.1.2]
*_Get1IxResource	$A80E	[6.3.3]
*_Get1IxType	$A80F	[6.3.3]
*_Get1NamedResource	$A820	[6.3.1]
*_Get1Resource	$A81F	[6.3.1]
_GlobalToLocal	$A871	[4.4.2]
_GrafDevice	$A872	[8.3.2]
_HandAndHand	$A9E4	[3.2.7]
_HandToHand	$A9E1	[3.2.6]
*_HClrRBit	$A068	[3.2.4]
*_HGetState	$A069	[3.2.4]
_HidePen	$A896	[5.2.3]
_HiWord	$A86A	[2.2.3]
_HLock	$A029	[3.2.4]
_HNoPurge	$A04A	[3.2.4]
_HomeResFile	$A9A4	[6.4.3]
_HPurge	$A049	[3.2.4]
*_HSetRBit	$A067	[3.2.4]
*_HSetState	$A06A	[3.2.4]
_HUnlock	$A02A	[3.2.4]
_InfoScrap	$A9F9	[7.4.2]
_InitAllPacks	$A9E6	[7.2.2]
_InitFonts	$A8FE	[8.2.4]
_InitGraf	$A86E	[4.3.1]
_InitPack	$A9E5	[7.2.2]
_InitPort	$A86D	[4.3.2]
_InsetRect	$A8A9	[4.4.4]
_InsetRgn	$A8E1	[4.4.7]
_InverRect	$A8A4	[5.3.2]
_InverRgn	$A8D5	[5.3.7]
_InverRoundRect	$A8B3	[5.3.3]
_InvertArc	$A8C1	[5.3.5]
_InvertOval	$A8BA	[5.3.4]
_InvertPoly	$A8C9	[5.3.6]
_IUDateString	$A9ED (0)	[2.4.4]
_IUTimeString	$A9ED (2)	[2.4.4]
_KillPicture	$A8F5	[5.4.2]
_KillPoly	$A8CD	[4.1.4]

Trap macro name	Trap word	Reference section
_Launch	$A9F2	[7.1.1]
_Line	$A892	[5.2.4]
_LineTo	$A891	[5.2.4]
_LoadSeg	$A9F0	[7.1.2]
_LocalToGlobal	$A870	[4.4.2]
_LodeScrap	$A9FB	[7.4.4]
_LongMul	$A867	[2.3.5]
*_Long2Fix	$A83F	[2.3.1]
_LoWord	$A86B	[2.2.3]
_MapPoly	$A8FC	[4.4.9]
_MapPt	$A8F9	[4.4.9]
_MapRect	$A8FA	[4.4.9]
_MapRgn	$A8FB	[4.4.9]
*_MaxApplZone	$A063	[3.3.4]
*_MaxBlock	$A061	[3.3.1]
_MaxMem	$A11D	[3.3.2]
*_MaxSizeRsrc	$A821	[6.4.3]
*_MeasureText	$A837	[8.3.4]
_MoreMasters	$A036	[3.2.5]
_Move	$A894	[5.2.4]
*_MoveHHi	$A064	[3.2.5]
_MovePortTo	$A877	[4.3.5]
_MoveTo	$A893	[5.2.4]
*_NewEmptyHandle	$A166	[3.2.1]
_NewHandle	$A122	[3.2.1]
_NewPtr	$A11E	[3.2.1]
_NewRgn	$A8D8	[4.1.6]
_NewString	$A906	[8.1.2]
_NumToString	$A9EE (0)	[2.3.7]
_OffsetPoly	$A8CE	[4.4.6]
_OffsetRect	$A8A8	[4.4.4]
_OfsetRgn	$A8E0	[4.4.7]
_OpenPicture	$A8F3	[5.4.2]
_OpenPoly	$A8CB	[4.1.4]
_OpenPort	$A86F	[4.3.2]
_OpenResFile	$A997	[6.2.1]
_OpenRgn	$A8DA	[4.1.6]
_Pack0	$A9E7	[7.2.1]
_Pack1	$A9E8	[7.2.1]
_Pack2	$A9E9	[7.2.1]
_Pack3	$A9EA	[7.2.1]
_Pack4	$A9EB	[7.2.1]
_Pack5	$A9EC	[7.2.1]

Trap macro name	Trap word	Reference section
_Pack6	$A9ED	[7.2.1]
_Pack7	$A9EE	[7.2.1]
*_Pack8	$A816	[7.2.1]
*_Pack9	$A82B	[7.2.1]
*_Pack10	$A82C	[7.2.1]
*_Pack11	$A82D	[7.2.1]
*_Pack12	$A82E	[7.2.1]
*_Pack13	$A82F	[7.2.1]
*_Pack14	$A830	[7.2.1]
*_Pack15	$A831	[7.2.1]
_PaintArc	$A8BF	[5.3.5]
_PaintOval	$A8B8	[5.3.4]
_PaintPoly	$A8C7	[5.3.6]
_PaintRect	$A8A2	[5.3.2]
_PaintRgn	$A8D3	[5.3.7]
_PaintRoundRect	$A8B1	[5.3.3]
_PenMode	$A89C	[5.2.2]
_PenNormal	$A89E	[5.2.2]
_PenPat	$A89D	[5.2.2]
_PenSize	$A89B	[5.2.2]
_PinRect	$A94E	[4.4.3]
_PortSize	$A876	[4.3.5]
_Pt2Rect	$A8AC	[4.1.2]
_PtInRect	$A8AD	[4.4.3]
_PtInRgn	$A8E8	[4.4.3]
_PtrAndHand	$A9EF	[3.2.7]
_PtrToHand	$A9E3	[3.2.6]
_PtrToXHand	$A9E2	[3.2.6]
_PtToAngle	$A8C3	[5.3.5]
_PurgeMem	$A04D	[3.3.2]
*_PurgeSpace	$A162	[3.3.1]
_PutScrap	$A9FE	[7.4.3]
_Random	$A861	[2.3.8]
_RealFont	$A902	[8.2.5]
_ReallocHandle	$A027	[3.3.3]
_RecoverHandle	$A128	[3.2.1]
_RectInRgn	$A8E9	[4.4.3]
_RectRgn	$A8DF	[4.1.7]
_ReleaseResource	$A9A3	[6.3.2]
*_RelString	$A050	[2.1.2]
_ResError	$A9AF	[6.6.1]
_ResrvMem	$A040	[3.2.5]
_RmveResource	$A9AD	[6.5.3]

Trap macro name	Trap word	Reference section
_ScalePt	$A8F8	[4.4.9]
_ScrollRect	$A8EF	[5.1.5]
_Secs2Date	$A9C6	[2.4.3]
_SectRect	$A8AA	[4.4.5]
_SectRgn	$A8E4	[4.4.8]
*_SeedFill	$A839	[5.1.6]
_SetApplLimit	$A02D	[3.3.4]
_SetClip	$A879	[4.3.6]
_SetDateTime	$A03A	[2.4.1]
_SetEmptyRgn	$A8DD	[4.1.7]
_SetFileInfo	$A00D	[7.3.3]
_SetFontLock	$A903	[8.2.7]
*_SetFScaleDisable	$A834	[8.2.8]
_SetHandleSize	$A024	[3.2.3]
_SetOrigin	$A878	[4.3.4]
_SetPBits	$A875	[4.3.4]
_SetPenState	$A899	[5.2.1]
_SetPort	$A873	[4.3.3]
_SetPt	$A880	[4.1.1]
_SetPtrSize	$A020	[3.2.3]
_SetRecRgn	$A8DE	[4.1.7]
_SetRect	$A8A7	[4.1.2]
_SetResAttrs	$A9A7	[6.4.2]
_SetResFileAttrs	$A9F7	[6.6.2]
_SetResInfo	$A9A9	[6.4.1]
_SetResPurge	$A993	[6.5.5]
_SetString	$A907	[8.1.2]
_ShowPen	$A897	[5.2.3]
_SizeRsrc	$A9A5	[6.4.3]
_SpaceExtra	$A88E	[8.3.2]
*_StackSpace	$A065	[3.3.4]
_StringToNum	$A9EE (1)	[2.3.7]
_StringWidth	$A88C	[8.3.4]
_StuffHex	$A866	[2.2.4]
_SubPt	$A87F	[4.4.1]
_TextFace	$A888	[8.3.2]
_TextFont	$A887	[8.3.2]
_TextMode	$A889	[8.3.2]
_TextSize	$A88A	[8.3.2]
_TextWidth	$A886	[8.3.4]

Trap macro name	Trap word	Reference section
_UnionRect	$A8AB	[4.4.5]
_UnionRgn	$A8E5	[4.4.8]
_UniqueID	$A9C1	[6.5.3]
*_Unique1ID	$A810	[6.5.3]
_UnloadSeg	$A9F1	[7.1.2]
_UnlodeScrap	$A9FA	[7.4.4]
_UpdateResFile	$A999	[6.5.4]
_UprString	$A854	[2.1.2]
_UseResFile	$A998	[6.2.2]
_WriteResource	$A9B0	[6.5.4]
_XOrRgn	$A8E7	[4.4.8]
_ZeroScrap	$A9FC	[7.4.3]

Trap Words

Here is the same list sorted numerically by trap word. Again, routine selectors are given in parentheses following the trap word for routines belonging to the standard packages, and routines marked with an asterisk (*) are available only on the Macintosh Plus.

Trap word	Trap macro name	Reference section
$A00C	_GetFileInfo	[7.3.3]
$A00D	_SetFileInfo	[7.3.3]
$A01C	_FreeMem	[3.3.1]
$A11D	_MaxMem	[3.3.2]
$A11E	_NewPtr	[3.2.1]
$A01F	_DisposPtr	[3.2.2]
$A020	_SetPtrSize	[3.2.3]
$A021	_GetPtrSize	[3.2.3]
$A122	_NewHandle	[3.2.1]
$A023	_DisposHandle	[3.2.2]
$A024	_SetHandleSize	[3.2.3]
$A025	_GetHandleSize	[3.2.3]
$A027	_ReallocHandle	[3.3.3]
$A128	_RecoverHandle	[3.2.1]
$A029	_HLock	[3.2.4]
$A02A	_HUnlock	[3.2.4]
$A02B	_EmptyHandle	[3.3.3]
$A02D	_SetApplLimit	[3.3.4]
$A02E	_BlockMove	[3.2.6]

Trap word	Trap macro name	Reference section
$A036	_MoreMasters	[3.2.5]
$A03A	_SetDateTime	[2.4.1]
$A03C	_CmpString	[2.1.2]
$A040	_ResrvMem	[3.2.5]
$A049	_HPurge	[3.2.4]
$A04A	_HNoPurge	[3.2.4]
$A04C	_CompactMem	[3.3.2]
$A04D	_PurgeMem	[3.3.2]
*$A050	_RelString	[2.1.2]
*$A061	_MaxBlock	[3.3.1]
*$A162	_PurgeSpace	[3.3.1]
*$A063	_MaxApplZone	[3.3.4]
*$A064	_MoveHHi	[3.2.5]
*$A065	_StackSpace	[3.3.4]
*$A166	_NewEmptyHandle	[3.2.1]
*$A067	_HSetRBit	[3.2.4]
*$A068	_HClrRBit	[3.2.4]
*$A069	_HGetState	[3.2.4]
*$A06A	_HSetState	[3.2.4]
*$A80D	_Count1Resources	[6.3.3]
*$A80E	_Get1IxResource	[6.3.3]
*$A80F	_Get1IxType	[6.3.3]
*$A810	_Unique1ID	[6.5.3]
*$A816	_Pack8	[7.2.1]
*$A817	_CopyMask	[5.1.4]
*$A818	_FixATan2	[2.3.6]
*$A81C	_Count1Types	[6.3.3]
*$A81F	_Get1Resource	[6.3.1]
*$A820	_Get1NamedResource	[6.3.1]
*$A821	_MaxSizeRsrc	[6.4.3]
*$A82B	_Pack9	[7.2.1]
*$A82C	_Pack10	[7.2.1]
*$A82D	_Pack11	[7.2.1]
*$A82E	_Pack12	[7.2.1]
*$A82F	_Pack13	[7.2.1]
*$A830	_Pack14	[7.2.1]
*$A831	_Pack15	[7.2.1]
*$A834	_SetFScaleDisable	[8.2.8]
*$A835	_FontMetrics	[8.2.6]
*$A837	_MeasureText	[8.3.4]
*$A838	_CalcMask	[5.1.6]
*$A839	_SeedFill	[5.1.6]
*$A83F	_Long2Fix	[2.3.1]

Trap word	Trap macro name	Reference section
*$A840	_Fix2Long	[2.3.1]
*$A841	_Fix2Frac	[2.3.3]
*$A842	_Frac2Fix	[2.3.3]
*$A847	_FracCos	[2.3.6]
*$A848	_FracSin	[2.3.6]
*$A849	_FracSqrt	[2.3.4]
*$A84A	_FracMul	[2.3.4]
*$A84B	_FracDiv	[2.3.4]
*$A84D	_FixDiv	[2.3.2]
$A854	_UprString	[2.1.2]
$A858	_BitAnd	[2.2.2]
$A859	_BitXOr	[2.2.2]
$A85A	_BitNot	[2.2.2]
$A85B	_BitOr	[2.2.2]
$A85C	_BitShift	[2.2.2]
$A85D	_BitTst	[2.2.1]
$A85E	_BitSet	[2.2.1]
$A85F	_BitClr	[2.2.1]
$A861	_Random	[2.3.8]
$A865	_GetPixel	[4.2.3]
$A866	_StuffHex	[2.2.4]
$A867	_LongMul	[2.3.5]
$A868	_FixMul	[2.3.2]
$A869	_FixRatio	[2.3.2]
$A86A	_HiWord	[2.2.3]
$A86B	_LoWord	[2.2.3]
$A86C	_FixRound	[2.3.1]
$A86D	_InitPort	[4.3.2]
$A86E	_InitGraf	[4.3.1]
$A86F	_OpenPort	[4.3.2]
$A870	_LocalToGlobal	[4.4.2]
$A871	_GlobalToLocal	[4.4.2]
$A872	_GrafDevice	[8.3.2]
$A873	_SetPort	[4.3.3]
$A874	_GetPort	[4.3.3]
$A875	_SetPBits	[4.3.4]
$A876	_PortSize	[4.3.5]
$A877	_MovePortTo	[4.3.5]
$A878	_SetOrigin	[4.3.4]
$A879	_SetClip	[4.3.6]
$A87A	_GetClip	[4.3.6]
$A87B	_ClipRect	[4.3.6]
$A87C	_BackPat	[5.1.1]
$A87D	_ClosePort	[4.3.2]
$A87E	_AddPt	[4.4.1]
$A87F	_SubPt	[4.1.1]

Trap word	Trap macro name	Reference section
$A880	_SetPt	[4.1.1]
$A881	_EqualPt	[4.4.1]
$A883	_DrawChar	[8.3.3]
$A884	_DrawString	[8.3.3]
$A885	_DrawText	[8.3.3]
$A886	_TextWidth	[8.3.4]
$A887	_TextFont	[8.3.2]
$A888	_TextFace	[8.3.2]
$A889	_TextMode	[8.3.2]
$A88A	_TextSize	[8.3.2]
$A88B	_GetFontInfo	[8.2.6]
$A88C	_StringWidth	[8.3.4]
$A88D	_CharWidth	[8.3.4]
$A88E	_SpaceExtra	[8.3.2]
$A891	_LineTo	[5.2.4]
$A892	_Line	[5.2.4]
$A893	_MoveTo	[5.2.4]
$A894	_Move	[5.2.4]
$A896	_HidePen	[5.2.3]
$A897	_ShowPen	[5.2.3]
$A898	_GetPenState	[5.2.1]
$A899	_SetPenState	[5.2.1]
$A89A	_GetPen	[5.2.4]
$A89B	_PenSize	[5.2.2]
$A89C	_PenMode	[5.2.2]
$A89D	_PenPat	[5.2.2]
$A89E	_PenNormal	[5.2.2]
$A8A1	_FrameRect	[5.3.2]
$A8A2	_PaintRect	[5.3.2]
$A8A3	_EraseRect	[5.3.2]
$A8A4	_InverRect	[5.3.2]
$A8A5	_FillRect	[5.3.2]
$A8A6	_EqualRect	[4.4.5]
$A8A7	_SetRect	[4.1.2]
$A8A8	_OffsetRect	[4.4.4]
$A8A9	_InsetRect	[4.4.4]
$A8AA	_SectRect	[4.4.5]
$A8AB	_UnionRect	[4.4.5]
$A8AC	_Pt2Rect	[4.1.2]
$A8AD	_PtInRect	[4.4.3]
$A8AE	_EmptyRect	[4.4.4]
$A8B0	_FrameRoundRect	[5.3.3]
$A8B1	_PaintRoundRect	[5.3.3]
$A8B2	_EraseRoundRect	[5.3.3]

Trap word	Trap macro name	Reference section
$A8B3	_InverRoundRect	[5.3.3]
$A8B4	_FillRoundRect	[5.3.3]
$A8B7	_FrameOval	[5.3.4]
$A8B8	_PaintOval	[5.3.4]
$A8B9	_EraseOval	[5.3.4]
$A8BA	_InvertOval	[5.3.4]
$A8BB	_FillOval	[5.3.4]
$A8BE	_FrameArc	[5.3.5]
$A8BF	_PaintArc	[5.3.5]
$A8C0	_EraseArc	[5.3.5]
$A8C1	_InvertArc	[5.3.5]
$A8C2	_FillArc	[5.3.5]
$A8C3	_PtToAngle	[5.3.5]
$A8C6	_FramePoly	[5.3.6]
$A8C7	_PaintPoly	[5.3.6]
$A8C8	_ErasePoly	[5.3.6]
$A8C9	_InvertPoly	[5.3.6]
$A8CA	_FillPoly	[5.3.6]
$A8CB	_OpenPoly	[4.1.4]
$A8CC	_ClosePgon	[4.1.4]
$A8CD	_KillPoly	[4.1.4]
$A8CE	_OffsetPoly	[4.4.6]
$A8D2	_FrameRgn	[5.3.7]
$A8D3	_PaintRgn	[5.3.7]
$A8D4	_EraseRgn	[5.3.7]
$A8D5	_InverRgn	[5.3.7]
$A8D6	_FillRgn	[5.3.7]
$A8D8	_NewRgn	[4.1.6]
$A8D9	_DisposRgn	[4.1.6]
$A8DA	_OpenRgn	[4.1.6]
$A8DB	_CloseRgn	[4.1.6]
$A8DC	_CopyRgn	[4.1.7]
$A8DD	_SetEmptyRgn	[4.1.7]
$A8DE	_SetRecRgn	[4.1.7]
$A8DF	_RectRgn	[4.1.7]
$A8E0	_OfsetRgn	[4.4.7]
$A8E1	_InsetRgn	[4.4.7]
$A8E2	_EmptyRgn	[4.4.7]
$A8E3	_EqualRgn	[4.4.8]
$A8E4	_SectRgn	[4.4.8]
$A8E5	_UnionRgn	[4.4.8]
$A8E6	_DiffRgn	[4.4.8]
$A8E7	_XOrRgn	[4.4.8]

Trap word	Trap macro name	Reference section
$A8E8	_PtInRgn	[4.4.3]
$A8E9	_RectInRgn	[4.4.3]
$A8EC	_CopyBits	[5.1.2]
$A8EF	_ScrollRect	[5.1.5]
$A8F3	_OpenPicture	[5.4.2]
$A8F4	_ClosePicture	[5.4.2]
$A8F5	_KillPicture	[5.4.2]
$A8F6	_DrawPicture	[5.4.3]
$A8F8	_ScalePt	[4.4.9]
$A8F9	_MapPt	[4.4.9]
$A8FA	_MapRect	[4.4.9]
$A8FB	_MapRgn	[4.4.9]
$A8FC	_MapPoly	[4.4.9]
$A8FE	_InitFonts	[8.2.4]
$A8FF	_GetFName	[8.2.5]
$A900	_GetFNum	[8.2.5]
$A902	_RealFont	[8.2.5]
$A903	_SetFontLock	[8.2.7]
$A906	_NewString	[8.1.2]
$A907	_SetString	[8.1.2]
$A94E	_PinRect	[4.4.3]
$A94F	_DeltaPoint	[4.4.1]
$A992	_DetachResource	[6.3.2]
$A993	_SetResPurge	[6.5.5]
$A994	_CurResFile	[6.2.2]
$A997	_OpenResFile	[6.2.1]
$A998	_UseResFile	[6.2.2]
$A999	_UpdateResFile	[6.5.4]
$A99A	_CloseResFile	[6.2.1]
$A99C	_CountResources	[6.3.3]
$A99D	_GetIndResource	[6.3.3]
$A99E	_CountTypes	[6.3.3]
$A99F	_GetIndType	[6.3.3]
$A9A0	_GetResource	[6.3.1]
$A9A1	_GetNamedResource	[6.3.1]
$A9A3	_ReleaseResource	[6.3.2]
$A9A4	_HomeResFile	[6.4.3]
$A9A5	_SizeRsrc	[6.4.3]
$A9A6	_GetResAttrs	[6.4.2]
$A9A7	_SetResAttrs	[6.4.2]
$A9A8	_GetResInfo	[6.4.1]
$A9A9	_SetResInfo	[6.4.1]

Trap word	Trap macro name	Reference section
$A9AA	_ChangedResource	[6.5.2]
$A9AB	_AddResource	[6.5.3]
$A9AD	_RmveResource	[6.5.3]
$A9AF	_ResError	[6.6.1]
$A9B0	_WriteResource	[6.5.4]
$A9B1	_CreateResFile	[6.5.1]
$A9B8	_GetPattern	[5.1.1]
$A9BA	_GetString	[8.1.2]
$A9BC	_GetPicture	[5.4.2]
$A9C1	_UniqueID	[6.5.3]
$A9C6	_Secs2Date	[2.4.3]
$A9C7	_Date2Secs	[2.4.3]
$A9E1	_HandToHand	[3.2.6]
$A9E2	_PtrToXHand	[3.2.6]
$A9E3	_PtrToHand	[3.2.6]
$A9E4	_HandAndHand	[3.2.7]
$A9E5	_InitPack	[7.2.2]
$A9E6	_InitAllPacks	[7.2.2]
$A9E7	_Pack0	[7.2.1]
$A9E8	_Pack1	[7.2.1]
$A9E9	_Pack2	[7.2.1]
$A9EA	_Pack3	[7.2.1]
$A9EB	_Pack4	[7.2.1]
$A9EC	_Pack5	[7.2.1]
$A9ED	_Pack6	[7.2.1]
$A9ED (0)	_IUDateString	[2.4.4]
$A9ED (2)	_IUTimeString	[2.4.4]
$A9EE	_Pack7	[7.2.1]
$A9EE (0)	_NumToString	[2.3.7]
$A9EE (1)	_StringToNum	[2.3.7]
$A9EF	_PtrAndHand	[3.2.7]
$A9F0	_LoadSeg	[7.1.2]
$A9F1	_UnloadSeg	[7.1.2]
$A9F2	_Launch	[7.1.1]
$A9F3	_Chain	[7.1.1]
$A9F4	_ExitToShell	[7.1.3]
$A9F5	_GetAppParms	[7.3.4]
$A9F6	_GetResFileAttrs	[6.6.2]
$A9F7	_SetResFileAttrs	[6.6.2]
$A9F9	_InfoScrap	[7.4.2]
$A9FA	_UnlodeScrap	[7.4.4]
$A9FB	_LodeScrap	[7.4.4]
$A9FC	_ZeroScrap	[7.4.3]
$A9FD	_GetScrap	[7.4.3]
$A9FE	_PutScrap	[7.4.3]

APPENDIX

Summary of Assembly Language Variables

System Globals

Listed below are all assembly-language global variables covered in this volume, with their hexadecimal addresses. *Warning:* The addresses given may be subject to change in future versions of the Toolbox; always refer to these variables by name rather than using the addresses directly.

Variable name	Hexa-decimal address	Reference section	Meaning
ApFontID	$984	[8.2.1]	True font number of current application font
ApplLimit	$130	[3.3.4]	Application heap limit
ApplZone	$2AA	[3.1.3]	Pointer to start of application heap
AppParmHandle	$AEC	[7.3.4]	Handle to Finder startup information
BufPtr	$10C	[3.1.3]	Pointer to end of application global space
CurApName	$910	[7.3.4]	Name of current application (maximum 31 characters)
CurApRefNum	$900	[6.2.2, 7.3.4]	Reference number of application resource file

Variable name	Hexa-decimal address	Reference section	Meaning
CurMap	$A5A	[6.2.2]	Reference number of current resource file
CurPageOption	$936	[7.1.1]	Integer specifying screen and sound buffers
CurrentA5	$904	[3.1.3]	Base pointer for application globals
CurStackBase	$908	[3.1.3]	Pointer to base of stack
DeskPattern	$A3C	[5.1.2]	Screen background pattern
FinderName	$2E0	[7.1.3]	Name of program to exit to (maximum 15 characters)
*FractEnable	$BF4	[8.2.8]	Use fractional character widths? (1 byte)
FScaleDisable	$A63	[8.2.8]	Turn off font scaling? (1 byte)
HeapEnd	$114	[3.1.3]	Pointer to end of application heap
Key1Trans	$29E	[8.4.4]	Pointer to keyboard configuration routine
Key2Trans	$2A2	[8.4.4]	Pointer to keypad configuration routine
Lo3Bytes	$31A	[3.2.4]	Mask for extracting address from a master pointer
MemTop	$108	[3.1.3]	Pointer to end of physical memory
ResErr	$A60	[6.6.1]	Result code from last resource-related call
ResLoad	$A5E	[6.3.4]	Load resources automatically?
ROMBase	$2AE	[3.1.3]	Pointer to start of ROM
ROMFont0	$980	[8.2.1]	Handle to system font
*ROMMapInsert	$B9E	[6.6.3]	Include ROM-based resources in search? (1 byte)
ScrapCount	$968	[7.4.2]	Current scrap count
ScrapHandle	$964	[7.4.2]	Handle to contents of desk scrap
ScrapName	$96C	[7.4.2]	Pointer to scrap file name
ScrapSize	$960	[7.4.2]	Current size of desk scrap
ScrapState	$96A	[7.4.2]	Current state of desk scrap
ScrnBase	$824	[3.1.3]	Pointer to start of screen buffer
SoundBase	$266	[3.1.3]	Pointer to start of sound buffer
SPFont	$204	[8.2.1]	True font number of default application font

Variable name	Hexa-decimal address	Reference section	Meaning
SysMap	$A58	[6.2.2]	True reference number (not 0) of system resource file
SysMapHndl	$A54	[6.2.2]	Handle to resource map of system resource file
SysResName	$AD8	[6.2.2]	Name of system resource file (string, maximum 19 characters)
SysZone	$2A6	[3.1.3]	Pointer to start of system heap
Time	$20C	[2.4.1]	Current date and time in "raw" seconds
*TmpResLoad	$B9F	[6.6.3]	Load resources automatically just this once? (1 byte)
TopMapHndl	$A50	[6.2.2]	Handle to resource map of most recently opened (not necessarily current) resource file
*WidthTabHandle	$B2A	[8.2.6]	Handle to global width table for current font

QuickDraw Globals

The QuickDraw global variables listed below are located at the given offsets relative to the QuickDraw globals pointer, which in turn is pointed to by address register A5.

Variable name	Offset in bytes	Reference section	Meaning
ThePort	0	[4.3.3]	Current graphics port
White	−8	[5.1.2]	Standard white pattern
Black	−16	[5.1.2]	Standard black pattern
Gray	−24	[5.1.2]	Standard gray pattern
LtGray	−32	[5.1.2]	Standard light gray pattern
DkGray	−40	[5.1.2]	Standard dark gray pattern
Arrow	−108	[II:2.5.2]	Standard arrow cursor
ScreenBits	−122	[4.2.1]	Screen bit map
RandSeed	−126	[2.3.8]	"Seed" for random number generation

GLOSSARY

The following is a glossary of technical terms used in this volume. *Note:* Terms shown in *italic* are defined elsewhere in this glossary.

A5 world—Another name for a program's *application global space*, located by means of a *base address* kept in processor register A5.

"above A5" size—The number of bytes needed between the *base address* in register A5 and the end of the *application global space*, to hold a program's *application parameters* and *jump table*.

access permission—The form of communication allowed for a particular *file*, such as read-only, write-only, or read/write.

allocate—To set aside a *block* of memory from the *heap* for a particular use.

and—A bit-level operation in which each bit of the result is a 1 if both operands have 1s at the corresponding bit position, or 0 if either or both have 0s.

Apple mark—A special *control character* (*character code* $14) that appears on the Macintosh screen as a small Apple symbol; used for the title of the menu of *desk accessories*.

AppleTalk—A network to which the Macintosh can be connected for communication with other computers.

AppleTalk drivers—The pair of *device drivers* used for communicating with other computers over the *AppleTalk* network.

application file—A *file* containing the executable code of an application program, with a *file type* of 'APPL' and the program's own signature as its *creator signature*.

application font—The standard *typeface* used by an application program; normally Geneva, but can be changed to some other typeface if desired.

application global space—The area of memory containing a program's *application globals, application parameters,* and *jump table;* normally situated just before the *screen buffer* in memory and located by means of a *base address* kept in processor register A5.

application globals—Global variables belonging to the running application program, which reside in the *application global space* and are located at negative offsets from the *base address* in register A5.

application heap—The portion of the *heap* available for use by the running application program.

application heap limit—The memory address marking the farthest point to which the *heap* can expand, to prevent it from colliding with the *stack.*

application parameters—Descriptive information about the running program, located in the *application global space* at positive offsets from the *base address* in register A5. The application parameters are a vestige of the Lisa software environment, and most are unused on the Macintosh; the only ones still in use are the *QuickDraw globals pointer* and the *startup handle.*

application resource file—The *resource fork* of a program's *application file,* containing *resources* belonging to the program itself.

arc—A part of an *oval,* defined by a given *starting angle* and *arc angle.*

arc angle—The angle defining the extent of an *arc* or *wedge.*

ascent—(1) For a text character, the height of the character above the *baseline,* in pixels. (2) For a *font,* the maximum ascent of any character in the font.

ascent line—The line marking a font's maximum *ascent* above the *baseline.*

ASCII—American Standard Code for Information Interchange, the industry-standard 7-bit character set on which the Macintosh's 8-bit *character codes* are based.

@ operator—An operator provided by Apple's Pascal compiler, which accepts a variable or routine name as an operand and produces a *blind pointer* to that variable or routine in memory.

attribute byte—The byte in a *resource map* entry that holds the *resource attributes.*

autograph—A *Finder resource* whose *resource type* is the same as a program's *signature,* and which serves as the program's representative in the *desktop file;* also called a *version data* resource.

background pattern—The *pattern* used for *erasing* shapes in a given *graphics port.*

base address—In general, any memory address used as a reference point from which to locate desired data in memory. Specifically, (1) the address of the *bit image* belonging to a given *bit map*; (2) the address of a program's *application parameters*, kept in processor register A5 and used to locate the contents of the program's *application global space*.

base of stack—The end of the *stack* that remains fixed in memory and is not affected when items are added and removed; compare *top of stack*.

base type—In Pascal, the data type to which a given pointer type is declared to point: for example, the pointer type ^INTEGER has the base type INTEGER.

baseline—The reference line used for defining the *character images* in a *font*, and along which the *graphics pen* travels as text is drawn.

"below A5" size—The number of bytes needed between the beginning of the *application global space* and the *base address* in register A5, to hold a program's *application globals*.

Binary/Decimal Conversion Package—A standard *package*, provided in the *system resource file* (or in ROM on the Macintosh Plus), that converts numbers between their internal binary format and their external representation as strings of decimal digits.

binary point—The binary equivalent of a decimal point, separating the integer and fractional parts of a *fixed-point number* or a *fraction*.

bit image—An array of bits in memory representing the *pixels* of a graphical image.

bit map—The combination of a *bit image* with a *boundary rectangle*. The bit image provides the bit map's content; the boundary rectangle defines its extent and gives it a system of coordinates.

bit-mapped display—A video display screen on which each *pixel* can be individually controlled.

blind pointer—A Pascal pointer whose *base type* is unspecified, and which can consequently be assigned to a variable of any pointer type. The standard Pascal constant NIL is a blind pointer; two nonstandard features of Apple's Pascal compiler, the POINTER function and the @ *operator*, also produce blind pointers as their results.

block—An area of contiguous memory within the *heap*, either allocated or free.

bottleneck procedure—A specialized procedure for performing a low-level drawing operation in a given *graphics port*, used for *customizing* QuickDraw operations.

boundary rectangle—(1) For a *bit map*, the *rectangle* that defines the bit map's extent and determines its system of coordinates. (2) For a *graphics port*, the boundary rectangle of the port's bit map.

bounding box—The smallest *rectangle* enclosing a *polygon* or *region* on the coordinate grid.

bozo bit—A *Finder flag* that prevents a file from being copied; named for the Apple programmer who invented it.

bundle—A *Finder resource* that identifies all of a program's other Finder resources, so that they can be installed in the *desktop file* when the program's *application file* is copied to a new disk.

bundle bit—A *Finder flag* that tells whether an *application file* has any *Finder resources* that must accompany it when it's copied to a new disk.

busy bit—A *Finder flag* that tells whether a file is currently in use (has been opened and not yet closed).

byte—An independently addressable group of 8 bits in the computer's memory.

Caps Lock key—A *modifier key* on the Macintosh keyboard, used to convert lowercase letters to uppercase while leaving all nonalphabetic keys unaffected.

chain—To start up a new program after reinitializing the *stack* and *application global space*, but not the *application heap*; compare *launch*.

change bit—A *Finder flag* that tells whether a file's contents have been changed and must be updated on the disk.

character code—An 8-bit integer representing a text character; compare *key code*.

character image—A *bit image* that defines the graphical representation of a text character in a given *typeface* and *type size*.

character key—A key on the keyboard or keypad that produces a character when pressed; compare *modifier key*.

character offset—The horizontal distance, in pixels, from the left edge of the *font rectangle* to that of the *character image* for a given character; equal to the difference between the character's leftward *kern* and the maximum leftward kern in the font.

character origin—The location within a *character image* marking the position of the *graphics pen* when the character is drawn.

character style—See *type style*.

character width—The distance in pixels by which the *graphics pen* advances after drawing a character; compare *image width*.

character-width table—An optional table in a *font record*, containing *fractional character widths* for the characters in the font. Used only by the Macintosh Plus Toolbox; ignored on earlier models.

check mark—A special *control character* (*character code* $12) that appears on the Macintosh screen as a small check symbol; used for marking items on a menu.

clip—To confine a drawing operation within a specified boundary, suppressing any drawing that falls outside the boundary.

Clipboard—The term used in Macintosh user's manuals to refer to the *scrap*.

clipping boundaries—The boundaries to which all drawing in a given *graphics port* is confined, consisting of the port's *boundary rectangle*, *port rectangle*, *clipping region*, and *visible region*.

clipping region—A general-purpose *clipping boundary* associated with a *graphics port*, provided for the application program's use.

clock chip—A component of the Macintosh, powered independently by a battery, that keeps track of the current date and time even when the machine's main power is turned off.

code segment—A *resource* containing all or part of a program's executable machine code.

Command key—A *modifier key* on the Macintosh keyboard, used in combination with *character keys* to type keyboard equivalents to menu items.

command mark—A special *control character* (*character code* $11) that appears on the Macintosh screen as a "cloverleaf" symbol; used for displaying *Command-key* equivalents of menu items.

compaction—The process of moving together all of the *relocatable blocks* in the *heap*, in order to coalesce the available free space.

complement—A bit-level operation that reverses the bits of its operand, changing each 0 to a 1 and vice versa.

control—An object on the Macintosh screen that the user can manipulate with the mouse, in order to operate on the contents of a window or control the way they're presented.

control character—An *ASCII* text character with a character code from $00 to $1F (as well as the character $7F). Most control characters have no special meaning and no visual representation on the Macintosh, but a few are defined as special-purpose symbols for use on the screen: see *Apple mark*, *check mark*, *command mark*, *diamond mark*.

creator signature—A four-character string identifying the application program to which a given *file* belongs, and which should be started up when the user opens the file in the *Finder*.

current port—The *graphics port* in use at any given time, to which most *QuickDraw* operations implicitly apply.

current resource file—The *resource file* that will be searched first in looking for a requested *resource*, and to which certain resource-related operations implicitly apply.

cursor—A small (16-by-16-bit) *bit image* whose movements can be controlled with the *mouse* to designate positions on the Macintosh screen.

customize—To redefine an aspect of the Toolbox's operation to meet the specialized needs of a particular program.

cut and paste—The standard method of editing used on the Macintosh, in which text, graphics, or other information is transferred from one place to another by way of an intermediate *scrap* or *Clipboard*.

dangling pointer—An invalid pointer to an object that no longer exists at the designated address.

data fork—The *fork* of a *file* that contains the file's data, such as the text of a document; compare *resource fork*.

date and time record—A data structure representing a calendar date and clock time, with fields for the year, month, day of the month, day of the week, hour, minute, and second; used for reading or setting the Macintosh's built-in *clock chip*.

dead character—(1) A text character with a zero *character width*, which doesn't advance the *graphics pen* when drawn. (2) A character (such as a foreign-language accent) that combines with the character following it to produce a single result character (such as an accented letter).

definition file—An assembly-language file containing definitions of Toolbox constants and global variables, to be incorporated into an assembly-language program with an .INCLUDE directive.

dereference—(1) In general, to convert any pointer to the value it points to. (2) Specifically, to convert a *handle* to the corresponding *master pointer*.

descent—(1) For a text character, the distance the character extends below the *baseline*, in pixels. (2) For a *font*, the maximum descent of any character in the font.

descent line—The line marking a font's maximum *descent* below the *baseline*.

desk accessory—A type of *device driver* that operates as a "mini-application" that can coexist on the screen with any other program.

desk scrap—The *scrap* maintained by the Toolbox to hold information being *cut and pasted* from one application program or *desk accessory* to another.

desktop—(1) The gray background area of the Macintosh screen, outside of any window. (2) The arrangement of windows, icons, and other objects on the screen, particularly in the *Finder*.

desktop file—A file containing *Finder*-related information about the files on a disk, including their *file types*, *creator signatures*, and locations on the Finder *desktop*.

detach—To decouple a *resource* from its *resource file*, so that the resource will remain in memory when the file is closed.

device code—An integer identifying the output device a *graphics port* draws on, used in selecting the appropriate *fonts* for drawing text.

device driver—The low-level software through which the Toolbox communicates with an input/output device; an important special category of device drivers are *desk accessories*.

diameters of curvature—The width and height of the *ovals* forming the corners of a *rounded rectangle*.

diamond mark—A special *control character* (*character code* $13) that appears on the Macintosh screen as a small diamond symbol. This symbol is a vestige of earlier versions of the Macintosh user interface and no longer has any specific use.

directory—A table containing information about the *files* on a disk. Under the *Hierarchical File System*, directories may in turn contain other directories, and correspond to *folders* displayed on the *desktop* by the *Finder*.

disk driver—The *device driver* built into ROM for communicating with the Macintosh's built-in Sony disk drive.

Disk Initialization Package—A standard *package*, provided in the *system resource file*, that takes corrective action when an unreadable disk is inserted into the disk drive, usually by initializing the disk.

dispatch table—A table in memory, used by the *Trap Dispatcher* to locate the various Toolbox routines in ROM.

document—A coherent unit or collection of information to be operated on by a particular application program.

document file—A *file* containing a *document*.

driver reference number—An integer between −1 and −32, used to refer to a particular *device driver*; derived from the driver's *unit number* by the formula refNum = −(unitNum + 1).

empty handle—A *handle* that points to a NIL *master pointer*, indicating that the underlying *block* has been *purged* from the heap.

empty rectangle—A *rectangle* that encloses no pixels on the coordinate grid.

empty region—A *region* that encloses no pixels on the coordinate grid.

emulator trap—A form of *trap* that occurs when the *MC68000* processor attempts to execute an *unimplemented instruction*; used to "emulate" the effects of such an instruction with software instead of hardware.

enclosing rectangle—The *rectangle* within which an *oval* is inscribed.

erase—To fill a *shape* with the *background pattern* of the *current port*.

error code—A nonzero *result code*, reporting an error of some kind detected by an *Operating System* routine.

event—An occurrence reported by the Toolbox for a program to respond to, such as the user's pressing the mouse button or typing on the keyboard.

exception—See *trap*.

exclusive or—A bit-level operation in which each bit of the result is a 1 if the corresponding bits of the two operands are different, or 0 if they're the same.

EXIT—A nonstandard feature of Apple's Pascal compiler that allows an immediate return from the middle of a procedure or function.

external reference—A reference from one *code segment* to a routine contained in another segment.

family record—A data structure containing information about a given *typeface;* used only by the Macintosh Plus Toolbox.

Fat Mac—A model of *Macintosh* introduced in Autumn 1984, with a memory capacity of 512K and a single-sided disk drive.

field—One of the components of a Pascal record.

file—A collection of information stored as a named unit on a disk.

file icon—The *icon* used by the *Finder* to represent a *file* on the screen.

file reference—A *Finder resource* that establishes the connection between a *file type* and its *file icon*.

file reference number—An identifying number assigned by the *file system* to stand for a given *file*.

file system—The part of the Toolbox that deals with *files* on a disk or other mass storage device.

file type—A four-character string that characterizes the kind of information a *file* contains, assigned by the program that created the file.

fill—To color a *shape* with a specified *pattern*.

fill pattern—A *pattern* associated with a *graphics port*, used privately by *QuickDraw* for *filling* shapes.

Finder—The Macintosh program with which the user can manipulate files and start up applications; normally the first program to be run when the Macintosh is turned on.

Finder flags—A set of Boolean flags associated with a *file*, specifying attributes of interest to the *Finder*; see *bozo bit, bundle bit, busy bit, change bit, init bit, invisible bit, lock bit, system bit.*

Finder information record—A data structure summarizing the *Finder*-related properties of a *file*, including its *file type, creator signature,* and location on the Finder *desktop*.

Finder resources—The *resources* associated with a program that tell the *Finder* how to represent the program's *files* on the screen. Finder resources include *autographs, icon lists, file references,* and *bundles.*

Finder startup handle—See *startup handle*.

Finder startup information—See *startup information*.

fixed-point number—A binary number with a fixed number of bits before and after the *binary point*; specifically, a value of the Toolbox data type Fixed, consisting of a 16-bit integer part and a 16-bit fractional part.

Floating-Point Arithmetic Package—A standard *package*, provided in the *system resource file* (or in ROM on the Macintosh Plus), that performs arithmetic on *floating-point numbers* in accordance with the *IEEE standard*, using the *Standard Apple Numeric Environment* (SANE).

floating-point number—A binary number in which the *binary point* can "float" to any required position; the number's internal representation includes a binary exponent, or order of magnitude, that determines the position of the binary point.

folder—An object in a disk's *desktop file*, represented on the screen by an icon or a window, that can contain files or other folders; used for organizing the files on the disk. Under the *Hierarchical File System*, folders correspond to *directories*.

folder number—The integer used by the *Finder* to identify a particular *folder*.

font—(1) A *resource* containing all of the *character images* and other information needed to draw text characters in a given *typeface* and *type size*. (2) Sometimes used loosely (and incorrectly) as a synonym for *typeface*, as in the terms *font number* and *text font*.

font height—The overall height of a font's *font rectangle*, from *ascent line* to *descent line*.

font image—A *bit image* consisting of all the individual *character images* in a given *font*, arranged consecutively in a single horizontal row; also called a *strike* of the font.

font information record—A data structure containing metric information about a *font* in integer form; compare *font metric record*.

font metric record—On the Macintosh Plus, a data structure containing metric information about a *font* in fixed-point form; compare *font information record*.

font number—An integer denoting a particular *typeface*.

font record—A data structure containing all the information associated with a given *font*.

font rectangle—The smallest rectangle, relative to the *baseline* and *character origin*, that would enclose all of the *character images* in a *font* if they were superimposed with their origins coinciding.

font scaling—The enlargement or reduction of an existing *font* to substitute for an unavailable font of a different size.

font width table—A *resource* containing all of the information on the *character widths* in a given *font*, but without the *character images* themselves; used for measuring the width of text without actually drawing it.

fork—One of the two parts of which every *file* is composed: the *data fork* or the *resource fork*.

fraction—A *fixed-point* value of the Toolbox data type Fract, consisting of a 2-bit integer part and a 30-bit fractional part.

fractional character widths—A new feature, available only on the Macintosh Plus, that allows the *character widths* for a font to be expressed as fractional, rather than integral, numbers of *points*. The resulting character positions are then rounded to the available resolution of whatever device they're drawn on (such as the screen or a printer).

frame—To draw the outline of a *shape*, using the *pen size*, *pen pattern*, and *pen mode* of the *current port*.

free block—A contiguous *block* of space available for allocation within the *heap*.

global coordinate system—The coordinate system associated with a given *bit image*, in which the top-left corner of the image has coordinates (0, 0); the global coordinate system is independent of the *boundary rectangle* of any *bit map* or *graphics port* based on the image.

global width table—A table used internally by the Macintosh Plus Toolbox, holding the fractional character widths and other low-level data about a font.

glue routine—See *interface routine*.

graphics pen—The imaginary drawing tool used for drawing lines and text characters in a *graphics port*.

graphics port—A complete drawing environment containing all the information needed for *QuickDraw* drawing operations.

handle—A pointer to a *master pointer*, used to refer to a *relocatable block*.

heap—The area of memory in which space is allocated and deallocated at the explicit request of a running program; compare *stack*.

heap zone—An independently maintained area of the *heap*, such as the *application heap* or the *system heap*.

HFS—See *Hierarchical File System*.

Hierarchical File System—The *file system* built into the Macintosh Plus Toolbox in ROM, designed for use with double-sided disks, hard disks, and other large-capacity storage devices; also available for older models in RAM-based form.

icon—A *bit image* of a standard size (32 pixels by 32), used on the Macintosh screen to represent an object such as a disk or file.

icon list—A *resource* containing any number of *icons;* commonly used to hold a *file icon* and its mask for use by the *Finder*.

identifying information—The properties of a *resource* that uniquely identify it: its *resource type, resource ID,* and (optional) *resource name*.

IEEE standard—A set of standards and conventions for *floating-point* arithmetic, published by the Institute of Electrical and Electronic Engineers.

image-height table—An optional table in a *font record*, containing information on the heights of the *character images* in the font. Used only by the Macintosh Plus Toolbox; ignored on earlier models.

image width—The horizontal extent of a *character image;* the width in pixels of a character's graphical representation. Compare *character width*.

ImageWriter—A dot-matrix impact printer manufactured and marketed by Apple Computer.

init bit—A *Finder flag* that tells whether the *Finder resources* belonging to an *application file* have been installed in the *desktop file* of the disk it resides on.

Inside Macintosh—The comprehensive manual on the Macintosh *Toolbox*, produced by Apple Computer and published by Addison-Wesley Publishing Company, Inc.

interface—A set of rules and conventions by which one part of an organized system communicates with another.

interface file—A text file that contains the declarations belonging to an *interface unit* in source-language form, to be incorporated into a Pascal program with a **uses** *declaration* (or a $i directive in some versions of Pascal).

interface routine—A routine, part of an *interface unit*, that mediates between the *stack-based* parameter-passing conventions of a Pascal calling program and those of a *register-based* Toolbox routine; also called a "glue routine."

interface unit—A precompiled *unit* containing declarations for Toolbox routines and data structures, making them available for use in Pascal programs.

International Utilities Package—A standard *package*, provided in the *system resource file*, that helps programs conform to the prevailing conventions of different countries in such matters as formatting of numbers, dates, times, and currency; use of metric units; and alphabetization of foreign-language accents, diacriticals, and ligatures.

interrupt—A *trap* triggered by a signal to the *MC68000* processor from a peripheral device or other outside source.

interrupt handler—The *trap handler* for responding to an *interrupt*.

invert—(1) Generally, to reverse the colors of *pixels* in a graphical image, changing white to black and vice versa. (2) Specifically, to reverse the colors of all pixels inside the boundary of a given *shape*.

invisible bit—A *Finder flag* that marks a file as invisible, so that the *Finder* will not display its *icon* on the screen.

jump table—A table used to direct *external references* between *code segments* to the proper addresses in memory; located in the *application global space*, at positive offsets from the *base address* kept in register A5.

K—See *kilobyte*.

kern—The amount by which a *character image* extends leftward beyond the *character origin* or rightward beyond the *character width*.

kerning table—An optional table in a *family record*, containing information on the amount of *kern* between pairs of characters in a typeface; used only by the Macintosh Plus Toolbox.

key code—An 8-bit integer representing a physical key on the keyboard or keypad; compare *character code*.

key map—An array of bits in memory representing the state of the keys on the keyboard and keypad.

keyboard configuration—The correspondence between keys on the Macintosh keyboard or keypad and the characters they produce when pressed.

keyboard driver—The low-level part of the Toolbox that communicates directly with the keyboard and keypad.

keyboard routine—A routine to be executed directly by the *keyboard driver* when the user types a number key while holding down the Command and Shift keys; stored on the disk as a *resource* of type 'FKEY'.

keypad—See *numeric keypad*.

kilobyte—A unit of memory capacity equal to 2^{10} (1,024) bytes.

LaserWriter—A high-resolution laser printer manufactured and marketed by Apple Computer.

launch—To start up a new program after reinitializing the *stack*, *application global space*, and *application heap*; compare *chain*.

leading—The amount of extra vertical space between lines of text, measured in pixels from the *descent line* of one to the *ascent line* of the next; rhymes with "heading," not "heeding." Although every *font* specifies a recommended leading value, the recommendation need not be followed when drawing text in a *graphics port*.

length byte—The first byte of a *Pascal-format string*, which gives the number of characters in the string, from 0 to 255.

LIFO—Last in, first out; the order in which items are added to and removed from the stack. Compare *LIOF*.

ligature—A text character that combines two or more separate characters into a single symbol, such as æ.

limit pointer—A pointer that marks the end of an area of memory by pointing to the address following the last byte.

line drawing—Drawing in a *graphics port* by moving the *graphics pen*, using the QuickDraw routines Move, MoveTo, Line, and LineTo.

LIOF—"Last in, OK, fine"; describes the allocation and deallocation of items in the *heap*, which can occur in any order at all. Compare *LIFO*.

Lisa—A personal computer manufactured and marketed by Apple Computer; the first reasonably priced personal computer to feature a high-resolution *bit-mapped display* and a hand-held *mouse* pointing device. Now called *Macintosh XL*.

List Manager Package—A standard *package*, provided in the *system resource file*, that displays scrollable lists of items from which the user can choose with the mouse (like the one used in selecting files to be read from the disk). This package was introduced at the same time as the Macintosh Plus, and is available only in versions 3.0 or later of the System file.

load—To read an object, such as a *resource* or the *desk scrap*, into memory from a disk file.

local coordinate system—The coordinate system associated with a given *graphics port*, determined by the *boundary rectangle* of the port's *bit map*.

local ID—The identifying number by which a *Finder resource* is referred to by other resources in the same *bundle;* not necessarily the same as its true *resource ID*.

localize—To tailor a program's behavior for use in a particular country.

location table—A table giving the horizontal position of each *character image* in a *font*, measured in pixels from the beginning of the *font image*.

lock—To temporarily prevent a *relocatable block* from being *purged* or moved within the heap during *compaction*.

lock bit—(1) A flag in the high-order byte of a *master pointer* that marks the associated block as *locked*. (2) A *Finder flag* that prevents a file from being deleted, renamed, or replaced.

logical shift—A bit-level operation that shifts the bits of a given operand left or right by a specified number of positions, with bits shifted out at one end being lost and 0s shifted in at the other end.

long integer—A data type provided by Apple's Pascal compiler, consisting of double-length integers: 32 bits including sign, covering the range ±2147483647.

long word—A group of 32 bits (2 *words*, or 4 *bytes*) beginning at a *word boundary* in memory.

Macintosh—A personal computer manufactured and marketed by Apple Computer, featuring a high-resolution *bit-mapped display* and a hand-held *mouse* pointing device.

Macintosh Development System—A 68000 assembler and software development system produced by Consulair, Inc., and marketed by Apple Computer.

Macintosh Operating System—The body of machine code built into the Macintosh *ROM* to handle low-level tasks such as memory management, disk input/output, and serial communications.

Macintosh Plus—An upgraded model of *Macintosh* introduced in January 1986, with a memory capacity of 1 megabyte (expandable to 4 megabytes) and featuring an updated and expanded version of the *Toolbox*, a double-sided disk drive, a redesigned keyboard, and a *SCSI* parallel port.

Macintosh Programmer's Workshop—A software development system produced and marketed by Apple Computer, including a Pascal compiler, C compiler, 68000 assembler, and other development tools.

Macintosh XL—A *Lisa* computer running Macintosh software under the *MacWorks* emulator.

MacWorks—The software "emulator" program that enables a *Lisa* to run Macintosh software without modification.

main entry point—The point in a program's code where execution begins when the program is first started up.

main segment—The *code segment* containing a program's *main entry point*.

master pointer—A pointer to a *relocatable block*, kept at a known, fixed location in the *heap* and updated automatically by the Toolbox whenever the underlying block is moved during *compaction*. A pointer to the master pointer is called a *handle* to the block.

MC68000—The 32-bit microprocessor used in the Macintosh, manufactured by Motorola, Inc.; usually called "68000" for short.

megabyte—A unit of memory capacity equal to 2^{20} (1,048,576) bytes.

menu—A list of choices or options from which the user can choose with the mouse.

MiniEdit—The extensive example program developed in Volume Two of this book.

missing character—A character for which no *character image* is defined in a given *font*; represented graphically by the font's *missing symbol*.

missing symbol—The graphical representation used for drawing *missing characters* in a given *font*.

modifier key—A key on the Macintosh keyboard that doesn't generate a character of its own, but may affect the meaning of any *character key* pressed at the same time; see *Shift key, Caps Lock key, Option key, Command key*.

mouse—A hand-held pointing device for controlling the movements of the *cursor* to designate positions on the Macintosh screen.

nonrelocatable block—A *block* that can't be moved within the heap during *compaction*, referred to by single indirection with a simple pointer; compare *relocatable block*.

numeric keypad—A set of keys for typing numbers into the computer. On the Macintosh Plus, the keypad is physically built into the keyboard unit; on earlier models, it's an optional separate unit that connects to the keyboard with a cable.

object module—The file containing the compiled code of a Pascal *unit*, to be linked with that of an application program after compilation.

offset/width table—A table giving the *character offset* and *character width* for each character in a given *font*.

one-deep operation—On the Macintosh Plus, a resource-related operation that applies only to the *current resource file*, rather than to all open resource files.

Operating System—See *Macintosh Operating System*.

Option key—A *modifier key* on the Macintosh keyboard, used to type special characters such as foreign letters and accents.

or—A bit-level operation in which each bit of the result is a 1 if either or both operands have 1s at the corresponding bit position, or 0 if both have 0s.

ORD—A standard Pascal function for converting any scalar value to a corresponding integer (for instance, a character to its equivalent integer character code); on the Macintosh, ORD will also accept a pointer and return the equivalent long-integer address.

origin—(1) The top-left corner of a *rectangle*. (2) For a *bit map* or *graphics port*, the top-left corner of the *boundary rectangle*, whose coordinates determine the *local coordinate system*.

oval—A graphical figure, circular or elliptical in shape; defined by an *enclosing rectangle*.

package—A *resource*, usually residing in the *system resource file* (or in ROM on the Macintosh Plus), containing a collection of general-purpose routines that can be loaded into memory when needed; used to supplement the Toolbox with additional facilities.

package number—The *resource ID* of a *package;* must be between 0 and 7 (0 and 15 on the Macintosh Plus).

package trap—A Toolbox *trap* used at the machine-language level to call a routine belonging to a *package.* In the original Toolbox there are eight package traps, named _Pack0 to _Pack7; on the Macintosh Plus there are sixteen, named _Pack0 to _Pack15.

paint—To fill a *shape* with the *pen pattern* of the *current port.*

Pascal-format string—A sequence of text characters represented in the internal format used by Apple's Pascal compiler, consisting of a *length byte* followed by from 0 to 255 bytes of *character codes.*

pattern—A small *bit image* (8 pixels by 8) that can be repeated indefinitely to fill an area, like identical floor tiles laid end to end.

pattern list—A *resource* consisting of any number of *patterns.*

pattern transfer modes—A set of *transfer modes* used for drawing lines or shapes or filling areas with a *pattern.*

pen—See *graphics pen.*

pen level—An integer associated with a *graphics port* that determines the visibility of the port's *graphics pen.* The pen is visible if the pen level is zero or positive, hidden if it's negative.

pen location—The coordinates of the *graphics pen* in a given *graphics port.*

pen mode—The *transfer mode* with which a *graphics port* draws lines and frames or paints shapes; should be one of the *pattern transfer modes.*

pen pattern—The *pattern* in which a *graphics port* draws lines and frames or paints shapes.

pen size—The width and height of the *graphics pen* belonging to a *graphics port.*

pen state—The characteristics of the *graphics pen* belonging to a *graphics port,* including its *pen location, pen size, pen mode,* and *pen pattern.*

picture—A recorded sequence of *QuickDraw* operations that can be repeated on demand to reproduce a graphical image.

picture frame—The reference *rectangle* within which a *picture* is defined, and which can be mapped to coincide with any other specified rectangle when the picture is drawn.

pixel—A single dot forming part of a graphical image; short for "picture element."

point—(1) A position on the *QuickDraw* coordinate grid, specified by a pair of horizontal and vertical coordinates. (2) A unit used by printers to measure type sizes, equal to approximately 1/72 of an inch.

point size—See *type size.*

POINTER—A function provided by Apple's Pascal compiler, which accepts a *long integer* representing a memory address and returns a *blind pointer* to that address.

polygon—A graphical figure defined by any closed series of connected straight lines.

pop—To remove a data item from the top of a *stack.*

port—(1) A connector on the back of the Macintosh for communication with a peripheral device, such as a printer or modem. (2) Short for *graphics port.*

port rectangle—The rectangle that defines the portion of a *bit map* that a *graphics port* can draw into.

printer driver—The *device driver* for communicating with a printer through one of the Macintosh's built-in ports.

pseudo-random numbers—Numbers that seem to be random but can be reproduced in exactly the same sequence if desired.

purge—To remove a *relocatable block* from the heap to make room for other blocks. The purged block's *master pointer* remains allocated, but is set to NIL to show that the block no longer exists in the heap; all existing *handles* to the block become *empty handles.*

purge bit—A flag in the high-order byte of a *master pointer* that marks the associated block as *purgeable.*

purgeable block—A *relocatable block* that can be *purged* from the heap to make room for other blocks.

push—To add a data item to the top of a *stack.*

pushdown stack—See *stack.*

QuickDraw—The extensive collection of graphics routines built into the Macintosh *ROM.*

QuickDraw globals pointer—A pointer to the global variables used by *QuickDraw,* kept at address 0(A5) in the *application global space* and initialized with the InitGraf routine.

RAM—See *random-access memory.*

random-access memory—A common but misleading term for *read/write memory.*

read-only memory—Memory that can be read but not written; usually called *ROM*. The *Skinny Mac* and *Fat Mac* have 64K of ROM containing the built-in machine code of the *Macintosh Operating System*, *QuickDraw*, and the *User Interface Toolbox*. The *Macintosh Plus* has an expanded 128K ROM that also includes some *packages*, *device drivers*, and other frequently used *resources*. Compare *read/write memory*.

read/write memory—Memory that can be both read and written; commonly known by the misleading term *random-access memory*, or *RAM*. The *Skinny Mac* has 128K of read/write memory; the *Fat Mac* has 512K; the *Macintosh Plus* has 1 megabyte, expandable to 4 megabytes. Compare *read-only memory*.

reallocate—To allocate fresh space for a *relocatable block* that has been *purged*, updating the block's *master pointer* to point to its new location. Only the space is reallocated; the block's former contents are not restored.

rectangle—A four-sided graphical figure defined by two *points* specifying its top-left and bottom-right corners, or by four integers specifying its top, left, bottom, and right edges.

region—A graphical figure that can be of any arbitrary shape. It can have curved as well as straight edges, and can even have holes in it or consist of two or more separate pieces.

register-based—Describes a Toolbox routine that accepts its parameters and returns its results directly in the processor's registers; compare *stack-based*.

release—To deallocate a *block* of memory that's no longer needed, allowing the space to be reused for another purpose.

relocatable block—A *block* that can be moved within the heap during *compaction*, referred to by double indirection with a *handle*; compare *nonrelocatable block*.

resource—A unit or collection of information kept in a *resource file* on a disk (or in ROM on the Macintosh Plus) and *loaded* into memory when needed.

resource attributes—A set of flags describing properties of a resource, kept in the *attribute byte* of its *resource map* entry.

resource bit—A flag in the high-order byte of a *master pointer* that marks the associated block as a *resource*.

resource compiler—A utility program that constucts *resources* according to a coded definition read from a text file.

resource data—The information a *resource* contains.

resource editor—A utility program with which *resources* can be defined or modified directly on the screen with the mouse and keyboard.

resource file—A collection of *resources* stored together as a unit on a disk; technically not a *file* as such, but merely the *resource fork* of a particular file.

resource file attributes—A set of flags describing properties of a *resource file*.

resource fork—The *fork* of a *file* that contains the file's *resources;* usually called a *resource file*. Compare *data fork*.

resource ID—An integer that identifies a particular *resource* within its resource type.

resource map—The table that summarizes the contents of a *resource file*, stored as part of the file itself and read into memory when the file is opened.

resource name—An optional string of text characters that identifies a particular *resource* within its *resource type,* and by which the resource can be listed on a *menu*.

resource specification—The combination of a *resource type* and *resource ID*, or a *resource type* and *resource name,* which uniquely identifies a particular resource.

resource type—A four-character string that identifies the kind of information a *resource* contains.

result code—An integer code returned by an *Operating System* routine to signal successful completion or report an error.

return link—The address of the instruction following a routine call, to which control is to return on completion of the routine.

ROM—See *read-only memory*.

rounded rectangle—A graphical figure consisting of a *rectangle* with rounded corners; defined by the rectangle itself and the dimensions of the *ovals* forming the corners.

routine selector—An integer used to identify a particular routine within a *package*.

row width—The number of bytes in each row of a *bit image*.

SANE—See *Standard Apple Numeric Environment*.

scrap—The vehicle by which information is *cut and pasted* from one place to another.

scrap count—An integer maintained by the Toolbox that tells when the contents of the *desk scrap* have been changed by a *desk accessory*.

scrap file—A disk file holding the contents of the *desk scrap*.

scrap handle—A *handle* to the contents of the *desk scrap*, kept by the Toolbox in a *system global*.

scrap information record—A data structure summarizing the contents and status of the *desk scrap*.

screen buffer—The area of memory reserved to hold the *screen image*.

screen image—The *bit image* that defines what is displayed on the Macintosh screen.

screen map—The *bit map* representing the Macintosh screen, kept in the QuickDraw global variable ScreenBits. Its *bit image* is the *screen image;* its *boundary rectangle* has the same dimensions as the screen, with the *origin* at coordinates (0, 0).

scroll—To move the contents of a *window* with respect to the window itself, changing the portion of a document or other information that's visible within the window.

scroll bar—A *control* associated with a *window* that allows the user to *scroll* the window's contents.

SCSI—Small Computer Standard Interface, a parallel interface built into the *Macintosh Plus* for communicating with peripheral devices; commonly pronounced "scuzzy" (or "sexy," according to personal temperament).

seed—The starting value used in generating a sequence of *pseudo-random numbers*.

segment header—Information at the beginning of a *code segment* identifying which entries in the program's *jump table* belong to this segment.

segment number—The *resource ID* of a *code segment*.

segment 0—A special *code segment* containing the information needed to initialize a program's *application global space*.

serial driver—The *device driver* built into ROM for communicating with peripheral devices through the Macintosh's built-in *serial ports*.

serial port—A connector on the back of the Macintosh for communicating with peripheral devices such as a hard disk, printer, or modem.

shape—Any of the figures that can be drawn with QuickDraw *shape-drawing* operations, including *rectangles, rounded rectangles, ovals, arcs* and *wedges, polygons*, and *regions*.

shape drawing—Drawing *shapes* in a *graphics port*, using the operations *frame, paint, fill, erase*, and *invert*.

Shift key—A *modifier key* on the Macintosh keyboard, used to convert lowercase letters to uppercase or to produce the upper character on a nonalphabetic key.

signature—A four-character string that identifies a particular application program, used as a *creator signature* on files belonging to the program and as the *resource type* of the program's *autograph* resource.

68000—See *MC68000*.

SIZEOF—A function provided by the Apple Pascal compiler, which accepts a variable or type name as a parameter and returns the number of bytes of memory occupied by that variable or by values of that type.

Skinny Mac—The original model of *Macintosh*, introduced in January 1984, with a memory capacity of 128K and a single-sided disk drive.

sound buffer—The area of memory whose contents determine the sounds to be emitted by the Macintosh speaker.

sound driver—The *device driver* built into ROM for controlling the sounds emitted by the Macintosh speaker.

source transfer modes—A set of *transfer modes* used for transferring pixels from one *bit map* to another or for drawing text characters into a bit map.

stack—(1) Generally, a data structure in which items can be added (*pushed*) and removed (*popped*) in *LIFO* order: the last item added is always the first to be removed. (2) Specifically, the area of Macintosh *RAM* that holds parameters, local variables, return addresses, and other temporary storage associated with a program's procedures and functions; compare *heap*. One end of the stack (the *base*) remains fixed in memory, while items are added or removed at the other end (the *top*); the *stack pointer* always points to the current top of the stack.

stack-based—Describes a Toolbox routine that accepts its parameters and returns its results on the *stack*, according to Pascal conventions; compare *register-based*.

stack pointer—The address of the current *top of the stack*, kept in processor register A7.

Standard Apple Numeric Environment—A set of routines for performing arithmetic on *floating-point numbers* in accordance with the *IEEE standard*; available on the Macintosh through the *Floating-Point Arithmetic Package*. Commonly called by the acronym *SANE*.

Standard File Package—A standard *package*, provided in the *system resource file*, that provides a convenient, standard way for the user to supply file names for input/output operations.

standard fill tones—A set of five *patterns* representing a range of homogeneous tones from solid white to solid black, provided as global variables by the *QuickDraw* graphics routines.

standard patterns—The 38 *patterns* included on the standard MacPaint pattern palette, available as a *pattern list* resource in the *system resource file*.

starting angle—The angle defining the beginning of an *arc* or *wedge*.

startup handle—A *handle* to a program's *startup information*, passed to the program by the *Finder* as an *application parameter*.

startup information—A list of *document files* selected by the user to be opened on starting up an application program.

strike—See *font image*.

string list—A *resource* consisting of any number of *Pascal-format strings*.

system bit—A *Finder flag* that marks files needed by the system for proper operation.

system font—The *typeface* (Chicago) used by the Toolbox for displaying its own text on the screen, such as window titles and menu items.

system globals—Fixed memory locations reserved for use by the Toolbox.

system heap—The portion of the *heap* reserved for the private use of the Macintosh Operating System and Toolbox.

system resource file—The *resource fork* of the file System, containing shared resources that are available to all programs.

text characteristics—The properties of a *graphics port* that determine the way it draws text characters, including its *text face, text size, text style*, and *text mode*.

text face—The *typeface* in which a *graphics port* draws text characters.

text file—A file of file type 'TEXT', containing pure text characters with no additional formatting or other information.

text font—A term sometimes used loosely (and incorrectly) as a synonym for *text face*.

text mode—The *transfer mode* with which a *graphics port* draws text characters.

text size—The *type size* in which a *graphics port* draws text characters.

text style—The *type style* in which a *graphics port* draws text characters.

Toolbox—(1) The *User Interface Toolbox*. (2) Loosely, the entire contents of the Macintosh *ROM*, including the *Macintosh Operating System* and *QuickDraw* in addition to the *User Interface Toolbox* proper.

top of stack—The end of the *stack* at which items are added and removed; compare *base of stack*.

Transcendental Functions Package—A standard *package*, provided in the *system resource file* (or in ROM on the Macintosh Plus), that calculates various transcendental functions on *floating-point numbers*, such as logarithms, exponentials, trigonometric functions, compound interest, and discounted value.

transfer mode—A method of combining *pixels* being transferred to a *bit map* with those already there.

translate—To move a *point* or a graphical figure a given distance horizontally and vertically.

trap—An error or abnormal condition that causes the *MC68000* processor to suspend normal program execution temporarily and execute a *trap handler* routine to respond to the problem; also called an *exception*.

Trap Dispatcher—The *trap handler* routine for responding to the *emulator trap*, which examines the contents of the *trap word* and jumps to the corresponding Toolbox routine in ROM.

trap handler—The routine executed by the *MC68000* processor to respond to a particular type of *trap*.

trap macro—A macroinstruction used to call a Toolbox routine from an assembly-language program; when assembled, it produces the appropriate *trap word* for the desired routine. Trap macros are defined in the assembly-language interface to the Toolbox and always begin with an underscore character (_).

trap number—The last 8 or 9 bits of a *trap word*, which identify the particular Toolbox routine to be executed; used as an index into the *dispatch table* to find the address of the routine in ROM.

trap vector—The address of the *trap handler* routine for a particular type of *trap*, kept in the *vector table* in memory.

trap word—An *unimplemented instruction* used to stand for a particular Toolbox operation in a machine-language program. The trap word includes a *trap number* identifying the Toolbox operation to be performed; when executed, it causes an *emulator trap* that will execute the corresponding Toolbox routine in ROM.

type size—The size in which text characters are drawn, measured in printer's *points* and sometimes referred to as a "point size."

type style—Variations on the basic form in which text characters are drawn, such as bold, italic, underline, outline, or shadow.

typecasting—A feature of Apple's Pascal compiler that allows data items to be converted from one data type to another with the same underlying representation (for example, from one pointer type to another).

typeface—The overall form or design in which text characters are drawn, independent of size or style. Macintosh typefaces are conventionally named after world cities, such as New York, Geneva, or Athens.

unimplemented instruction—A machine-language instruction whose effects are not defined by the *MC68000* processor. Attempting to execute such an instruction causes an *emulator trap* to occur, allowing the effects of the instruction to be "emulated" with software instead of hardware.

unit—A collection of precompiled declarations that can be incorporated wholesale into any Pascal program.

unit number—The *resource ID* of a *device driver*; an integer between 0 and 31, related to the *driver reference number* by the formula refNum = −(unitNum + 1).

unload—To remove an object, such as a *code segment* or the *desk scrap*, from memory, often (though not necessarily) by writing it out to a disk file.

unlock—To undo the effects of *locking* a *relocatable block,* again allowing it to be moved within the heap during *compaction.*

unpurgeable block—A *relocatable block* that can't be *purged* from the heap to make room for other blocks.

update—(1) To write a new version of a *resource file* to the disk, incorporating all changes made in the file's resources in memory. (2) To redraw all or part of a *window* that has been exposed to view on the screen as a result of the user's manipulations with the mouse.

update region—The *region* defining the portion of a *window* that must be redrawn when *updating* the window.

user—The human operator of a computer.

user interface—The set of rules and conventions by which a human *user* communicates with a computer system or program.

User Interface Guidelines—An Apple document (part of the *Inside Macintosh* manual) that defines the standard *user interface* conventions to be followed by all Macintosh application programs.

User Interface Toolbox—The body of machine code built into the Macintosh *ROM* to implement the features of the standard *user interface.*

uses declaration—A declaration that incorporates the code of a precompiled *unit* into a Pascal program.

vector table—A table of *trap vectors* kept in the first kilobyte of RAM, used by the *MC68000* processor to locate the *trap handler* routine to execute when a *trap* occurs.

version data—Another name for a program's *autograph* resource, so called because its *resource data* typically holds a string identifying the version and date of the program.

visible region—A *clipping boundary* that defines, for a *graphics port* associated with a *window,* the portion of the *port rectangle* that's exposed to view on the screen.

wedge—A graphical figure bounded by a given *arc* and the radii joining its endpoints to the center of its *oval.*

wide-open region—A rectangular *region* extending from coordinates $(-32768, -32768)$ to $(+32767, +32767)$, encompassing the entire QuickDraw coordinate plane.

window—An area of the Macintosh screen in which information is displayed, and which can overlap and hide or be hidden by other windows.

word—A group of 16 bits (2 *bytes*) beginning at a *word boundary* in memory.

word boundary—Any even-numbered memory address. Every *word* or *long word* in memory must begin at a word boundary.

Index